The Minister's Annual Manual
for Preaching and Worship Planning
2006-2007

Compiled and Edited by
Rebecca H. Grothe

Logos Productions Inc.
6160 Carmen Avenue East
Inver Grove Heights, MN 55076-4422
1-800-328-0200
www.logosproductions.com

First Edition
Twentieth Annual Volume

Scripture listings in this publication are from The Revised Common
Lectionary, copyright © 1992 by the Consultation on Common Texts
(CCT). All rights reserved. Used by permission.

Scripture quotations, unless otherwise noted, are from the New Revised
Standard Version of the Bible, copyright 1989 by the Division of Christian
Education of the National Council of Churches of Christ in the USA.
Used by permission. All rights reserved.

Published in the US by Logos Productions Inc.
6160 Carmen Avenue East
Inver Grove Heights, Minnesota 55076-4422
Phone: 800-328-0200
Fax: 651-457-4617
www.logosproductions.com

ISBN: 1-885361-84-X
ISSN: 0894-3966

Contents

Children's Time

Appendices

FREE Children's Sermon Index

Your paid subscription now includes FREE access to the *Children's Sermon Index* – **a database of children's sermons based on the Revised Common Lectionary for each Sunday of the year.** You can search by theme, season of the church year, or keyword.

- ◆ **Your activation code is MA284.**
- ◆ **In the US visit www.logosproductions.com** and click on "Online subscriptions."
- • **In Canada visit www.woodlakebooks.com** and click on "Church resources."
- ◆ Follow the instructions to receive FREE access to the *Children's Sermon Index* for as long as you subscribe to *The Minister's Annual Manual.*

How to Use This Book

Using the CD-ROM

Although the book may be the easiest way to read weekly material, if you wish to reprint prayers or worship material in your Sunday bulletin, using the CD-ROM will save you time and effort. As a purchaser of *The Minister's Annual Manual 2006-2007,* you have permission to use and reprint the entire contents of this book. Following are some simple hints for using the CD-ROM:

- This CD can be used in both IBM-compatible and Macintosh computers.
- Insert the CD into your computer's CD-ROM drive and select your preferred word-processing application. Click on "File" and then "Open." Be sure the "List Files of Type" drop-box says "All Files (*.*)." For additional help, refer to your software manual.
- Select the week of materials you are interested in viewing or copying and double-click on that file.
- Once the file has opened, you will see a plain text version of the manuscript. You may highlight any or all of the information, then copy and paste it into another document – for example, into your worship bulletin.
- Once the material is in place, change the type font and size to match the document.

This book is intended for use from August 2006 through July 2007.

Because many ministers plan for the year during the summer, this manual is designed to assist in summer-to-summer planning. Included in this book are helpful suggestions to guide your worship planning for each Sunday and several additional worship occasions, such as Thanksgiving and Ash Wednesday.

The Contents of This Resource

Every minister develops her or his own style of preaching and worship planning. Methods, planning, study, writing, and delivery are unique. Use this book in whatever ways will benefit your worship and sermon preparation most fully.

As you study the texts, you may find David H. Schmidt's "Resources for Preparing to Preach" on page 412 to be helpful. A variety of resource materials, commentaries, and translations are listed there to aid in exegesis.

The following materials are included for each worship experience:

- **Lessons.** A listing of appointed readings is given for Revised Common Lectionary, Roman Catholic, Episcopal (Book of Common Prayer), and Lutheran use.
- **Introduction to the Lessons.** A brief explanation and introduction is provided for each appointed text. Consider using these notes in your Sunday bulletins or providing them to lectors or lay readers.
- **Theme.** The overall theme of the day's materials is noted here.
- **Thought for the Day.** A nugget is provided for your own reflection or to help set the tone for preaching.
- **Call to Worship and Prayers.** Prayers provided by the writers fit with the theme for each day. You may copy these prayers for use with your congregation.
  - *Call to Worship*
  - *Pastoral Prayer*
  - *Prayer of Confession*
  - *Prayer of Dedication of Gifts and Self*
- **Sermon Summary.** Key points from the sermon are noted here.
- **Hymn of the Day.** A suggestion for hymn of the day is provided, along with background information.
- **Children's Time.** Pastors who are planning conversations with children during worship or church school time will find ideas here.
- **The Sermon.** The sermon materials are based on one of the Sunday readings appointed by the Revised Common Lectionary.

A Note about the Revised Common Lectionary

A majority of denominations now follow the Revised Common Lectionary. The worship materials provided in this book reflect the texts appointed by the Revised Common Lectionary. You should have no difficulty adapting these materials to your own church calendar. The Consultation on Common Texts asks that we provide this information for you:

> For the Sundays following Pentecost, the Revised Common Lectionary provides two distinct patterns for readings from the Old Testament. One pattern offers a series of semi-continuous Old Testament readings over the course of these Sundays. The other pattern offers paired readings in which the Old Testament and gospel reading for each Sunday are closely related. In adopting the Revised Common Lectionary, the Presbyterian Church U.S.A., United Church of

Christ, and The United Methodist Church elected to use the pattern of semi-continuous Old Testament readings. The other pattern of paired readings is found in *The Revised Common Lectionary* (Nashville: Abingdon Press, 1992).

—The Revised Common Lectionary, 1992
Consultation on Common Texts (CCT)

Not all preachers use appointed lectionary lessons on a regular basis. If you don't use these texts for your preaching, the materials in this book can still be useful in providing sermon ideas and illustrations on specific texts appropriate for the time of year. On the other hand, if you are accustomed to using the lectionary lessons, you will find these materials especially suited to your preaching needs.

Resources for Worship Music
"Hymn of the Day" selections were chosen from the following hymnals:
- *Common Ground: A Song Book for all the Churches,* Edinburgh, UK: Saint Andrew Press, 1998.
- *The New Century Hymnal,* Cleveland, OH: Pilgrim Press, 1995.
- *Presbyterian Hymnal,* Louisville, KY: Westminster John Knox Press, 1990.
- *The Faith We Sing,* Nashville, TN: Abingdon Press, 2000.
- *The United Methodist Hymnal,* Nashville, TN: United Methodist Publishing House, 1989.
- *This Far by Faith: An African American Resource for Worship,* Minneapolis, MN: Augsburg Fortress, 1999.
- *Voices United: The Hymn and Worship Book of the United Church of Canada,* Toronto: United Church Publishing House, 1996.
- *With One Voice: A Lutheran Resource for Worship,* Minneapolis, MN: Augsburg Fortress, 1995.

Many of the hymns suggested are available for congregational use through LicenSing: Copyright Cleared Music for Churches.™ For information on LicenSing go to www.LicenSingOnline.org.

Planning Calendars
A four-year church year calendar is included on page 422, followed by calendars for 2006 and 2007 on page 423.

For More Worship Planning Helps . . .

For even more worship planning helps, check out the 2006 May/June planning issue and the regular monthly issues of *The Clergy Journal*. These resources include additional sermon materials and hymn selections. The planning issue also includes more children's time ideas. Preachers who use *The Minister's Annual Manual 2006-2007* and also subscribe to *The Clergy Journal* will have valuable resources for worship planning that include:

- Three sets of sermon materials for every Sunday of the year and ten additional worship occasions. (The sermon materials in all three publications are cross-referenced so you will know at a glance which publication to use for a particular passage.)
- Two sets of children's time ideas.
- Hymn selections to coordinate with the lectionary readings.
- Prayers and calls to worship.

Thank you for including *The Minister's Annual Manual 2006-2007* in your planning for worship and preaching.

Rebecca Grothe, editor
Spring 2006

August 6, 2006

9th Sunday after Pentecost (Proper 13)
RC/Pres: 18th Sunday in Ordinary Time

Lessons

RCL	2 Sam 11:26—12:13a	Eph 4:1-16	Jn 6:24-35
Roman Catholic	Ex 16:2-4, 12-15	Eph 4:17, 20-24	Jn 6:24-35
Episcopal (BCP)	Ex 16:2-4, 9-15	Eph 4:17-25	Jn 6:24-35
Lutheran	Ex 16:2-4, 9-15	Eph 4:1-16	Jn 6:24-35

Introduction to the Lessons
Lesson 1
(1) 2 Samuel 11:26—12:13a (RCL)
David has abused the power of his position. Uriah is dead. The widowed Bathsheba is the king's wife. But through the parable of the ewe lamb, the prophet Nathan reveals David to stand under judgment.

(2) Exodus 16:2-4, 12-15 (RC); Exodus 16:2-4, 9-15 (Epis/Luth)
The newly delivered Israelites murmur against Moses in the wilderness. They are hungry. They long for Egypt, where slaves were fed. God offers a gift and a test in the provision of quail and manna.

Lesson 2
Ephesians 4:1-16 (RCL/Luth); Ephesians 4:17, 20-24 (RC); Ephesians 4:17-25 (Epis)
Paul celebrates Christian unity experienced in the midst of the Spirit's diverse gifts. The purpose of those gifts is growth and maturity for both the individuals who practice them and the community built by them.

Gospel
John 6:24-35 (RCL/RC/Epis/Luth)
Following their miraculous feeding, crowds seek Jesus. Jesus' "I am the bread of life" is one of several such sayings in John. *I am* resembles the divine name spoken to Moses at the burning bush.

Theme

God provides the bread needed for faith's journey.

Thought for the Day

What (who) is the "bread" that feeds your life, faith, and hope?

Call to Worship

One: Gather in this place, where grace would feed our spirit's hunger.

All: We come to feed on the grace God gives.

One: Gather in this place, where Spirit would quench our thirsting for God.

All: We come to drink in the joy of God's presence.

One: Gather in this place, and find the One you seek.

All: We come to meet Christ in company with one another.

Pastoral Prayer

God of all Creation, we thank you for the gift of this day: a day you have entrusted to us, a day you promise to journey with us, a day you provide for us what we most need for life. We pray, O God, for those whose lives pass through difficult times and places. For those who hunger, whether for bread or hope, we pray for their filling. For those who face pain of body or spirit, we pray for comfort and healing. We pray for this world: for peace where conflict rages, for justice where oppression rules, for mercy where kindness seems distant. And in offering these prayers, make us mindful that we may be the instruments through whom your Spirit would respond to these needs. We pray in the name and hope of Jesus the Christ, the Bread of life. Amen.

Prayer of Confession

We confess, O God, that we sometimes settle for filling our lives with things that do not fill, or satisfy, or endure. We may jam activity and busyness into every corner and moment as we can, and still find ourselves empty, anxious, and hungering. And so we come to you. We come having heard those whispers of bread of life. We come wondering if those promises of never hungering again could possibly be true. We come to you. Nourish us with your grace. Empower us for your service. In the name of Jesus, who is life's bread. Amen.

Prayer of Dedication of Gifts and Self

You are the giver of every good gift, Holy One. From your hands we have received life and breath, spirit and senses. Receive now these gifts your people bring. Guide this congregation in the wise and faithful use of these offerings in your service: that as you bring life to us, these gifts may bring life to others. Consecrate the lives of those whose gifts today are but symbols of the giving of ourselves into that same service of Christ Jesus. Amen.

Sermon Summary

Bread serves as a powerful image of God's grace, yet one easily overlooked because of its ordinariness. In Jesus Christ, God provides us with living bread for nourishment of our spirits and commissioning of our lives.

Hymn of the Day

"Bread of the World in Mercy Broken"

Based upon Jesus' self-description as "the bread of life," this hymn, written by British Anglican priest Reginald Heber, first appeared in print one year after his death. The collection in which it appeared, *Hymns Written and Adapted to the Weekly Service of the Church Year,* had been compiled by the author, but published through the efforts of his widow. This collection became a significant source of 19th-century Anglican hymnody. The hymn, sung in connection with the Lord's supper or on other occasions, can serve as a rich reminder of the Christian's true source of spiritual nourishment.

Children's Time

Believing in Jesus

Ask the children about questions they have asked this week. What did they ask? If they could ask Jesus a question, what would it be? Affirm their curiosity and comment that asking questions is a good way to learn new things.

Explain that in our Bible story today some people asked Jesus a very important question, "What does God want us to do?" Ask the children what they think Jesus said. Affirm their answers and indicate that Jesus gave a very simple answer: "Believe in me."

17

Explain that to believe in Jesus means to trust him. Comment that when you trust someone, you believe that what he or she says is true. Jesus said many things, but the most important thing he said was that God loves everyone.

Another way to show that we trust someone is to do what he or she asks us to do. What does Jesus ask us to do? Share God's love with others. Exclaim that when we believe that God loves everyone and we share God's love with others, then we are doing what God wants us to do.

Pray with the children, giving thanks for Jesus and his wonderful message of love.

The Sermon

Bread of Life

Hymns
Beginning Worship: "Let All Things Now Living"
Sermon Hymn: "Break Thou the Bread of Life"
Closing Hymn: "Guide Me, O Thou Great Jehovah"

Scripture
John 6:24-35 (For additional sermon materials on this passage, see the April 2006 issue of *The Clergy Journal;* for sermon materials on Ephesians 4:1-24, see the 2006 May/June planning issue of *The Clergy Journal.*)

Bread. How common and ordinary an element of food it is. It might even be unusual anymore to think of eating bread alone, unless it's still warm from the oven. We tend now to think of bread smeared with jelly to flavor it, or covered with slices of lunchmeat to add substance, or spread with butter. It makes some people wonder why on earth anyone would want to eat plain dry bread.

Bread has become a mere accessory to meals. Perish the thought of making a single meal of bread, much less depending on it entirely. Yet bread alone was the diet of some people. For bread alone was, and sometimes still is, the only food consistently available for long periods of time. The diet of the Jewish people in biblical times started out that way. Their very language reveals bread's importance. In Hebrew, the word for ordinary bread and the word for food is the same word. Variety may be the spice of our eating life, but bread was the basis of theirs.

The most famous story of bread in the Hebrew Scriptures is the gift of manna in the wilderness. It's worth remembering that manna's gift came not because the Israelites had such great faith – but because they had become such complainers. "If only we had died by the hand of the Lord in the land of Egypt," they complained to Moses, "when we sat by the fleshpots and ate our fill of bread" (Ex 16:3). Yet to this community of murmurers, the manna descended from heaven.

People who collapse images of God in the Old and New Testaments as "justice versus grace" are hard-pressed by stories like this. A just God would have given the Israelites a good swift kick in their collective back-sides, with a parting word to enjoy their Egyptian slave menus for the next generation or so. Instead, God's response to their ingratitude is one of grace: "I am going to rain bread from heaven for you; and each day the people shall go out and gather enough for that day" (16:4). So God provided bread and life to this people.

Now there are curious – and instructive – things worth noting about the qualities attributed to this bread. For starters, the daily gift of manna was sufficient to feed everyone who hungered, sufficient for that day's journey. Secondly, this bread could not be stored away for either profit or gluttony. "Some left part of it until morning, and it bred worms and became foul" (16:20). The manna was given by God for one day: no more, no less. It was, literally, *daily* bread.

Now where have we heard that before? "Give us this day our daily bread." Daily bread. Manna. The prayer Jesus teaches us to pray is not one that invokes overladen tables and multiple refrigerators stocked to overflowing. The prayer is for daily bread – bread that is sufficient for that day's need. Manna that is sufficient for our sojourn in the wilderness.

In our text from John's gospel, a crowd searches out Jesus. This immediately follows Jesus' feeding of the multitude, so it is likely that many if not most of this crowd had been fed with the loaves multiplied in the miracle. Jesus himself declares this to be part of their motive: "You are looking for me, not because you saw signs, but because you ate your fill" (Jn 6:26).

They enter into dialog with Jesus. He tells them to work for food that endures – perhaps a between-the-lines reference to manna that lasted only one day. The people ask what such work requires. Jesus says the work is belief in the One whom God sends. But before such belief is to be given or considered, the crowd by the sea remembers the wilderness story. "What sign are you going to give us . . . Our ancestors ate the manna in the wilderness; as it is written, 'He gave them bread from heaven to eat'" (6:30-31). Once again, the subject is manna, bread. Only now, the crowd confronts Jesus: Are you up to what Moses did? Can you rain bread from heaven?

Jesus' response is twofold. First, he tells them that it was not Moses but God who provided bread from heaven. And that bread, he goes on to clarify, comes to give life to the world. When the crowd pleads for this bread always – much as the Samaritan woman at the well had earlier pleaded to drink always of living water – Jesus offers the passage's climax. "I am the bread of life" (6:35). The bread that feeds, the bread that sustains life in the wilderness, the bread sufficient for each day's need, the bread that reminds us to trust in the grace of its provider rather than in our own anxious and frenzied attempts to secure life: if you want to know that bread's identity, Jesus says *I am*. Not even manna in the wilderness, not even pages of scripture, can compare to the One who is the Bread of Life.

I am the bread of life. We take these words to heart when we come to the table of communion. At this table, we use bread to remember the One who is life's bread. When broken bread invokes the remembrance and recognition of living bread, we find our manna: all that is necessary for the needs of our spirits, for the nurture of our faith.

But there is a catch. The bread we receive at communion is not intended to merely fill us, but also to commission us. For the bread of life here broken and offered is bread for our living. The gift we *receive* in this meal imparts the gift we are to *become:* the very image of God in a world too often seen as devoid of God's presence. We have this calling because we have this Christ, the bread of life, come down from heaven to give life to the world!

– John Indermark

August 13, 2006

10th Sunday after Pentecost (Proper 14)

RC/Pres: 19th Sunday in Ordinary Time

Lessons

RCL	2 Sam 18:5-9, 15, 31-33	Eph 4:25—5:2	Jn 6:35, 41-51
Roman Catholic	1 Kgs 19:4-8	Eph 4:30—5:2	Jn 6:41-51
Episcopal (BCP)	Deut 8:1-10	Eph 4:(25-29), 30—5:2	Jn 6:37-51
Lutheran	1 Kgs 19:4-8	Eph 4:25—5:2	Jn 6:35, 41-51

Introduction to the Lessons

Lesson 1

(1) 2 Samuel 18:5-9, 15, 31-33 (RCL)

David had fled Jerusalem in the face of a rebellion led by his son Absalom. David's followers counseled him not to lead his troops into battle with the rebels. He stayed back. Absalom did not.

(2) 1 Kings 19:4-8 (RC/Luth)

Elijah's victorious contest with the prophets of Baal resulted in Jezebel's promise to kill Elijah. In fear, he fled Israel and entered the Judean wilderness. Alone, and despairing, he prays to die.

(3) Deuteronomy 8:1-10 (Epis)

Moses' second address to Israel at the end of the wilderness sojourn intends to prepare them for life in the promised land. Key to that life will be faithful remembrance of what God has done.

Lesson 2

Ephesians 4:25—5:2 (RCL/Luth); Ephesians 4:30—5:2 (RC); Ephesians 4:(25-29), 30—5:2 (Epis)

The faith witnessed to in the opening chapters of this epistle now finds translation into the practicalities of how one is to live. These verses list imperatives of action in relationship.

Gospel
John 6:35, 41-51 (RCL/Luth); John 6:41-51 (RC); John 6:37-51 (Epis)

Jesus' self-revelation of his identity as "the bread of life" evokes connections with the Old Testament gift of manna, not only in the meaning of the gift but in the expression of complaint.

Theme
God meets our laments with an invitation to live.

Thought for the Day
Faith beckons us to move from complaint – justified or not – to trust in God's life-offering grace revealed in Jesus the Christ.

Call to Worship

One: Come to the One who hears our praise and tears, who knows our joys and sorrows.

All: We wait for God, our spirits wait in hope.

One: Open the deep places of your life to God, places of light and shadow.

All: We wait for God, more than those who watch for the morning of a new day.

One: Taste and see that God is good; blessed are those whose refuge is God.

All: We trust in God's steadfast love and great power to redeem.

– adapted from Psalms 130 and 34

Pastoral Prayer
You are the One to whom we may bring the whole of our lives, for you know us already. And so we bring to you this day our gratitude for life, grace, and creation. Receive our thanks. And so we bring to you this day what grieves us: children who starve, wars that go on and on, injustice that favors the rich and ignores the poor. Receive our lament. And so we bring to you this day our trust. For you are the One who seeks the good of us and all. You are the One in whose hands rest creation and the

future. You are the One whose love is our hope and our home. Receive our trust – and enable us to serve as those through whom you bring answer to prayer and faith to life. In Jesus Christ. Amen.

Prayer of Confession

For spirits closed to the movement
    and newness you would bring to our lives,
forgive us, O God.
For hearts unwilling to name to you
    what we complain about among ourselves,
forgive us, O God.
For hands clenched too tightly around
    the abundance of gifts we enjoy when others go wanting,
forgive us, O God.
For faith that presumes we can only pray
    about what is good and not lament what is wrong,
forgive us, O God.
May your Holy Spirit grace us with forgiveness
    that heals, that opens, that encourages,
in Jesus Christ. Amen.

Prayer of Dedication of Gifts and Self

God of Manna, who pours out upon us what we need for life, receive these gifts we bring to you and the lives of which they are but symbols and signs. May we give all that we offer with a grateful heart. We pray that you would use these gifts in your service, even as you would receive and commission us in that same service. And may we always find our ability and willingness to give growing out of your gracing of our lives. In Jesus Christ. Amen.

Sermon Summary

Complaint arises out of dissatisfaction. Lament couples complaint with trust in the one to whom complaint is brought. Some complain about Jesus' claim to be the bread of life. Their complaint stops short of trust. Even so, Jesus leaves the offer of grace open, even to those who complain.

Hymn of the Day
"I Am the Bread of Life"
This is another beautiful hymn emphasizing Christ as the bread of life. Written by Sister Suzanne Toolan, this hymn was first used during a Eucharist service in the Archdiocese of San Francisco in 1967. In addition to the "bread of life" emphasis, the hymn reminds us of the teaching of Jesus that he is also the "resurrection and the life." We also remember that on the last day, Jesus Christ will raise up all who have eaten of the bread of life, believed, and followed him; and that they shall live forever. Having a soloist or choir sing a stanza can be a meaningful and moving introduction to this hymn.

Children's Time

Living Bread

Bring some freshly baked bread. Express appreciation for the gift of bread. Break open the loaf and let the children smell it. Break it into smaller pieces and share a piece with each one, being sensitive to those who may have food allergies. While you are doing this, discuss bread: What is your favorite kind? How do you like to eat it? Invite the children to share any experiences of baking bread.

Comment that in our gospel reading today, Jesus said something interesting about himself. Read or paraphrase verse John 6:35a. (You may wish to set Jesus' words into context by recalling that Jesus had just fed 5000 people.) Ask the children what they think Jesus means by "the bread of life."

Explain that in Jesus' day, bread was very important to people. It was served at almost every meal, it tasted good, it filled empty tummies, and for those people who did not have much food, it kept them alive.

Make the observation that in many ways bread can remind us of Jesus. Whenever we eat bread we can remember how important Jesus is to us. Just as bread keeps us healthy, so Jesus' teachings help us to be strong and to grow.

Pray with the children, giving thanks for Jesus the living bread.

The Sermon

Complaining about the Food

Hymns

Beginning of Worship: "If Thou But Trust in God to Guide Thee"
Sermon Hymn: "Come O Thou Traveler Unknown"
Closing Hymn: "How Firm a Foundation"

Scripture

John 6:35, 41-51 (For additional sermon materials on this passage, see the
April 2006 issue of *The Clergy Journal;* for sermon materials on Ephesians
4:25—5:2, see the 2006 May/June planning issue of *The Clergy Journal.*)

You may remember hearing the words. You may remember speaking the
words: *What? This again! You know I don't like* _____ – and here you can
fill in any number of things: broccoli, spinach, rutabaga, salmon surprise
(my own personal dread). Complaints about food are as old as school
cafeterias and military rations . . . and the Bible. In our gospel lesson,
the people complained about Jesus because he claimed to be the bread
of heaven.

It is an intriguing and theologically loaded word that John uses for
complain. In the Greek versions of the Old Testament, the word in John
is the same word used to describe the complaining "murmuring" of the
people of Israel in the wilderness. Then, too, the complaint had been
about food, or the lack thereof. The taste of freedom did not seem to
satisfy. The people wanted better food, even if it came at the expense of
slavery in Egypt. "If only we had died by the hand of the Lord in the
land of Egypt, when we sat by the fleshpots and ate our fill of bread"
(Ex 16:3). Like Elijah under the broom tree, they would rather be dead.
And so they complain.

Before we cast accusing fingers in their direction, however: have you
ever hungered, really hungered? Sometimes, complaints may be in order.
Sometimes, there is good reason to grieve the passing of what has been.

The death of Absalom moves David to pour out his heart in the grief of *if only:* "O my son Absalom, my son, my son Absalom! Would that I had died instead of you, O Absalom, my son, my son!" (2 Sam 18:33). A great number of the psalms of Israel are laments, whose verses often open with complaints to God of "why" or "how long." The faith we inherit from Judaism bares life and emotion before God, even the complaints.

But in practically every case, the laments in the psalms conclude with an affirmation of trust in God. After crying out to God in protest, bewilderment, or wondering, the psalmist avers that hope remains in God. Lament becomes an act of faith, precisely because it holds onto God even in the midst of complaint.

In that sense, the complaints raised in the gospel lesson against Jesus do not rise to the standard of laments in the psalms. For the murmuring against Jesus does not lead to or seemingly even seek a holding onto him, but rather a letting go. There is distancing here, disengagement. The people complain against Jesus' claim – because they know who and whose he is. They define Jesus solely by family of origin, and thus put limits on who he could be because they know from where he has come. Misunderstanding is a common dynamic in the gospel of John.

Perhaps what most separates their complaint about Jesus from the positive expression of lament may be seen in Jesus' first words to them. "Do not complain among yourselves" (Jn 6:43). Complaint is one thing when addressed to the individual or group who aggrieve us. At least then, there is opportunity for response and dialog. The impression left by Jesus' words is that their complaining had been done without bothering to address him.

When complaint is not shared, how can change come? When we clutch our resentments close to our hearts, not willing to give them a sounding to see if they are valid or can evoke a change – but hold on and nurse them – nothing good will come. Our opinions of those we blame or resent will only worsen, for our conversations are only with others who share our complaints – or if none can be found, we will simply roll those things over and through our minds until they gnaw away at our spirits.

It is likely not coincidental that, at the end of this chapter, the complaining "among yourselves" leads to its logical conclusion. Folks begin to leave. In fact, in verse 61, the complaining has spread. It is not merely Jesus' opponents but "many of his disciples" who separate themselves from Jesus. Complaint can be contagious . . . and deadly to relationship.

Many experiences in life evoke complaint and many times the complaint is justified. In the face of injustice suffered, in the face of pain, whether our own or others, complaint may be exactly what is needed. Lament to God may be the most faithful thing we can do in those moments. Yet, the key is to hold onto the One to whom we cry, to keep together our expression of lament with trust in God. Jesus concludes his words to the complainers, not by slamming a door in their faces but by leaving open the invitation: "I am the living bread that came down from heaven. Whoever eats of this bread will live forever" (6:51). How and why can he do that? Jesus speaks out of the tradition of wilderness murmuring – and wilderness feeding. For when manna falls from heaven, it does not feed only those who remain faithful and trusting. It does not fall only on those who, even if they are hungry, keep their mouths shut and keep their pain to themselves. Manna is given to all, including the murmurers and the complainers.

Such is the nature of God's grace. God seeks our good. And it is that affirmation, and that grace, that allows us to hold together our crying out in lament with our trust in the God who will hear us and receive us – and feed us with grace that will not fail.

– John Indermark

August 20, 2006

11th Sunday after Pentecost (Proper 15)

RC/Pres: 20th Sunday in Ordinary Time

Lessons

RCL	1 Kgs 2:10-12; 3:3-14	Eph 5:15-20	Jn 6:51-58
Roman Catholic	Prov 9:1-6	Eph 5:15-20	Jn 6:51-58
Episcopal (BCP)	Prov 9:1-6	Eph 5:15-20	Jn 6:53-59
Lutheran	Prov 9:1-6	Eph 5:15-20	Jn 6:51-58

Introduction to the Lessons

Lesson 1

(1) 1 Kings 2:10-12; 3:3-14 (RCL)

The old king, David, is dead. The new king, Solomon, now sits on Israel's throne. Young and inexperienced, he has survived the intrigue that led to his rule. But how will he rule? God offers a choice.

(2) Proverbs 9:1-6 (RC/Epis/Luth)

Proverbs has personified Wisdom before as one who invites individuals to life (1:20-33) and who was present at God's work of creation (8:22-30). Now Wisdom invites others to join her in the banquet she provides.

Lesson 2

Ephesians 5:15-20 (RCL/RC/Epis/Luth)

Paul addresses the Christian community with wisdom teachings that encourage faithful living. This passage prefaces a more extensive "ordering" of the Christian household (5:21—6:4).

Gospel

John 6:51-58 (RCL/RC/Luth); John 6:53-59 (Epis)

While John's Gospel contains no narrative of the last supper, this passage brings strong hints of the meal's meaning. Jesus' "flesh" promises life to those who partake of this gift.

Theme

We are promised Jesus' abiding presence.

Thought for the Day

The presence of Christ in communion is not a debating point – it is an invitation to experience community with God and with one another in Jesus.

Call to Worship

One: God beckons us to come, with arms opened in love.
All: We thank you, O God, for love that receives us.
One: Christ welcomes us as sisters and brothers, at a table set with grace.
All: We thank you, O Christ, for grace that provides a place for us.
One: Spirit fills us and sends us, in service of the One who calls.
All: Lead us, O Spirit, in our worship and into our living.

Pastoral Prayer

Abiding God, we entrust to you the needs that weigh on our hearts. Not so that we can escape them or the ways in which we might help meet them, but so we may be reminded of your care and grace that goes with us and works through us as we are able – and beyond what we alone can do. We bear to you the needs for peace in this world. Redirect the hearts and wills of those who can make a difference, and do not let us think that we cannot. Bring in your Spirit a renewed spirit among us for justice coupled with mercy and compassion. We come to you in the joy your presence brings to us and promises to this world. May we be joyful in your service, fervent in your hope, and ever mindful that you are not only here among us, but here for us and for all. In Jesus Christ. Amen.

Prayer of Confession

Holy God, you have come to us with such grace, in such a gracious One. How, then, do we come to neglect the body that is called by Christ's name? Forgive us, O God, for that neglect: by our withdrawal in times of confusion and anger, by disunity when our ways get confused with your ways and your invitations become overridden with our ultimatums. Grant healing to us, as individuals and communities. Restore us to relationship with you and with one another. Renew our faith and discipleship by your Spirit's presence, working among and within us. Lead us to honor your presence and grace by being present and gracious to those with whom we share this life and Christ's calling. This we pray in the name of Jesus. Amen.

Prayer of Dedication of Gifts and Self

One: For the beauties of creation, for the joys of relationship, for your gracing of our lives:

All: We give you our thanks.

One: For your service in this world, for your children's needs, for earth's hope and renewal:

All: We bring these gifts.

One: Direct the use of these gifts, that they may be instruments of your peace and food for your people.

All: Direct our lives, that we may bear your grace to this world. Amen.

Sermon Summary

Jesus' invitation to "eat my body" and "drink my blood" invites us to experience God's abiding presence with us. The presence Christ offers in communion is grace for life, not a call to divisive hairsplitting. The signs of Jesus' abiding presence are love, restoration, compassion, and the Spirit's empowering gift.

Hymn of the Day
"There's a Spirit in the Air"

Not many seven-stanza hymns are sung in present-day worship services. This hymn, written by the influential British-born contemporary American hymn writer Brian Wren, should be an exception. The hymn was written for Pentecost in 1974 to celebrate the Holy Spirit at work in our world. Its seven stanzas can effectively serve as a call for Christians around the world to allow the Holy Spirit to fill our praise, guide our thoughts, and change our ways as we seek to influence the world in the name of Jesus Christ.

Children's Time

Bread from Heaven

Encourage the children to tell about some things they have heard that are difficult to understand. Explain that sometimes Jesus said some things that were hard to understand. Recall what Jesus said about being the living bread that came down from heaven (Jn 6:51a).

Mention that when Jesus talked about the bread that came from heaven, he was thinking of something that had happened to the Hebrew people many years before. It was the story of how God gave the people special bread, called manna. The manna was sent from heaven to keep the people alive in the wilderness.

Explain that in many ways Jesus was just like the bread sent from heaven. At the right time, God sent the manna to the people; in the same way God sent Jesus to us. The manna was a sign of God's love, and so is Jesus. The manna gave life and hope to the people, and so does Jesus.

Comment that whenever we celebrate communion we use bread. When we come to God's table and eat the bread, we can remember that Jesus was sent from God to tell us of God's love.

Pray with the children, giving thanks for Jesus who was sent as a sign of God's love.

The Sermon

Abiding in Jesus

Hymns
Beginning of Worship: "God Himself Is Present"
Sermon Hymn: "Let All Mortal Flesh Keep Silence"
Closing Hymn: "I Was There to Hear Your Borning Cry"

Scripture
John 6:51-58 (For additional sermon materials on this passage, see the April 2006 issue of *The Clergy Journal;* for sermon materials on Ephesians 5:15-20, see the 2006 May/June planning issue of *The Clergy Journal.*)

"Those who eat my flesh and drink my blood abide in me, and I in them" (Jn 6:56).

One of Jesus' parables concludes with the declaration that the first shall be last and the last shall be first. I long to invert the order of this verse from John's Gospel to make the last phrase first and the first phrase last! If only we could get to our abiding with Jesus first, and then out of that experience of unity and communion deal with the more difficult matters of how exactly we understand "eat my flesh" and "drink my blood." Because for too many of us, we bog down in our differing interpretations and disagreements over those first nine words and never get to the gift and grace of abiding. We war over the words of Jesus' presence in the meal of communion – sometimes figuratively and on occasion in history even literally – and in those warrings we tend to lose touch with Jesus' abiding presence in the community fractured as a result.

The Gospel of John is famous for reporting misunderstandings of what Jesus says. So Nicodemus responds to Jesus' teaching of another birth: "Can one enter a second time into the mother's womb?" (3:4) So a Samaritan woman responds to Jesus' offer of living water: "Sir, you have no bucket, and the well is deep" (4:11). The misunderstanding of verse 54 belongs not just to this original audience who found the teaching difficult and wondered who could accept it. The misunderstanding continues to haunt us today in the hundreds of ecclesial fragments of Jesus' abiding.

Please do not think this sermon intends to pronounce a single word and solution to the mystery of eating Jesus' flesh and drinking Jesus' blood. It is a mystery. Those who approach the sacrament with faith that would receive in the elements the true blood and body of Jesus remind us of the "high nature" of these words in John's gospel. We encounter Presence that exceeds explanatory words and moves us into the realm of worship and awe. Then again, those who approach the sacrament with faith that these elements are but symbols of Christ's presence among us remind us that God exceeds all attempts to confine or "place" God. And those who approach the sacrament as a meal of remembrance remind us of God's once and for all action in Jesus Christ. No one of these approaches, or any others that could be suggested, to "eat this flesh" and "drink this blood" exhausts the whole truth. None of them, either, are devoid of truth.

But where these views of communion, even as Jesus' own words that set our misunderstanding and limited perspective into motion, intend to lead us is that second half of verse 56: "abide in me, and I in them." *Abide* translates a Greek word that means "to dwell" or "take up residence." And it is not the only time John records Jesus using this word. In a later time, when the community worried over Jesus' announcement of his imminent departure, Jesus said this: "I am the vine, you are the branches. Those who abide in me and I in them bear much fruit" (Jn 15:5).

Abiding in Jesus is not a solitary act. Abiding in Jesus is an act that makes us community: with Christ, with one another. It is a *gift* Jesus offers, not a hurdle we set up for others to measure up to according to how closely their ideas of Jesus and communion and church polity accord to our (obviously right!) ideas. Abiding in Jesus is *grace:* given to us, given for us, from Jesus' own hands.

It is something like John's account of the miraculous feeding at the outset of this chapter, which set all this conversation into motion. Unlike the synoptic gospels, where the disciples hand out the loaves and fish, Jesus distributes them in John and gives the people as much as they want. The detail sets up an intriguing precedent for when the narrative reaches our passage and Jesus says he will abide in those who eat Jesus' flesh and drink Jesus' blood. For who determines whether the "eating" and "drinking" is done in a right spirit or proper understanding? It is the one who feeds the multitudes, the one who offers in himself the bread of life and living water. The eating and drinking of these gifts will bring us the gift of Jesus' abiding.

"Those who eat my flesh and drink my blood abide in me, and I in them." *Abide* is at the heart of this verse, even as it is at the heart of this gospel. God's abiding with us in Jesus Christ drives practically every story one will read in John. It is an abiding whose purpose is to reveal the love and grace of God, as revealed in the encounter with Nicodemus and its watershed verse, John 3:16. It is an abiding whose power to heal, restore, and make new shines through every one of the miracles ("signs" as John speaks of them) that give structure to the first half of this gospel. It is an abiding whose compassion wells up in Jesus' prayer for the disciples in his time and every time in chapter 17 and his entrusting of Mary to the beloved disciple at the cross. It is an abiding whose presence continues even after death and resurrection by the bestowal of the Spirit and commissioning of the apostles to feed the sheep of Jesus' flock.

So when we gather at Christ's table, let us remember its invitation comes not in the credentials of merit or understanding that we bring. Jesus invites us to come, eat, and drink and in doing so to experience the gift of Christ's abiding among all who gather at the table in Jesus' name.

– John Indermark

August 27, 2006

12th Sunday after Pentecost (Proper 16)
RC/Pres: 21st Sunday in Ordinary Time

Lessons

RCL	1 Kgs 8:(1, 6, 10-11), 22-30, 41-43	Eph 6:10-20	Jn 6:56-69
Roman Catholic	Josh 24:1-2, 15-17, 18	Eph 5:21-32	Jn 6:60-69
Episcopal (BCP)	Josh 24:1-2a, 14-25	Eph 5:21-33	Jn 6:60-69
Lutheran	Josh 24:1-2a, 14-18	Eph 6:10-20	Jn 6:56-69

Introduction to the Lessons
Lesson 1
(1) 1 Kings 8:(1, 6, 10-11), 22-30, 41-43 (RCL)
The temple God commanded David not to build has been completed by Solomon. Solomon offers this prayer of dedication, which invites God to hear the prayers not only of Israel but also of foreigners.

(2) Joshua 24:1-2, 15-17, 18 (RC); Joshua 24:1-2a, 14-25 (Epis); Joshua 24:1-2a, 14-18 (Luth)
The tribes of Israel stand poised to possess the land long promised. The kept covenant promise of land now summons a renewed covenant choice of whom Israel will serve in this place.

Lesson 2
(1) Ephesians 6:10-20 (RCL/Luth)
Drawing on the imagery of the armor and weaponry of an imperial soldier in the service of Caesar, Paul depicts the qualities of spiritual life that are to "equip" those in the service of Christ.

(2) Ephesians 5:21-32 (RC); Ephesians 5:21-33 (Epis)
Lists of household responsibilities were common in the secular world of Paul's day. Paul uses this device to depict the relationship of wife and husband, a relationship grounded in *mutual* subjection.

35

Gospel
John 6:56-69 (RCL/Luth); John 6:60-69 (RC/Epis)

Misunderstood words of "eating the flesh of the Son of Man and drinking his blood" have disintegrated into dispute and complaint and abandonment of Jesus. Will the rest walk away – and if not, why?

Theme

Faith may be a gift of grace, but discipleship is a choice of will.

Thought for the Day

Why do you choose to follow Jesus?

Call to Worship

One:	Why have *you* come here?
All:	We have come for the hope and wholeness we find in God.
One:	But why have you *come* here?
All:	We have come because we are pilgrims, and Christ is found on the journey.
One:	But why have you come *here*?
All:	We have come because this place and these people offer the Spirit's sanctuary.

Pastoral Prayer

Holy God, Living Christ, Present Spirit: be present to us and to those we name in prayer, whether in words spoken aloud or in sighs of the Spirit too deep to be heard or uttered by us. We are grateful for life's gift: we pray for those whose experience of its giftedness is tempered by illness, loneliness, violence, or hunger. Remind us that our prayers for such individuals and groups lay us open to being the ones through whom you would respond. And help us to receive that not as ominous news, but as joyful opportunity to be the body of Christ through whom you reach, touch, feed, lift up, and embrace. For we would follow you, as those who have gone before us, and for the sake of those who wait to learn from us the ways of discipleship. In Jesus Christ. Amen.

Prayer of Confession

Forgive us, O God, when your words and ways seem difficult. Soften us when we harden our views about you and about others into rigid opinions from which we will not back down. Refresh us when we parch ourselves and others dry with formulas instead of relationships, with offense taken instead of understanding granted. Remind us through your Spirit that even when we stumble into these impasses, you are there to renew our spirits, to enlighten our minds, to cast away that which holds us and others back and under, and to take on that which leads to life in Jesus Christ. We choose to follow Christ, not because we must but because we may. Amen.

Prayer of Dedication of Gifts and Self

Receive, O God, these gifts we choose to render to you through this congregation. May this congregation choose wisely where and how to expend these gifts in your service. And remind us always how you have chosen to entrust us as stewards with creation's gift, love's grace, and discipleship's call. May our wills tend faithfully to what you have already bestowed and to what may still come. In Jesus Christ. Amen.

Sermon Summary

Choice is foundational to following Jesus. The choice is not made once and for all time, but repeated throughout life as we confront situations that ask us again if we will follow. Yet even when our willingness falls short, God remains faithful in God's choice to grace us.

Hymn of the Day
"Eternal Ruler of the Ceaseless Round"

Considered by some as a hymn of superior merit, this American hymn text was written in 1864 by John White Chadwick for his graduation class at Harvard Divinity School. The next year Chadwick began a 39-year tenure as pastor of the Second Unitarian Church in Brooklyn, New York. An altered text appears in many current hymnals, making this hymn more ecumenically accessible. In this hymn we have a prayer that God would rule in our hearts so that we, by virtue of the Son and the power of the Holy Spirit, may love and do all that we should as we follow and serve.

Children's Time

Words of Life

Bring a large dictionary and show that it is a book of words. When we need help understanding what a particular word means, we can look in a dictionary. Comment that some words are used often and others hardly ever. Explain that there must be thousands of words in the book.

Mention that in our Bible reading today we hear about some very special words. Set the scene by explaining that Jesus had been teaching the people, and some of them had left because they thought it was too difficult to follow Jesus. Jesus asked his special friends if they wanted to leave him too. Paraphrase Peter's response in verse 68.

Comment that a dictionary is very useful because it has many words in it, but if we want to find the most important words we have to go to Jesus. Jesus has the words that give life and hope. Ask the children and the congregation if they can remember some of the things Jesus said. Affirm all the answers and explain that we can find Jesus' words in the Bible.

Pray with the children, giving thanks for Jesus who gives us words of life.

The Sermon

To Whom Shall We Go?

Hymns
Beginning of Worship: "Holy God We Praise Thy Name"
Sermon Hymn: "Lord, I Want to Be a Christian"
Closing Hymn: "O Master, Let Me Walk with Thee"

Scripture
John 6:56-69 (For additional sermon materials on this passage, see the April 2006 issue of *The Clergy Journal;* for sermon materials on Ephesians 6:10-20, see the 2006 May/June planning issue of *The Clergy Journal.*)

A recent book that deals with religious life in the Pacific Northwest has for its subtitle: "The None Zone." A line on the back cover explains: "When asked their religious identification, more people answer 'none' in the Pacific Northwest than in any other region of the United States" (*Religion and Public Life in the Pacific Northwest,* edited by Patricia O'Connell Killen and Mark Silk, AltaMira Press, 2004). One of the points made by the authors from the data collected is that "choice" looms large for those who checked something other than "none." Church affiliation is not a given, not an expectation of tradition. One has to choose.

Then again, that is neither new nor unique to the Pacific Northwest. In our reading from Joshua, the tribes of Israel stand ready to finally possess the land promised and now conquered. You'd think it would be time to let out with a sigh of relief after the 40-year sojourn in wilderness and the battle through Canaan. But no, Joshua says, it's time to choose. Choose the gods of the Amorites; or the gods from where Father Abram and Mother Sarai first set out; or the gods back in Egypt who nearly sucked the life out of you; or choose the God who brought you into this land. Joshua understood that "none zones" are few and far between. The problem for those who would be religious is not the death of gods, but their multiplicity – not their absence from contemporary life, but the issue of their relevance to it.

I believe that more than a few opt for "none" based on that last issue: the relevance of God or religious community to their lives. To be honest, the church has sometimes given ample justification to that choice. Folks come looking for spiritual guidance or holy encounter, and walk in on us squabbling over who gets to use the fellowship hall for free and who has to pay. Others come seeking new ways and partners for serving God through serving others, only to find us refusing to budge from comfortable pews and unwilling to risk reserve funds. Some come in search of a place to belong and hear endless debates on who doesn't belong.

"None" can become an understandable choice. Until it comes time for a child to be married. Until it comes time for an elder to be buried. Weddings typically are not performed by "none." Funerals are rarely officiated or hosted by "none." In times of passage and crisis, Peter's response to Jesus in our text from John becomes a lively question: "to whom can we go?" Look around you this morning – and not just at the peculiar furniture and windows that makes this place different from your living room or the Elks lodge. Look around at the memories imbedded here of those who have come in hope of finding sanctuary. Perhaps, at some time or another, it was you. Perhaps it was even while your checkmark was still in the "none" box.

"Lord, to whom can we go? You have the words of eternal life" (Jn 6:68). Peter's response arose out of conflict. The troops were deserting. Jesus said things that were difficult to hear, and in John's reporting, "Many of his disciples turned back and no longer went about with him" (6:66). "To whom can we go?" is not a question with only one possible answer – then or now. "To whom can we go?" is not a question to which the church has any monopoly on the response. We live in a culture filled with choices of things to do and movements to follow and gurus to heed.

"To whom can we go?" Perhaps the more important question is to whom *will* we go? Following and discipleship are acts of the will. Peter spoke these words in response to Jesus asking the twelve: "do you also wish to go away" (6:67). *Wish* is a very weak translation of a verb that means "to will." The world is full of options for religious meaning and affiliation, among which our wills must choose. Religion in the "none zone" simply reminds us that a lot of us live in places where those choices may have less presumptions of *everybody who's anybody goes to the Methodist church in this town.* (Feel free to substitute any brand or flavor, including the currently in vogue "non- (as in *none*) denominational" one.)

"To whom will we go?" Peter opts for Jesus, in whom he finds words of eternal life. But let us also remember that the willful choices we make concerning faith and following Jesus are not one-time-and-for-all-time matters. Peter chooses to say to Jesus, "you have the words of eternal life" now. And Peter later chooses to say to Jesus, "I will lay down my life for you" (13:37). But then, in a courtyard outside the interrogation place of Jesus, Peter chooses to deny that he knows Jesus. Three times, Peter chooses denial. In the courtyard, Peter discovered "to whom can we go" does have other options. Safer ones. Easier ones. But are those the reasons we follow?

Following Jesus is a choice of the will, made again and again. The good news and grace of it all, however, is that even when our choices and wills betray us, God's grace does not. Grace does not excuse our failings. Grace simply, yet profoundly, receives with open arms those who answer, "to whom can we go" with the choice and will to follow Jesus. Not because it is the traditional thing to do, for that may or may not be true. Not because it is the acceptable thing to do, for that may or may not be true. Not because we will be part of a growing and vibrant community, for that may or may not be true. But because we find in Jesus the words of life, and in those words the grace for living.

To whom will you go?

– John Indermark

September 3, 2006

13th Sunday after Pentecost (Proper 17)
RC/Pres: 22nd Sunday in Ordinary Time

Lessons

RCL	Song 2:8-13	Jas 1:17-27	Mk 7:1-8, 14-15, 21-23
Roman Catholic	Deut 4:1-2, 6-8	Jas 1:17-18, 21-22, 27	Mk 7:1-8, 14-15
Episcopal (BCP)	Deut 4:1-9	Eph 6:10-20	Mk 7:1-8, 14-15, 21-23
Lutheran	Deut 4:1-2, 6-9	Jas 1:17-27	Mk 7:1-8, 14-15, 21-23

Introduction to the Lessons
Lesson 1
(1) Song of Solomon 2:8-13 (RCL)
This book as a whole contains love songs that some hear as parables of God's love for us. Today's passage contains an invitation to the beloved, set in the context of spring and new life.

(2) Deuteronomy 4:1-2, 6-8 (RC); Deuteronomy 4:1-9 (Epis); Deuteronomy 4:1-2, 6-9 (Luth)
This text serves as the conclusion to Moses' first address to Israel as they are poised on the edge of Canaan. It is an invitation to faithfully observe and do the commandments of God.

Lesson 2
(1) James 1:17-27 (RCL/Luth); James 1:17-18, 21-22, 27 (RC)
James is a collection of early Jewish-Christian wisdom materials. As with earlier wisdom writings, it emphasizes wisdom not so much as what one knows about God but how one lives in response to God.

(2) Ephesians 6:10-20 (Epis)
The author transforms the equipment of a Roman soldier into a metaphor for the life of faith. The "mystery" of the gospel (6:19) recalls the "plan" to gather up all things in Christ (1:9-10).

Gospel
> **Mark 7:1-8, 14-15, 21-23 (RCL/Epis/Luth);**
> **Mark 7:1-8, 14-15 (RC)**

Jesus turns criticism of allegedly not keeping laws about cleanliness into a critique of attending to God in "words only," while neglecting what one does in life and what one harbors in the heart.

Theme
Be doers of the word and not hearers only.

Thought for the Day
If charged with the crime of being Christian, would our actions provide sufficient evidence to convict us?

Call to Worship
One:	What does God seek of those who seek the Lord?
All:	To walk with a clear conscience and do the right thing;
One:	To speak truth from the heart and do no harm to neighbors;
All:	To stand by one's word even when waffling might be advantageous;
One:	To not make another's misfortune a cause for one's own profit;
All:	To not use words as weapons;
One:	To not put one's judgment up to the highest bidder.
All:	Those who do these words will be found in the One they seek.

– based on Psalm 15

Pastoral Prayer
Creator God, your word calls life into being and your action seeks life for all creation. Attend to the words we bring to you in prayer, even as you would shape our actions in faithful response. Hear the words we offer for those who are ill, who face isolation or estrangement. Be present to them

in ways that bring healing and wholeness. Hear the words we offer for this church community. May your Spirit move through us in forming our ministries and witness to your grace and love. Hear the words we offer for this world: for peace, for justice, for compassion. Shape us in word and deed as your servant people, that the faith we offer in sanctuary resonates with the lives we live in workplace, home, and community. All these things we pray in the name of Christ, your Word incarnate among us and for us. Amen.

Prayer of Confession

Gracious God, how easy it can be to coast on the words of faith, to bask in the grace of your love – and to neglect the truth that those words and that grace come with a purpose for our lives: to change, to renew, to heal, to challenge. Forgive us when we divorce faith from service, grace from ministry. Forgive us when we confuse obsession with words with devotion to your Word. By your Spirit's working inside our lives and inside our communities, restore wholeness to us so that speech and action may flow seamlessly and that word and deed may give a common witness to your uncommon grace. The world needs to hear your word in Jesus Christ. May our witness be complemented, not contradicted, by the word we proclaim and demonstrate. This we pray, and thus we would live, in Jesus Christ. Amen.

Prayer of Dedication of Gifts and Self

Receive, O God, these offerings we bring from our labors, from the work of our hands and minds. Guide this congregation to see how we may best embody the words of service to which you have commissioned us as the body of Christ. As you receive these gifts, receive us into that same service. For we would join our words of praise with deeds of ministry through the offering of these gifts and of our lives. This we pray in the name of Christ. Amen.

Sermon Summary

Faith is not just what we hear or say about God. Christian faith involves how we live and act in response to the God revealed in the Word incarnate, Jesus Christ. Faith's best witness comes in the integrity of word set to deed.

Hymn of the Day
"I Sing the Almighty Power of God"

Written by Isaac Watts (1674-1748), considered to be the father of the English hymn, this hymn finds its basis in the Genesis account of creation. Watts wrote this for inclusion in *Divine Songs Attempted in Easy Language for the Use of Children*, published in 1715, with the title "Praise for Creation and Providence." The hymn can serve to impress upon worshipers that God is to be seen in God's works and God's Word. We can celebrate this creative power in song. This is not "nature worship," but a confident statement that all of life is in God's care.

Children's Time

A Letter from James

Before worship, prepare an envelope and piece of paper. On the envelope print, "To all God's people." On the paper print, "Dear friends, If you want to follow in God's way, find out what God wants you to do and then do it! What does God want us to do? Look after others, especially those in need. From James, a servant of God." Fold and put it in the envelope.

Ask the children if they like to get cards and letters in the mail. Explain that people have been sending and receiving letters for thousands of years. In the early church, people would encourage one another by writing letters about living in God's way. Some of these letters became part of our Bible.

Explain that our Bible reading today is part of a letter written by a church leader called James. Show the envelope and say that it is addressed to the people of God and that means us. Open the letter and read the message. Talk about some of the ways your faith community is looking after those in need. How might we help?

Pray with the children, asking God to help you as you learn to follow in God's ways.

The Sermon

Practicing What We Preach

Hymns
Beginning of Worship: "I Would Be True"
Sermon Hymn: "Jesu, Jesu, Fill Us with Your Love"
Closing Hymn: "Lord, Whose Love through Humble Service"

Scripture
James 1:17-27 (For additional sermon materials on this passage, see the 2006 May/June planning issue of *The Clergy Journal;* for sermon materials on Mark 7:1-8, 14-15, 21-23, see the April 2006 issue of *The Clergy Journal.*)

Do as I say, not as I do.

Have you ever been tempted to lay that line on someone? The problem with the phrase is the mixed signals it sends. On the one hand, it can be an honest expression that we don't always live up to our expectations. On the other hand, it may give the impression of approving double standards of behavior. Telling a son or daughter not to do drugs while the parent goes on abusing alcohol is not likely to carry much freight. "Do as I say and not as I do" can create a mindset that assumes when one becomes an adult, one is free to have one's actions contradict one's words.

Perhaps the best antidote to the abuses of "do as I say and not as I do" resides in another proverb: *practice what you preach.* If the words are good enough to say, then they're good enough to do. It is interesting that the antidote contains within it the language of the church. Education teaches, politics persuades – but the church preaches. "Practice what you preach" assumes that there is the possibility of doing the opposite: of not practicing the preaching, of not putting into action the words of faith. That should come as no surprise to anyone, especially given the tendency to sometimes limit questions about faith to questions about words. Consider, for example, the typical question one might ask about joining a church. In my experience, "what do you believe" far outnumbers "what do you do" in such inquiries. Now we may assume that in knowing what is believed we will know what is being done. But that isn't necessarily the case. Words can

46

be differently interpreted and acted upon. Or, they can be flat out ignored. "Practicing the preaching" means that the words of faith are expressed in the actions of faith as best we are able by the Spirit's leading.

You can search through biblical concordances and never find Jesus, Moses, or anybody else in the biblical witness commanding us to "practice what you preach." Our text in James is about as close as those words come to being said outright: "Be doers of the word, and not merely hearers" (Jas 1:22). James' theme is more inclusive, for some might say that "practicing what you preach" is limited to the responsibility of preachers. There is a certain truth to that. Those set apart by the church in ordained ministry do have expectations placed upon their lives for modeling their words. Having said that, however, is not to declare that only clergy have a responsibility of seeking consistency in words and actions. James does not call upon us to be "doers of the word and not preachers only." James calls us to be "doers of the word and not hearers only." Consistency between word and action, between preaching and practice, is the responsibility of everyone in the church. God's word – whether we preach it or hear it – is the word we are to do, the word we are to express in our actions.

James describes the difference between hearing and doing by using parallel illustrations. The one who is only a hearer of the Word is like someone who stares at herself or himself in a mirror. There are ways in which the word of the gospel is like a mirror held up before us. In its light, we see not only who we have been and who we are, but also who we can be by the grace of God. To hear that word is to look into that mirror. But to only look in a mirror is to accomplish no change. The one who only hears is able to walk away and forget, untouched by the experience. An alcoholic can be shown exactly what is happening to her or him. But unless the word heard gets inside and acted upon, he or she will walk away from that mirror image unchanged. The end result of hearing only in James' text is deception. The word literally means to "reason wrongly." To be a hearer only is to mislead oneself.

In contrast, the one who is a doer of the word also looks into the mirror held up to us in the word God speaks and in the Word God made incarnate in Jesus Christ. Instead of observing and then "going away," that person "perseveres." Instead of forgetting what was seen, that person keeps at the hard but necessary task of acting out the mirror's vision in daily life. The vision given by God's word does not dissolve in the mist of unutilized memory. Rather, it becomes the blueprint for one's own words, actions, and decisions. The living Word incarnate in Christ and revealed to us through scripture is a word not just taken to heart but acted out in life. The end result for the doer of the word is not deception but blessing.

For James, "do as I say and not as I do" is not an adequate philosophy. It may express the weakness that will at times surface in our lives – the gap between the words of our faith and the actions of our lives. However, we cannot be content to leave the matter there. We are called to be doers of the word, practitioners of the gospel's preaching.

Integrity is a good word to sum up the desired relationship between our words and our actions, our profession and our practice of the faith. This kind of integrity makes it possible for us to affirm "do as I say and as I do," not out of self-righteous pride, but out of the simple truth that faith's best witness is the doing of Christ's word. For in our doing of that word lies the purpose of God for us and the blessing of God upon us. Amen.

– John Indermark

September 10, 2006

14th Sunday after Pentecost (Proper 18)
RC/Pres: 23rd Sunday in Ordinary Time

Lessons

RCL	Prov 22:1-2, 8-9, 22-23	Jas 2:1-10, (11-13), 14-17	Mk 7:24-37
Roman Catholic	Isa 35:4-7	Jas 2:1-5	Mk 7:31-37
Episcopal (BCP)	Isa 35:4-7a	Jas 1:17-27	Mk 7:31-37
Lutheran	Isa 35:4-7a	Jas 2:1-10, (11-13), 14-17	Mk 7:24-37

Introduction to the Lessons
Lesson 1
(1) Proverbs 22:1-2, 8-9, 22-23 (RCL)
This passage from Proverbs reminds us to care for the poor, and in so doing we will be blessed as well. God's concern for those who are poor, disenfranchised, and oppressed is evident throughout scripture.

(2) Isaiah 35:4-7 (RC); Isaiah 35:4-7a (Epis/Luth)
The prophet Isaiah serves as God's messenger, telling all to have faith that God will deliver them from affliction. The prophets in Hebrew Scriptures generally comfort the afflicted and afflict the comfortable.

Lesson 2
(1) James 2:1-10, (11-13), 14-17 (RCL/Luth); James 2:1-5 (RC)
James is a series of moral teachings and wisdom sayings directed to Jewish-Christian congregations. Departing from Paul's assertion that salvation is by faith alone, James contends that faith is reflected by one's actions.

(2) James 1:17-27 (Epis)
The writer of James tells Christians how they ought to live. Over half the verses are commands! The strength of this letter is derived from its direct language and vivid metaphors.

Gospel
Mark 7:24-37 (RCL/Luth); Mark 7:31-37 (RC/Epis)
The Gospel of Mark includes numerous accounts of Jesus' miraculous healings. Despite Jesus' attempts to remain inconspicuous, people of various origins seek his healing touch and reveal Jesus' ability to heal.

Theme
Jesus' touch has healing power.

Thought for the Day
While the Syrophoenician woman is assertive in her plea for healing, the deaf man with a speech impediment appears passive toward Jesus. Nevertheless, Jesus heals both.

Call to Worship
One: O Lord, we come to you seeking healing.
All: Great is your faithfulness.
One: We know our destiny is in your hands.
All: Great is your faithfulness.
One: Our confidence is based on your love and mercy.
All: Great is your faithfulness. Amen.

Pastoral Prayer
Lord Jesus, great are your powers! We stand in awe of your majesty. We respect the quiet nature of your ministry. We are amazed at your abilities to heal a multitude of disabilities. Our faith is strengthened by your power to defeat death. We are empowered by your willingness to heal those who come to you in search of healing. As we come before you today in worship, remind us of your willingness and ability to touch our souls and bring wholeness to our lives. Open our ears, remove our impediments, and feed us as children of God. Amen.

Prayer of Confession
Gracious God, healer of all, despite the witness of your wonders, we find ourselves searching for healing. We deplore our addictions and find ourselves immersed in their powers. We suffer afflictions and continue

trying to heal ourselves. We often ignore your healing powers. In our hearts we know that you are the source of all that is good, yet our heads lead us into confusion and doubt. Too often we put our lives in jeopardy forgetting that we, indeed, reap whatever we sow. Now we come to you in humility, begging you to strengthen our faith. Feed us with the crumbs of your goodness that we might resist temptations and avoid what is evil. Restore us and forgive our sins. Help us to rely on you, that we might again delight in your will and walk in your ways. Amen.

Prayer of Dedication of Gifts and Self

Heavenly Provider, we give you thanks and praise for your vigilance over the lives of your people. You have redeemed us from the consequences of our own sin through the gift of your Son, Jesus Christ. Your gift of life eternal prompts us to be grateful in our prayers and generous in our giving. Our hearts abound in thankfulness and our lives reflect your goodness. Use your powers to instill in us the need to give. Amen.

Sermon Summary

We desire healing for ourselves as well as for others. Jesus' healing of the gentile woman's daughter represents a change in the understanding that Jesus' ministry was to the Jews. While Jesus' healing of the man with speech and hearing difficulties raises several questions, the main significance is that Jesus heals.

Hymn of the Day
"Jesu, Jesu, Fill Us with Your Love"

While serving as a missionary to Ghana, Thomas Colvin (born in Glasgow, Scotland, 1925) translated a series of native hymns into English. This simple and spiritually stimulating Ghana folk hymn is one of the most popular of his 24 translations published by the Iona Community in 1968. It speaks of our neighbors as "rich and poor, black and white, near and far." This hymn illustrates Christ's example of true servanthood. Colvin suggests that a variety of available percussion instruments be used with the congregation's singing of this tune. The ideal tempo will not be too slow.

Children's Time

Jesus Heals

Invite the children to close their eyes and listen carefully. Ask: What can you hear? Listen once more, what else can you hear?

Have some conversation about the sense of hearing. What kinds of things do you hear everyday? Being sensitive to those who are hearing impaired, ask the children to imagine what it would be like if their ears didn't work well. How would life be different? Comment that the Bible story today is about a man who could not hear anything at all.

Tell the story about Jesus healing the man who was deaf and mute. Comment that the man was healed because some people asked Jesus to help. Explain that these people had heard many stories about Jesus and knew he could heal with just a touch or a word.

Comment that just like the people who brought the man to Jesus, we can ask Jesus to help those we know who are sick. We do this through prayer.

Ask the children to think about the people they know who are sick. Pray, holding up those who need God's healing touch in their lives.

The Sermon

A Healing Touch

Hymns
Beginning of Worship: "Seek Ye First"
Sermon Hymn: "Healer of Our Every Ill"
Closing Hymn: "Go My Children, with My Blessing"

Scripture
Mark 7:24-37 (For additional sermon materials on this passage, see the April 2006 issue of *The Clergy Journal;* for sermon materials on James 2:1-10, (11-13), 14-17, see the 2006 May/June planning issue of *The Clergy Journal.*)

Have you ever finished explaining something to others – perhaps your children or employees – only to discover later they didn't understand? Most frustrating, wouldn't you agree? Well, in the verses preceding today's gospel reading, Jesus had just finished speaking to the crowd about what defiles a person, only to discover that not only did the crowd not understand what he was saying, but neither did his disciples! So, Jesus explained it again to his disciples and then sought refuge in the region of Tyre. Despite his best efforts to find seclusion, it was not to be.

A Gentile, a Syrophoenician woman, sought out Jesus for the sake of her daughter. Have you ever wanted something for your child – something as important as healing? At what point would you have stopped seeking? Most parents would do anything to see that healing is accomplished. This mother is no different. She prostrates herself at Jesus' feet and begs him, not just asks or requests, but *begs* him to cast out the demon that inhabits her daughter. In the Gospel of Matthew this same incident is recorded, and the mother's plea is desperate: "Lord, help me."

The mother's persistence is not surprising. What is surprising is Jesus' initial response. Jesus casts her aside, contending that the children (meaning Israel) should be first. The early Christian church followed that same thinking, so Jesus' refusal to heal this woman's daughter – as harsh as it seems – was consistent with the practices of the early church. The apostle Paul declared that the gospel should be preached first to the Jews and then to the Gentiles (Rom 1:16) and followed that practice as well. (Acts 13:46; 18:6.) Considering the context, Jesus' belittling reference to the Gentiles as "dogs" seems consistent.

But the mother's persistence paid off! Her willingness to be called a dog does not defer her quick-thinking response, and in that response Jesus recognizes her faith and grants her plea for her daughter's deliverance.

The significance of Jesus granting this request is the shift in Jesus' ministry. From this point forward, the gospel is seen as intended for all. The Syrophoenician woman persuades Jesus to enlarge the dimensions of who are to be called the people of God.

From the episode with the distraught mother, Mark immediately tells of another event of healing, this time of a man who has a speech impediment and is deaf as well. There are many details about this account that are ambiguous and unknown to us, but the main thrust and meaning of the story is unmistakable: Jesus heals.

The group of people who brought this man to Jesus is not identified, nor do we know their motives. Is it an attempt to test Jesus' ability to heal? Is it a trap? Or is it simply compassionate concern? We do not know, though we note that they implored Jesus with great energy to heal this man. Jesus heals the man of both his deafness and speech impediment.

The exact nature of the man's impediment is also unknown to us. Biblical scholars have debated the meaning of the word *impediment*, ranging from "coarseness in speech" to "stammering." His difficulty in speaking and inability to hear are not what is important. What is important, of course, is Jesus' compassion, as evidenced by his sigh, and the healing he performs.

Why did Jesus use the Aramaic command, *Ephphatha* ("be opened")? Again, we're not sure. It may have been the fulfillment of the prophecy from Isaiah, chapter 35:5-6, "Then the eyes of the blind shall be opened, and the ears of the deaf unstopped; then the lame shall leap like a deer, and the tongue of the speechless sing for joy."

And why did Jesus order the crowd not to tell anyone of what they had seen? Some have suggested the command to remain silent was a plan of reverse psychology. A more reasonable explanation suggests that the right time for these disclosures had not yet come. Perhaps the healing has the symbolic intent of showing that the Gentiles, once "deaf and dumb" towards God, are now capable of hearing God. While we can ponder these suppositions, the real significance of these events is this: Jesus heals!

The healing of this man is the second of three healings in Mark in which an unidentified group brings someone to Jesus to be cured (2:1-12 and 8:22-26). While these healings demonstrate faith, it is not really the faith of the sick that is the focus of attention, but rather the faith of those who witness these cures. What is the effect on the mother, whose daughter is freed from the demons who torment her? What is the effect of the crowd who observes the transformation of the man who now hears and speaks without any imperfection in his speech? What is the effect upon us when we witness healing?

Yes, Jesus heals our bodies and our souls, heals our children as well as our elders. Jesus heals, heals us from the penalty of our sins, heals the emotional wounds left by others in our relationships.

We, of course, are left to wonder and ask: Why aren't all our maladies healed? Why aren't the ills of the world removed? Why doesn't justice prevail? Human bondage to sin began a long time ago. Because of human-kind's disobedience, we are confined to live in an era of inconsistencies and impediments, not only in speech but in our very nature. We are not privileged to know the answers to our questions.

While God works to provide us with healing, we are blessed to have professionals to aid us in our healing. God's grace in healing comes through the tenderness and nurture of friends and family. We are shep-herded and ministered to by those who care for us. Jesus heals us through the work and love of others as well as through divine intervention that defies explanation. For us, this healing must be sufficient. Our ultimate healing will come when we approach the judgment seat of God, and Jesus will say to the Father, "This is one of mine."

– Rod Broding

September 17, 2006

15th Sunday after Pentecost (Proper 19)
RC/Pres: 24th Sunday in Ordinary Time

Lessons

RCL	Prov 1:20-33	Jas 3:1-12	Mk 8:27-38
Roman Catholic	Isa 50:4-9	Jas 2:14-18	Mk 8:27-35
Episcopal (BCP)	Isa 50: 4-9	Jas 2:1-5,	Mk 8:27-38
		8-10, 14-18	or Mk 9:14-29
Lutheran	Isa 50:4-9	Jas 3:1-12	Mk 8:27-38

Introduction to the Lessons
Lesson 1
(1) Proverbs 1:20-33 (RCL)
The book of Proverbs gives insights on coping with life. These moral and religious instructions, written primarily for Jewish youth, speak as a prophet making strong threats against those who do not listen.

(2) Isaiah 50:4-9 (RC/Epis/Luth)
The servant brings a word of comfort to the weary Israelites. With a strong emphasis on obedience, the servant is confident of God's support and vindication.

Lesson 2
(1) James 3:1-12 (RCL/Luth)
James emphasizes the need for us to "tame the tongue," which he names a "restless evil."

(2) James 2:14-18 (RC); James 2:1-5, 8-10, 14-18 (Epis)
While the writings of Paul emphasize the importance of faith, James stresses the importance of works, which should emanate from faith. Proclaiming that God shows no partiality, James stresses the need for impartiality among us.

Gospel
Mark 8:27-38 (RCL/RC/Epis/Luth)

What begins as an ordinary journey for the disciples moves to a startling revelation. Jesus' provocative question, "Who do you say that I am?" causes each of us to consider our own answer to this important question.

Theme

Jesus speaks openly about what it means to follow him.

Thought for the Day

"Those who want to save their life will lose it, and those who lose their life for my sake, and for the sake of the gospel, will save it" (Mk 8:35).

Call to Worship

One:	We have come here today to worship the One who has saved us from our sins.
All:	"You are the Messiah," Peter answered.
One:	We thank you, Jesus!
All:	"You are the Messiah," Peter answered.
One:	We praise your name.
All:	"You are the Messiah," Peter answered.
One:	Our hope rests in you, Jesus.
All:	"You are the Messiah," Peter answered.
One:	Jesus, you have called us to follow you.
All:	"You are the Messiah," we answer.

Pastoral Prayer

Gracious Lord, you have shown us by your example what it means to deny ourselves and take up your cross. Thank you for bringing about our salvation. Despite your willingness to surrender your life upon the cross, we confess that we are reluctant to deny ourselves, take up our cross, and follow you. Because we are selfish and weak, we are delighted that our salvation does not depend upon us, but on you, for you are the Messiah. You are the way, the truth, and the life. Do not abandon us to the follies of our own strength and wisdom, but keep us in the folds of your garments that we may wear the robe of righteousness that you have won for us. We come to you, O Lord, for we have nowhere else to go. Accept our praise. Amen.

Prayer of Confession

As we come before you, O Christ, we want to speak confidently that you are the Messiah. We give you thanks and praise that through the power of the Holy Spirit you give us the courage to speak boldly. Words of proclamation may come to our lips, but so often our actions lack consistency with our speech. We confess that we are fearful of what it means to follow you. We regret our tendency to put ourselves ahead of others. We desire to repent, but we know that true repentance comes with a cost we'd rather avoid. We beg your forgiveness for our reluctance to follow. Have mercy on us. Give us confidence in you and make us willing and eager to follow you regardless of the cost. Amen.

Prayer of Dedication of Gifts and Self

O God, you have given us life eternal.
> What may we offer in return?

O God, you sustain us through the bounty of the earth.
> What may we offer in return?

O God, you have given us the Holy Spirit as a comforter.
> What may we offer in return?

O God, you have provided for every one of our needs.
> What may we offer in return?

Strengthen us to offer ourselves as a thank-offering. Amen.

Sermon Summary

Jesus speaks openly to his disciples and his followers regarding what is in store for him, as well as what it means to be a disciple of Jesus Christ.

Hymn of the Day
"New Every Morning"

Written by British Anglican pastor John Keble, this hymn is drawn from the opening 16-verse poem of his famous work *The Christian Year,* first published in 1827. While emphasis is given, particularly in stanza five, on the denying of self to follow Christ (Mk 8:34), the hymn strongly highlights the freshness of God's daily blessings. Stanzas one and two are reminiscent of Lamentations 3:22-23: "The steadfast love of the Lord never ceases . . . they are new every morning." The tune MELCOME has been generally associated with the hymn since 1861.

Children's Time

Who Am I?

Invite the children to play "Who am I?" Choose someone from the congregation that the children would know. Give a few clues, such as "I play the organ and I have brown hair – who am I?" Invite the children to guess the identity of the mystery person.

Comment that in the Bible story today Jesus wasn't playing a guessing game, but he did ask his disciples a similar question, "Who do people say that I am?" Ask the children to tell how they would describe Jesus to someone else.

Explain that Jesus' friends had been listening to what the people had been saying about Jesus. Many people thought that Jesus was Elijah, or one of the other prophets, come back to life. Some people thought Jesus might be John the Baptist in disguise! Jesus then asked his disciples, "Who do you say that I am?" Invite the children to guess what the disciples said.

Paraphrase Peter's response in verse 29. Peter knew that Jesus was sent from God to tell of God's love for everyone. Comment that this is a great way to describe Jesus.

Pray with the children, giving thanks for Jesus who came to tell us about God's love.

The Sermon

Speaking Openly

Hymns
Beginning of Worship: "Rise, Shine You People"
Sermon Hymn: "Praise and Thanksgiving"
Closing Hymn: "Now Thank We All Our God"

Scripture
Mark 8:27-38 (For additional sermon materials on this passage, see the April 2006 issue of *The Clergy Journal*; for sermon materials on James 3:1-12, see the 2006 May/June planning issue of *The Clergy Journal*.)

"How am I doin'?" he asked hesitantly. I panicked. I knew what he was asking. I knew he was looking for reassurance. But I could see the quality of his work was lacking. What was I to say – "It could be better;" "Fine;" "O.K."? Speaking openly requires not only precision in language and some degree of courage; it also requires speaking truth.

Jesus spoke openly whether he was speaking to the Pharisees or a Gentile, his enemies or his closest friends. And Jesus spoke openly and plainly to his disciples.

When Jesus began to speak openly with his disciples about what was to come, they were unable to accept his words. They probably were stunned. Suffering? Rejection? And be killed? No way!

"This simply could not be," they may have reasoned. "There must be some mistake. We must have heard incorrectly." Their concept of a messiah did not include suffering, rejection, and murder. Nothing could be more foreign to their understanding.

In disbelief, Peter, speaking for the rest of the disciples, pulled Jesus aside and began to reprimand him. For three years, these disciples had witnessed miracle upon miracle. They had seen Jesus give sight to the blind and hearing to the deaf. They had witnessed the exorcism of demons, the forgiveness of sins, the calming of the sea, the raising of the dead. They had observed the compassion of this man, even when he was exhausted. They had seen Jesus expose the hypocrisy of the Pharisees and cure the lepers. Surely this man was the one of whom the prophets spoke. Suffering? Rejection? Killed? No way!

Perhaps some doubt crept into their thinking at this point: "Have we followed the wrong one? Have we left our homes and families and jobs to follow someone who isn't what we thought?"

The degree of Peter's protest demonstrates how Jesus' teaching about his mission and his fate represented a new way of thinking. A new direction in the way of Jesus was being forged. A new view of discipleship was required.

We all understand how ambiguous messages can be misunderstood. But when someone speaks openly and directly as Jesus did here, there is little room for misunderstanding. The problem is that, despite their relationship with Jesus, the disciples did not understand what Jesus was really about. Somehow they had missed the point.

Of course, the disciples had a preconception of what a messiah should be. The scriptures they had heard from their childhood told them of one who would be God's chosen one, one in whom God delighted. This One would bring forth justice and blot out their sins. This One would open the eyes of the blind and redeem the lost. Had they not witnessed all this in Jesus? Of course they had.

The disciples could repeat the prophecies of Isaiah and the others by heart.

"Is not this the fast that I choose:
to loose the bonds of injustice,
to undo the thongs of the yoke, to let the oppressed go free,
and to break every yoke?
Is it not to share your bread with the hungry,
and bring the homeless poor into your house;
when you see the naked, to cover them,
and not to hide yourself from your own kin?" (Isa 58:6-7)

"Yes," the disciples would say to one another. "We have seen these things taking place." But did they miss the prophecies of Isaiah and the others who spoke of one who would be despised and rejected; one who would be oppressed and afflicted; one who would be wounded for our transgressions, crushed for our iniquities; a man of suffering and acquainted with grief? Did they miss that the messiah would enter Jerusalem, "humble and riding on a donkey" (Zech 9:9)?

The disciples' concept of Jesus' identity and mission was much like the crowd that followed Jesus. Despite the clarity with which Jesus spoke, the disciples just didn't get it.

What do you think the atmosphere in that room was like as Jesus began to expound on what the future would hold? I imagine Peter's face must have paled, his composure evaporated. Peter must have felt like a pebble instead of a rock. Peter's response caused a response in Jesus that must have cut deeply into the disciples: "Get behind me, Satan! For you are setting your mind not on divine things but on human things" (Mk 8:33).

From there Jesus lays it on the line quite openly about what it takes to be one of his disciples. "Those who want to save their life will lose it, and those who lose their life for my sake, and for the sake of the gospel, will save it" (Mk 8:35). It is a three-point plan. Deny yourselves. Take up your cross. Follow me.

Unlike the disciples, the elders understood and fumed. The priests understood and spit on the ground. The scribes understood and shouted, "Blasphemy!" They grasped his call and knew his mission. And the truth of Jesus' words was so threatening to the religious and political powers of that time that they decided to kill him. That is just what they did. Fulfilling what the prophets had forecast, they looted his clothes, mocked his name, and crucified him.

This leaves us to decide just as the disciples and the crowds had to decide. Jesus asks each one of us, "Who do you say that I am?" The answer and what happens next is up to you and to me.

– Rod Broding

September 24, 2006

16th Sunday after Pentecost (Proper 20)
RC/Pres: 25th Sunday in Ordinary Time

Lessons

RCL	Prov 31:10-31	Jas 3:13—4:3, 7-8a	Mark 9:30-37
Roman Catholic	Wis 2:12, 17-20	Jas 3:16—4:3	Mark 9:30-37
Episcopal (BCP)	Wis 1:16—2:1, (6-11), 12-22	Jas 3:16—4:6	Mark 9:30-37
Lutheran	Jer 11:18-20 or Wis 1:16—2:1, 12-22	Jas 3:13—4:3, 7-8a	Mark 9:30-37

Introduction to the Lessons
Lesson 1
(1) Proverbs 31:10-31 (RCL)
This wife, the personification of wisdom, is lauded as one who demonstrates a series of worthwhile characteristics. Among other virtues, she "opens her hand to the poor and reaches out her hands to the needy."

(2) Jeremiah 11:18-20 (Luth)
This is the first of Jeremiah's six personal laments and reflects Jeremiah's deep conviction to serve God.

(3) Wisdom of Solomon 2:12, 17-20 (RC); Wisdom of Solomon 1:16—2:1, (6-11), 12-22 (Epis)
Called a "covenant of death," these words foretell what tests and traps await the Righteous One who is to come.

Lesson 2
James 3:13—4:3, 7-8a (RCL/Luth); James 3:16—4:3 (RC); James 3:16—4:6 (Epis)
James expands the meaning of wisdom, culminating in the proclamation that true wisdom is a gift from God. A series of admonitions encourages us to resist worldly wisdoms and draw closer to God.

Gospel
Mark 9:30-37 (RCL/RC/Epis/Luth)
After hearing Jesus' teaching about what is to come, the disciples are concerned about who is the greatest among themselves. Taking a child in his arms, Jesus reminds all that greatness is accomplished through serving.

Theme
"Whoever wants to be first must be last of all and servant of all" (Mk 9:35).

Thought for the Day
In God's eyes, our greatness is determined by our willingness to serve those considered by humankind as the least.

Call to Worship
One:	Let us lie in wait for the righteous man.
All:	For if the righteous man is God's child, God will help him.
One:	The Son of Man is to be betrayed into human hands, and they will kill him.
All:	And three days after being killed, he will rise again.
One:	Let us condemn him to a shameful death.
All:	For their wickedness blinded them, and they did not know the secret of God.

– Based on Wisdom of Solomon 2:12-22

Pastoral Prayer
Oh, God, we give you thanks and praise for your word, which enlightens us and points us toward Jesus the Christ, who has saved us from our sin. We pray that your word would be known throughout the world, that all may know your salvation. Give us your wisdom so that we may not be led astray by worldly wisdom. Keep us mindful that greatness does not come through power and might, but through serving. Amen.

Prayer of Confession
Merciful Lord, we confess that we have sought greatness at the expense of servanthood. We have considered ourselves great while those who are poor and needy have stood among us with outstretched hands. We confess that

we have kept for ourselves that which you have given to us so that we might share. We have depended on our wisdom instead of yours. Destroy our sin of self-centeredness and replace it with a desire to put others ahead of ourselves, for we know that we are unable to do this good work in and of ourselves. Send your Holy Spirit that we might trust in your power and in the assurance of your goodness. Amen.

Prayer of Dedication of Gifts and Self

Almighty God, thank you for your goodness and lovingkindness, given to us and to all whom you have made. Accept our gifts this day. Make us more aware of your mercies so that we praise you with our lips and also with our works. Lead us in paths of holiness and righteousness all of our days. Amen.

Sermon Summary

The wisdom of God calls us to put ourselves last and be a servant to all.

Hymn of the Day
"The Church of Christ in Every Age"

The late Fred Pratt Green (1903-2000) is considered by some to be the most important hymn writer of Methodism since Charles Wesley. Although a British Methodist pastor, Green's influence as a hymn writer has gone far beyond the walls of Methodism. Most recent hymnals in North America include his hymns. This hymn, written in 1969, calls the church to be an agent of change and reconciliation in the world. It reminds us that we, as the church, "have no mission but to serve in full obedience to our Lord." Perhaps using an already familiar LM hymn tune for the singing of the hymn will facilitate its introduction.

Children's Time

Who Is the Greatest?

Bring some pictures of some well-known cartoon superheroes. Place the pictures on a sheet of newsprint. Have some conversation about the characters and invite some discussion about which one is the greatest and why. Write down the words the children mention such as strongest, fastest, and bravest. If there is disagreement, explain that arguments about who is the greatest are not unusual.

Retell the story of the disciples' argument in Mark 9:33-34. You might use your imagination to present some of the arguments the disciples could have used to defend their position: "I met Jesus first" or "I walked on the water with Jesus."

Mention that when Jesus heard what his friends had been quarreling about, he said something very surprising. Paraphrase verse 35. You may have to explain that a servant is someone who takes care of the needs of others.

Invite the children to name some ways to serve others at home, at school, or at church. Affirm their ideas and comment that every time we serve someone else, we are a hero in God's eyes, and that makes us great.

Pray with the children, asking God to help you as you learn to serve others.

The Sermon

Knowing Better

Hymns
Beginning of Worship: "God of Grace and God of Glory"
Sermon Hymn: "Be Thou My Vision"
Closing Hymn: "Son of God Eternal Savior"

Scripture
Mark 9:30-37 (For additional sermon materials on this passage, see the July/August 2006 issue of *The Clergy Journal;* for sermon materials on James 3:13—4:3, 7-8a, see the 2006 May/June planning issue of *The Clergy Journal.*)

"You know better than that!" This is one of my favorite lines whether I'm disciplining my students, my children, or my dog. "Use some common sense!" is another. I've tried to push others to a higher degree of wisdom. It doesn't always work, and sometimes my patience becomes very limited.

Jesus, on the other hand, seems infinitely patient, especially with his disciples. Picture the setting of our gospel reading. As they passed through Galilee, Jesus was teaching the disciples, telling them how he was going to be handed over to a group of people who would kill him. And this was not the first time he had told them this.

Here Jesus is telling his closest friends of his upcoming suffering and death. Can you imagine the pain and emotion of that interchange? What energy did Jesus need to disclose such painful information? And his disciples, well, they didn't understand. If they were like most of us, they probably didn't want to know. Besides, they were busy discussing and arguing which of them was the greatest!

Maybe Jesus wasn't sure what their subject of conversation had been. Maybe he hadn't heard them. Maybe he was just testing them. Nevertheless, Jesus asked what they had been talking about. At least the disciples had the decency to keep quiet. (Maybe it was their embarrassment.) Don't you wonder what length of time elapsed before Jesus, in his mercy, broke the awkward silence?

Apparently, Jesus didn't chew them out for their lack of sensitivity. He didn't waggle his finger at them or lecture them. He didn't just stand there and stare them down. He didn't even tell them they should know better or to use some common sense. Apparently, Jesus didn't even raise his voice. Instead, he sat down, called them together, took a child in his arms, and spoke to them.

It is not recorded for us how Jesus was able to determine their earlier conversation. Maybe the disciples finally admitted what they had been talking about. Maybe Jesus had caught enough of their conversation to fill in the blanks. Maybe their silence gave the disciples away. Whatever it was, Jesus makes it clear that if we want to be first in the eyes of God, we must put ourselves last. If we want to be a hotshot in the kingdom of God, we'll have to be a servant here on earth.

This is not news to most of us. If you've been in the church very long at all, you've heard this call to servanthood before. But why did Jesus take a child to illustrate his point? It may have been that children were so vulnerable and defenseless. In that day and culture, children were not highly regarded. Of more value was one's cattle or sheep—at least animals provided an income. Maybe the way Jesus treated children, here and elsewhere, initiates a new era in the value of children. But most certainly, the illustration is clear: we belong at the bottom of our own priority list.

I wonder how many times God has looked upon my words and deeds and thought, "You know better than that!" But instead of raking me over the coals, instead of giving me a lecture, God sits down with me and gathers me in, reminding me once again what I need to remember and what I need to be. Even when I thought I knew better.

We are called to be servants of all. We are called to have servant hearts. We are called to welcome even those with whom we'd rather not share a cup of coffee. We are called to offer others the head of the table and not to think too highly of ourselves. We know all that. We are plagued not so much with a lack of wisdom as with a lack of obedience. We desire to be great among others. We are caught in the sin of putting ourselves first. Conformed to a worldly definition of greatness, we are tempted to make friends with the world and flaunt the risk of becoming an enemy of God. We know better than that. Oh, yes! We are not dumb or naïve! Our problem is not one of knowledge, but of obedience. Left to ourselves and our earthly wisdom, we invite God's disapproval, God's disappointment, and, possibly, God's wrath. And we know that, too.

We have no way to estimate or determine the limits of God's patience. But we do know that throughout his earthly mission, Jesus constantly identified himself with the underdog, the forsaken, the oppressed, the servant, the child. Despite our pretense that we know better, God continues to uphold that mission.

It is told that when Ghandi traveled around India and entered a village, the first thing he would do would be to gather all the scattered human feces into a place away from their water supply. While his followers pleaded with him to let them do this work of serving while he did more important work, Ghandi contended that this was "the most important work."

Ours is a call to realign our priorities. Ours is a call to obedience. Our call is to realize that greatness is achieved not through political pandering but through service to others, most of all to those who might be considered "less than." Ours is a call to believe that dignity is not derived from pride but from humility. We are called to treat others as Jesus did. We can do no better than that. And we know that. Amen.

– Rod Broding

October 1, 2006

17th Sunday after Pentecost (Proper 21)
RC/Pres: 26th Sunday in Ordinary Time

Lessons

RCL	Esth 7:1-6, 9-10; 9:20-22	Jas 5:13-20	Mk 9:38-50
Roman Catholic	Num 11:25-29	Jas 5:1-6	Mk 9:38-43, 45, 47-48
Episcopal (BCP)	Num 11:4-6, 10-16, 24-29	Jas 4:7-12, (13—5:6)	Mk 9:38-43, 45, 47-48
Lutheran	Num 11:4-6, 10-16, 24-29	Jas 5:13-20	Mk 9:38-50

Introduction to the Lessons
Lesson 1
(1) Esther 7:1-6, 9-10; 9:20-22 (RCL)

The purpose of this book is to demonstrate the certainty of how justice can retaliate against oppression and the need for the oppressed to act with confidence and shrewdness. Here, the wicked leader Haman receives his deserved reward.

(2) Numbers 11:4-6, 10-16, 24-29 (Epis/Luth);
Numbers 11:25-29 (RC)

Doing the Lord's work is not limited to the people of God. Despite the Israelite's discouragement, God's Spirit came upon 70 of the elders as well as two others who remained in the camp.

Lesson 2
(1) James 5:13-20 (RCL/Luth)

The practical nature of this letter ends with a series of pastoral concerns, culminating in the assertion that God's truth leads to righteousness.

(2) James 5:1-6 (RC); James 4:7-12, (13—5:6) (Epis)

These verses contrast godliness with worldliness, and demonstrate the futility of putting one's own faith and emphasis in the things of this world.

Gospel
Mark 9:38-50 (RCL/Luth);
Mark 9:38-43, 45, 47-48 (RC/Epis)
We are forewarned that the seriousness of our sin cannot be ignored without risk of eternal punishment. We are encouraged to work for others for the good of the kingdom.

Theme
Do not discourage the good that is done by those outside the church.

Thought for the Day
Much good is accomplished in this world by those who claim no allegiance to Jesus Christ.

Call to Worship
One:	Your word, O Lord, revives the soul.
All:	The law of the Lord is perfect.
One:	You make wise the simple.
All:	The decrees of the Lord are sure.
One:	You enlighten our eyes.
All:	The commandment of the Lord is sure.
One:	The ordinances of the Lord are true and righteous.
All:	More to be desired are they than gold.

– Based on Psalm 19:7-10

Pastoral Prayer
Gracious God, source of all goodness and mercy, we give you thanks for your care and keeping. Continue to bestow on us your love and devotion. Strengthen your church that we might be witnesses of your glory by the good that others see in us. Remind us, Lord, that we are not the only providers of good in the world. Help us to look with favor upon other helpers and offer assistance where it is desired and needed. Keep us from being prideful of our works, but mindful that all we have is a gift from you. Teach us to share. In the name of Jesus Christ we pray. Amen.

Prayer of Confession

You, O Christ, are the vine; we are but branches. We have difficulty remembering that. You, O Christ, are the cornerstone; we are but bricks. We often forget that, too. You, O Christ, are perfect and whole; we are woefully incomplete. So, in our helplessness and weakness, we cast ourselves upon the altar of your mercy. Turn our inadequacies into powers that will benefit others, and motivate us to care for your environment. Support our efforts and the efforts of others to relieve misery in the world and keep our world safe from destruction. Replace our tendency to destroy with a desire to build. Transform us from haters into healers. In your name, we pray. Amen.

Prayer of Dedication of Gifts and Self

Mighty Creator, you have made all that exists. You have blessed us beyond measure. And so, we offer ourselves to your service and dedicate our lives to the care and redemption of all you have made. We return to you this portion of what you have first given us. Receive our gifts of time, talent, and treasure for the sake of Christ, who offered himself for us. Amen.

Sermon Summary

The stark words of Jesus warn us of the gravity of our sin. We are not called to judge others in their efforts to do good, but rather join them in ministry – remembering that "whoever is not against us is for us" (Mk 9:40).

Hymn of the Day
"Where Cross the Crowded Ways of Life"

Written by American Methodist pastor Frank Mason North in 1903, this American hymn is one of the earliest social gospel hymns. It promotes Jesus' teaching to offer the cup of living water to all and to honor all who do so in his name. The author's long ministry in New York City opened his eyes to situations of social neglect, including the many ways that human needs and civil rights can be ignored. These images enabled him to provide us with a powerful expression of Christian concern that may be applied in our time.

Children's Time

Like Salt

Bring some salted and unsalted crackers. Being mindful of possible food allergies, invite the children to try both kinds of crackers and talk about the difference between the two. While they are eating, have some conversation about salt: When do you use salt in your family?

Talk about some of the ways in which salt is used to make our lives better. For example: Salt is used to prevent food from spoiling. It is used in factories to help make paper and plastic. It is used in the process of making brightly colored fabrics. Admire some of the colors in the children's clothes, noting that without salt those beautiful colors would just rinse away in the washing machine.

Explain that in our Bible reading today, Jesus said that we should be like salt in the world. As followers of Jesus we can add the flavor of God's love to our world and make it a better place for everyone to live. What kinds of things could our church family do to share God's love and help others?

Pray with the children, asking for help as you share God's love this week.

The Sermon

A Cup of Cold Water

Hymns
Beginning of Worship: "I, the Lord of Sea and Sky"
Sermon Hymn: "We Are All One in Mission"
Closing Hymn: "There's a Wideness in God's Mercy"

Scripture
Mark 9:38-50 (For additional sermon materials on this passage, see the July/August 2006 issue of *The Clergy Journal* and the 2006 May/June planning issue of *The Clergy Journal*.)

"It is better for you to enter life maimed . . ." (Mk 9:43). Shocking words. These dire warnings of Jesus shock us. This blunt and devastating language helps us recognize Jesus' hatred of sin. Now, obviously this hand chopping, eye plucking, and foot severing would never work, if for no other reason than that we don't have enough body parts to atone for our sins! Besides, after all this dismembering, we'd still have our thoughts and tongue to control. And, as far as I can determine, we haven't done too well on that count. No, do not take these words of Jesus as literal commands, but view them as a way to see ourselves for what we really are – sinners in desperate need of redemption. In his love for us, Jesus wants us to see the ramification of our acts, thoughts, and attitudes.

Our destination should not be hell, but heaven. In fact, in times of biblical antiquity, hell was never unanimously believed to be a place or state of eternal punishment. It was often regarded as the necessary impasse of the soul when it had to reckon with its misdeeds and rebellion. While nearly every religion believes in the existence of a hell, not every religion considers hell to be a place of punishment. For some it is a form of purgation, a process of purification. Hell is universally described as "fire" because fire cleanses, and fire is painful. Pain and purification are always linked together.

God does not desire that we perish, but that, "everyone be saved and come to the knowledge of the truth" (1 Tim 2:4). Our problem is that we insist on our own way instead of God's. That was the problem with John in our text today. John was so sure that any exorcism had to be done by Jesus or the disciples that John stopped this unknown exorcist because he didn't belong to "the group." When John told Jesus what he had done, Jesus' response was a surprise.

"Do not stop him!" Jesus commanded, "for no one who does a deed of power in my name will be able soon afterwards to speak evil of me" (Mk 9:39). Then Jesus announces, "Whoever is not against us is for us" (9:40). Whoever is not against us is for us! Exclusivity among his followers was something Jesus could not tolerate. The disciples tried to define and limit those who could work so that God's will might be done. The lesson here is that we should not build barriers around those who can do God's work. From Jesus, it is obvious that it matters more that the work gets done than who does it.

We can see a similar self-centeredness in the church today. Egos abound – sometimes among denominations; sometimes among synods or parishes; sometimes within a congregation. Who is going to get the credit? Who is the healer, minister, or prophet of privilege? Jesus says that "who" is not the issue.

The issue is that the job gets done. Someone has said that when no one is concerned about who gets the credit, a lot can be accomplished.

God works within the church; God also works outside the church. Everyone can be a worker in the kingdom of God. For, "Whoever is not against us is for us."

All the world is God's creation. "The earth is the Lord's and all that is in it," the psalmist proclaims (Ps 24:1). Let's not limit the work that God desires. As the hymn "There's a Wideness in God's Mercy" declares, "For the love of God is broader than the measures of our mind."

It is easy for us to confuse the means with the end. It is the end that should determine the means and those who work toward that goal. The churches' approval is nonessential. What matters is that God's will gets done. We are not to be obstructionists or obstacles to that endeavor, but partners in it.

The church has no monopoly on God's grace nor on God's will. In addition to sanctifying the work of God by all who labor in God's behalf, we are obligated to accept those who wish to work with us. If all sinners are not welcome in the church, then none of us belong. And, who among us is called to be a judge of that? Whom do we stop at the door? To whom do we say, "You don't belong here"?

The wonderful news is that acceptance of others does not dilute our own faith. Jesus made it clear that it is not our task to "separate the weeds from the wheat." Who among us is qualified or even able to tell the difference? (I have enough difficulty in my garden doing that!) The Lord has made us all. Claim that. Ponder that. Rest in that.

More wonderful news is that we are not obligated or limited to doing only "big" works. No, our call is not to eliminate single-handedly all the world's poverty or injustices or illnesses. We are called to "bloom where we are planted." We are to do "mustard seeds" worth of good. Every little bit helps. Even an action as small as a cup of cold water given to one who thirsts is remembered. Jesus tells us that when we do a good work to another, we do the kindness to him.

So, we don't judge. We minister. And we welcome those who may not be part of us. We join together in our efforts to do whatever we can to fulfill the mission Jesus gave us. We work hand in hand offering our energy, our time, and our possessions, even a cup of cold water. Amen.

– Rod Broding

October 8, 2006

18th Sunday after Pentecost (Proper 22)
RC/Pres: 27th Sunday in Ordinary Time

Lessons

RCL	Job 1:1; 2:1-10	Heb 1:1-4; 2:5-12	Mk 10:2-16
Roman Catholic	Gen 2:18-24	Heb 2:9-11	Mk 10:2-16
			or 10:2-12
Episcopal (BCP)	Gen 2:18-24	Heb 2:(1-8), 9-18	Mk 10:2-9
Lutheran	Gen 2:18-24	Heb 1:1-4; 2:5-12	Mk 10:2-16

Introduction to the Lessons
Lesson 1
(1) Job 1:1; 2:1-10 (RCL)
This book deals with a question that has concerned both ancient and modern thinkers: why is there suffering in the world, when it seems so unfair? This passage sets the scene for the rest of the book.

(2) Genesis 2:18-24 (RC/Epis/Luth)
The Lord, deciding that the human God created should have a partner in life, creates a woman from the man's side. This passage moves the people of God to an understanding of oneness.

Lesson 2
(1) Hebrews 1:1-4; 2:5-12 (RCL/Luth)
The anonymous author opens this letter (addressed to those who have been persecuted) with a firm statement about the superiority of Christ above all creation.

(2) Hebrews 2:(1-8), 9-18 (Epis); Hebrews 2:9-11 (RC)
To a suffering church, these words from an anonymous author must have brought great comfort – Christ himself suffered and calls all of them brothers and sisters.

Gospel
Mark 10:2-16 (RCL/Luth); Mark 10:2-16 or 10:2-12 (RC); Mark 10:2-9 (Epis)

The Jesus of the gospels put a high standard on marriage and a particularly high standard on the care and nurture of children. Here he treats children as full human beings loved by God.

Theme
Children are loved by God.

Thought for the Day
Churches often assume children will only "someday" serve and love God. Jesus shows us that children are God's people now.

Call to Worship

One:	Lord, defend me because I have lived an innocent life. I have trusted the Lord and never doubted.
All:	Lord, try us and test us; look closely into our hearts and minds.
One:	I raise my voice in praise and tell of all the miracles you have done. I love the temple where you live, where your glory is.
All:	Lord, we stand in a safe place. We praise you in the great meeting.

– based on Psalm 26

Pastoral Prayer
O great and loving God, who has created human beings for relationship, and who enters into relationship with all your people, we give you thanks for all the people who make our lives interesting and full. Thank you for families who love us, friends who make us laugh, children who show us the delight of discovery, youth who remind us of the importance of asking questions, adults who have much wisdom to share.

We pray, O Lord, for those whose relationships are troubled, those who have no one in their lives to love them, those who live in homes where abuse or neglect reign in an evil departure from your holy design. Teach all of us to seek relationships that are healthy and show us how to reflect your love to those around us. Amen.

Prayer of Confession

Gracious God, whose love is beyond our understanding, forgive us for taking our relationships too lightly, for treating those close to us with coldness, for treating the stranger with contempt. We have not loved wholeheartedly; we have not guarded our words as we should; we have refused to let the interests of others interfere with our own self-interest. Teach us through the example of Jesus how to love, how to share, how to be in community with others. Amen.

Prayer of Dedication of Gifts and Self

Our gratitude for life and its gifts overflows, O Lord, into the giving of ourselves – what we have and what we are. Take these gifts we offer, and use them to bless others. Then make of us the type of people who are always looking for ways to share in the name of Jesus. Amen.

Sermon Summary

Children, often relegated to the outskirts of our faith, were treated as insiders by Jesus. Jesus wants us to know that there is something to be said for being like children. To be childlike in our faith is to recognize a spiritual truth: we are indeed dependent upon God.

Hymn of the Day
"Tell Me the Stories of Jesus"

Knowing of Jesus' love for children, it is fitting that we sing a hymn that was written in response to children's requests for stories of Jesus. The hymn was written around 1885 by William Henry Parker, an insurance executive who assisted with children's Sunday school work in Nottingham, England. The hymn highlights events in the life and ministry of Jesus. We can imagine being beside Jesus, in language that both children and adults can easily comprehend and sing together. The tune STORIES OF JESUS was written in 1903 as the prize-winning tune in a competition sponsored by the national Sunday School Union of England.

Children's Time

Let the Children Come

Bring a variety of baby dolls. Invite the children to hold them if they wish. Ask the children: "What's great about being a child?" Explain that in Jesus' time, children, even though they were loved by their parents, were not considered very important. But Jesus knew that everyone is important to God and he wanted to teach the disciples about this.

Tell the story of Jesus rebuking the disciples and blessing the children.

Invite some discussion of the story. What do you think the disciples said to each other when they heard what Jesus said? What do you think Jesus said when he blessed the children? What do you think the children said to Jesus?

Comment that Jesus knew that everyone is important to God – children and grown-ups, girls and boys, old and young. We are all part of God's family and that makes us very special. In fact, we are amazing. Invite the children to share this message with the whole congregation. Make a group huddle, have a whisper practice first, face the congregation and shout, "We are amazing!"

Pray with the children, giving thanks for Bible stories that help us understand how important we are to God.

The Sermon

Let Them Come

Hymns
Beginning of Worship: "All Things Bright and Beautiful"
Sermon Hymn: "I Want to Walk as a Child of the Light"
Closing Hymn: "Jesus Loves Me"

Scripture
Mark 10:2-16 (For additional sermon materials on this passage, see the July/August 2006 issue of *The Clergy Journal* and the 2006 May/June planning issue of *The Clergy Journal*.)

I started out my adult life as an elementary school teacher, so I feel I have a fairly strong understanding of and appreciation for children. I've taken courses and read books on childhood development. As a Christian educator and then pastor, I have watched individual children grow and develop into teens and adults. As they mature, great physical, emotional, and spiritual changes have come over them. I am always amazed by the miracle of growing up. I love looking at a young adult and thinking, "I remember when you were in the first grade! My, how you've changed!"

Of course, that is no surprise to anyone. We all change as we mature. As children, nearly all of us (except Peter Pan) thought growing up would be a wonderful thing. "When I'm big, I can ride my bike down the street to my friend's house." "When I grow up, no one can tell me what to do." "Someday I can eat chocolate cake for breakfast if I want to!"

Though some would wish to turn back the clock on the aging process, very few would go back to childhood even if they could. Nearly everyone enjoys the independence of being a grown-up.

So if adulthood is the desirable state for nearly all of us, why does Jesus say, " . . . it is to such as these that the kingdom of God belongs . . . Whoever does not receive the kingdom of God as a little child will never enter it" (Mk 10:14-15). Shouldn't Jesus be saying something like, "Aren't they cute? I can't wait until they grow up and can have a mature faith!"

But, as is often the case, Jesus turns our ideas of what ought to be into his better purpose. It's important to see that Mark couples this teaching about children with one about marriage. There is no question that Jesus had a higher view of marriage than some others did in his day. Family ties were important, and should not be broken on a whim.

Right upon the heels of this strong statement on marriage, we have a story about children being brought to Jesus for his blessing. The disciples "spoke sternly to them" (10:13). It is unclear whether "them" refers to the adults bringing the children or to the children themselves. In either case, Jesus "was indignant" and responded by declaring that no child should be hindered in such a way. Then, he calls them examples of how to approach and receive the kingdom of God.

It may be hard for us to imagine children as examples. Don't we usually point the children around us to older youth or adults as models of faith and behavior? Children are wonderful, to be sure. They are fun, loving, creative, fresh. But they are also sometimes petty, argumentative, and in need of correction or guidance. Does God want us to be like that?

I believe the answer may be found in that very thing we try to work out of ourselves as we grow: dependence. Every child longs to be able to do things on her own, to make his own decisions. From the time we learn to say no, we say it often as a way of trying to assert our minimal but growing independence. As teenagers we can hardly stand that we still have to get our parents' permission to attend a certain movie or to stay out late with friends. We begin to strive against the fact that we still must rely on parents for financial help and for emotional support. Becoming independent adults means breaking away from those constraints and finding our own way.

However, Jesus wants us to know that there is something to be said for being like children. To be childlike in our faith is to recognize a spiritual truth: we are indeed dependent upon God. Just as a child must rely on others for even the most basic of needs such as food, shelter, love, and security, so do we all truly rely upon God, whether we consciously realize it or not. And the more conscious we are of that dependence, the more we understand what it means to be a child of God.

Like children, we are utterly dependent upon God for everything: for life, for breath, for love, for redemption. It is not that God calls us to be dependent; we already are. God calls us to *recognize* our dependence.

How would it make a difference in our lives if we were constantly to recognize our dependence before God? If we can live continually, actively in the mindset of dependence, then we are reminded of God's presence in every area of our lives. Though we may try to be cognizant of our physical needs before God, we often forget to remember that we depend on God for our emotional well-being, our relationships with family and neighbor, our ability to get along in the world.

Sadly, it seems the more successful (read: independent) we become – the more we achieve goods, comfort, and influence – the less likely we are to attribute those things to God. When we have more than enough to eat, nice houses, and more than one car in the driveway, we tend to forget who is the source of life itself and its barest necessities. The single parent who has three kids and an unsteady job may be more likely to be aware that everything comes from God than is the person who is financially stable and physically healthy. When need of any kind – a loss, fiscal difficulty, health problems, relational strain – hits us, we are more likely to return to God. That's when we give thanks for the understanding landlord, pray for the healing of a sick spouse, and hope for something good to happen if God wills it.

Those of us who have plenty are no less dependent upon God than those who have little. We may simply have a stronger need to recognize that dependence. That is when we learn to receive the kingdom of God as a little child.

– Melissa Bane Sevier

October 15, 2006

19th Sunday after Pentecost (Proper 23)
RC/Pres: 28th Sunday in Ordinary Time

Lessons

RCL	Job 23:1-9, 16-17	Heb 4:12-16	Mk 10:17-31
Roman Catholic	Wis 7:7-11	Heb 4:12-13	Mk 10:17-30 or 10:17-27
Episcopal (BCP)	Amos 5:6-7, 10-15	Heb 3:1-6	Mk 10:17-27, (28-31)
Lutheran	Amos 5:6-7, 10-15	Heb 4:12-16	Mk 10:17-31

Introduction to the Lessons
Lesson 1
(1) Job 23:1-9, 16-17 (RCL)
Job, after listening to his friends' "explanations" of why bad things had happened to him, complains that God's presence has been hidden during the entire ordeal.

(2) Wisdom 7:7-11 (RC)
All good things come with God's wisdom, a gift more precious than gold and jewels.

(3) Amos 5:6-7, 10-15 (Epis/Luth)
Amos, the shepherd-turned-prophet, rails against the attitudes of injustice and the lack of faithfulness in those around him.

Lesson 2
(1) Hebrews 4:12-16 (RCL/Luth); Hebrews 4:12-13 (RC)
The writer of the letter to the Hebrews expresses an exalted understanding of Christ to encourage readers who may be suffering.

(2) Hebrews 3:1-6 (Epis)
Suffering brothers and sisters in Christ are reminded that Christ reigns over all.

Gospel

Mark 10:17-31 (RCL/Luth); Mark 10:17-30 or 10:17-27 (RC); Mark 10:17-27, (28-31) (Epis)

The gospel of Mark shows Jesus' love for and challenge to one who questions him. The text moves from a specific person to all the wealthy, then to all persons.

Theme

Faithfulness requires examining heart and motive.

Thought for the Day

Love for God requires digging deeply into our psyches to see what things hinder our faithfulness.

Call to Worship

One: My God, my God, why have you rejected me? You seem far from saving me, far from the words of my groaning.

All: My God, I call to you during the day, but you do not answer. I call at night; I am not silent.

One: Praise the Lord, all you who respect God. All you descendants of Jacob, honor God; fear God, all you Israelites.

All: God does not ignore those in trouble. God does not hide from them, but listens when they call out.

– based on Psalm 22

Pastoral Prayer

O God, whether we are in a time of crisis or of relative normalcy, help us to see all the good things we have received from you. Let us draw our loved ones close and breathe a prayer of thanks for their safety. Let us look around our homes and wonder why we have so much when so many others have little or nothing. Let us put on our clothing and eat our meals and sleep in our beds, and realize how often we take those simple things for granted.

We thank you for giving us hearts that are pulled by the needs of others. We pray for those today who are grieving loss, for the elderly and weak, for the sick and depressed, and for those who have lost all hope. Show us how we may share the love of Christ in whatever way we can. Amen.

Prayer of Confession

Loving and forgiving God, you have reached into our souls and have seen us as our true selves. You know where we have been faithful and where we have come up short. Forgive us when we believe we have kept all your commandments, but have forgotten to remember the poor, the weak, the stranger, and the hurting. Instill in us an understanding of your love and grace, so that as we are forgiven we may reach out to others and share that same love with them. Amen.

Prayer of Dedication of Gifts and Self

Thank you, O God, for all your good gifts. In response, we bring to you the results of our work and the intentions of our hearts. Receive our offerings and use them for the work of this congregation in your world. Receive our very lives and make us willing servants who are always listening for the call to help those in need. Help us dedicate ourselves anew to efforts of love. Amen.

Sermon Summary

Like the man in the story, we enthusiastically run after Jesus, only to find that often we are held back by our own desires and presuppositions. Even though we are imperfect in our obedience, with God real faithfulness is possible.

Hymn of the Day
"O Jesus, I Have Promised"

This musical prayer of commitment, written for the confirmation of youth, easily serves as an expression of commitment for the congregation. The major focus of the hymn is the dedicated commitment to Christ-centered service. It was written by Anglican priest John Ernest Bode of Cambridgeshire, England in 1866 for the confirmation of his three children. Although the hymn emphasizes dedicated servanthood, it reminds us that even as Jesus is our master, he is also our friend. As we sing this hymn, we may perhaps identify with the disciples' relationship to Jesus and their desire to "follow him to the end."

Children's Time

Leave It Behind

Bring a knapsack packed to overflowing with things that would not be useful on a day hike (electric kettle, movie) and things that would be (water bottle, sunscreen, map). Show the bag and explain that you are going on a hike later, so you packed a bag. Lift the bag and exclaim that it's too heavy to take on a long walk. Let the children feel the weight.

Comment that you will have to leave some things behind. Unpack everything and ask the children to help you decide what to leave behind. As the children make their suggestions give some ridiculous reasons for keeping everything. Reluctantly follow the children's directions and repack the bag. Let the children feel the reduced weight.

Explain that in the Bible story today, Jesus was talking to some people about what it meant to be a disciple. Jesus said that if we want to follow him we might have to leave some things – like selfishness – behind. Comment that sometimes it can be hard to decide what is important and what is not as we follow Jesus. As a church family we can help each other decide.

Pray, asking God to help you as you learn more about following Jesus.

The Sermon

You Lack One Thing

Hymns

    Beginning of Worship: "God of Grace and God of Glory"
    Sermon Hymn: "Great God, Your Love Has Called Us Here"
    Closing Hymn: "Jesu, Jesu, Fill Us with Your Love"

Scripture

Mark 10:17-31 (For additional sermon materials on this passage, see the July/August 2006 issue of *The Clergy Journal;* for sermon materials on Hebrews 4:12-16, see the 2006 May/June planning issue of *The Clergy Journal.*)

Shirley goes to church every Sunday. She teaches a class of four-year-olds how much God loves them. She serves on the mission committee and raises money for both local and international projects. For a year she was on the board of the Habitat for Humanity chapter for her county, spending one night a month and several Saturdays giving her time "for a good cause." As a businesswoman, she sees to it that her small corporation invests wisely and fairly.

Last year, Shirley's mother became ill. Her mother lives a half-hour away, but Shirley went to visit only once over a period of about six months. With no family to help, the mother relied on friends and taxis to get her to the doctor, and had someone come in several times a week to look after her. Though the daughter was well-equipped and energetic when it came to helping all sorts of other people, she felt emotionally paralyzed and incapable of responding in the face of her own mother's needs. Events from her past kept her from helping, even though if it had been a neighbor she would have been free with her assistance.

Some people know Bob as a guy who is generous with his money. It's not that he's public about it; he's helped out many in very quiet ways. Bob's church put out an appeal for help for hurricane survivors, and he gave half his salary for the month. An old friend comes by on a regular basis and Bob always pulls out his wallet – the guy has fallen on hard times. At Christmas, Bob responds to every request for money from an agency he respects. He gives money for toys, food, emergency aid, and funds a Christmas party for the nursing home down the street. But, even though Bob has plenty of spare time (he is retired) and is in great health, he never responds to requests for volunteering. He has said no to helping at the Christmas party, to delivering meals, and to working a fund-raiser event for the hurricane survivors. He even avoids conversation with the friend who always needs money. Bob's point of view is that he doesn't have to give his time because he gives his money. He has his own pursuits and interests, and he just likes having his time at his own disposal, without demands from others. Writing a check is easy; giving up a Saturday – that's another thing altogether.

When Bill and Marge discuss their retirement, they realize they will be very comfortable. They plan to travel to Europe and Asia. They want to buy a lake house and a boat. They have good health insurance and long-term care insurance, so they don't worry about their future. They have good relationships with their family members and friends. They work hard at their jobs and are respected in them. They feel they have earned every penny they've made, and they've invested wisely. But they decided long ago to stop giving to charities and those in need. They love to read accounts of churches and not-for-profits who have handled money poorly and illegally; these incidents give them additional reasons never to trust their contributions to any organization. And individuals, they say, like the homeless they pass on their way to work, will just use the money to buy drugs and alcohol. So, they enjoy the financial rewards of their labors and plan how they will spend their retirement income.

When Jesus encountered the man in today's story, Mark tells us Jesus looked at him and "loved him" (Mk 10:21). He was one of us – our neighbor, our coworker, our fellow pew-sitter; he was us. He was a normal guy, a very good guy who was happy with his life. "Is there anything lacking?" he asked. I think he knew what was lacking. He seemed to be faithful in so many ways. Jesus told him to keep the commandments. "I do all that," he said eagerly. "You know what's required," said Jesus, loving him. "What's the one thing you have trouble with?"

"Give up your money," said Jesus. "Give away all of it to the poor."

"All of it?" he gasped.

"All of it."

This rich man was shocked. Shocked. It was impossible to imagine that, after all he had done for God, there would be this one, enormous, unreasonable thing asked of him.

When he realized Jesus was serious, he went away. He grieved, because he could not believe this would be required of him. He wanted to do all for God, but this was just too much. This was over the edge. Maybe Jesus wasn't from God after all. The God he knew would not require such a thing – possessions are blessings, aren't they?

Jesus watched this man and loved him. And the disciples watched, slack-jawed. If this is true, then who in the world can get into the kingdom? "With God," smiled Jesus, "all things are possible." And he loved them.

Each of us, no matter how faithful we are, has the potential to hold something back. We have the potential of keeping one door of our hearts closed to God. We have the potential to love one thing too much to allow God to use it, because only we know how best it should be used. We have the potential of letting that one thing – small though it may be – grow in importance to such an extent that it overshadows our faithfulness. But we also have the potential of learning to let go of that one thing, of making small beginnings to be more faithful and more open to God and others. We have this possibility because all things are possible with God. And because, even when we are shocked that this one last stronghold must now be opened to God's intrusion, and when we turn away in sadness and grief – grief that we are losing that one last thing – Jesus looks after us and loves us.

– Melissa Bane Sevier

October 22, 2006

20th Sunday after Pentecost (Proper 24)

RC/Pres: 29th Sunday in Ordinary Time

Lessons

RCL	Job 38:1-7, (34-41)	Heb 5:1-10	Mk 10:35-45
Roman Catholic	Isa 53:10-11	Heb 4:14-16	Mk 10:35-45 or 10:42-45
Episcopal (BCP)	Isa 53:4-12	Heb 4:12-16	Mk 10:35-45
Lutheran	Isa 53:4-12	Heb 5:1-10	Mk 10:35-45

Introduction to the Lessons

Lesson 1

(1) Job 38:1-7, (34-41) (RCL)

God's response out of the whirlwind to all Job's questions about suffering consists of more questions.

(2) Isaiah 53:10-11 (RC); Isaiah 53:4-12 (Epis/Luth)

The servant portrayed by the prophet suffers for the people and is exalted by God because of his sufferings.

Lesson 2

(1) Hebrews 5:1-10 (RCL/Luth)

Jesus, though he suffered greatly, was elevated to the rank of high priest, as was the ancient priest of Salem, Melchizedek.

(2) Hebrews 4:14-16 (RC); Hebrews 4:12-16 (Epis)

The writer of the letter to the Hebrews exalts Christ to encourage readers who may be suffering.

Gospel

Mark 10:35-45 (RCL/Epis/Luth);
Mark 10:35-45 or 10:42-45 (RC)

Jesus answers a question about power by teaching that, in God's kingdom, power is of a different sort.

Theme
Power is not what we think.

Thought for the Day
The true power of God's love is expressed in humility.

Call to Worship

One: Bless the Lord, O my soul. O Lord my God, you are very great.

All: You are clothed with honor and majesty, wrapped in light as with a garment. You stretch out the heavens like a tent.

One: O Lord, how manifold are your works! In wisdom you have made them all; the earth is full of your creatures.

All: Bless the Lord, O my soul. Praise the Lord!

— based on Psalm 104

Pastoral Prayer
Creator God, when we look at all you have made and the great beauty of it, we feel small in comparison. We see your vastness in the sea, hear your power in the wind, experience your genius in the first cry of an infant, know your wildness in the howl of the leopard. We thank you for the blessings of the people we hold dear, the love we experience, the gifts of life and security. May these blessings lead us to reach out to others who have no one who holds them dear, whose lives are empty or unhealthy or unsafe, who reach out for faith or justice or help and find none. Teach us to love with compassion, to aid while preserving dignity, to share with delight. Amen.

Prayer of Confession
O God of great power, how often we have abused the power you have given us. We have hurt family members; we have ignored the poor; we have refused to share what we have; we have not cared about the feelings of others. Forgive us our sins, show us where we have been wrong, and give us the ability to acknowledge and address those wrongs. Help us to live as people who have much to share. Through Jesus Christ our Lord. Amen.

Prayer of Dedication of Gifts and Self

For gifts of love, O God, we offer our compassion to others. For gifts of possessions, we offer what we have to help those in need. For the gift of time, we offer our days of service. For the gift of life, we offer our selves to be your servants. Amen.

Sermon Summary

Personal power raises many issues within us. Jesus teaches a different way.

Hymn of the Day
"Immortal, Invisible, God Only Wise"

The combination of this hymn text with the Welsh tune ST. DENIO makes for a grand and majestic statement about the splendor of Almighty God. Based on 1 Timothy 1:17 ("To the King of the ages, immortal, invisible, the only God, be honor and glory forever and ever") the hymn provides images of God as unchanging and hidden. Yet, it also presents God as being visible in creation and as the God of righteousness. Walter Chalmers Smith, a Scottish pastor of the Free Church, wrote the hymn in 1867.

Children's Time

Servant Leaders

Bring a toy crown and have some conversation about who might wear it. Ask for a volunteer to wear the crown. When you have crowned your volunteer, ask what he or she would do as a king or queen.

Explain that in the Bible story today two of Jesus' disciples ask Jesus if they could be leaders with him in God's realm. They wanted to be like two kings sitting with Jesus. Comment that they probably wanted to be in charge! Jesus suspected they didn't really understand what he expects leaders to do, so he called the disciples together and began to teach them about being a leader in God's realm.

Paraphrase Mark 10:42-43. Ask the children if they know what a servant does. (If the children don't seem to have a good understanding, describe a servant as someone who works to take care of someone else.) Comment that in God's realm if we want to lead, we have to be servants.

Talk about how you might care for the needs of others at home, at school, or in the community this week.

Pray with the children, asking that God would help you become servant leaders.

The Sermon

How to Have Influence

Hymns

Beginning of Worship: "Celebrate with Joy and Singing"
Sermon Hymn: "Called as Partners in Christ's Service"
Closing Hymn: "Lord, Make Us Servants of Your Peace"

Scripture

Mark 10:35-45 (For additional sermon materials on this passage, see the July/August 2006 issue of *The Clergy Journal;* for sermon materials on Hebrews 5:1-10, see the 2006 May/June planning issue of *The Clergy Journal.*)

A version of an ancient story is told in many cultures: The monarch is challenged to consider the poor in the kingdom who have sometimes been forgotten. So one day the monarch decides to see what it is like to live as a poor commoner. In disguise, he spends time walking among the poor, seeing what it is like to live under the sometimes oppressive laws of the government. Returning to the palace, the king is changed by the experience, and the state becomes more friendly to those under its rule.

Why has this tale been so popular in so many places for so long? I think it is because people want those in authority to know what it's like to live under that authority. And I think it is because people don't see that kind of understanding very often. This can be true in nations, work environments, even in churches.

Two brothers, followers of Jesus, came to him to ask a question. Mark puts this story in an interesting place – after a couple of chapters in which Jesus has predicted his passion three times and has set a child in front of these same followers as an example of humility. Perhaps we're to see the brothers as waiting, biding their time to ask Jesus this question. They are so interested in what they want to ask of Jesus that they have failed to listen to what he's been saying. "Teacher, we want you to do for us whatever we ask of you . . . Grant us to sit, one at your right hand and one at your left, in your glory" (Mk 10:35, 37).

They had in mind, of course, some earthly or heavenly palace, a throne, a couple of extra scepters, a great deal of authority where they would reign as benevolent yet firm co-leaders with their Lord. The minds of Mark's readers, though, jump forward to the only place in this gospel where we are given a vision of people on Jesus' right and on his left – the cross and the two thieves who join him there. This is hardly a realization of anyone's definition of glory. If I had to guess, it's not the kind of glory James and John were thinking of when they asked Jesus for a favor. Jesus asked them if they could drink that cup, meaning the cup of suffering; they said of course they could drink that cup, meaning the cup of glory. He told them they would indeed share in his fate.

Now the other ten followers, who had been watching and listening to this conversation, got very angry with the two brothers, and Jesus used the moment to speak to all of them about leadership. It's almost certain Mark chose to record this interchange as a lesson to leaders in the early church of which he was a part.

Don't be like those worldly rulers you see around you, Jesus told them, and they knew what he meant. They could see Herod's palace, the governors, and even the priests who did not consider those over whom they had authority. I'm sure that the Twelve believed they could be *different* rulers. If *they* had authority, they'd use it wisely, take care of people; they'd be benevolent rulers.

But for Jesus, leading goes far beyond benevolence. A benevolent ruler waves from the rooftop to adoring crowds. Jesus walked among the crowds so that they pressed upon him and wore him out. A benevolent ruler sends servants to care for important invited guests. Jesus invited everyone to the banquet, then washed their feet himself when they arrived. A benevolent ruler hopes that people will be fed. Jesus broke enough bread and fish to feed a crowd. A benevolent ruler sees that laws are applied as fairly as possible to as many as possible. Jesus taught about God's love as the law by which we live. A benevolent ruler may even give up something for others. Jesus gave his life as a ransom for many.

So, if the followers of Jesus are supposed to move into a different type of leadership role – that of servant – what does that mean?

Ron Heifetz, a leader in the field of leadership training, tells a story of when he and his wife were in England on their way to a speaking engagement. Rosh Hashanah, the Jewish New Year, was approaching, and they had hoped to observe the holiday at a synagogue in London. The day came, however, and they found themselves still in the English countryside, nowhere near a synagogue. On a bit of a whim, they decided to enter a small, empty Anglican church for a time of spiritual reflection. At the front of the church was a crucifix, and Ron found himself in a bit of spiritual conflict. Here he was, a Jew well-aware of the abuses of Christians toward his people, confronted with the figure of Jesus on the cross. Nevertheless, he asked "Reb Jesus" to tell him about the experience of the cross. Suddenly, he asked his wife to go outside with him for a small experiment. They sat together near a tree in the deserted churchyard. He asked her to spread out her arms in a cruciform pose, which they both did. After a few moments, he asked her how she felt, to which she replied, "Really vulnerable." That was it! For this expert in leadership, the experience was a lesson in vulnerability. Jesus was such a great leader because he was open and vulnerable to the experiences of life. (Ronald A. Heifetz and Marty Linsky, *Leadership On the Line*, Harvard Business School Press, 2002, pp. 228-229.)

That is exactly what we see and know from the life of Jesus. He inspires all of us to follow him because he was willing to give up equality with God for a time in order to become one of us; he walked with us and was vulnerable just as we are. That is the kind of leader we should be.

– Melissa Bane Sevier

October 29, 2006

21st Sunday after Pentecost (Proper 25)

RC/Pres: 30th Sunday in Ordinary Time

Lessons

RCL	Job 42:1-6, 10-17	Heb 7:23-28	Mk 10:46-52
Roman Catholic	Jer 31:7-9	Heb 5:1-6	Mk 10:46-52
Episcopal (BCP)	Isa 59:(1-4), 9-19	Heb 5:12—6:1, 9-12	Mk 10:46-52
Lutheran	Jer 31:7-9	Heb 7:23-28	Mk 10:46-52

Introduction to the Lessons

Lesson 1

(1) Job 42:1-6, 10-17 (RCL)

Job responds to God's message to him. God honors Job and dismisses the responses of Job's friends.

(2) Jeremiah 31:7-9 (RC/Luth)

God will bring the people of Israel back to their homeland.

(3) Isaiah 59:(1-4), 9-19 (Epis)

Judah has not kept covenant with God. God calls them to repent.

Lesson 2

(1) Hebrews 7:23-28 (RCL/Luth)

Jesus, the Son of God, is the great high priest of our faith. Here are his attributes.

(2) Hebrews 5:1-6 (RC); Hebrews 5:12—6:1, 9-12 (Epis)

Jesus, though he suffered greatly, was elevated to the rank of high priest, as was the ancient priest of Salem, Melchizedek.

Gospel
Mark 10:46-52 (RCL/RC/Epis/Luth)
This is the story of a blind man named Bartimaeus, restored to his sight by Jesus.

Theme
Jesus came to help us through our hopeless situations.

Thought for the Day
Though a situation may seem hopeless, God cares about each person and each situation.

Call to Worship

One: I will praise the Lord at all times; praise for God is always on my lips.

All: My whole being praises the Lord. The poor will hear and be glad.

One: Glorify the Lord with me, and let us praise God's name together.

All: I asked the Lord for help, and God answered me, saving me from all that I feared.

One: The angel of the Lord camps around those who fear God, and God saves them.

All: Examine and see how good the Lord is. Happy is the person who trusts God.

— based on Psalm 34

Pastoral Prayer
Loving and giving God, you have made us and all things. We thank you for the hope we find in the smallest and grandest of things: an October morning; a baby's cry in worship; a phone call from a good friend; a decent night's rest. When hope is lost, when rest does not come and morning takes too long to arrive, when friends are nowhere to be found, and when life seems empty, speak to us, O God, even as Jesus spoke to Bartimaeus. May your word of kindness and hope bring us back to our feet and enable us to walk with full sight. Today we remember all who

struggle with a lack of hope and who long for a decent job, a roof over their children's heads, a day without pain, a life of freedom and security. Show us, we pray, how to bring your hope to them. Amen.

Prayer of Confession

O God of hope, how often we have lived as if there were no hope to be found. We neglect to see Christ in the other person; we do not look for the brightness of Christ's love in the shadows. We have forgotten how to share hope with those in need. Forgive us our short-sightedness, and give us the vision to see you at work in the world around us. And when we see others who are hurting, enable us to find ways of bringing your hope to others. Jesus, Son of David, have mercy on us. Through Christ we pray. Amen.

Prayer of Dedication of Gifts and Self

For gifts of hope, O God, we give you thanks. Enable us to see – in the places we live and work and go to school – the desperate and obvious needs of some, and the silent, hardly noticeable needs of others. Then strengthen our hearts to respond to what we discover. In Christ our Lord. Amen.

Sermon Summary

Bartimaeus begged by the side of the road. When Jesus saw him, he had mercy on the man's physical situation and also on his emotional and spiritual needs. In the same way, God cares about our needs and gives us hope in the midst of crisis.

Hymn of the Day
"O For a Thousand Tongues to Sing"

Written by Charles Wesley in 1739 to celebrate the first anniversary of his Christian conversion, this hymn has become somewhat of an "anthem" for Methodist and other Wesleyan churches. Included in most every other hymnal as well, the hymn enjoys a broad ecumenical usage, perhaps making it the most popular of Wesley's some 6500 hymns. Most current hymnals contain from four to seven of the hymn's original eighteen stanzas. In addition to the standard tune AZMON, the hymn tune RICHMOND is often used with this hymn, lending fresh insights to the text. British Methodists often use the tunes LYDIA and UNIVERSITY.

Children's Time

Blind Bartimaeus

Invite the children to play a game of "I spy." Explain how to play the game and start by giving an example, "I spy with my little eye something that is *(name the color)*." The children guess the object. The one who guesses correctly takes the next turn. Play several times.

Explain that you would like to change the game a little. Comment that God has given us many ways to explore the world around us. Suggest that this time you use your ears. Start by giving an example, "I hear with my little ear something that rings." Play several times. If you have time move onto the sense of touch, "I feel with my hands something that is *(rough, smooth, sticky . . .)*"

Comment that the Bible story today is about a man who could not see anything at all. He had to use his other senses to explore the world. Tell the story about Jesus healing blind Bartimaeus. Ask the children to imagine what it was like to be Bartimaeus after his eyes were healed. What might he like to look at the most? How would his life be different?

Pray with the children, giving thanks for the gifts of eyes, ears, noses, and fingers.

The Sermon

Blindness and Hope

Hymns
Beginning of Worship: "I Greet Thee Who My Sure Redeemer Art"
Sermon Hymn: "Seek Ye First"
Closing Hymn: "We Walk By Faith and Not By Sight"

Scripture
Mark 10:46-52 (For additional sermon materials on this passage, see the July/August 2006 issue of *The Clergy Journal* and the 2006 May/June planning issue of *The Clergy Journal*.)

It is hard, sometimes, to preach from the healing stories of Jesus, for in just about any congregation someone sits, wondering, "Why would Jesus heal Bartimaeus, but God seems to ignore my pain?" It's a legitimate question. There is certainly enough pain to go around in this world, and we all imagine that if we were God, we wouldn't allow it. We'd do something about it.

The question of pain is an ancient one, as old as the world itself, and the question never has an answer – at least not the kind of answer we wish we could hear. There is no explanation, no resolution, no key to understanding why Bartimaeus and all of humankind find ourselves in need of physical healing and not receiving it.

Though the healing stories from Jesus' ministry do not provide us with an answer to human pain, or even a promise that, if we have enough faith, we can be healed just like Bartimaeus, they do give us a look into the work and mercy of God.

"Jesus, Son of David, have mercy on me!" (Mk 10:47) cried the blind man beside the crowd, at the fringes of society. This was his place, where his blindness had put him. This was where he could get the only help available to him – handouts from passersby. He cried out, as he always did, for alms. But when he heard that Jesus was in the crowd, his pleas changed. I don't know if he even held out hope for healing or if he expected something else from Jesus. Perhaps he'd heard of other healings. Those who wanted to protect Jesus told the man to be quiet, but he was determined to be heard. "Son of David, have mercy on me!"

That is when we see it: not the answer to all our pain, but one who pays attention. Though others tried to shush the crier, Jesus stood and turned. "Call him here" (10:49) he said. And they did. Those who had previously told Bartimaeus (not a little meanly) to be quiet, now followed the merciful example of Jesus: "Take heart; get up, he is calling you."

And Bartimaeus did. He didn't just amble, but threw off his cloak, jumped to his feet, and came to Jesus, who asked, "What do you want me to do for you?" (10:51)

"My teacher, let me see again" (10:51). And so it happened. Bartimaeus was healed of his blindness and became a disciple, following Jesus along with the crowd that had, a few moments before, told him not to bother Jesus.

The story of Jesus' healing of a blind man is a story of mercy and hope. There is more emotion in this story than in many others, expressed through both words and actions: the crowd first "sternly ordered" Bartimaeus into silence and later told him to "take heart;" Bartimaeus shouted and cried for mercy, threw off his cloak and sprang to his feet, then followed. Far from refusing to deal with hurting people, Jesus responded to the shouts and cries and enthusiastic hopes of a man in need.

What for us, then?

There is much about the workings of human pain within a community in this story, workings that many will recognize. The blind man, in great need, continually calls out for help, not just on this day, but every day. He is there, by the side of the road, asking for aid. Just as we often do, the people walk on by. And some of them try to get him to be quiet. Are they worried Jesus will be disturbed? Or are they using that as an excuse to quiet him because *they* are disturbed? They are disturbed by the reminder that there is pain in the world; they are disturbed by how close that pain has come to them – close enough to reach out and touch them – and they would just as soon not hear about it.

But the one in need is wise enough not to keep the pain bottled up inside. He shouts; he cries out to Jesus; and Jesus recognizes and responds to his cries.

The crowd's response is interesting, isn't it? Once protective (of Jesus, ostensibly), after they see how Jesus responds, they too turn to Bartimaeus and tell him to take heart, get up, and draw close, because his cries have been heard and Jesus wants to see him.

I see in this story a human being in pain, who thankfully isn't afraid to talk about it, and a community that initially is reluctant to hear his pain but eventually is willing to listen and to help the man get the help he needs. What would it be like in our churches and communities if we encouraged those in pain to talk about it, if we made a space for those who are troubled to be heard? Would we start support groups, open our fellowship hall as a place where social workers could mingle with street people, set up a program for lay people to visit with the elderly and sick, just to listen? And once we truly listen, we have no other way to go than to begin to show them the mercy and hope of Christ, to encourage them to take heart because Jesus has heard their cries.

No, there may not be an answer to pain and suffering, but there is indeed hope. This is what the community of Christ does: we watch for those by the side of the road; we listen to them; and we offer them hope. Nothing less is expected of us, because we are following the example of Jesus.

– Melissa Bane Sevier

October 31, 2006

Reformation Day

Lessons
Lutheran   Jer 31:31-34   Rom 3:19-28   Jn 8:31-36

Introduction to the Lessons
Lesson 1
Jeremiah 31:31-34
God has offered us an eternal covenant: God's own law written on our hearts so that we do not need to stand separate from God, but can be one with the Most Holy.

Lesson 2
Romans 3:19-28
Although humanity is broken by sin, faith becomes the path by which we can rest confidently in God's righteousness.

Gospel
John 8:31-36
Jesus calls us out of slavery to sin into the freedom of discipleship.

Theme
The Reformation is not about an event or an era; it is about committed discipleship and the willingness to be who God needs us to be here and now.

Thought for the Day
Once an old woman at my church said the secret is God loves us *exactly* the way we are *and* that [God] loves us too much to let us stay like this, and I'm just trying to trust that.

— Anne Lamott, *Operating Instructions*
(quoted in *The New Beacon Book of Quotations by Women*,
Beacon Press, 1996)

Call to Worship

One: We come together not as perfect people,
All: But as people seeking God's re-formation of our souls,
One: Of our hopes and visions,
All: And of our words and deeds.
One: As clay in the potter's hands,
All: We offer ourselves to be shaped anew.

Pastoral Prayer

Reforming God, you offer us the grace of beginning each day anew with a heart, soul, mind, and spirit freshly born into the universe. Help us to stop dragging the burdens of past mistakes and past glories behind us, so that we may be free to become faithful sisters and brothers of the One who defined himself only by your image in him. Grant us the grace to be a re-formed people, not once only, but day after day until your peace is accomplished here on earth as it is in the eternal places. Amen.

Prayer of Confession

Merciful God, we acknowledge all the ways we cling to our old selves and to the image of you we were called to reveal yesterday. We admit our fear of losing the comfort of what we have been. We confess our resistance to accepting the new self you are offering and the image of you we are called to reveal today. Forgive us our anxiety and inspire us to trust so that we can hold ourselves lightly, letting go of the outworn and receiving the new self you are continually promising. Amen.

Prayer of Dedication of Gifts and Self

Accept these gifts, Gracious God, offered back to you from the bounty you have shared with us. Form them into tangible hope for your needy world and re-form us to become ever more bounteous givers. Amen.

Sermon Summary

We are accountable to God to be persons fitting lightly to our identity in this moment, so that we can become the vessels and instruments God requires to bring the realm of Shalom to fulfillment. Thus we will never "be," because we are always "becoming."

Hymn of the Day
"A Mighty Fortress Is Our God"

Here is another popular hymn that transcends denominational boundaries. "Ein feste burg ist unser Gott" was written by German Reformation leader Martin Luther, probably between the years of 1527 and 1529. The German text has been translated into over fifty languages, including some 100 English versions. Based on Psalm 46, the hymn expresses confidence in God and may be used as a source of strong encouragement for the advancement of the entire church. Singing the tune EIN FESTE BURG in a joyful, moving tempo allows an expression similar to that associated with Luther's original rhythmic setting of the tune.

Children's Time

God's Love

Bring a large hoop and ask the children to tell you what shape the hoop makes. Gather around the ring and observe that there is no beginning or ending to the circle. Trace the ring with a finger and observe that a circle just goes on and on and on. Encourage the children to join you saying "on and on . . . "

Comment that this circle reminds you of God's love. God's love has no beginning and no end. God has always loved us and always will. Even when we make a mistake, God still loves us. Just like a circle, God's love for us goes on and on. Express excitement that God loves us no matter what.

Ask the children to search for circles in the church. Comment that every time we see a circle we can remember God's amazing love for us. Mention that today is Reformation Sunday. On this day we celebrate the lives of people through the ages who wanted to share the good news of God's love. If you have time, you might want to tell the story of Martin Luther or other reformers who have influenced your church.

Pray with the children, giving thanks for the good news of God's love.

The Sermon

Held Accountable

Hymns
Beginning of Worship: "Fire of God, Undying Flame"
Sermon Hymn: "How Clear Is Our Vocation, Lord"
Closing Hymn: "As a Chalice Cast of Gold"

Scripture
Romans 3:19-28 (For sermon materials on John 8:31-36, see the July/
August 2006 issue of *The Clergy Journal;* for sermon materials on Jeremiah
31:31-34, see the 2006 May/June planning issue of *The Clergy Journal.*)

Here in the epistle to the Romans, Paul wrestles with an old, old issue for
the Christian community: Are we under the law or under grace? Are we
saved by our own works or by God's unconditional love? For a long time, I
worried about this and I broke out in a cold sweat every time I needed to
preach one of these texts because the preacher is always – to some greater
or lesser extent – translating. The idiom of another time and place must
be made accessible in the language of the time and place in which we
find ourselves right now, so that the light of scripture is reflected into the
corners of our daily lives.

Law or grace? Our own works or God's unconditional love? We ask
this as if pinning it down to one thing that is essential for faithful living.
We ask as if it is – or needs to be – the same thing for everyone. Or as if it
is the same for each person at all times in his or her life.

Are we under the law or under grace? Yes, we are. Does our salvation
depend on our own works or God's unconditional love? Yes, it does. It
depends on both.

This is Reformation Day. It is assuredly a celebration of an historical
event that has marked our own faith journeys. But if that is all it is, the
remembrance has failed in its true purpose. When we speak of reformation, we are speaking not only of an event or of a time in the life of the
corporate church, but of an ongoing process within our own individual
hearts, minds, souls, spirits. We are speaking of the process of being

shaped by God – reshaped and reshaped yet again as a potter shapes clay. Here the clay becomes a chalice, there a basin. Here, a pitcher or a flowerpot; there, a statue. It is shaped now for the sacred; then, for the mundane. What is necessary today will not be tomorrow. The vessel needed yesterday is not the one needed today.

What remains unchanging is that we who call ourselves followers of Jesus are accountable to God to be shaped as God needs. We are accountable to God to be God's servant people, to be available to God for God's use to bring the divine realm to fulfillment. We are accountable under the law *and* under grace. We are accountable in our works *and* as the recipients of God's unconditional love.

We have it from the gospel according to Matthew that Jesus said, "Do not think that I have come to abolish the law or the prophets; I have come not to abolish but to fulfill" (5:17). We are accountable for what we have heard, learned, and done as a result of being graced to receive prophetic wisdom. In some things we will act as persons transformed and in others we won't. Yet even under the weight of sin, we are accountable to God to resist despair and to embrace confidence because God promises that in the divine universe death and sin are not the last word – abundant life in the resurrection is the last word. We are accountable to God to act on God's behalf, reflecting the divine image that God entrusted to us in our creation.

We are accountable to God to be people of *faith,* not merely people of *belief.* A faithful disciple is not in a passive or abstract relationship with God. Rather, a faithful disciple is anticipatory and eager. That means we are *beings* in the process of *becoming.* I'm not sure that the term "Reformation Day" does justice to what we are about. Perhaps "Reforming Day" describes it better. We are a people covenanted with God to being formed and re-formed as many times as God needs us to be.

We are not spiritual infants. We should not cling to our image of God as a baby clings to a favorite blanket, shrieking in terror if anyone tries to take it away. We are spiritual adults growing into the full maturity of Christ, able to meet God as God chooses to become. We are not concrete, operational children fiercely resisting any and every change of language, liturgy, hymnody, and ministry that God offers through the wild tempest of the Spirit blowing through human history. We are spiritual adults, able to recognize and embrace that God is bigger than all our thoughts, our words, our ideas, our theories, and our doctrines. God may choose to be revealed through the least expected persons and the most radical notions, just as God has always done.

We are a people being re-formed in the thought of the Holy One. We are useless to God unless we are malleable enough to be reshaped by the divine hands and the divine vision for the service God needs here and now. In another place Paul says, "I have become all things to all people, so that I might by any means save some" (1 Cor 9:22b). On this Reformation Day, looking back at our life since last October 31, have we acted as persons committed to such wholehearted service? Have we acted as persons willing to give up the comfortable and the familiar to meet God's needy people in the words and deeds they require here and now? Or have we resisted all re-formation? Can we say with Paul that we are willing to become now Jew, now Gentile, now radical, now conservative, now foolish, now wise? Or must we acknowledge that our own opinions and our self-illusions are more important to us than God's startling word and holy image in our lives?

As we sit in prayerful quiet with these questions, I invite you to inhale God's divine breath that animated creation and, thus, to hold yourself as lightly as breath exhaled at rest. I invite you to still yourself into an attentive tranquility where the echoing silence of God's word can name you into new being and, thus, resonate with more profound harmony. I invite you to risk the grace of transformation from who you are to who you might become. In the name of God, may it be so.

– Andrea La Sonde Anastos

November 1, 2006

All Saints' Day

Lessons

RCL	Wis 3:1-9 or Isa 25:6-9	Rev 21:1-6a	Jn 11:32-44
Roman Catholic	Rev 7:2-4, 9-14	1 Jn 3:1-3	Mt 5:1-12
Episcopal (BCP)	Sir 44:1-10, 13-14	Rev 7:2-4, 9-17	Mt 5:1-12
Lutheran	Isa 25:6-9 or Wis 3:1-9	Rev 21:1-6a	Jn 11:32-44

Introduction to the Lessons
Lesson 1
(1) Wisdom 3:1-9 (RCL/Luth)
God watches over the souls of the righteous forever.

(2) Isaiah 25:6-9 (RCL/Luth)
Isaiah describes God calling the people to a feast on the mountain where "death will be swallowed up forever."

(3) Sirach 44:1-10, 13-14 (Epis)
The well-known passage beginning, "Let us now sing the praises of famous [people] . . . " is a description of those who are godly. It reminds us that their names will continue forever because of the way they lived as a blessing to others.

(4) Revelation 7:2-4, 9-14 (RC)
This vision includes the multitude of the saints rejoicing before the throne of God, praising God and worshiping with angels and elders.

Lesson 2
(1) Revelation 21:1-6a (RCL/Luth)
John offers a vision of the new heaven and the new earth and the joy that will wipe away all sorrow.

(2) 1 John 3:1-3 (RC)
We have been granted the greatest of gifts in being received by God as God's own children, which, in time to come, will reveal us to be like God, reflecting the divine image.

(3) Revelation 7:2-4, 9-17 (Epis)
This vision includes the multitude of the saints rejoicing before the throne of God, praising God and worshiping with angels and elders.

Gospel
(1) John 11:32-44 (RCL/Luth)
Jesus comes to Martha and Mary in their time of grief.

(2) Matthew 5:1-12 (RC/Epis)
This passage is the beatitudes – Jesus' mandate to the community he calls to walk in God's ways – as recorded by the Gospel of Matthew.

Theme
To be new is not merely to be changed; it is to blossom from a vine that grows from different roots completely.

Thought for the Day
Eternity is not something that begins after you are dead. It is going on all the time. We are in it now.

– Lily Dougall, "The Undiscovered Country"
(quoted in *The New Beacon Book of Quotations by Women*,
Beacon Press, 1996)

Call to Worship *(Unison)*
Come, sisters! Lift up your heart and mind with me!
Come, brothers! Lift up your soul and strength with me!
Come! Let us climb the holy mountain.
Come! Let us join the company of those who seek the God of Glory.

Pastoral Prayer

Alpha and Omega, you are our beginning and our end. You are our pathway and our goal. You are companion and journey. Help us to see through the veil of time to the eternal now in which your hope for creation already exists, whole and holy. Guide us to live as citizens of that new heaven and new earth in this time and place and, in so doing, to bring your shalom to radiant fulfillment. Amen.

Prayer of Confession

We confess before you, Eternal One, our temptation to use our burdens and tears to gain us attention and sympathy. We confess our temptation to use our apathy to make us comfortable and our sins to make us interesting. We stand before you, clinging to a self that has grown dusty and outworn. Wipe away the old, Eternal One, and make us new that we may faithfully bear the name, "Saint of God." Amen.

Prayer of Dedication of Gifts and Self

Create in us such wise and generous stewardship of your gifts that these offerings may become new life for those to whom they are committed. Amen.

Sermon Summary

God has called us into a new creation right here, right now. God has called us to be saints of God now and here. Our baptism births us anew and commissions us for that vocation.

Hymn of the Day
"For All the Saints"

As we sing this hymn we are praising God for the Christian believers who have lived and died in all eras of history. We are giving thanks for those who have fought the good fight, remained faithful, and now live in bright array. We are reminded of the vastness of the family of saints, as gathered from the earth's widest bounds and ocean's farthest coast. Anglican bishop William W. How, in the year 1864, based this hymn on the Apostles' Creed statement: "I believe in the communion of saints." The tune SINE NOMINE by Ralph Vaughan Williams provides a powerful musical expression when sung with energy and rhythmic drive.

Children's Time

God's Dream

Have a brief conversation about dreams: What was the best dream you ever had? Comment that the Bible has many stories about people who heard God's voice in a dream.

Hold up a Bible and show the children how to find the book of Revelation. Explain that many years ago God shared a dream with John. It was a wonderful dream about the kind of world God wants for us. Paraphrase verses 3-4.

Invite the children to imagine what it would be like to live in a world where there was no sadness and everyone loved each other. What might it be like?

Comment that today is All Saints' Day. On this day we celebrate the lives of all the people who followed in God's way and worked to make the world a better place. These people wanted to see God's dream come true. (If you have time you might want to give an example of someone who worked hard to bring God's love into the world.) Invite the children to name ways we might make our world a happier place to live.

Pray, giving thanks for all those who show us how make the world a better place to live.

The Sermon

Making All Things New

Hymns

Beginning of Worship: "Give Thanks for Life"
Sermon Hymn: "O Holy City, Seen of John"
Closing Hymn: "O Day of Peace"

Scripture

Revelation 21:1-6a (For sermon materials on Matthew 5:1-12, see the July/August 2006 issue of *The Clergy Journal;* for sermon materials on John 11:32-44, see the 2006 May/June planning issue of *The Clergy Journal.*)

"And the one who was seated on the throne said, 'See, I am making all things new'" (Rev 21:5).

In this vision of John of Patmos, God proclaims something we mortals have a difficult time comprehending. God does not say, "See, I am making all things better." God does not say, "See, I am making all things bigger . . . " or "different" or "beautiful" or, even, "perfect." God does not say, "See, I am changing all things." God says, "See, I am making all things *new*."

God is saying that everything we have understood about the creation in which we are currently living is or will be (it isn't clear what the correct verb tense is here) no longer valid. God is describing the creation the prophets were trying to tell us about when they talked about the lion lying down with the lamb and the child putting her hand in the adder's nest. This is the creation that doesn't make any sense under the rules as we understand them. This is the creation that Jesus was trying to explain to us when he talked about the owner of the vineyard hiring the workers at different times of day, but paying them all the same (abundant) wages, and about the first being last, and about a servant monarch. This is the creation that just doesn't compute in our worldly economies or earthly power structures.

It's hard for us to understand this new universe because we have only our human experience to inform us. No matter how hard we try, we can't imagine something beyond the laws of physics of the universe in which we live. We may *think* we are imagining truly new things, but I defy you to start from nothing and create something that you don't have to describe as "*like* an armadillo but with eight arms and fur." But *new* means a creation without fur or eight or sound, and we simply can't get there from here via the brain synapses and neurological pathways we already have!

"And the one who was seated on the throne said, 'See, I am making all things new'."

Perhaps we will just have to wait until we are there to comprehend – whatever "comprehend" means in that universe. Perhaps we will just have to be where all things are new in order to understand it. And maybe it is just not important to worry about it at the moment.

There is, however, something that I suspect God really needs us to work on understanding right here and right now, on this specific All Saints' Day in the year of our Lord 2006. This is the day on which we annually remember and honor the saints of God, those people most of us consider extraordinary and rare, people like Francis and Mary (any one of them) and Mother Teresa of Calcutta, or like Paul or the martyrs of Uganda or Japan or New Guinea, or someone like the Venerable Bede or Clare or Dominic or Bernard. "What amazing people," we think to ourselves. "This is what it is like to be *real* disciples." We think how lucky we are to have such role models. And somewhere deep in our subconscious, where we truly believe our thoughts are masked even from God, we heave a huge internal sigh and think, "Thank God I am not religious enough to be among them!"

Uh, uh, uh . . . Put that thought away right now. Because guess what? If you are a baptized Christian, God is simply waiting for you to offer your name to be put on the calendar along with all the rest of them. "Wait," you say, "what is this about baptism and sainthood?" In baptism you and I and the person beside you in the pew were all made new. We were not made bigger, better, different, more beautiful, more perfect; we were not even changed (in the way most of us use that word), *we were made new.* We were told that in entering the waters of baptism, we died to the old self; and in rising from those waters, we were born anew of one being with Christ. We are told that we have been rooted or grafted to a different vine entirely. We are *new* creatures of a *new* creation. The fact that we are given the amazing baptismal present of being allowed to inhabit this creation for the purpose of incarnating that newness here and now seems to be part of God's plan for making "all things new" one creature at a time. That means you and me, folks.

"And the one who was seated on the throne said, 'See, I am making all things new.'"

See, I am making *all* things new. On this All Saints' Day, we are not only remembering and honoring those who chose to *believe* that they were new and to *live as if* they were new, we are reminding ourselves and each other that God is waiting for us to believe it and live it, too. I have said this before and I suspect I will say it many more times before I preach my last sermon: the saints of God are not some other people who lived in some other place or some other time. We – you, me, our parents, our children, our friends and, yes, even our enemies – are the saints of God. The difference between Francis or Mary and me is that they took up the vocation to which they had been commissioned . . . and I am still thinking about it.

What am I waiting for? This seems the ideal day to stop waiting and to say yes to the One who created me and then created me anew. It seems the ideal day for any of us who are still waiting to accept our sainthood, to stop dragging our heels, to start dancing with the angels and that great company of witnesses who surround us and uphold us.

My friends, my fellow saints of God, look! Listen! God speaks, "I am making all things new . . . It is done!" May it be so. Hallelujah! Hallelujah!

– Andrea La Sonde Anastos

November 5, 2006

21st Sunday after Pentecost (Proper 26)
RC/Pres: 31st Sunday in Ordinary Time

Lessons

RCL	Ruth 1:1-8	Heb 9:11-14	Mk 12:28-34
Roman Catholic	Deut 6:2-6	Heb 7:23-28	Mk 12:28-34
Episcopal (BCP)	Deut 6:1-9	Heb 7:23-28	Mk 12:28-34
Lutheran	Deut 6:1-9	Heb 9:11-14	Mk 12:28-34

Introduction to the Lessons
Lesson 1
(1) Ruth 1:1-8 (RCL)
The opening of this book introduces Naomi and the life events through which she becomes the means for Ruth, a Moabite woman, to journey to Judah and eventually become an ancestor of Jesus.

(2) Deuteronomy 6:1-9 (Epis/Luth); Deuteronomy 6:2-6 (RC)
Moses tells the people to keep God's commandments as they pass into the land promised to them, carrying the commandments in their hearts and teaching them to their children.

Lesson 2
(1) Hebrews 9:11-14 (RCL/Luth)
The personal sacrifice of Christ is infinitely preferable to the animal sacrifices previously offered; this sacrifice purifies all things for all time.

(2) Hebrews 7:23-28 (RC/Epis)
Jesus is described as high priest, eternally available as an intercessor for humankind because, unlike the priests of Levi, Christ is recognized permanently by God.

Gospel
Mark 12:28-34 (RCL/RC/Epis/Luth)
Jesus converses with one of the scribes about the two great commandments. This episode contradicts the simplistic understanding that *all* the religious authorities were enemies of Jesus.

Theme
Disciples live the blessing that was, that is, and that is to be in each moment that unfolds before them. They do not wait for some other life; they live holiness now.

Thought for the Day
God has no other hands than ours.

— Dorothee Sölle, *Suffering*
(quoted in *The New Beacon Book of Quotations by Women,*
Beacon Press, 1996)

Call to Worship
One: We come with what strength we have of heart, mind, and soul,
All: To learn to love the God who first loved us into being.
One: In joy, God returns that love with abundance,
All: Through the hands and hearts of our neighbors. Praise God from whom all blessings flow!

Pastoral Prayer
You call me your servant.
Grant me the grace this day to speak every word with your voice,
To greet each person with your compassion,
To make each decision with your wisdom,
To see every opportunity with your vision.
In every breath I take, may others see your glory revealed. Amen.

Prayer of Confession
Self-giving God, you loved us by taking on the fullness of our humanity. We confess that we would rather forget what you taught us about being fully human! We confess our halfhearted love of our neighbor, our mindless

115

grasping after pleasure, our soul-numbed response to another's need, our weak excuses in the face of injustice. We pray for forgiveness, but we also pray that we may be awakened, startled, shocked into remembering that others will know you through our actions. Amen.

Prayer of Dedication of Gifts and Self

Bless the offerings we bring, beloved God, that they may reflect not our imperfect love, but your boundless charity. May our hearts and souls be graced in the giving, as we have been graced by receiving from others. Amen.

Sermon Summary

To love God with our whole hearts, minds, souls, and strength is our true vocation. Our vocation is made manifest through loving the sisters and brothers that God has put beside us with our whole hearts, minds, souls, and strength.

Hymn of the Day
"Spirit of God, Descend upon My Heart"

Written by Irish pastor George Croly in 1867, this hymn recounts the Holy Spirit's descent on Christ's baptism and at Pentecost. It also offers a prayerful request for personal indwelling of the Spirit. This prayer is not for a dramatic display, but simply for the Spirit to "take the dimness of my soul away." The fourth line of the fourth stanza presents a request that may not be too popular, when we sing, "teach me the patience of unanswered prayer." Sing the hymn with a sense of quiet confidence, growing in intensity on the final stanza in singing of our commitment to God.

Children's Time

The Most Important Rule

Bring three large paper hearts and a marker.

Invite the children to think of some important rules or laws where you live. (You may have to recruit the help of some of the adults.) Do you have any family rules? Is there any rule that is more important than any other?

Open the Bible and mention that in today's Bible story Jesus talks about the two most important rules of all. Tell the story of Jesus' conversation with the Pharisees.

Show the three hearts and ask the children what Jesus said about love. Who are we to love? Print one of these words on each heart: God, Self, Others.

Explain that the first rule about love was a commandment written in the Hebrew Scriptures. This meant it was very special to Jesus and all Jewish people. Jesus added the second commandment because he knew it was very important for us to love one another.

Hold up each heart in turn and invite the children to name ways that we might show love to God, to ourselves, to others. Observe that there are many different ways of showing love.

Pray with the children, asking God to help you as you learn to love God, others, and yourselves.

The Sermon

All My Heart; All My Soul

Hymns
Beginning of Worship: "As Those of Old Their First-Fruits Brought"
Sermon Hymn: "Here I Am, Lord"
Closing Hymn: "Go Forth for God"

Scripture
Mark 12:28-34 (For additional sermon materials on this passage, see the July/August 2006 issue of *The Clergy Journal* and the 2006 May/June planning issue of *The Clergy Journal*.)

Listen, my sisters and brothers, to the words of that long-ago scribe of Israel. Listen to the words of one person whose heart was yearning to share in the life-giving teaching of Rabbi Jesus who was traveling the dusty roads of the countryside with his followers and preaching. Listen to the scribe: "'To love one's neighbor as oneself' – this is much more important than all whole burnt-offerings and sacrifices"(Mk 12:33b).

117

We are drawing near the end of the long season of Pentecost and preparing ourselves in these November days to conclude one liturgical year and begin a new one. In these final weeks of Pentecost, the gospel moves decisively toward apocalyptic readings. Our hearts and souls are invited to dance and to pray in *kairos* (God's paradoxical time), holding side by side the expectant longing of Advent and a prayerful consideration of the end time (the time not of the Incarnation, but of the *second* coming of Christ.) In that context, this encounter sits on a fulcrum between past and present: between the ancient riches and wisdom of Judaism in which Jesus was steeped, and the yet-to-be riches and wisdom of the Christian way that he visioned with his disciples.

It can be far too easy for 21st-century Christians to assume that every time Jesus spoke to the religious authorities, there was conflict and antagonism. This, in turn, encourages many faithful churchgoers to believe that Jesus taught that Judaism was no longer valid as a path for God's covenanted people. Such misunderstanding of scripture leads some to disdain the spiritual wealth of Jewish practice and learning, or, even worse, to scapegoat Jews and permit in themselves an anti-Semitism that breeds violence.

We need to look again at our preconceptions. This dialog is not hostile; on the contrary, it is built around the blessing of tradition (represented by the scribe) on the new teaching that God is offering (represented by Jesus). The scribe invites Jesus to express the deepest, most holy truth of his belief and practice. Jesus responds with the *Shema*, one of the principle statements undergirding Judaism – a proclamation of the Holy as the center from which all creation flows and toward which all creation looks, "Hear, O Israel, the Lord our God, the Lord is one!" Then, in what is almost a duet, Jesus and the scribe trade additional statements about how God's people respond to God's outpouring, each building on the choices of the other in a soaring proclamation of what the kingdom of shalom will be like.

The passage ends with Jesus gathering the blessing from his past and casting it over the future. He tells the scribe, "You are not far from the kingdom of God" (12:34). What was the statement of the scribe that brought this blessing? Listen! "'To love one's neighbor as oneself' – this is much more important than all whole burnt-offerings and sacrifices."

Whatever else can be said about burnt-offerings and sacrifices, they are personal and individual, they are an offering back to God from me on my own behalf, from you on your behalf. Yes, burnt-offerings and sacrifices were sometimes (in times of famine or exile or at the High Holy Days) made for the *whole people;* but 99 times out of 100, they were pretty private and pretty exclusive.

Jesus, standing firmly rooted in the prophetic Jewish tradition, was not about being private and exclusive! Jesus was about community. Jesus was about discovering the presence of God in community. Jesus was about Immanuel – God with us. The scribe doesn't say, nor does Jesus, that burnt-offerings and sacrifices don't have their place. They do. A sacrifice is a way I practice with God what God is training me to do: love others.

Think of it this way: Have you ever watched a parent and child play what I call the "Give-Give Back" game? The parent gives the child something (a book, a blanket, a toy) and then asks for it back. The child gives it back and the parent says, "Thank you." Then the parent holds it for a moment and asks, "Would you like it back?" The child reaches for it and the parent prompts, "What do you say? Thank you?" The child attempts the words. The parent invites the child to offer the object again and says, "Thank you!" and the game continues. Some time later (weeks, months) the parent and child are with another child and now the parent invites the child to give the book, blanket, toy, to the "neighbor." The initial game was practice for this much more important skill of sharing.

Most of us have seen this parenting technique so often that we don't think about how strange it is. Why should the parent say, "Thank you"? The object *came* from the parent in the first place! The child didn't buy this object or earn it. But each time the parent receives the object, she or he says, "Thank you!" We understand that the parent is modeling gratitude and inviting the child to mimic it. The parent is teaching the child how to receive with grace and how to give with generosity.

In the same way, a sacrifice or a burnt offering is God's way of teaching us how to receive with grace and give with generosity. God invites us to practice this easier generosity (giving back to God directly) so that we will mature into our real vocation, which is practicing generosity with one another – with friend and stranger and, yes, with enemy. Listen! "'To love one's neighbor as oneself' – this is much more important than all whole burnt-offerings and sacrifices."

This gospel reading is about the end time. It is about what that holy commonwealth will be like. In that glorious realm, the One God will be loved and praised with all our hearts and all our minds and all our souls, and every neighbor will be loved as we love ourselves. What Jesus was about in his earthly ministry was teaching us that "then" is really "now." There is nothing about "then" that we can't be doing right now. We are not far from the kingdom because it is among us, around us – beneath, above, and before us – in the neighbor we dare to love. May we live what we await. Amen.

– Andrea La Sonde Anastos

November 12, 2006

22nd Sunday after Pentecost (Proper 27)
RC/Pres: 32nd Sunday in Ordinary Time

Lessons

RCL	Ruth 3:1-5, 4:13-17	Heb 9:24-28	Mk 12:38-44
Roman Catholic	1 Kings 17:10-16	Heb 9:24-28	Mk 12:38-44 or 12:41-44
Episcopal (BCP)	1 Kings 17:8-16	Heb 9:24-28	Mk 12:38-44
Lutheran	1 Kings 17:8-16	Heb 9:24-28	Mk 12:38-44

Introduction to the Lessons
Lesson 1
(1) Ruth 3:1-5, 4:13-17 (RCL)
The story of Ruth continues with her marriage to Boaz and the birth of Obed, father of Jesse, grandfather of David.

(2) 1 Kings 17:8-16 (Epis/Luth); 1 Kings 17:10-16 (RC)
This story of Elijah and the widow at Sidon recounts a miracle in the midst of famine.

Lesson 2
Hebrews 9:24-28 (RCL/RC/Epis/Luth)
This reading is a further description of Jesus as high priest, who has acted to save humanity with his voluntary sacrifice of self and who will come again to save humankind at the end of time.

Gospel
Mark 12:38-44(RCL/RC/Epis/Luth)
Jesus sits opposite the temple with his disciples and observes the widow and her offering of all that she has.

Theme

The condemnation in which we live right now, right here, is not from God, but from our own refusal to give up the illusions of the world for the clarity and joy of shalom.

Thought for the Day

We always attract into our lives whatever we think about most, believe in most strongly, expect on the deepest level, and imagine most vividly.

– Shakti Gawain, *Reflections in the Light*
(quoted in *The New Beacon Book of Quotations by Women,*
Beacon Press, 1996)

Call to Worship

One: It is not enough to gather in this sanctuary made by human hands,
All: Because God is calling us to make all the world a holy sanctuary.
One: We come in to be strengthened to go out,
All: So that, at the end of time, all creation will be ready to be born again, whole and glorious.

Pastoral Prayer

Loving God, you willingly sacrificed yourself so that we could learn that not even death will separate us from you. You remind us again and again that our sins are already forgiven and redeemed and that Christ comes again not to judge, but to save. You invite us to lay aside the fears that hold us back from becoming your whole and holy servant people. Grant us the confidence to believe your promise and to accept your invitation so that the commonwealth for which we wait eagerly may become reality in this world today. Amen.

Prayer of Confession

For choices grown selfish, forgive us.
For inner radiance grown dim, forgive us.
For expectancy grown apathetic, forgive us.
For hope grown cold, forgive us.

For vision lost, for love hoarded, for justice abandoned, forgive us.
Inspire us to begin again, Holy God, aware of the riches you have
bestowed on us and ready to use them to bring heaven to earth. Amen.

Prayer of Dedication of Gifts and Self

Gracious God, what you have given abundantly for the good of all, receive
back from overflowing hearts and open hands as a gift of salvation for those
in need. May you bless us with the same fullness that we give. Amen.

Sermon Summary

When we turn our minds from fear to eager anticipation, we discover that
God is waiting eagerly to welcome us into God's own realm of glory – not
in the distant future, but here on earth in this day.

Hymn of the Day
"Seek Ye First the Kingdom of God"

In the year 1971 contemporary American singer/song writer Karen Laf-
ferty was inspired to write the first stanza and music of this scripture
song after attending a Bible study on Matthew 6:33. The second stanza
appeared as an anonymous addition in 1980. The song became popular
in the "Jesus movement" of the 1970s and early 1980s, helping to pave
the way for today's "contemporary Christian music" movement. The text
and simple tune call our attention to the eternal things of God and away
from the material things of this world. This provides a convenient way of
memorizing scripture; thus, the term "scripture song."

Children's Time

Jesus Stands in God's Presence

Wear some shoes with the shoelaces undone. If there are older children
in the group, invite them to help you tie your shoelaces. If not, tie them
yourself. Mention that tying shoelaces is tricky and is something you have
to learn to do for yourself. Ask: Who ties (or used to tie) your shoelaces
for you?

Comment that when you are a child, there are lots of things that you can't do for yourself. Perhaps they are too dangerous or too difficult. Comment that we learn from the Bible reading today that Jesus stands in the presence of God for us because we can't do that for ourselves yet, no matter how old we are.

Ask the children to recall a time they went somewhere that was a little scary – maybe to the dentist for the first time. Who went with you? Did you feel better knowing there was an adult with you? Explain that when we die we will stand in the presence of God, but we won't do it alone. Jesus will there with us.

Pray with the children, giving thanks for Jesus who stands in God's presence on our behalf.

The Sermon

Eagerly Waiting

Hymns
Beginning of Worship: "The Head That Once Was Crowned"
Sermon Hymn: "Come, Thou Long-Expected Jesus"
Closing Hymn: "When Morning Gilds the Skies"

Scripture
Hebrews 9:24-28 (For sermon materials on Mark 12:38-44, see the July/August 2006 issue of *The Clergy Journal* and the 2006 May/June planning issue of *The Clergy Journal*.)

The liturgical year draws steadily to its close and we hear these words about those who are anticipating the reappearance of the Christ, who is coming "not to deal with sin, but to save those who are eagerly waiting for him" (Heb 9:28).

Eagerly waiting. *Eagerly* waiting. My most profound wish as a pastor and preacher is that the people of God would stop worrying about divine judgment and punishment in the life to come and focus, instead, on the great joy of welcoming Christ here and now – into their family relationships, their date books, their wallets, and their voting booths. I would like to suggest that we don't need God to punish us at the judgment seat; we are doing a superlative job all by ourselves while we are still alive on this glorious earth.

What do we call it if not "punishment" every time we fill our calendars with schedules that require us to multitask nine hours out of every twelve, that deny us the sleep and spiritual renewal we need for healthy bodies and souls, that invite us to treat our children or our spouse or our friends as objects to be moved from one place to another in their own (eternal) round of activities? What is it if not punishment every time we make choices that increase the speed of our lives at the expense of meaning? What are we doing if not punishing ourselves when we are moving so fast that we "have to" consume, use up, and throw away because there is "no time" to maintain and sustain the earth and its resources?

Isn't it punishment when we vote to support systems that create and nurture poverty for our sisters and brothers, or for ourselves? Isn't it punishment when we make choices that condemn all of us to terminal anxieties such as: How will I feed my family? How do I protect my family from the people who need to steal from me in order to feed their families? How do I look my neighbor in the eye when I hate him for oppressing me? How do I look my neighbor in the eye when I know I have condemned her to the indignity of bankruptcy or the shame of depending on welfare?

We punish ourselves when we put up gated communities and live behind their walls. Is this the freedom we think God was offering when our mothers and fathers in faith were led out of slavery? Is it really freedom to live in smaller and smaller enclaves because we fear for the physical safety of ourselves or our children? In the late 1930s and early 1940s, we called six or eight or fifteen acres of housing protected by manned security gates and high brick walls with hidden razor wire on the top "ghettos" or "concentration camps." Such places still are ghettos, no matter how luxurious the housing. To live in fear of anyone who is different is more horrible and life-sapping than anything Dante imagined in *The Inferno.*

In the midst of this strange, self-inflicted agony in which we live, we read in the letter to the Hebrews: "So Christ, having been offered once to bear the sins of many, will appear a second time, not to deal with sin, but to save those who are eagerly waiting for him" (Heb 9:28).

Once and for all time until the end of time, Christ has shown us who we can be and what life we can have. He lived among us, sharing that wisdom with unconditional generosity and love, and then he voluntarily went to the cross rather, than deny the holy vision he had received and offered. All we have to do is stop condemning ourselves to life sentences of violence and imprisonment and, instead, look with open eyes, listen with open ears, and love with open hearts while we wait eagerly for the icing on the cake.

For some among us, this may happen as a sudden conversion of manners (as the Benedictines would say). Some of us may be able to shift in the blink of an eye into that life-giving, liberating paradigm that was, is, and always will be God's hope for us. Others among us may need to do it more slowly, initially committing ourselves to a single act of eager anticipation each day, gradually strengthening our hearts and minds to receive the light of glory radiating around us.

Perhaps you can plunge with nothing but relief into a simplicity of lifestyle that allows you the time and focus to recognize the blessing in every breath. But if not, perhaps you can take a smaller step and manage to clear 30 minutes today to watch the sunset with a loved one. Or perhaps you can commit 1 percent more of your income to sustainable living: to planting trees, supporting organic farmers, taking a job closer to home so that you can walk to work. Perhaps you can listen to that piece of music (not listen while driving, listen while cooking, listen while dusting, but only listen). Perhaps you can sell the SUV and buy a smaller car and, in the process, give up the decision to own the SUV in order to transport the soccer team. Perhaps all the time you are devoting to your children's activities can go to one-on-one time with those children – *your* time, not the coach's time – or to giving your children permission to listen to that piece of music or watch that sunset or play some unplanned game or run merely for the joy of running.

Perhaps, in those brief moments of pause, you can begin to feel what it feels like to wait eagerly and, in the waiting, to be in a place of meaning as a person of infinite value and meaning to God. Perhaps you will discover that you have intentionally centered yourself in the presence of the God who loves you and who is eagerly waiting for your release from the burden of those sins you keep hanging on to, into the joy of God's own realm. May it be so.

– Andrea La Sonde Anastos

November 19, 2006

23rd Sunday after Pentecost (Proper 28)
RC/Pres: 33rd Sunday in Ordinary Time

Lessons

RCL	1 Sam 1:4-20	Heb 10:11-14, (15-18), 19-25	Mk 13:1-8
Roman Catholic	Dan 12:1-3	Heb 10:11-14, 18	Mk 13:24-32
Episcopal (BCP)	Dan 12:1-4a, (5-13)	Heb 10:31-39	Mk 13:14-23
Lutheran	Dan 12:1-3	Heb 10:11-14, (15-18), 19-25	Mk 13:1-8

Introduction to the Lessons
Lesson 1
(1) 1 Samuel 1:4-20 (RCL)
Amid gross misunderstanding – barrenness was wrongly considered spiritual disfavor and sincere prayer was falsely equated with drunkenness – God's servant, Hannah, received assurance of God's favor.

(2) Daniel 12:1-3 (RC/Luth); Daniel 12:1-4a, (5-13) (Epis)
Though no one knows the time and circumstances of the final reality of history, we can be certain of God's identity as "loving deliverer," even in the midst of the most trying circumstances.

Lesson 2
Hebrews 10:11-14, (15-18), 19-25 (RCL/Luth);
Hebrews 10:11-14, 18 (RC); Hebrews10:31-39 (Epis)
Through the ministry of Christ, God removed for all time the need for any intercessor to stand between God and us in order to secure forgiveness for our sins. No more offerings for sin are required.

Gospel
Mark 13:1-8 (RCL/Luth); Mark 13:14-23 (Epis); Mark 13:24-32 (RC)

Using the language of apocalyptic literature to describe disturbing developments related to the end time, Jesus assures his followers that not even the worst that happens can invalidate the promise of God's word regarding salvation.

Theme
Our identity as followers of Christ is that of priests to each other.

Thought for the Day
The priesthood bestowed upon us by Christ takes the form of a blessing as we claim our individual access to God and the form of a responsibility as we serve as priests to each other.

Call to Worship

One:	Our hearts are glad, our bodies secure, and our souls rejoice.
All:	We bless you, O God.
One:	You, O God, show us the path of life and grant us the pleasures of living.
All:	We worship you, God, and sing your praises now and forever.

– based on Psalm 16

Pastoral Prayer
Holy God, sustain within us the praise appropriate to you as Creator and Redeemer. Strengthen us by the teachings of your written word. Energize us through our realization of your forgiveness. Stretch the reach of our compassion by extending the breadth of our vision of need. Elicit from us actions of generosity and helpfulness. And, please God, keep vital our prayers and actions by the fidelity of your presence with us, that we may be as faithful, healing, and loving in our lives as was Jesus in his life, during good days and bad. Amen.

Prayer of Confession

O God, sometimes that for which we want to pray is buried so deep
within us – mired in fear, sunk in embarrassment, wedged in sorrow –
that we cannot find and form words to convey it. For some of us, the
subject about which we long to speak to you is wrapped in so much hurt
that to give words to it seems to be more painful than we can stand. Dear
God, you have promised that when we cannot voice our prayers, you will
understand our pained groans, our deep sighs, and even our silence. So,
look into our souls, God. Please sense the tremors of our spirits. Touch the
turbulence of our thoughts. Listen to our silence. Interpret the emptiness
of the space where ordinarily words fit, and know the reality of our lives
that exists beyond where words form. Hear our prayers, O God. Amen.

Prayer of Dedication of Gifts and Self

Though, in our giving, we never can come close to equaling the ultimate
offering made by Jesus, O God, we do seek to emulate Jesus by offering
to you right now – for your glory and for the good of others – all that we
are and all that we have. Amen.

Sermon Summary

Jesus, the great high priest, commissions us to serve as priests offering
forgiveness, exuding confidence, confessing hope, prompting love, and
providing encouragement to one another.

Hymn of the Day
"O Love, How Deep, How Broad, How High"

Having the organ or other instrument announce this hymn in a majestic
manner introduces us to an in-depth description of Christ's self-sacrificing
love. The hymn is an 1854 translation by Anglican minister Benjamin
Webb of an anonymous 15th-century Latin hymn. The hymn illustrates
Christ's deep, broad, and high love through his incarnation, baptism,
ministry, passion, death, resurrection, and exalted reign. We enjoy a grand
climax of directed praise and thanksgiving as we sing the sixth stanza's "all
glory to our Lord and God . . . " The name of the tune DEO GRACIAS
(once named AGINCOURT) means "thanks be to God."

Children's Time

God's Forgiveness

Bring a small whiteboard, dry-erase markers, and eraser. Talk briefly about the board and show the children how it works. Explain that you like to use the board because you don't have to worry about making mistakes. Draw a simple picture and make an obvious mistake, then erase it. Comment that the wonderful thing about the whiteboard is that you can try over and over again. The eraser always works.

Comment that this whiteboard and eraser remind you of God's love. Sometimes in our lives we make mistakes. (Write "oops!" on the board.) We forget to live in God's loving ways. When that happens all we have to do is ask God to forgive us and God erases the mistake. (Erase the board.) We can start over and try again.

Comment that the Bible tells us that God will forgive us every single time we ask. (Write the word "oops!" on the board several times and invite the children to take turns erasing the board.) We get a fresh new start every time. Isn't God's love amazing?

Pray with the children, giving thanks for God's amazing love.

The Sermon

Commissioned as Priests

Hymns

> **Beginning of Worship:** "Love Divine, All Loves Excelling"
> **Sermon Hymn:** "There's a Wideness in God's Mercy"
> **Closing Hymn:** "Called as Partners in Christ's Service"

Scripture

Hebrews 10:11-14, (15-18), 19-25 (For sermon materials on Mark 13:1-8, see the July/August 2006 issue of *The Clergy Journal* and the 2006 May/June planning issue of *The Clergy Journal*.)

Reading the exquisite promises from the writer of Hebrews makes me a bit uncomfortable. Oh, to be sure, I am grateful beyond measure for affirmation of the truth about Christ's priestly work – its singular sufficiency for everybody, its comfort and assurance personally, its revolutionary promise regarding forgiveness. Then I ponder the implications of this blessing – the responsibility that is mine as a beneficiary of Christ's offering. The ministry of Jesus has become my ministry and yours. We have been made priests. We are priests called by God and commissioned by Christ. We are priests to each other. And what a priesthood it is!

Frankly, my first reaction to this realization of priesthood was a sense of heaviness imposed by an anticipation of more responsibilities stacked on top of an already large pile of duties. After further reflection, however, I realized that the basic issue here is not more tasks to be assumed, but a basic identity to be embraced and enjoyed – a recognition of who we are that prods us to be all we can be, all that God created us to be. That understanding of our priesthood births a sense of excitement and expectation.

Though not included among the readings today, 1 Peter 2:9-10 and 4:8-11 read like an insightful commentary on the Hebrews text. Christ, who extended grace to us, in turn appointed us as stewards of grace. Just as we received mercy from him, we are to extend mercy to others. Having been blessed by the unique priestly ministry of Jesus, we also have been charged to bless others through our shared ministry as Christ-appointed priests. The author of 1 Peter writes with a clarity that leaves no room for doubt or confusion regarding our identity and ministry: "You are a chosen race, a royal priesthood . . . Once you were not a people, but now you are God's people" (1 Pet 2:9-10).

What does this mean? Since Jesus has offered the ultimate sacrifice and cleared the way for us to relate to God personally, what is left for us to do? What is the nature of the priesthood to which we have been called? Look carefully – the characteristics of this priesthood are enumerated by the author of the Hebrews text.

First, Jesus commissions us to a priesthood of forgiveness (Heb 10:18). What we see in Jesus points us to the nature of God and to the nature of our lives as the people of God. In other words, what Jesus did, we are to do – namely, serve as facilitators of forgiveness.

Be forewarned that, at times, this can be scandalous work. Almost everyone can name somebody whom they think does not deserve forgiveness. Jesus, though, reveals to us the God who is not a moralist, not an accountant, not a rules-maker, not a power-broker, not a law enforcement officer, but a graceful lover eager to take the burden of sin off people's backs. Such an identity for God combined with such a ministry from Jesus must inform our priestly efforts.

No priest of God rightly can withhold from an individual who has sinned that which God freely offers to everybody, that for which Jesus made the once-and-for-all offering described in the Hebrews text. To withhold the grace of God from a person who has sinned is a sin every bit as serious as the sin to which the withholding is a response. Acting as a miser of grace contradicts ministry inspired by the priesthood of Jesus.

Second, Jesus commissions us to a priesthood characterized by humble confidence (10:19). The work of Jesus fills us with confidence regarding our ability to experience forgiveness and our opportunity to engage God in the "holy of holies" of life. Herein is all of the authority that we need to function as priests to each other. Confidence, however, must not be confused with arrogance. Our responsibility is to serve each other, not to try to play God or to take on the authority of Jesus in relation to each other.

Knowing with confidence the all-sufficient work of Jesus allows us to speak boldly about Jesus – commending him to others – and to serve others compassionately in Jesus' name without attempting to take unto ourselves work that only Jesus can do. So confident are we of Jesus that humbly we refrain from judging other people and proclaiming who is and who is not acceptable to God.

Third, Jesus commissions us to a priesthood of hopefullness (10:23). What good news we have been given to share with people! God keeps promises, and the promise of the work of Jesus is forgiveness, reconciliation with God, and meaning in life for all of us.

Recently I have spent a good deal of time among hurricane survivors – people for whom hope seems scandalous. Life has not been easy for these folks. Things have gone badly for them. Depression seems more fitting than positive expectation. Such individuals will not listen to an easy optimism or be moved by promises based only on hunches.

Among priests commissioned by Jesus, the substance of hope consists not of a Pollyanna view of the future but of a realistic view of the past. Look what God has done through Christ. Consider the provisions made for us in the priestly ministry of Jesus. We have every reason to live with vibrant, expectant hope and to encourage others to do the same.

Fourth, Jesus commissions us to a priesthood provocative of love (10:24). Because we have been loved so lavishly, we love responsibly. To experience the love of God through the revelation and actions of Jesus is to live by love ourselves and to seek to prompt love among others.

Virtually nothing in this whole Hebrews passage on priesthood makes sense apart from recognition of its foundation of love. Both the gift of God and the offering of Jesus were profound expressions of love. Our subsequent priesthood reeks with a lack of authenticity if both its words and actions are not transparent to a similar love within us and a desire for such love within others.

Finally, Jesus commissions us to a priesthood that is encouraging (10:25). To us is given the happy responsibility, rooted in the love of God and the grace of Jesus, of enabling others to feel better about themselves, to see previously unrecognized possibilities in their lives, and to face the future with eager anticipation. Conversely, any priesthood that trades primarily in prohibitions, judgment, negatives, and condemnation is not the priesthood commissioned by Jesus.

Our commission as priests is accompanied by a positive promise. Though we work every day at the responsibilities assigned to us by Jesus – offering forgiveness, exuding confidence, confessing hope, prompting love, and providing encouragement – we need not worry about the success of our efforts. The results of our priestly work already have been assured by the one who calls us to this work and makes us strong in the faith that allows us to live as the righteous people of God. Thanks be to God! Amen.

– C. Welton Gaddy

November 23, 2006

Thanksgiving (U. S. A.)

Lessons

RCL	Joel 2:21-27	1 Tim 2:1-7	Mt 6:25-33
Roman Catholic	Sir 50:22-24	1 Cor 1:3-9	Lk 17:11-19
Episcopal (BCP)	Deut 8:1-3, 6-10, (17-20)	Jas 1:17-18, 21-27	Mt 6:25-33

Introduction to the Lessons

Lesson 1

(1) Joel 2:21-27 (RCL)

The prophet Joel calls the people of God to exultant praise, sure that even pestilence and war fail to prevent a proliferation of blessings and goodness from God. Let there be no doubt that God is among us.

(2) Sirach 50:22-24 (RC)

From the heart of wisdom literature comes this soaring benediction that responds to the essence of spiritual wisdom derived from God and inspires a profound personal expression of wise thanksgiving to God.

(3) Deuteronomy 8:1-3, 6-10, (17-20) (Epis)

The writer of Deuteronomy reminds us that thanksgiving for items like bread and power pales in comparison to thanksgiving for the joy of keeping God's commandments.

Lesson 2

(1) 1 Timothy 2:1-7 (RCL)

The joy of thanksgiving is made full when we obey God as revealed in the scriptures and give thanks for other people.

(2) 1 Corinthians 1:3-9 (RC)

Thanksgiving for other people inexorably leads into thanksgiving for Christ who strengthens people with spiritual gifts and sustains them to the end of life, and thanksgiving for God who is faithful to all of us beyond measure.

(3) James 1:17-18, 21-27 (Epis)
Since every good gift comes from God, our thanksgiving is to God and for God. Such thanksgiving finds its loftiest expression not in words alone, but also in actions that evidence our faithfulness to God.

Gospel
(1) Matthew 6:25-33 (RCL/Epis)
Jesus described God as the faithful provider and the great caregiver. Acknowledging this identity of God stills anxieties within us and increases our praise and thanksgiving to God.

(2) Luke 17:11-19 (RC)
After healing ten lepers, only one returned to thank Jesus for the gift of healing. Jesus acknowledges the importance of the spiritual discipline of giving thanks; thanksgiving is an expression of faith as well as gratitude.

Theme
Experiencing grace and embracing life as a gift move us to thanksgiving.

Thought for the Day
We are blessed by God in order to live as a blessing to others.

Call to Worship
> **One:** It is good to give thanks to God.
> **All:** How great are God's works!
> **One:** It is good to give thanks for God's steadfast love and faithfulness.
> **All:** We will worship God with thanksgiving!
> – based on Psalm 92

Pastoral Prayer
Great loving and giving God: What are we to do when it is time to give thanks and not all is well? Deliver us, God, from a chauvinistic gratitude that says, "We are thankful that we are so much better off than other people." Spare us the thanksgiving of cynicism that says, "This is probably as good as things can ever be, so we are thankful." Mute the thankful impulses in our hearts that have been stirred by pessimism that

says, "There is nothing we can do but give thanks; it doesn't matter much anyway."

O God, nurture within us sensitivity to your love and the resources of your presence that, even in the worst of situations, we may know how to give thanks for your gifts. Amen.

Prayer of Confession

O God, sometimes, most of the time, actually, we feel caught between competing emotions – between praise and protest, between gratitude and cynicism, between optimism and despair, between thanksgiving and complaints. The dilemma is not merely a subjective one; our lives are pulled in diametrically different directions. We feel spiritually stretched as if on a rack. Relief looks possible only if we relieve the tension and go with one emotion alone. But such a mode of relief poses problems for our integrity; we can't simply close our eyes to difficulties in order to mouth praises. Yet, total cynicism is not a possibility because we know that underneath that which fills us with anxiety are realities that properly evoke gratitude. Great God, enable us to tolerate ambivalence and speak to you as honestly about our thankfulness as about our complaints. God, help us, please. Amen.

Prayer of Dedication of Gifts and Self

O God, you have blessed us with gifts beyond measure and love that defies understanding. We give you now a portion of our possessions, a promise of our devotion, and the commitment of our lives, daring to hope that you will feel blessed by us. Amen.

Sermon Summary

The gratitude that we feel – evoked by recognition of the primacy of grace and a realization that life is a gift – moves us to practice grace and to offer gifts gratefully.

Hymn of the Day
"For the Fruit of All Creation"

This hymn by Fred Pratt Green originally bore the title "Harvest Hymn" with the opening line, "For the fruits of his creation." The hymn also appears in some hymnals with the title "For the Fruits of This Creation" and in

others as "For the Fruits of His Creation." The original hymn was written
by Green for the purpose of supplying a fresh text for the hymn tune EAST
ACKLAM, composed by Francis Jackson in 1957. First printed in the British
publication *Methodist Recorder* in 1970, the hymn has enjoyed widespread use
as a thanksgiving hymn with a strong social gospel accent.

Children's Time

Thanksgiving

Show a variety of thank-you cards and tell how you might use them
to write thank-you notes. Ask: How else might you say "thank you" to
someone? Has anyone said "thank you" to you this week? How did you
feel when that person thanked you?

Comment that our story today is about someone who thanked Jesus.
Tell the story of the person who was healed and came back to thank Jesus.
Talk about the story: How do you think the man felt when Jesus made
him better? Why did he come back to say thank you to Jesus? How do you
think Jesus felt when the man said thank you?

Comment that this story reminds us that it's good to give thanks. We
can thank other people when they help us, and we can thank God for all
the things God has done.

Observe that today is Thanksgiving, a special day when we say thank
you for the all the ways God has blessed us. Mention that Thanksgiving
Day is just one day in the year, but we can remember to say thank you
to God every day.

Pray with the children, giving thanks for all of God's blessings.

The Sermon

Grace, Gifts, and Gratitude

Hymns
Beginning of Worship: "Joyful, Joyful, We Adore You"
Sermon Hymn: "We Praise You, O God"
Closing Hymn: "Now Thank We All Our God"

Scripture

Luke 17:11-19 (For sermon materials on Matthew 6:25-33, see the July/ August 2006 issue of *The Clergy Journal* and the 2006 May/June planning issue of *The Clergy Journal.*)

Recently I heard a young, Native American woman observe that "The most profound spiritual act is to teach people to be thankful." In the realm of spirituality and faith, no attitude exceeds in importance that of gratitude, and no act transcends in significance that of giving thanks.

So, how does it happen? How does gratitude develop? How does living gratefully become a basic trait of one's character?

Addressing those questions honestly requires a recognition that actually functions as a word of warning. Self-help books will be of no benefit in this endeavor of developing gratitude. The same is true of personal determination. Gratitude is not the product of a person simply psyching herself up to be more grateful or firmly resolving to say "thank you" more often. Gratitude is not a learnable issue of etiquette, consideration, or politeness – "Be nice and always say 'thank you.'"

Both the mentality of gratitude and the articulation of thankfulness spring from a fundamental orientation to life, a basic way of looking at life. On the basis of the narrative about Jesus healing ten lepers whom he encountered on the road to Jerusalem, one could conclude that approximately only one out of ten people develop this orientation to life and give themselves fully to the wonderful experience of giving thanks.

It all starts with recognition of the primacy of grace. That, in itself, is a serious challenge for people preoccupied with entitlements, merits, rights, and earnings. You know the pervasiveness of the popular attitude: "I have a right to property, a right to make as much money as possible, and a right to own everything I can buy." Individuals who hold such attitudes hardly can tolerate grace.

Grace is not just the opposite of rights, entitlements, and earnings; it does not even exist within the same realm as those phenomena. Grace responds only to what is needed, to what is best, to what is helpful, as it motivates contributions for the good of a person.

From beginning to ending, the Bible depicts the primacy of grace that is illustrated so dramatically in Jesus' healing the ten lepers. The lepers asked nothing more of Jesus than that he respond to them with mercy – treat them as persons rather than as diseased bodies to be avoided. But Jesus gave them more – what they needed rather than what they requested. Jesus took away their disease and made their bodies whole again. The whole experience was one of grace. Grace is primary in the Bible generally and in the ministry of Jesus specifically.

Once we know that reality, once we recognize the prevailing primacy of grace, we develop an awareness of the gifts of life, indeed, an acknowledgment of life as gift. The only way we ever know the most important aspects of life, as well as the meaning of life itself, is to see ourselves as recipients of gifts. Life is not about ownership and entitlement. Life is about gifts. Life reaches its zenith in our awareness of gifts. We can't merit faith. We can't buy love. We can't earn joy. We can't achieve happiness. We experience all that makes life truly worth living not as a result of personal accomplishments, financial purchases, or honorary rewards, but as gifts.

To understand life as gift is to experience a radical transformation in how we live. Recognizing that we have no more claim on living than we have inalienable rights to comfort, affluence, property, and happiness, we give thanks for the life that is ours. Every day is a gift.

Now, we have reached the birthplace of gratitude. To understand the primacy of grace and the nature of life as a gift is to experience and express gratitude.

We never will find gratitude among persons who think life owes them something or that others should be impressed by their rights and worth. Gratitude is stillborn among individuals who offer gifts to woo affections, to make an impression, or to accomplish a selfish goal. Do not expect gratitude in the lives of people who give things while protecting or withholding themselves.

Gratitude arises out of awareness of the grace that touches us and the gifts that enrich us. At its essence, gratitude is a response to a gift for which we realize that we want to give thanks.

This realization may take time. The recognition of the importance of grace and gifts runs counter to popular culture and conventional wisdom. Perhaps the maturation of this realization explains, in part, the time lapse between the lepers being freed from their disease by Jesus and one of them coming to the realization that he had to return to Jesus and give thanks for the grace and gift extended to him. Maybe the other nine lepers simply never "got it" – never allowed the recognition of life as grace and gifts to develop – thus never even sensed, much less acted upon, the moral urgency of offering thanksgiving and praise.

More is involved here than just a good attitude about life or a healthy outlook on life. The gratitude that we feel evoked by a recognition of the primacy of grace and a realization of life as a gift moves us to practice grace and to offer gifts gratefully. Thankfulness inspires and empowers a lifestyle of gracefulness.

I must warn you that only in frightening vulnerability and with a risk of being changed forever will anyone fully know the depths of life's gifts and the expanse of grace-oriented gratitude. We must know something else as well, though. Only in such vulnerability laced with risk does anyone ever really know love – the ultimate gift, the essence of grace – that causes its recipient, either in the exultant shout of a primal scream or in the quiet whisper of an intimate word, to exclaim, "Thanks be to God" and to resolve to live every day and in every way lovingly and thankfully. Amen.

– C. Welton Gaddy

November 26, 2006

Reign of Christ/Christ the King

Lessons

RCL	2 Sam 23:1-7	Rev 1:4b-8	Jn 18:33-37
Roman Catholic	Dan 7:13-14	Rev 1:5-8	Jn 18:33-37
Episcopal (BCP)	Dan 7:9-14	Rev 1:1-8	Jn 18:33-37
			or Mk 11:1-11
Lutheran	Dan 7:9-10, 13-14	Rev 1:4b-8	Jn 18:33-37

Introduction to the Lessons
Lesson 1
(1) 2 Samuel 23:1-7 (RCL)
Through words attributed to King David, his last words we are told, this popular ruler of Israel describes the essence of civil leadership – a ruler who fears God, a ruler that advances justice.

**(2) Daniel 7:9-10, 13-14 (Luth); Daniel 7:9-14 (Epis);
Daniel 7:13-14 (RC)**
With mind-boggling metaphors and fiery images, the writer of Daniel describes how all realms of sovereignty will pass away until the realm of God's rule is established forever.

Lesson 2
**Revelation 1:1-8 (Epis); Revelation 1:4b-8 (RCL/Luth);
Revelation 1:5-8 (RC)**
The book of Revelation opens with a cosmic burst of praise for the Messiah. Christ is recognized as supreme among all who rule and lauded as the sovereign who loves us, frees us, and calls us into a realm of obedient service to God.

Gospel
(1) John 18:33-37 (RCL/RC/Epis/Luth)
In response to Pontius Pilate's concern about the reign of Christ, Jesus explains that the realm of his rule is not in this world. Indeed, all who

141

know the truth understand the nature of Christ's reign as well as the nature of his identity as a ruler.

(2) Mark 11:1-11 (Epis)

Jesus dramatizes the nature of his place in the lineage of King David by entering the holy city of Jerusalem on a donkey. Though the crowd shouted as if welcoming a king, Jesus came, and forever comes, in the name of God, as a servant whose reign is marked by humility.

Theme

A review of the life of Christ prompts affirmation of the sovereignty of Christ.

Thought for the Day

The reign of Christ is a reign of love.

Call to Worship

One:	Lift up your heads, people of God. Behold the King of glory.
All:	Who is this King of glory?
One:	The Lord of hosts, the eternal God, is the King of glory.
All:	We lift our heads, we bow our knees, and we open our hearts to worship the King of glory, our God, graceful and mighty.

– based on Psalm 24:7-10

Pastoral Prayer

O God, we celebrate the reign of the Christ who wipes away our tears and joins our laughter, comforts our grief and draws us into joy. Keep us always mindful of the sovereignty that allows us to experience intimacy with Christ in the shadows of our lives as well as in the sunlight, when spiritually lost in a wilderness even as when gloriously found in a service of worship. Make us ever mindful of the provisions inherent in a realm in which the governing law is the spirit of love, and a beloved community in which all are included is the goal of every person devoted to the Christ. Amen.

Prayer of Confession

We are so busy, God. Our calendars are so full. Why, we don't even
have time for you – to study, to worship, to commune, to serve. Thank
you for having time for us, God. Forgive us for any momentary lapse in
our recognition of your providence. Forgive us as well for a presumption
of busyness that leaves no time for focused experiences with you. How
foolish can we get? Please, God, stop us, quiet us, and make us be still.
Grant us the courage to say "no" to any commitment on our calendars
that leaves us without time to meditate, to pray, to worship, to count our
blessings, to confess our sins, to realize that we are not alone, to express
our love for you – to be reborn. Amen.

Prayer of Dedication of Gifts and Self

Divine Giver of all that is good, we seek freedom from the cultural
philosophy of possessions as power and money as a means of control. That
is why we dedicate to you not only who we are but what we have, praying
that you will use our possessions, our money, and, indeed, our very lives
as instruments of compassion and service for the betterment of others and
for your glory. Amen.

Sermon Summary

According to Jesus, dominion is shaped by compassion. Love is supreme
– king or queen, if you will. Its goal is a fellowship of redemption. Its
strategy involves forgiveness and reconciliation. Its mode of operation is
humble service.

Hymn of the Day
"Jesus Shall Reign"

This hymn is a paraphrase of the second part of Psalm 72, written by
Isaac Watts. It was included by Watts in his *Psalms of David, Imitated in
the Language of the New Testament* in 1719. One of Isaac Watts's major
contributions to English hymnody is his Christian interpretation of Psalms.
Although Psalm 72 is a prayer for the king of Israel, Watts makes Jesus the
subject of his paraphrase. Even though Watts intended his Psalm paraphrase
as an adaptation to address the circumstances of 18th-century Christians, it
applies just as easily to the Christians of the 21st century.

Children's Time

Jesus the King

Bring a paper crown for each child and a children's book that has a story about a king or queen. Show the book and ask the children to tell you what they know about queens and kings: What do they do? Where do they live? What do they wear?

Explain that in Jesus' time the people of Israel had been hoping and praying for a long time. They wanted God to send a new king to lead them. God heard their prayers and sent Jesus, but Jesus was not the kind of king the people expected. Discuss this notion by asking: Was Jesus born in a palace? Did he sit on a throne? Did he have a golden crown to wear? Did Jesus boss people around? What kinds of things did Jesus do? Comment that Jesus was a very different kind of king.

Observe that today is Reign of Christ/Christ the King Sunday. It's a time to remember what kind of leader Jesus was and how we can follow his example.

Give each child a paper crown to wear as a reminder to love and help others like Jesus did.

Pray with the children, giving thanks for Jesus the king, who came to show God's love.

The Sermon

Tell It Again!

Hymns
Beginning of Worship: "Lift Up Your Heads, O Mighty Gates"
Sermon Hymn: "Crown with Your Richest Crowns"
Closing Hymn: "Amen, Amen"

Scripture
John 18:33-37 (For sermon materials on Revelation 1:4b-8, see the July/August 2006 issue of *The Clergy Journal* and the 2006 May/June planning issue of *The Clergy Journal*.)

Several years ago, I had the good fortune to share worship leadership responsibilities with the outstanding African American actor and musician Jester Hairston. We took the theme for the service from the gospel song that is almost synonymous with Jester's name – that wonderful, rollicking choral piece, "Amen." Likely you know the rhythm and the text: "A-a-amen, a-a-amen, a-a-amen, amen, amen." This piece of music reviews the life of Jesus from beginning to end, following every reference to history with the ringing refrain "amen," meaning "let it be so" or "so be it."

The whole story of Jesus' role in salvation history is right there in Jester's words – Christmas morning, Easter, "talkin,' baptizin,' prayin,' and savin.'" There is a recognition of deepest sorrow, knowing that Jesus was led before Pilate and an exclamation of "Hallelujah" recognizing that Jesus rose and lives forever. The whole gospel story is there and every part of it is followed with a resounding "Amen."

In the more formal liturgy of Christians gathered in public worship, the grand story of salvation unfolds through a pilgrimage guided by the worship-oriented road map through time that we call the Christian year – Advent, Christmas, Epiphany, Lent, Holy Week, Easter, Pentecost, and the long stretch of spirit-filled Ordinary Time following Pentecost. On the calendar of the Christian year, today is designated "Reign of Christ Sunday" or "Christ the King Sunday." Significantly, this is the last Sunday of the church year, the Sunday before the entire cycle begins again with the First Sunday of Advent. The message is quite clear – after a review of the entire sweep of the major events in the life of Jesus, we sound a soaring "amen" and laud Christ as the sovereign of all history, as well as of our personal lives.

In that spirit – reflecting on the scope, spirit, and substance of the ministry of Jesus – people of Jesus' day who were well-versed in ancient hopes and prophecy immediately began to apply to Jesus the expectations of spiritual dominion and political sovereignty. This association, I am sure, motivated those who gave the title "Christ the King Sunday" to the last Sunday of the church year. It was a spiritual conclusion, a personal conviction, and a liturgical affirmation.

Yes, followers of Jesus properly called him "Lord," a term that acknowledged his sovereignty. Yes, the gospel writers dramatized Jesus' dominion over all creation. However, neither the dominion nor the sovereignty of Jesus was of the nature envisioned in ancient hopes and desired by the earliest disciples.

Look carefully at the conversation between Jesus and Pilate reported in the gospel text for today. From this exchange, there is much to learn that can prevent the exalted title of "King" from distorting the meaning of Jesus' ministry and leading to misunderstanding about the nature of Christianity.

A political sovereign named Pilate interviewed the spiritual leader named Jesus, who was accused of political crimes that warranted capital punishment. When Pilate quizzed Jesus about his kingship, Jesus insisted that Pilate make up his own mind about the identity and the authority of the one standing before him. Freedom prevailed. Jesus would have it no other way.

Faith is never about compliance with a decree from sovereignty. Authentic belief can never be imposed, compelled, or forced. Faith is always a consequence of a decision made with free will.

In his conversation with Pilate, even as at other pivotal moments in his life, Jesus turned the traditional understanding of religion upside down. According to Jesus, the story of salvation is not about individual success, personal elevation, national supremacy, political authority, or social/cultural superiority. In the way of Jesus, dominion is shaped by compassion. Love is supreme – king or queen, if you will. Its goal is a fellowship of redemption. Its strategy involves forgiveness and reconciliation. Its mode of operation is humble service.

The story of God's work in the world consists both of hope and despair – not hope in the absence of despair, but hope in the face of despair and, often, *through* despair. The soaring carols of joy evoked by Jesus' birth did not mute haunting echoes of Rachel weeping for her children. Simeon and Anna celebrated Jesus' presentation in the temple, though each had more years behind them than in front of them to enjoy the fulfillment of the hope that they had held tenaciously for a lifetime. Jesus' inviting message of freedom and inclusion lofted across the plains and hills of Galilee amid harsh exclamations of prejudice, strident calls for exclusion, and ugly acts of hatred. Many of the same voices that sought to shout the good news of Jesus' resurrection must have been hoarse from their earlier shouts demanding Jesus' crucifixion.

Do you see the implications of this truth? Do you catch a glimpse of what all of this means? Our worst moments do not disqualify us as recipients of God's grace. Indeed, God's grace is for people mired in their worst moments. Our suffering does not occur outside the realm of God's love. Often God's love finds its most memorable expression in suffering or through suffering.

The story of God's work in the world enables us to realize that the essence of meaning in our lives resides not in what we can do, but in what all God can do in us, through us, and with us. Then, it becomes clear to us that what we receive from God – the hope, the strength, the encouragement, the assurance – is available nowhere else, from no one else. No other story can make the promises and deliver the fulfillment that can be found in God's story.

As we look back over the dramatic sweep of God's story of salvation – seeing love with flesh on it; sin as an opportunity for forgiveness; suffering as a cradle for hope; war as a context in which to discover the meaning, importance, and ways of peace; darkness as a prelude to light; and the sufficiency of faith in all situations – we find that it is almost too much for us. We don't know whether to laugh or to cry.

Thoughts of Jester Hairston's music rush in again. After the whole story has been told and affirmed by exciting outbursts of "Amen," the lyrics of the music rush to declare, "Sing it over." Our sentiments precisely! Like a two-year-old child having heard her favorite bedtime story, we say passionately, "Please tell it again." This time, not only do we want to hear it, we want to live it. And so, laughing and crying at the same time, we begin to tell the story again – singing it and living it. Amen. So be it! Amen.

– C. Welton Gaddy

December 3, 2006

1st Sunday of Advent

Lessons

RCL	Jer 33:14-16	1 Thess 3:9-13	Lk 21:25-36
Roman Catholic	Jer 33:14-16	1 Thess 3:12—4:2	Lk 21:25-28, 34-36
Episcopal (BCP)	Zech 14:4-9	1 Thess 3:9-13	Lk 21:25-31

Introduction to the Lessons

Lesson 1
(1) Jeremiah 33:14-16 (RCL/RC)
God promised a leader to establish righteousness and bring safety and salvation to the people of God. And God keeps promises.

(2) Zechariah 14:4-9 (Epis)
The highest and grandest of divine visions is that of one God with one name who reigns over all people and things.

Lesson 2
1 Thessalonians 3:9-13 (RCL/Epis);
1 Thessalonians 3:12—4:2 (RC)
The fondest hope among Christians involves being together, growing in holiness, pleasing God, and abounding in love.

Gospel
Luke 21:25-36 (RCL); Luke 21:25-31 (Epis);
Luke 21:25-28, 34-46 (RC)
Through many signs, sayings, parables, and actions, Jesus offers assurance that God's word will remain and redemption will come. He urges all to stay alert so as not to miss any aspect of the advent of God.

Theme
God comes among us in good times and bad times, amid ugliness as well as beauty.

Thought for the Day

Christmas is to be celebrated as our response to the gift of God's grace, not as God's response to our fevered preparations.

Call to Worship

One: God comes among us to be known by us.
All: Let us show the salvation of God.
One: In the day of trouble, God will deliver us.
All: Come among us, God. O come, O come, Immanuel. We will greet you with praise and worship you with our lives.

– based on Psalm 50

Pastoral Prayer

God, seldom do we brazenly complain, but this morning we must tell you that Advent seems a bit out of place in our world right now. Some of us are hurting so badly that we find it offensive to speak of hope, and joy is nowhere in our sight. Many of our friends, grieving the absence of members of their families, flash angry resentment when they hear comments about a reign of peace. Frankly, we don't care to hear much more about the lofty nature of love; we will settle for just a little kindness and the possibility that someone might like us. If you insist on Advent, God, please show us one solid reason that we should expect you to come into this world and help us. If that cannot happen, we ask you to understand our lack of talk about your coming and the absence of "hallelujahs" in our talking and singing. Amen.

Prayer of Confession

God of hope, a fight is raging in our souls. We are pushing hard to hold back Advent, resisting with all our might thoughts of singing angels or, for that matter, any messengers of goodwill. You know us. We live in a world in which skies don't open, stars don't guide, and people don't stop what they are doing to go to see a baby, to greet the Messiah, or to do anything that they (that *we*) don't want to do. Our cynicism has a headlock on our faith. Our spirituality is gasping for breath. We need a serious encounter with holiness. The best that we can do at the moment is to offer a simple, but sincere prayer. If this is not enough, please forgive us. Come among us, God. Come, O long-expected Jesus. Amen.

Prayer of Dedication of Gifts and Self

O God, on the front edge of a season marked by the frantic selling and buying of gifts among people concerned that each gift will be big enough, attractive enough, and expensive enough to impress and please the recipient, give us wisdom regarding the value of what we give to others and to you. We give our love to you and, in the name of the Christ, we give a portion of our possessions to be used as expressions of your love to other people. Amen.

Sermon Summary

Christ's arrival is not about decorations, but about revelation; not about perfect conditions, but about divine compassion. The advent of Jesus is nothing less than the revelation of God's incredible love for all people, whatever their life situations or social conditions.

Hymn of the Day
"Lo, He Comes with Clouds Descending"

This Charles Wesley hymn emphasizes the second appearing of Jesus Christ on the earth. It was first printed in Wesley's *Hymns of Intercession for All Mankind* in 1758 under the heading "Thy Kingdom Come." Wesley may have written this hymn as a "refinement" of a hymn by Moravian hymn writer John Cennick. The tune HELMSLEY has most always been associated with this hymn. It first appeared in John Wesley's tune book *Select Hymns and Tunes Annext* (2nd edition, 1765) under the name OLIVERS. Realizing the tune's longevity, some authorities believe the tune may be the greatest musical achievement of Methodism.

Children's Time

Signs

Invite the children to look around the church and spot the changes in your worship space. What is different this week? Take a quick tour around the church to look at the Advent decorations. Explain that all these changes are signs that something special is coming. Ask the children if they know what it might be. Affirm all answers and explain that in the church, Advent is a special time of waiting as we get ready to celebrate Jesus' birthday.

Have some conversation about other signs at church, in the community, or at home that tell us that preparations for Christmas are underway. Conclude your discussion by observing that there are many signs telling us that it's time to get ready to welcome Jesus.

Explain how Jesus promised that one day he would return, but no one knows when that will be. Jesus told his followers that they needed to get ready for his return. We can get ready by living the way that Jesus taught us. When we do that, we become living signs pointing to Jesus!

Pray with the children, giving thanks for this special Advent waiting time.

The Sermon

A Different View of Advent

Hymns

Beginning of Worship: "We Hail You God's Anointed One"
Sermon Hymn: "Isaiah the Prophet Has Written of Old"
Closing Hymn: "Come, O Long-Expected Jesus"

Scripture

Luke 21:25-36 (For sermon materials on Jeremiah 33:14-16, see the September 2006 issue of *The Clergy Journal;* for sermon materials on 1 Thessalonians 3:9-13, see the 2006 May/June planning issue of *The Clergy Journal.*)

What is this text, today's gospel reading from Luke? It certainly does not evoke thoughts of Christmas! What is going on here? This biblical text is crammed full of words that conjure up thoughts of cataclysm rather than revelation!

Most of us associate very specific sights and sounds with Christmas. Some may envision a favorite ornament to hang on a Christmas tree, while others think of a cherished toy always displayed at this time of the year. Whatever the specifics, most of the images of Christmas that fill our minds involve rich colors, fine fabrics, sparkling stars, favorite foods, glittering ornaments, costly stones, shimmering tinsel, and beautiful lights.

But, there is another side to the season, a different view of Christmas. For some people, Christmas looks dull and sparse rather than sparkling and rich, rugged rather than polished, dark rather than light, futile rather than festive.

151

Here is the critical question: Can the truth of Christmas be experienced devoid of any festive symbols of the season? What kind of preparations must be made, what kind of decorations must be displayed in order for Immanuel to enter our lives – for God to be with us? Grasping correct answers to these questions is crucial to understanding the meaning of the season.

From the perspective of the holy scriptures, Advent – the coming of Christ – is much more about disorder than about order. God's visitation to earth is not contingent upon burning candles and shimmering stars. Look at Luke's message. The gospel writer employed words and images that seem to have nothing to do with the advent of Jesus in order to declare that these very words and images – and the harsh conditions that they suggest – should be viewed as sure signs that the advent of Jesus is imminent.

Decorations that adorn the seasons of Advent and Christmas rightfully signal a celebration – an unfurling of joy, an explosion of happiness, an eruption of beauty to honor the Christ who comes to give glory to God. As a means of response to the event that gives rise to the season, decorations are in order – the more the better, the more glorious the more appropriate.

But, must everything be beautiful for Christ to be born? God help us if that is the case! Look at the text from Luke. The worst of conditions may hold out the greatest promise of the nearness of the presence of God in our midst. The arrival of Christ is not deterred by scenes of the bloated bellies of hungry kids, the squalor of a refugees' village, or the misery that shrouds an AIDS ward in a charity hospital. Indeed, God invades the ugliest situations in life as well as the most glorious.

Every year during Advent I hear some people say almost frantically, "I have so much to get done before Christmas; I don't believe I'm going to make it. Christmas just can't come; I don't have my house decorated, my food prepared, my presents bought." We will do well to listen to ourselves even as we listen to Luke. A subtle, though profoundly important, misperception pervades the attitude reflected in our comments: "Christmas comes most meaningfully to those who have prepared for it most lavishly." Wrong!

God's entrance into our lives occurs at God's initiative. Christ arrives in our midst not as a reward for detailed preparations, but as a result of divine compassion. God comes to us whether or not we have made ready for the divine presence. The success of Christmas is not contingent on how well we have decorated for the event. God comes amid darkness and despair as readily as amid light and happiness. Christmas is an expression of God's grace.

Many years ago I came across an exceptionally fine essay focused on that biblical phrase, "When the fullness of time had come, God sent his Son" (Gal 4:4). The writer skillfully made the point that Jesus was born when the world was fully prepared. He wrote of the unification of the world under the Roman peace, the value of new avenues for travel and communication for spreading the word about the Bethlehem event, a right moment in the international economy, and a previously-unexcelled moral and spiritual readiness for revelation. The conclusion of the essayist was that, from the beginning of time, God had been waiting for people to get the conditions of the world and the sentiments in their souls just right for Jesus to appear on earth.

Recently I reread that essay and responded to it with a resounding, "No." I think the author is wrong. Jesus' arrival in the world did not depend upon the world having everything ready for divine revelation to occur. Then and now, God shows up in people's lives not in response to their preparations, but out of mercy and grace that is responsive to the immense needs of humankind.

On this first Sunday of Advent, please be freed from the deception that the success or failure of Christmas rests upon us. Christ's arrival is not about decorations, but about revelation; not about perfect conditions, but about divine compassion. The advent of Jesus is nothing less than the revelation of God's incredible love for all people, whatever their life situations or social conditions.

If you have been able to tie ribbons, fly banners, hang wreaths, adorn trees, and display lights to celebrate Christ's birth or if you plan such decorations, great. But, if your days are devoid of joy and your habitat stark and sparse – if your life seems blighted with ugliness rather than blessed with beauty – no matter. No matter! Christ still will come to you. Christmas will arrive in your life.

Read again the narratives about God in the gospels. God is not partial to finery or impressed by extravagance. God's grace ignores prerequisites. The God who joined the world in a smelly cattle stall somewhere down a back street in a little-known village called Bethlehem arrives where no lights blink and no flags fly, in hospital wards as well as in cathedrals, among mourners as well as amid carolers. God comes where everything seems to be ending as well as where everything appears to be beginning.

Let us be done with any thought that the success or failure of Christmas, much less assurance of the fundamental reality of Christmas, depends upon how we get ready. Neither a gala nor a concert, neither a banquet nor a finely decorated tree is a prerequisite to Christ's advent among us. Christmas is about God's response to our needs, not God's reaction to our decorations.

The Christ who has come *will* come. Christ will come among us! Let us open our hearts and make him welcome. Amen.

– C. Welton Gaddy

December 10, 2006

2nd Sunday of Advent

Lessons

RCL	Bar 5:1-9 or Mal 3:1-4	Phil 1:3-11	Lk 3:1-6
Roman Catholic	Bar 5:1-9	Phil 1:4-6, 8-11	Lk 3:1-6
Episcopal	Bar 5: 1-9	Phil 1:1-11	Lk 3:1-6

Introduction to the Lessons

Lesson 1

(1) Malachi 3:1-4 (RCL)

The prophet indicates God's weariness with Israel's cynicism. God speaks:
A messenger is coming. Indeed, who can stand in the presence of Yahweh?

(2) Baruch 5:1-9 (RCL/RC/Epis)

God will lead Israel with joy, in the light of God's glory.

Lesson 2

Philippians 1:3-11 (RCL); Philippians 1:4-6, 8-11 (RC); Philippians 1:1-11 (Epis)

The Philippian church was the first European congregation. Paul gives
thanks for them, but does not merely reminisce. God is still working,
he assures them, and will not stop until history itself culminates in the
fullness of Jesus Christ.

Gospel

Luke 3:1-6 (RCL/RC/Epis)

In this text, Luke makes a radical distinction between the political conven-
tions of nations and the ways of God. Luke gives us a list of who is
in charge of the world. However, God skirts the powerful and picks a
messenger from the desert.

Theme

God wants you to step up and live your life.

Thought for the Day
Take back your life from all the personalities and competing interests that have claimed you, and prepare for living with God.

Call to Worship
One: When the Lord restored the fortunes of Zion, then we were like those who dream.

All: Then our mouths were filled with laughter, and our tongues with shouts of joy;

One: Then it was said among the nations, "The Lord has done great things for them."

All: The Lord has done great things for us, and we rejoice!

– based on Psalm 126:1-3

Pastoral Prayer
We have just begun a new season of watching for your coming, O God, and already some of us are tired. Advent is barely one week old, and some of us feel so much older, bone-weary, bent low. Can we make it until Christmas Eve? Look at us and see how we rest our heads in our hands, slumber in our pews, and mumble our prayers.

Come now and bless us – look past the mess of our celebrations and expectations – and bless us. We need you, Holy One of Israel, to shine upon us, to lift us, to bring us up out of the depths and set us again on a firm, dry rock. We would like so much to sing aloud and sing for joy, but we have lost our voices and "Joy to the World" is still so distant and faint to our hearing. Still, we belong to you. So come, Lord Jesus, come. Come quickly!

Prayer of Confession
Dear Lord, who hears and listens even to our muttering, hear now our confession. We could say that we are too busy, that we have forgotten the "reason for the season," and that our priorities are really out of whack. Probably, they are. The truth, however, is much worse, O Lord. The truth is, we don't much care. We've been attending services for too long, listening to lengthy prayers, singing un-singable songs, and boasting unwavering smiles through innumerable and intolerable sermons.

The truth is, we often haven't a clue as to how you can help us. The truth is, we are not all that sure that you even want to help us. But, if you can hear this prayer and not strike us down, then perhaps you are the kind of God we could get to know, and even grow to love. If you can hear just how bored we are with religion and this annual Christmas gruel, and not lash us to the mast, then maybe, just maybe, what they say about you is true. Maybe you are a longsuffering and merciful God who cares for us. We pray that it is true. In the holy name of Jesus, may it be so! Amen.

Prayer of Dedication of Gifts and Self

Blessed are you, O God. We are bringing what we can, and maybe more than we should, for fear you will not accept us unless we give all to you. Sort through our offerings – where there is vanity and pride, may these gifts advance your kingdom without the stain of our sin. Where these gifts come with needs for love and assurance, grant these in abundance to those of us bent low in shame and scandal. Where these gifts are given without due thought as to the real needs of our world, shake our foundations. For the sake of our world, our church, our souls, and our Lord Jesus Christ we pray. Amen.

Sermon Summary

Our lives are made for God. Most of us, however, live second-hand lives through endless cycles of headline news, celebrity scandal, sporting events, and political intrigue. John the Baptist preached a message of "personal agency." We are responsible for our lives. It is time we take back our lives, and prepare for God to come live in us.

Hymn of the Day
"Love Divine, All Loves Excelling"

This hymn first appeared in Charles Wesley's collection, *Hymns for Those That Seek and Those That Have Redemption in the Blood of Jesus Christ,* in 1747. In addition to being a prayer that emphasizes the indwelling of the Holy Spirit, it is a positive statement of faith in the "joy of heaven to earth come down." This hymn, with its thirteen biblical references, illustrates well the way in which Wesley's hymns are so firmly based on theological and biblical themes. Singing the text to an alternate tune, such as BLAENWERN or LOVE DIVINE, can provide a refreshing change from the tune BEECHER, normally used with the hymn in American churches.

Children's Time

Get Ready!

Bring some items that could be used for sending, receiving, and passing on messages. These might include a message pad, a printed email message, a cell phone text message, and an answering machine. Have some conversation about these items, noting how these can all be used in conveying a message. Ask the children when they have had to take a message and then give it to someone else. Comment that in our Bible story today we meet someone who brought messages to people from God. Tell the children about John the Baptizer and his special message.

Mention that in the Bible story, the people were getting ready to welcome Jesus. In this Advent waiting time, we also are getting ready to welcome Jesus. Explain that the best way to do this is by living the way that Jesus taught us.

Observe that John's message to the people was never forgotten. It has been passed from one person to another down through the years. Now it's our turn to pass on John's special message. Show the children how to make megaphones by cupping their hands around their mouths. Together call out, "Get ready! Get ready! Jesus is coming!"

Pray with the children, giving thanks for John the Baptizer and his message.

The Sermon

Take Back Your Life and Prepare for God

Hymns
Beginning of Worship: "Praise the Lord Who Reigns Above"
Sermon Hymn: "Comfort, Comfort Now My People"
Closing Hymn: "Lift Up Your Heads, O Mighty Gates"

Scripture

Luke 3:1-6 (For sermon materials on Malachi 3:1-4, see the September 2006 issue of *The Clergy Journal;* for sermon materials on Philippians 1:1-11, see the 2006 May/June planning issue of *The Clergy Journal.*)

When I turn on my computer in the morning, I am greeted with headline news. When I pick up the paper, there again are the large print headlines. As I drive to work, the all-news radio repeats the same information, along with traffic and weather. If I watch TV, perhaps at work or in the gym, many of the same headlines will once again clamor for my attention. News, news, news. Everywhere I look there are headlines, bulletins, banners, and pop-up windows.

With no real effort to speak of, I can learn about politicians, rock stars, movie stars, and business moguls. I can locate my discourse and orient my activity on any given day within a frame of reference drawn from a list of celebrity birthdays, "this day in rock-and-roll history," or "soon-to-be-released" cinematic features. However, if I choose to live as a political junkie, rock groupie, or sports fan, my actual life loses significance. My world will increasingly mirror their world. I will dress like them, wear clothes bearing their name, and repeat their jokes and stories. I will mouth their opinions on food, sex, politics, extraterrestrial life-forms, religion, and relationships. Of course, my own self will wither in doing so, and eventually die.

Luke draws a similar frame of reference in verses one and two of the third chapter of his gospel. He positions the major players of his day. Herod, brutal son of the even more brutal Herod the Great, rules Galilee. Brother Philip holds court over two lesser regions. Someone named Lysanias is the governor of Abilene. Collectively, these regions represent the geographic area in which most ordinary peasants of Jesus' day would have lived. Of course, in addition to knowing who ruled over them in the immediate sense, they needed to know that over the entire known world – that is, the ultimate realm of significance – reigned Emperor Tiberius. They also would have known that over the religious life of Israel, Annas and Caiaphas held preeminent power. These two high priests presided over the Temple in Jerusalem, the center of the universe according to ancient Jewish teaching. Tiberius, Herod, Philip, Lysanias, Annas, and Caiaphas: these six – together with their wives, children and, as John the Baptist would later discover, their lovers – were the players, the movers, and the shakers.

Of course, no one had explained these important facts to God. God appears to be living out of the wrong frame of reference. God had at least six significant leaders who were available for serving up the "Word of God." Even Luke knew this much. There were at least a dozen or more different palaces from which official announcements could have been issued. And, each of these weighty leaders had massive military and police presence throughout the region for enforcing the Word of God as official government policy.

It seems like God messed up, and not just in terms of whom God selected to carry the message – who, after all, was John the Baptist? God chose the wilderness as the first forum for issuing the Word of God. Jerusalem or Rome would have provided far more extensive coverage and initial public exposure. John the Baptist in the wilderness? It made no human sense. Not only did God pick a poor point-man to launch the Word of God campaign as well as a sparsely populated and hostile desert venue, God also issued an upsetting press release of rather harsh demands: repentance, baptism, and personal agency.

In a nutshell, that is what God wanted of Israel then and what God wants from us now. God, you see, is not about to excuse our sordid and messy affairs on the basis that we have "died" and let some celebrity have control. God is not going to set aside our sins of omission and commission on the plea that we have not attended to our own life because we've been consumed with the loves, labors, and laughs of politicians and athletes. Giving up our lives for notable religious leaders won't get us any favors either. God gave us life and is quite upset that we've squandered it by handing it over to others.

God wants us to step up and live our life. This is what is termed *personal agency*. I am responsible for me. You are responsible for you. There is no one else who will be held accountable for you – only you! Only you can live your life in the company of God who formed and fashioned you in God's own image. Only you can shut off the news, tune out the appeals of celebrities, and make haste for the river Jordan. Only you can walk down into the waters, confess your sins, put your head in the hands of John the Baptist, and plunge beneath the running waters of God's unending mercy. Only you can get serious about living your life before God. Take back your life, and prepare for God.

Palaces are unworthy places for announcing this good news. Emperors and governors have no credibility to call people to repentance. Celebrities cannot wash us clean. We need ascetics – what the church calls spiritual athletes – to hear our confession, cut our hair, bathe our bodies, lay balm on our sores, and feed our souls. We need Isaiah, Jeremiah, and Malachi to turn our hearts to God. We need John to lead us to the water.

If we know what is good for us this Advent season, we will quit our office festivities, forsake our political parties, abandon our Christmas-as-usual cycle of gift and drink, and get ourselves down to the nearest river. If we are wise, we will turn off the repetitious cacophony of carols, pick up a prophet, and bow low. In a word, we should begin to take our bodies, minds, wills, and souls seriously. God does; we should too.

"Get ready," John the Baptist says. "Tear down every obstacle between you and God – or God will tear it down. Fill in every ditch between you and God – or God will fill it in. Straighten the blind curves in your attitude and the twisting ways in your behavior toward others – or God will straighten you out. Get to work smoothing God's way home, for God is surely coming home to live in you!"

That is the message of John the Baptist, and his message lives: "Get ready!"

– William L. Mangrum

December 17, 2006

3rd Sunday of Advent

Lessons

RCL	Zeph 3:14-20	Phil 4:4-7	Lk 3:7-18
Roman Catholic	Zeph 3:14-18a	Phil 4:4-7	Lk 3:10-18
Episcopal (BCP)	Zeph 3:14-20	Phil 4:4-7, (8-9)	Lk 3:7-18

Introduction to the Lessons
Lesson 1
Zephaniah 3:14-20 (RCL/Epis); Zephaniah 3:14-18a (RC)

The promises of salvation in this reading must not be proclaimed in isolation from earlier warnings. This important "Day of the Lord" message is two-sided. God will come – both to save and to judge!

Lesson 2
Philippians 4:4-7 (RCL/RC); Philippians 4:4-7, (8-9) (Epis)

Theology for Paul is never merely speculative and always immediately practical. Rightly transmitted, doctrine gives shape to the Christian life and forms the Christian community. Here Paul motivates the community by emphasizing, "the Lord is near."

Gospel
Luke 3:7-18 (RCL/Epis); Luke 3:10-18 (RC)

John's message is one of personal accountability before God for our actions, words, and attitudes. We make straight the "way of the Lord" by making straight our lives. We get right with God by repenting and "bearing good fruit."

Theme

Christians may say, "The Lord is near," but does their conduct betray their disbelief?

Thought for the Day

Set a place at the table today for Jesus. How do your preparations, your family relations, and your attitudes change when you imagine the Lord coming to your house for dinner?

Call to Worship

One: Show us your steadfast love, O Lord, and grant us your salvation.

All: Let us hear what God the Lord will speak, for God will speak peace to the people, to God's faithful, to those who turn to God in their hearts.

One: Surely God's salvation is at hand for those who fear the Lord, that God's glory may dwell in our land.

All: The Lord will give what is good, and our land will yield its increase. Righteousness will go before God, and will make a path for holy steps.

– based on Psalm 85

Pastoral Prayer

Holy God, to you we come, and ask you to come! Come down in power; burst from the air before us in radiance. O God, do not stay hidden, quiet, sedate, and withdrawn. We beg you. Show yourself to us! Aloofness is not becoming of you who sought Adam and Eve in the Garden. Come, call us by name and walk with us. You visited Mary's womb that you might take flesh and keep company with fishermen, Susanna, Joanna, and little children. Visit this sanctuary, let us be your womb. Be born through us so that the people of our streets might see you, that the children of our neighborhood might play with you, that the angry ones of our church might be forgiven and set free from violence, that the lonely and bitter in our families, our church, and our community might be loved by you.

Do this we pray, in the powerful name of Jesus Christ, who lives and reigns with you in the unity of the Holy Spirit, one God, now and forever. Amen.

Prayer of Confession

We speak now to you in truth, God, for you see and know all truth and all falsehood. So, in courage and boldness, we name our sins:

We are all sitting here in one place, but we are not one. Within a stone's throw of where we sit are those whom we have stoned with our words. We are murderers.

We are eager for the church to do more to help those is need, those displaced, those without. But we have not taken our full measure before the cross of Jesus Christ. If we did, we would know that we are the needy, we are the displaced, we are those without. Instead, we mock your teachings and scorn your Christ.

Then there is tax fraud, lust, bitterness, and sloth — all of this and more is the story of our lives. So you see, God, we are really fine sinners. Save us, we pray. Amen!

Prayer of Dedication of Gifts and Self

Most high and holy God, in the quietness of the night, when we are most afraid, when we face overwhelming difficulty, we make promises to you in return for your assistance. This morning we acknowledge that you need nothing from us, for you are complete and without need. Still, we are grateful. So, accept in the precious name of Jesus Christ our lives, our loves, our hopes, our dreams, our plans, and our gifts. Take us and use us for the sake of this most desperate and hurting world. Amen.

Sermon Summary

Winter warnings are issued to prepare motorists and others for the dangers they will face when venturing outside in difficult conditions. Paul warns, "The Lord is near" to alert Christians. The nearness of Christ brings comfort to the suffering. It also should prod us to do good and walk humbly.

Hymn of the Day
"Hark! The Glad Sound! The Savior Comes"

This excellent Advent hymn text has maximum impact when coupled with a suitable tune. Most congregations will catch on to the tune RICHMOND more readily than they will to BRISTOL, the tune often associated with this text. The hymn's author is Philip Doddridge, a British Congregational minister. The hymn was first published in 1755, four years after his death, although it's believed to have been written in 1735. While not as popular today as it once was, this hymn lends itself quite well to 21st-century worship, reminding us that "He comes the broken heart to bind, the bleeding soul to cure."

Children's Time

Let Us Rejoice!

Bring a small bell or jingle bell loop for each child. (Thread a couple of large jingle bells onto a pipe cleaner and form the pipe cleaner into a circle.) Comment that today is the third Sunday of Advent, sometimes known as "Rejoice Sunday." On this day we are reminded that Jesus' birth brought joy to people's lives. We are invited to rejoice and be glad. Invite the children to discuss what makes them happy and excited as they get ready to celebrate Jesus' birthday. How do they show that joy? Comment that in the Bible reading today the apostle Paul encourages us to rejoice in God's love every single day of the year, not just at Christmas.

Distribute bells and encourage the children to ring their bells and move in a joyful way. If you have time, finish by singing "Joy to the World." Invite children to ring their bells and dance to the music.

Pray with the children, giving thanks for the gift of joy at Christmas.

The Sermon

The Lord Is Near

Hymns
Beginning of Worship: "Rejoice, Ye Pure in Heart"
Sermon Hymn: "Put Peace into Each Other's Hands"
Closing Hymn: "He Comes to Us as One Unknown"

Scripture

Philippians 4:4-7 (For sermon materials on Zephaniah 3:14-20, see the
September 2006 issue of *The Clergy Journal;* for sermon materials on Luke
3:7-18, see the 2006 May/June planning issue of *The Clergy Journal.*)

Living in the Northeast has been a new experience for my family and me.
We are not accustomed to muggy weather. Lacrosse is strange, as is sprint
football. Where we lived before, doctors and insurance agents have their
offices in medical plazas and business parks. In our new community, the
house next door is likely to be both office and home to the podiatrist
while the home across the street might house a tailor shop. Towns are
really villages stitched together along paved-over carriage roads, and the
toll-turnpike system still puzzles us.

New too, for us, are the "winter is near" notices sent courtesy of our
automobile insurer. The first flyer I pulled from my mailbox shocked me!
In all the years I lived in California, I never received a reminder from
my insurance agent to wash and wax my vehicle as protection against the
corrosive effects of ice and snow. Never did my agent write with advice
to change my car's wiper blades, check the tire tread and air pressure,
and install a new battery before winter arrived. In California, I paid my
quarterly premiums on time and fully expected to hear nothing from the
company save a notice that rates were going up. But in the Northeast, it is
different. "Winter is near" notices are not for laughs. Lives are at risk, they
warn, if seasonal advice is not followed. I feel an urgency to check off each
item on the list. "Winter is near," say these colorful little flyers. "Don't be
caught ill-prepared. Act now!"

On this third Sunday of Advent, our sermon is drawn from the New
Testament epistle to the Philippians. When these verses are set alongside
the urgency of "winter is near" notices, today's text may seem a bit placid,
perhaps even anaesthetizing in its general exhortations to "don't worry, be
happy." It feels like the same tired message the church has been handing
out for centuries: be nice, be happy, be patient, be peaceful.

God is good – both good to us and good for us. And we are lucky
to have Jesus. There, if that is all you wish to hear for a sermon this
morning, then you have heard it: You are now free to scan the pew Bible,
look up your favorite hymn, make your shopping list, or text message
your girlfriend. But before you tune me out, I ask you to consider this

question. What if Paul is at least as serious, and maybe more, in the warning that "the Lord is near" as my insurance agent is when notifying me that "winter is near"?

Why don't we take Paul seriously when he says, "the Lord is near"? I think we should. I've purchased new tires and installed new wiper blades. I've had my car in for its pre-winter safety inspection. I think Paul ought to be afforded, at the very least, the same level of respect as my insurance agent. They both know of what they speak. My insurance agent knows something about winter storms, vehicular safety, and driver awareness. My insurance agent knows something of the correlation between slick tires, ice, and death. The apostle Paul knows something about Jesus, his proximity to our lives, and our soul's ill-preparedness. Paul knows that personal practices affect congregational habits. Churches where each member personally attends to disciplines of forgiveness, scripture study, tithing, and forbearance are likely to be healthier congregations than those where everyone expects the minister to be "holy" while the rest excuse themselves as merely "human."

Paul is giving us a heads-up, an urgent bidding to wash, wax, and polish our churches and our own souls for protection against winter's fierce approach. When Paul writes, "Do not worry," it is as if he warning: "Check you blood pressure and your ego; you may be either overheated or over-inflated or both. Take your lead foot off the accelerator; your aggressiveness on the road, at work, in the parking lot late on Thursday nights after the building and grounds meeting, and in your parenting habits dishonors God. You'll get into an accident; unless you lighten up, many will be injured, some may even die. Be different; let your gentleness be known to everyone."

People of God, our faith community is more precious than our cars in the parking lot. It is to our shame if we pay more attention to our cars than to our congregations. We are all traveling together in one vehicle. We must attend to the integrity of this vehicle in which we are riding. The health and well-being of the congregation is everyone's work. Don't pass it off to the pastor, the choir director, or the janitor.

"The Lord is near." It will not do to dismiss your neighbor's anger in hopes that they will overlook your anxiety. Anger and anxiety both kill the soul and destroy the body. We are all in one vehicle, the church. When we are baptized into the body of Christ we become members of one another. Because we belong to each other we are not merely asked, but obligated, to wash each other from head to toe in joy and celebration. We must wax and polish each other's souls gently until we shine like the children of God we are. We must drive safely, wisely, purposively, for, "The Lord is near!"

"The Lord is near." Do not squander your resources on trivial goodies and distractions when the life of your community and the well-being of your family demand immediate attention. Cease your petty squabbling and start celebrating that you are loved – both in Christ and through this family of God. Drive with discernment; go gently. "The Lord is near!"

– William L. Mangrum

December 24, 2006

4th Sunday of Advent

Lessons

RCL	Mic 5:2-5a	Heb 10:5-10	Lk 1:39-45, (46-55)
Roman Catholic	Mic 5:1-4a	Heb 10:5-10	Lk 1:39-45
Episcopal (BCP)	Mic 5:2-4	Heb 10:5-10	Lk 1:39-49, (50-56)

Introduction to the Lessons
Lesson 1
Micah 5:2-5a (RCL); Micah 5:1-4a (RC); Micah 5:2-4 (Epis)
The book of Micah is an oscillating mix of judgment and salvation. Salvation comes into a situation of dire need as the people of God are surrounded by their enemies and walled in by their foes.

Lesson 2
Hebrews 10:5-10 (RCL/RC/Epis)
The book of Hebrews is an extended discourse on the person and work of Jesus. Today's reading urges Christians to cling to the superiority of Jesus' death as a "once for all" sacrifice trumping other competing claims.

Gospel
Luke 1:39-45, (46-55) (RCL); Luke 1:39-45 (RC); Luke 1:39-49, (50-56) (Epis)
Advent began with readings of Jesus' teachings about the future, then worked backward through John's preaching and Jesus' baptism to today's story within a story. This narrative of Mary and Elizabeth is set within a larger story of God sending the promised Messiah.

Theme
If ever we flee from God, God will go before us and meet us.

Thought for the Day

Bring up a picture in your mind's eye of those who have known you to the core, yet still welcomed you. Imitate their embrace.

Call to Worship

One:	Give ear, O Shepherd of Israel,
All:	You who lead Joseph like a flock!
One:	Stir up your might,
All:	And come to save us!
One:	Restore us, O God;
All:	Let your face shine, that we may be saved.

– based on Psalm 80

Pastoral Prayer

Blessed are you, O God, Father, Son, and Holy Spirit. From you springs all creation, by you alone is there any mercy, and only in you have we any strength. Blessed are you, Name above all Names, Immanuel, Comforter. Only by your imagination are we alive. Only by your death do we live again. Only by your eternal upholding have we any hope of living eternally with you.

Blessed are you, God of Abraham, Isaac, and Jacob, for by our mothers' wombs we are born and by the fruit of Mary's womb are we born again. You see through our eyes into our very souls, yet welcome us home. You know our darkest thoughts this very morning, yet embrace us. Before we arrived, you were here preparing to meet us, to greet us, to love us in Jesus Christ. To you be all majesty, honor, and praise forever and ever. Amen.

Prayer of Confession

Shame on us, God, for squandering your creation. Shame on us, Holy One of Israel, for our slothful living in squalid and squalor. Shame on us, Lord of the universe and Lord of our bodies, for our philandering and our carousing. Shame on us, Alpha and Omega, for our shameless storing away of your commands and stoning of your prophets, for drawing up our own plans and pursing our own purposes. Of you and your goodness, we are not worthy. But, in Christ, we are taken up, bathed, and presented anew before your throne. Blessed are you that in Christ, our shame is no more. Blessed are you that in Jesus' death, our "No" is canceled. Blessed are you that in Jesus' resurrection we hear and receive your final "Yes." Amen.

Prayer of Dedication of Gifts and Self

Dear God, you hear every prayer, know all intentions, and read well our hidden fears – we are afraid of giving too much and having too little. We are ennobled by the sacrifice of so many and pledge in passion to surrender all. Yet in the light of the morning after, we renege. So, here we are again asking you to take what we can barely part with and stretch it. Take our hearts, too, and stretch them so that in the future we will give ever more, welcome ever more, forgive ever more, feed ever more, and clothe ever more than we have thus far. In the name of Christ we pray, Amen.

Sermon Summary

Perhaps Mary had some doubts about her "Yes" to God, and this is why she went to visit her cousin Elizabeth in the Judean hills. If this is true, her doubts and her flight render her more human – more like us. In Elizabeth, God meets Mary and welcomes her. God meets and welcomes us, doubts and all.

Hymn of the Day
"Away in a Manger"

What simpler, more familiar, or more beautiful hymn could we want? Although Martin Luther has sometimes been attributed as the author, evidence suggests that it is of anonymous, American origin. The first known printing was in 1885. Two tunes are associated with the text: AWAY IN A MANGER, written by James R. Murray in 1887, and CRADLE SONG, written by William J. Kirkpatrick around 1895. The hymn provides an opportunity for children to sing by themselves, or for an appreciative intergenerational congregational expression. Each one may sing to Jesus, "I ask thee to stay close by me forever, and love me, I pray."

Children's Time

Special Babies

Bring a manger (box), a bag of clean straw or shredded paper, and some baby items. Show the baby items and comment that people often get very excited when they find out they're going to have a baby. Talk about the kinds of preparations people make as they get ready to welcome a new baby.

The Bible story today is about two special mothers. Mary was going to be the mother of Jesus. Mary was so excited when she found out that she was going to have a baby that she went to visit her cousin Elizabeth to share the good news. Elizabeth was also getting ready to welcome a special baby. Elizabeth was going to be the mother of John the Baptizer.

Mary and Elizabeth would have done many things to get ready to welcome their special babies. They probably prepared special beds for them. Gather around the manger and remind the children that Jesus' first bed was a manger. Invite the children to help prepare a bed for the baby Jesus. Have each child take a handful of hay and place it into the manger.

Pray, giving thanks for the birth of Jesus and John.

The Sermon

For All Who Sometimes Run

Hymns
Beginning of Worship: "Come, Thou Long-Expected Jesus"
Sermon Hymn: "My Soul Proclaims with Wonder"
Closing Hymn: "In the Bleak Midwinter"

Scripture
Luke 1:39-45, (46-55) (For additional sermon materials on this passage, see the 2006 May/June planning issue of *The Clergy Journal;* for sermon materials on Micah 5:2-5a, see the September 2006 issue of *The Clergy Journal.*)

There is a Native American saying about the value and worth of a story, which suggests that the first business for listeners is to make room in themselves for the story to stay. "So now the story has made camp in you," the proverb reads. "If you let it, it will hunt meat for you, and at night its campfires will keep you warm."

We are deep into the most storied season of the Christian year. By this fourth Sunday of Advent, we have sung or heard dozens of Christmas hymns and carols. When we listen to Christmas carols straight from Thanksgiving to Baptism of Jesus Sunday, the music makes camp in us. The melodies get inside our heads, settle down into our bones, build themselves a home in our memories. They warm us; their lyrics feed us. Quite often we will hear a stanza differently than before – then the story is hunting meat.

If you lean in closely, soon the lyrics will have a meal for you. I am fed yearly by verse two of "In the Bleak Midwinter:" "Heaven cannot hold him, nor the earth sustain; heaven and earth shall flee away when he comes to reign." As I chew on this, I reflect on the obvious truth that nothing I say, write, sing, or even believe wholly contains God. God may condescend to use my words, but God will not be contained by my words. Heaven cannot hold the Triune God. Neither will our prayers, passions, and petty offerings sustain Immanuel – God with us – here on this earth. God is bigger than you, me, this church, our denomination, this country, planet, solar system, galaxy, and universe. Nothing contains God, yet God contains all.

Now, while talking about music I am talking about scripture, too. Take the familiar story before us today. It sings. Once inside us, this story feeds us. Pregnant, unwed Mary bolts for the hills. Dazed or dazzled by the startling message that she was carrying a child by a Father not of this earth, Mary gets out of town. If heaven cannot hold God, Nazareth cannot hold Mary. She makes "haste," Luke says. With burning zeal, she beat a path for the Judean hills.

Where cousin Elizabeth lived remains a mystery. Luke is silent on this subject. Do we need to know exactly where Mary was headed to know that Mary was intently headed somewhere far away from where she had heard the word of the Lord? In this regard, Virgin Mary reminds me of Jonah. Jonah heard the word of the Lord in Gath-Hepher, which is just three miles to the northeast of Nazareth – the little town where God "shocked and awed" Mary into giving the Word room in her womb. God also "shocked and awed" Jonah who promptly fled for Tarshish – the exact location of which is also unknown.

Mary and Jonah: who would think them neighbors or alike in any significant way except that both were visited by God? Yet, I think Jonah and Mary are alike. God chose each to give birth: Jonah to the word of the Lord; Mary to the God's Word Incarnate. Before each, the heavens split wide, and each – having heard God's will for them – leaves town.

It is not until the end of Jonah's story that we learn why Jonah fled. As it turns out, Jonah was displeased that God showed mercy to the Ninevites. But why Mary fled is still a mystery, though the church has made plenty of assumptions. After Mary settles into Elizabeth's house she speaks such beautiful words, the Magnificat, that we've all assumed she went there to ponder the glory of God. Yet, what if she were fleeing? What if she is like those of us who put our hand to the plow and then turn back? What if Mary says, "Yes, here I am Lord," and then has second thoughts?

We modern folks have over-romanticized desert retreats. We fashion our retreat weekends around prayer, solitude, and silence. We then assume Mary went out into the wilderness for the same reason – namely to get closer to God. Only in Mary's case, God was, I think, already a bit too close. After all, the angel had said God would "overshadow" her. Perhaps, all she wanted was to get away from God.

Mary was human. We also. We all have our moments. No matter how confident we are when first we hear God speak to us and no matter the sincerity of the baptismal vows we make, we all have doubts, moments of failing, fears. When fear strikes, when doubts grow, when our promises exceed our resolve, we run for places not easily found. When God gets just a bit too close, we decide it is time to get away.

So, hear the good news. Wherever we flee, God has gone there before us and will be waiting. Mary was "overshadowed by the Most High" and when the angel left her, perhaps her courage went also and she ran. Do not hold this against her. We would probably do the same. Like the prophet Elijah, Mary ran to the wilderness. But God was already there before her – not in wind, earthquake, or fire, but in gentleness. She met one who looked deep into her eyes, knew her soul, took her in, blessed her, and loved her.

Jonah booked fare for Tarshish and met God in a pitched storm and the stinky stomach of a giant sea creature. Elijah stood up to 400 prophets of Baal and 450 prophets of Asherah, then wilted in fear before one woman, turned, and ran. Yet, God embraced Elijah at the mouth of a cave. God blessed Mary in the welcome of her cousin. God met Elijah in a cave, Jonah in a fish, and Mary in the arms of Elizabeth.

Wherever we run, God is there. God asks for our hearts. This is so, so much harder than just giving money. Even when we say yes and then flee, God will go before us. In the voice of those who look through our eyes and see our soul, then welcome us, bless us, and give us lodging – in them we meet God.

– William L. Mangrum

December 24, 2006

Christmas Eve

Lessons

RCL	Isa 9:2-7	Titus 2:11-14	Lk 2:1-14, (15-20)
Roman Catholic	Isa 9:1-6	Titus 2:11-14	Lk 2:1-14
Episcopal (BCP)	Isa 9:2-4, 6-7	Titus 2:11-14	Lk 2:1-14, (15-20)

Introduction to the Lessons
Lesson 1
Isaiah 9:2-7 (RCL); Isaiah 9:1-6 (RC); Isaiah 9:2-4, 6-7 (Epis)
The prophet foretells an heir to the throne who will break the rule of military, political, and economic oppression. The resulting new age will be characterized by joy, light, peace, celebration, and justice.

Lesson 2
Titus 2:11-14 (RCL/RC/Epis)
Titus remains in Crete to continue the work of establishing the Christian church. Paul writes to encourage him and to remind him that grace pays our fine for debts incurred, as well as our tuition to the school of righteous living.

Gospel
Luke 2:1-14, (15-20) (RCL/Epis); Luke 2:1-14 (RC)
The gospel of Luke offers an orderly account of the details surrounding Jesus' birth.

Theme
Because we are reticent to be quiet, we often miss the voice of God.

Thought for the Day
Go for a walk, and notice something ordinary and common. Then find a quiet place and hold your observation quietly for fifteen minutes in your mind. Ponder it; let God speak to you.

Call to Worship

One: Ascribe to the Lord, O families of the peoples,
All: Ascribe to the Lord glory and strength.
One: Ascribe to the Lord the glory due God's name; bring an offering and come into the courts of the Lord.
All: Worship the Lord in holy splendor; tremble before God, all the earth.

– based on Psalm 96

Pastoral Prayer

We are gathered to hear, see, and feel you move among us, O Most High and Holy God. On this night, we join with billions of your children who long for another miracle. Though we have heard it a hundred times before, we marvel yet again at the simple story of your son's coming, of Mary's "yes," of Joseph's trust, of the shepherd's visit, of ranks of angels crying out, "Holy, holy, holy. Glory to God in the highest!"

This story carries all of our hopes and dreams, and we long for it to work in us one more time. Though we are not completely convinced it will, we are full of hope. Though we are not fully certain about Jesus' mission, we are certain that we would like to meet him. Though we are not ready to meet you, in Jesus we accept that you have come to meet us. So, come Lord Jesus, come. Come tonight, meet us, in this place. Amen.

Prayer of Confession

We confess to you, O God, that we have not always kept well the treasure you have entrusted to us on this sacred night. Sometimes we have locked this story in our hearts of stone, so that it is not heard. Often we have squandered Jesus on our own frivolous nationalistic agendas, and frittered away his majesty on petty church politics. We have tried to master the story of Jesus, rather than seeing the living examples you provide of what it means to be mastered by the story. We pray that we might be forgiven. Take us up into the holy community of those who have been faithful and have obeyed. Holy God, let the story of Jesus come down upon us, bathe us, and possess us, so that we might belong not to ourselves, but to you. Amen.

Prayer of Dedication of Gifts and Self

Hear now, O God, our prayers of dedication. We are moved by candle and song, procession and decoration, story and silence to renew again our vows of allegiance. We belong not to ourselves, but to you. We belong not to our jobs, but to you. We belong not to our country, but to you. We belong not to our dreams, but to you. We belong not to our institutions and endowments and investments, but to you. Accept now these gifts we offer, through your Son, our Lord Jesus Christ. Amen.

Sermon Summary

God wishes to speak with us, too! The problem in hearing God is not on God's side, but on ours. We are chatty and gossip about every event of our day. To hear God, we must practice reticence, silence, and the lost art of pondering. Through the recovery of these spiritual disciplines, our soul's ear can be opened to hear God's voice.

Hymn of the Day
"On Christmas Night"

What a delightful, bright, and uplifting nativity carol! The authorship of the text and tune is unknown. They are of "traditional English" origin, probably of the early 1930s. This makes an excellent carol for antiphonal singing. Either a soloist or choir may sing the first two lines of each stanza, with the congregation responding with the singing of lines three through six. Perhaps the Christmas Eve service could start with a soloist or choir singing the first two lines from the back of the sanctuary and another soloist or choral group responding from the front. The entire congregation could join on the final stanza.

Children's Time

Jesus Is Born

Bring a flashlight and a variety of Christmas cards with scenes from the Christmas story. If you are expecting a lot of children you may want to bring extra cards. Don't worry if some scenes are duplicated.

Recruit some volunteers to help. (Older children or youth might enjoy being your helpers.) Invite the children to choose one card to hold. Explain that you will use the pictures to tell the story of the Jesus' birth.

Ask the children to listen carefully to the story and decide if the picture on their card shows what you are describing. When it does, they can hold the card up for everyone to see. Explain that there will probably be more than one card held up at any given time, and some cards may be held up more than once.

Slowly retell the story of Jesus' birth, pausing between each scene. Direct your volunteers to help cue the younger children when it is time to hold up their cards. Give the flashlight to another volunteer and ask her or him to shine it on each card as it is held up.

Pray with the children, giving thanks for the wonderful story of the birth of Jesus.

The Sermon

Ponder This . . .

Hymns
Beginning of Worship: "People Look East"
Sermon Hymn: "Savior of the Nations, Come"
Closing Hymn: "Sing We Now of Christmas"

Scripture
Luke 2:1-14, (15-20) (For additional sermon materials on this passage, see the September 2006 issue of *The Clergy Journal* and the 2006 May/June planning issue of *The Clergy Journal.*)

I was unemployed and living in a strange town. My wife held a good job and my daughter was in school – both of them were thriving in this new place. I, however, was sinking into a deep dark well of doubt and self-pity. I had no friends and little to occupy my energies during the day. I sought work with a theological institution, but did not have sufficient credentials. I sought work with area churches, but had too many credentials for entry-level positions. I finally found work – waiting tables for private dinners held at a local seminary.

One day I served lunch at a gathering of 25 denominational leaders. These were the movers and shakers of several regional districts. Many of them had reviewed my résumé for possible placement within their boundaries. A couple of them recognized me; most never noticed those who waited upon their needs. After they departed, the other waiters and I cleared away the cups and plates, gathered up the dirty linens, and tossed out the table scraps. As was permitted, I then prepared a parcel of leftovers for my family's evening meal.

It was drizzling as I walked the two miles across the campus and through town to our apartment. Along the path home I tried calling my wife, but she was away from her desk. I looked in vain at my cell phone directory and realized I had no one else to call. I was alone with my thoughts and my fears. I was afraid of the future – walking alone in a mid-day mist with a bag of pan-seared salmon and two pieces of chocolate cake. I was troubled. Yet, I had no one with whom I could immediately share either my worries or the good news of supper secured. It was just me – with my under employment, my sense of being an outsider, my desire to serve, and my banquet leftovers.

Somehow, as I walked I thought of Mary: Mary in her singleness, with her chastity; Mary – still childlike and yet now herself with child; Mary with her surprise visit from an angel and her questions about her future; Mary pondering. Scripture tells us that Mary pondered. She stored up all that happened and set to thinking about her life and God's claim on her body. Mary had no cell phone, instant messaging, or blogging. Mary was alone with her cascading thoughts, angelic voices, and celestial visions. Mary was without peers, for who could comprehend her story?

In that lonely moment on that drizzling afternoon, I knew what kept Mary sane. I saw the pathetic state of my own soul cowering alongside the radiant brilliance of her strength. I grasped the difference between us and understood why, as of yet, God have not yet been born through me. In her heart, Mary pondered and thus cleared the land for God to plant. The reason we are so unable to approximate Mary's virtue in our own lives is because we have accepted it as impossible to live with a thought unexpressed, a sorrow unshared, a vision of God unheralded to a vast network of friends and acquaintances. We moderns barely taste the newly poured wine before we begin pronouncing on its body and color. Everything that happens to us is turned into news. We lack reticence. So little is held in reserve. So little is deeply pondered.

What are you pondering this evening? What mysterious unveilings of God are you hiding away in your soul? What visitations of beauty capture your eye, holding your gaze in reverential awe? What "Word of the Lord" has settled into your heart, taken root, and grown to harvest? What message are you pondering? Or do you ponder?

The secret to pondering is secrecy. Mary was good at keeping her thoughts to herself and so she was good at pondering. Too often pastors, ministers, social workers, therapists, counselors, and teachers espouse a different way to mental health. "Talk about it," we say. "Get your feelings out. Share your frustration or your anger or your doubts." Now, maybe that "let it all out" approach is good for us. Or maybe not.

Perhaps we should ponder pondering. Pondering is a little advocated spiritual discipline and I, for one, would like to commend the renewal of pondering as a regular practice. I should like to suggest that the next time we find ourselves pregnant with God that we shut up. I should like to suggest that the next time the pizza delivery man comes knocking at our door in the middle of the night, saying, "God sent me here with this pizza 'cuz you're going to have a divine birthing real soon," that we take the pizza, latch the door, and be still. I should like to suggest that the next time we are afraid and can't "reach out and touch someone" by phone, that we accept the moment as God's ringing call for us to ponder.

You see, I believe God still speaks, though what God says is often difficult to discern. However, the most obvious difficulty with divine-human communication is not God's silence, it's our steady muttering of our hurts, feelings, and opinions. I should like to suggest that the difference between Mary and all the others who marched to their home towns that same month according to the dictates of the Emperor's Office of Imperial Tax Assessments, is that Mary "pondered" all. She didn't chat up her anger; she kept silence. She didn't gossip round her visitation; she held it in reverence. While others were complaining and arguing, Mary pondered deeply all that she heard, and saw, and knew of God.

I believe there are many Christmas Evenings still to come and many Christs waiting to born if only we would ponder his coming and prepare him room. This is what Mary did. She pondered his coming and prepared him room. We are called to do no less. Perhaps this strikes you has a dangerous thought, but it is not such a heretical notion. "O holy Child of Bethlehem, descend to us, we pray; cast out our sin, and enter in; be born in us today."

Ponder this . . . and may you find Christ being born in you tonight.

– William L. Mangrum

December 25, 2006

Christmas Day

Lessons

RCL	Isa 52:7-10	Heb 1:1-4, (5-12)	Jn 1:1-14
Roman Catholic	Isa 52:7-10	Heb 1:1-6	Jn 1:1-18
			or Jn 1:1-5, 9-14
Episcopal (BCP)	Isa 52:7-10	Heb 1:1-12	Jn 1:1-14

Introduction to the Lessons
Lesson 1
Isaiah 52:7-10 (RCL/RC/Epis)
All seems well as the promised ruler approaches Zion. All are ready for a show of power befitting a King of eternal majesty.

Lesson 2
Hebrews 1:1-4, (5-12) (RCL); Hebrews 1:1-6 (RC); Hebrews 1:1-12 (Epis)
This sermon was written to sustain a young Christian community facing difficult, even hostile challenges. Christ can be trusted as the true Word of God. In fact, Christ is superior to both prophets and angles.

Gospel
John 1:1-14 (RCL/Epis); John 1:1-18 (RC)
This prolog to the Gospel of John presents two themes repeated throughout John. First, Jesus is a real human being. Second, Jesus lived in daily contact with people. In Christ, the Word of God is "flesh," and this flesh lived among others.

Theme
In Christ, God comes home. In this birth, the King returns to claim his kingdom.

Thought for the Day

Picture a bug. Imagine fitting your whole being inside this bug, and then being birthed by this bug. Now, imagine how great a distance God covers to enter us through Mary's womb.

Call to Worship

One: O sing to the Lord a new song, for God has done marvelous things.

All: God has remembered, with steadfast love and faithfulness, the house of Israel.

One: All the ends of the earth have seen the victory of God.

All: Let the sea roar, and all that fills it; the world and those who live in it.

One: Let the floods clap their hands; let the hills sing together for joy at the presence of the Lord.

All: God is coming to judge the world with righteousness and the peoples with equity.

– based on Psalm 98

Pastoral Prayer

The noise of the morning is now fading, O God. We bless you for calling us together and for all your many gifts to us this Advent season. Some of us have come here to give thanks for family who are still slumbering at home. Some of us have come to give thanks for friends and loved ones still en route, or unable to meet us this Christmas. Some of us have come to see a friendly face on what will be a very lonely day. Some of us have come for your love, mercy, and forgiveness. We know you will not be stingy.

May your plan for the salvation of the world – already complete in Jesus Christ – be now completely within us. May the hope we feel grow and burst forth in new songs of praise, new words of encouragement, new eyes to see you already before us and at work in the world. Take us and make us whole and holy servants of your Word. Amen.

Prayer of Confession

O God who rules all creation, hear now our confession.

It would be so easy for us to say, "We have ignored your teachings." The fact is, we can no longer even recall the Ten Commandments without prompting, nor are we able to fathom their virtue and significance for our well being.

We could say, "We have stoned your prophets." What we should say is, "We think the Hebrew Scriptures are boring; we don't even bother to read the prophets anymore."

We want to say, "Let our pastor bring us some good news." Instead we should say, "We pay little attention to your message and your messenger except when the message confirms our beliefs and your messenger coddles our hurts."

Hear, then, a straight word from us: We have failed to heed you, your word, your teachers, and your Son. Save us from sin and restore us to the purposes for which you created us. Amen.

Prayer of Dedication of Gifts and Self

Blessed are you, O Lord of Hosts and through the birth of Jesus Christ, our Friend. We dedicate ourselves to Jesus – to love him always and to leave upon his shoulders every pride and ill-gotten gain, every despairing moment and malicious word, every slothful act and indolent attitude. As you receive the gifts we bring, take our lives as well – change us, renew us, and restore us to yourself. Through Jesus Christ we pray. Amen.

Sermon Summary

Popular images of God depict an absent yet benevolent and somewhat powerless figure who watches us from a distance. In the gospel we read not of a God who is distant, but of a God who in Christ overcomes the distance. We encounter a God who comes home and a King who arrives and intends to live – up close and in person – with his people.

Hymn of the Day
"Joy to the World"

This hymn provides a grand musical announcement for the opening of Christmas Day worship. The text by Isaac Watts is a paraphrase of Psalm 98:4-9. It first appeared in his book, *The Psalms of David, Imitated in the Language of the New Testament,* of 1719. The hymn helps us join with heaven and earth in rejoicing in the coming of Christ. Of course the hymn can be effective when sung at times other than Christmas. An explanation of its Psalm 98 origin would be especially helpful at such times. The fourth stanza also can be a reference to Philippians 2:10: "at the name of Jesus every knee should bend."

Children's Time

God's Amazing Gift

Bring a nativity crèche. Place the baby Jesus figure into a gift box. Print the words, "To the world, with love from God" on a gift tag and attach it to the box. Invite the children to gather around the nativity crèche. Have a brief discussion about Christmas gifts: What was your favorite gift this year? What kinds of gifts did you give to others? Comment that giving and receiving gifts is a wonderful Christmas tradition.

Mention that the Bible passage today tells about a wonderful gift God gave to the world on the very first Christmas. Show the gift box and read the tag. Ask the children what they think might be inside. Invite a volunteer to unwrap the package and carefully place the baby Jesus figure in the manger.

Explain that God's special gift to the world was Jesus. Jesus came to tell us that we are all God's children and that God loves us very much. Express excitement for God's amazing gift.

Pray with the children, giving thanks for Jesus, who came to tell us about God's love.

The Sermon

Up Close and In Person

Hymns
Beginning of Worship: "New Songs of Celebration"
Sermon Hymn: "Long Ago, Prophets Knew"
Closing Hymn: "Break Forth, O Beauteous Heavenly Light"

Scripture

John 1:1-14 (For additional sermon materials on this passage, see the September 2006 issue of *The Clergy Journal* and the 2006 May/June planning issue of *The Clergy Journal.*)

A few years ago a popular song proclaimed, "God is watching us." Well-known singers such as Bette Midler, Nanci Griffith, and Kathy Mattea have offered moving renditions of this song, "From a Distance." Perhaps you will recall that the lyrics speak of beautiful snowcapped mountains, lush green forests, and deep blue waters encircling the globe. This view, the songwriter tells us, is of our planet from space – "from a distance." Such is God's perspective of this terrestrial ball because God lives at an immense distance from us.

Up close to the action, down here on earth, it is in fact quite a different story. The snowcaps are melting because of global warming. The forests are decimated as are hundreds of mammal, reptile, and insect species. The streams, rivers, and seas are polluted. And we humans reserve our greatest powers of ingenuity and creativity for humiliating and destroying other human beings. When viewed up close and in person, our world is messy.

The song appeals to God's view of us, and asks us to become who we are when viewed "from a distance." From a distance we are one, no one is in need, harmony echoes through the land, and hope dwells abundantly in every home. If only we could see ourselves the way God sees us, all wars would immediately cease, enemies would fast become friends, and the noble character of humanity would shine undimmed in every endeavor henceforth and forever more. If only we could see ourselves as God sees us, we would desire to be different.

Now, "From a Distance" is a great song. In fact, it reminds me a bit of the apostle Paul who, when addressing the Philippian congregation, urges them on to repentance, change, and holy living by intoning, "The Lord is near" (Phil 4:5b). Obviously, both the apostle Paul and Julie Gold, the songwriter, hold that belief in God is a powerful motivator of human transformation.

However, for the songwriter, we must climb up and out of the hole we are in. God is "up there" and "looking down." The song suggests that God cannot save us; only we can save ourselves. The changing, the peacemaking, the forgiving, the healing, and the saving is our work. Paul is also concerned about the gap between humans and God. However, unlike the song, the unified thrust of the biblical writers is this: the gap is closing, and from God's side. God is coming closer. For example, Paul motivates real, substantive change among his parishioners in Philippi by announcing, "The Lord is near." God's increasing nearness is not because we have climbed up, but because God has climbed down.

John the Baptist, in the tradition of the prophet Isaiah, appealed to God's proximity to humankind – to God's eventual and certain coming – as a way of urging humans to live justly and mercifully with each other. "Prepare the way of the Lord," John shouted. "Make his paths straight." God will come, John announced, and in that day "all flesh shall see the salvation of God" (Lk 3:6).

In fact, in today' lesson from the Gospel of John we are told that God is not content to watch from a distance as we go on bungling creation and mangling each other. Rather, God is coming; the gap is closing.

There is, to be sure, a very real distance between God and us, as there must always be between Creator and creature. We are the work of God's hands; we are not now and will never be God. There is a very certain divide between God and us. The "stuff" of God is different than the "stuff" of humankind. Now, this distinction between God and us is so grand and infinite that many assume it is insurmountable, unbridgeable. This Christmas morning, however, I proclaim to you the good news that this gap has been breached. Last night, God rushed into the world to meet us. Last night, soaked in sweat and covered in straw, Mary birthed God for us. Last night, God traversed a great distance and came home. Last night, God arrived up close and in person – Infinite, Almighty Creator squeezed into a human child. Last night, God took flesh and entered this messy world. Last night, "the Word became a human being and came to live here with us" (Jn 1:14 CEV).

In the light of Christmas morning we can tell the truth. And this is the truth: Once our King lived in a land far away. Darkness fell upon the land. Though from a distance, our King watched over us, others ruled, and often despotically. But from the beginning our King always intended to return. As time passed, our King sent messengers to announce his impending arrival. Some of us mocked the King's agents, some of us even threw stones, and most all of us ignored the announcements of the King's approach. Yet still our King approached and would not relent in his plans to rule, to restore the glories of his kingdom.

Last night, our King returned. Now our King is no longer out there, but here – next to you, and you, and you, and me. Our King no longer watches over us from a distance, but has come to live with us. This is not merely a visit. Our King has returned. In Jesus Christ, God lives – up close and in person. Amen.

– William L. Mangrum

December 31, 2006

1st Sunday after Christmas

(RC: The Holy Family, Not Listed)

Lessons

RCL	1 Sam 2:18-20, 26	Col 3:12-17	Lk 2:41-52
Episcopal (BCP)	Isa 61:10—62:3	Gal 3:23-25; 4:4-7	Jn 1:1-18

Introduction to the Lessons
Lesson 1
(1) 1 Samuel 2:18-20, 26 (RCL)

The boy Samuel, an offering to God from his mother Hannah, is serving God by helping Eli, the priest. Love, gratitude, the grace of God, and the fruits of obedience are seen here.

(2) Isaiah 61:10—62:3 (Epis)

Isaiah, nearing the end of a long career, speaks powerful words expressing the great joy of belonging to God. He paints a vivid picture of the gifts this relationship yields.

Lesson 2
(1) Colossians 3:12-17 (RCL)

How should Christians think about the qualities they are to embody in daily life? Paul uses the concept of clothing oneself as a metaphor for how Christians should behave. His persuasive words are great reminders to us all.

(2) Galatians 3:23-25; 4:4-7 (Epis)

Paul continues to admonish the Galatian church to live by faith, not works. Here he addresses the difference between the law of God and faith in God. The role and effect of Christ is highlighted.

Gospel
(1) Luke 2:41-52 (RCL)
Mary and Joseph are in Jerusalem to celebrate the Passover. Jesus, on this trip, does something surprising that signals a new phase of his growth and human ability to take on the mission for which he has been born.

(2) John 1:1-18 (Epis)
John, by the time he wrote this, was probably one of the last surviving eyewitnesses of Christ. He writes in the first century and opens with his own introduction of who Christ is.

Theme
Do you know where Christ is?

Thought for the Day
We do not need to search for Christ. He says, "Listen! I am standing at the door, knocking; if you hear my voice and open the door, I will come in to you and eat with you, and you with me" (Rev 3:20).

Call to Worship
One: The Lord is present in this sanctuary.
All: And we are present with the Lord.
One: The Lord will search for those who are lost, who strayed away.
All: The Lord will bring them safely home again, and will bind up the injured.
One: The Lord will strengthen the weak and feed them.
All: The Lord is present in this sanctuary and we are present with the Lord.

– based on Ezekiel 34:16

Pastoral Prayer
We come to you, O Lord, as humbly as we know how, thanking you for your constancy and presence without fail. You know where we are at all times and never lose track of us or what we are going through. We thank you for the grace of your Holy Spirit that ministers to us in difficulties, your unconditional love that holds us up, and your power that carries us

through. We pray for those who do not know you, O God, who are lost in the dark and are looking for peace where it will not be found. Use us, Lord. May our light shine as a beacon, that we may lead people into the light of your holy presence, so they may know the great joy of truly being found. In the name of Jesus the Christ, who keeps us and saves us. Amen.

Prayer of Confession

God, we confess our weakness before you. In this world that brings so much pain to so many, we seek an easy way out. We seek to protect ourselves by surrounding ourselves with things that can take us away from the hard work of faith. We hoard items of comfort, live vicariously through others as we watch television or movies. We look for our share of the pie, instead of looking to give to others from the blessing of your goodness to us. Help us to remember that true joy is found in you. Open our hearts, that we may not hold on so tightly to temporal things, but to the treasures that are everlasting. Help us to enrich the lives of others, knowing that richness of spirit is far more valuable than earthly possessions. In the name of Jesus Christ, we pray. Amen.

Prayer of Dedication of Gifts and Self

We dedicate these tithes and offerings to the work of the kingdom. May they be used to feed the hungry in body and spirit, and to find the lost, that they may come to know you, Lord. Amen.

Sermon Summary

Losing track of a child can be a heart-wrenching experience. To find that loved-one again brings great joy. When we lose track of our true source of joy and happiness, we can look for it in the wrong places; but when we look to Christ our happiness is fulfilled.

Hymn of the Day
"Once in Royal David's City"

The hymn text was written by Cecil Frances Alexander and published in her *Hymns for Little Children* in 1848. Alexander, married to an Irish pastor, wrote this hymn and others as a way of teaching children the meaning of the Apostles' Creed. This hymn is centered on the phrase "who was conceived by the Holy Spirit, born of the Virgin Mary." The stately tune IRBY, written for this text, lends itself well for using this hymn as a processional hymn. Perhaps a single child's voice or a children's choir could sing the first stanza, followed with the congregation singing the remaining stanzas as the processional.

Children's Time

Learning and Growing

Bring photographs that show you or a family member at different ages. Show the photographs. Enjoy noticing all the changes. Invite the children to share stories they have of growing, changing, and learning. Marvel at all the ways you have grown since you were born.

Observe that, just like us, Jesus didn't stay a baby. He learned and grew, just like any other child. Today's Bible story is about something that happened to Jesus when he was twelve. Tell the story of Jesus in the temple.

Comment that in this story Jesus was both a learner and a teacher. Ask: What questions might Jesus have asked the Jewish teachers about God? What kinds of questions do you have about God? What do you think Jesus may have taught the leaders about God? Affirm that asking questions is a great way to learn.

Comment that, just like Jesus, we are all learners and teachers. There are so many wonderful things to discover about God and we can work together at learning them.

Pray with the children, giving thanks for the marvelous ways in which we all learn and grow.

The Sermon

Do You Know Where Christ Is?

Hymns
Beginning of Worship: "When Morning Lights the Eastern Skies"
Sermon Hymn: "I Want Jesus to Walk with Me"
Closing Hymn: "Go with Us, Lord"

Scripture
Luke 2:41-52 (For additional sermon materials on this passage, see the September 2006 issue of *The Clergy Journal;* for sermon materials on Colossians 3:12-17, see the 2006 May/June planning issue of *The Clergy Journal.*)

The festival of the Passover was the most important of the three great Jewish celebrations that also include Pentecost and Tabernacles. Passover, of course, is the festival commemorating the night the angel of death killed the Egyptian firstborn while passing over the homes of the Jews. Against the great horde of pilgrims making the sojourn to Jerusalem, the backdrop to this celebration of God's blessing included entrepreneurs and merchants who offered their wares to the travelers. Imagine the array of people selling food, souvenirs, clothing, and toys while others were offering housing. There would have been a great deal of hustle and bustle with many things to see and do. The sights, sounds, colors, smells, and tastes would have filled those present with an excitement one did not experience daily in humdrum hometown life.

There must have been a throng of young people present. Jesus, a very human boy, no doubt would have been as outgoing as anyone there. You can imagine that he wanted to meet others and explore his surroundings with them. Perhaps checking in with mom and dad from time to time, he was allowed to venture away, as long as they knew his general whereabouts. It must also be acknowledged that in Jesus' day a twelve-year-old boy was considered almost an adult and would not be expected to tag along everywhere with his parents. It would be the next year that he would be presented as one ready to take his place in the religious community.

In addition, on the trip to and from Jerusalem, it was customary for the women and children to travel in the front of a caravan with the men bringing up the rear for protection. It would have been acceptable for Jesus to be in either place. It is, as you see, quite understandable that his whereabouts were easily assumed, given the social norms. It was in this delicate dance of freedom and security that Jesus turned up missing.

Those who have been through the experience of temporarily losing track of a child in the grocery store, or at a baseball game, or at some other event with crowds of people know the feeling that sits in the pit of your stomach, marking the terror and fear you experience in that moment or realization. It is a parent's worst nightmare to lose a child. The news reports of a missing child are heartbreaking to hear no matter whose child has been lost. I would imagine this human response was the same in Jesus' day, even if the community was somewhat safer than our own times.

The Bible says they found Jesus after the third day. It is not absolutely clear whether the scenario includes the days of travel to get back to Jerusalem. If so, then Joseph and Mary looked first among the extended family and friends. They had already traveled a day's distance and so took a second day to get back to Jerusalem. The third day was spent looking for their son. However, the biblical account could also mean that it took three days from the time they arrived back in Jerusalem. In either case their concern is not mitigated by length of time. The Amplified Bible adds that they felt distressed and tormented.

Now, Mary and Joseph knew their son was unique, that God had given him to them for a special purpose. That did not prevent them from fearing for his safety, for they did not know how or when his unique mission would actually take effect and make itself known.

Where do you think they looked for Jesus? They probably checked the marketplace with its many shops and the homes of friends and/or acquaintances. After agonizing hours passed they finally looked in the right place. They found him in the temple! And they were amazed. Upon questioning him, no doubt relieved and upset, they were even more amazed at Jesus' response to them. He reminded them of his life's mission and pointed to the temple as the logical place he would be. It seemed Mary and Joseph looked many other places before trying the temple. Jesus seems to be saying it should have been the first place.

Mary and Joseph had lost something precious to them. It was Jesus. This story becomes a powerful analogy when we connect it to our own losses in life. When we lose something important in our lives – love, wealth, happiness, beauty, security, or peace of mind – we can be tempted to search for them in all the wrong places. Many people look for their salvation in the wrong places. Some look in the marketplace, in the world of things, in money and possessions. The market advertises itself as a place where you can purchase that which will make you happy and perfect. It says, "Buy this toothpaste to get the perfect smile." Or, "Buy these clothes to attract the woman and man of your dreams." Or, "Live here for the best life." Furthermore, people pay expensive fees for cosmetic surgeries, looking for salvation in youthful appearance.

Just as Mary and Joseph may have looked in homes to find what they were looking for, we too can think, when we look in others' homes, that if we had what someone else has, our lives would be better and happier. Some even go as far as to covet another man's wife or another woman's husband, thinking it to be a solution to make up for the lack one may be experiencing in his or her own marriage. Solomon's wisdom, however, warns against this folly in Proverbs 5:15-23.

Jesus' response to his parents is also his response to those looking for Christ today. He says, in essence, that he is not difficult to find. He is in the temple of the heart. For those who have already taken Christ into their hearts, we sometimes forget that Christ is in us, close by. We must remember the words of 1 John 4:4 and claim them for ourselves: "For the one who is in you is greater than the one who is in the world."

The outside world can take away our peace, joy, and sense of stability; and we can respond without first looking in the right place for sustenance and spiritual renewal. When life tosses us around and we lose sight of our happiness and joy, we must remember that Jesus says, "I have said this to you, so that in me you may have peace. In the world you face persecution. But take courage; I have conquered the world" (Jn 16:33).

As a new year dawns, whatever challenges, doubts, or fears you may have about the future, know that Christ is in the temple of your own soul. Christ is always there – never lost – and ready to give you the resources of wisdom, unconditional love, grace, mercy, peace, joy, and power for life. Amen.

– David P. Sharp

January 6, 2007

Epiphany

Lessons

RCL	Isa 60:1-6	Eph 3:1-12	Mt 2:1-12
Roman Catholic	Isa 60:1-6	Eph 3:2-3a, 5-6	Mt 2:1-12
Episcopal (BCP)	Isa 60:1-6, 9	Eph 3:1-12	Mt 2:1-12

Introduction to the Lessons
Lesson 1
Isaiah 60:1-6 (RCL/RC); Isaiah 60:1-6, 9 (Epis)
Isaiah, a prophet in the eighth century before Christ, encouraged the people of Judah while under foreign rule and in exile. In times of hardship, an encouraging word is welcome. Isaiah speaks words of promise and prosperity as he seeks to inspire faith.

Lesson 2
Ephesians 3:1-12 (RCL/Epis); Ephesians 3:2-3a, 5-6 (RC)
Written in the final decade of the first century after Christ, this text is a manual of Christian living. Is this plan only for some? It is a mystery waiting to be revealed.

Gospel
Matthew 2:1-12 (RCL/RC/Epis)
All did not welcome Jesus' birth. As the star shone, darkness filled the hearts of some. Deceit and intrigue are in play here. Will wisdom rule or will treachery win in the battle over the baby Jesus' life?

Theme
Wise people listen to God.

Thought for the Day
Rebellion to tyrants is obedience to God.
> – Thomas Jefferson (1743-1826); this is the motto on his seal

Call to Worship
One: God is the king of justice.
All: And Jesus the prince of peace.
One: God judges with righteousness.
All: God defends the poor, delivers the needy, and is against oppression.
One: May God be to you like soft rain falling on grass, and like showers that water the earth.
All: And may righteousness and peace flourish in our lives and in the world.
> – based on Psalm 72

Pastoral Prayer
We thank you, O God, for the privilege of coming to you in prayer. We honor and praise you for your love and power and mercy. We pray that you bless us with wisdom for the days ahead and the years to come, that we might move in the direction you would have us move. Help us to meet the challenges of each moment with grace and compassion. May we hear you, Lord, as you lead and guide us.

Open the ears of our hearts, that we might hear your voice clearly, listen with eagerness, and respond with complete trust. May we create the spaces in our day to pray, to meditate on your word, and to seek your presence, lest we lean to our own understanding and lose our way. We ask these things in the name of Jesus, our Lord and Savior. Amen.

Prayer of Confession
We confess, Lord, that we want to go our own way. We prefer to listen to our own voices instead of yours. We confess our need for power and our unwillingness to submit ourselves to you. It feels good to do things our way – to think we cause our own success and to believe we are powerful in our own right. Forgive us, Lord, and help us to have a more humble spirit. We know that your wisdom is better than our own, and your direction

for us will lead to a better destiny. Help us to have more desire and commitment to receiving the grace and wisdom of your Holy Spirit. In the name of Jesus Christ, the One whose path we follow. Amen.

Prayer of Dedication of Gifts and Self

We bring these gifts to you, O God, as an ongoing sign of our knowing that all blessing comes from you. As you have given us the priceless treasure of life, we return a portion to give life to the work of church. We thank you for our jobs, and the skills and health to provide for our family and loved ones. We humbly ask for increase both of spirit and material, that we may be more able to bless others as you bless us. Amen.

Sermon Summary

The wise men came to Jesus, honored and worshipped him. Obeying God's direction, they did not go back the same way; they left going in a different direction – one that would be better for them. Likewise, when people go to church, they should not go out the same way they came in. Christ changes us, every time we come into his presence.

Hymn of the Day
"As with Gladness Men of Old"

This hymn celebrating the coming of the wise men was written around 1858 by Scottish insurance executive, William Chatterton Dix. The first three stanzas of the hymn detail the Epiphany story. Stanzas four and five serve as a prayer that we will be kept in the narrow way and admitted to heaven where we will "ever sing alleluias to our King." The popularity of the hymn began with its inclusion in the first edition of the esteemed British hymn collection, *Hymns Ancient and Modern,* published in 1861. The tune Dix has been associated with the text since 1861.

Children's Time

Special Gifts for Jesus

Bring a baby doll and a basket containing a few baby items. Bring some sticky notes. Show the doll and invite the children to take turns holding it if they wish. Comment that people often celebrate the birth of a baby with special gifts. Show the basket of baby items. Have the children take each item out of the basket and say how the parents of a young child might use it.

Mention that the Bible story today is about a time when some wise people gave gifts to Jesus. Relate the story and ask the children what they think about the gifts Jesus received. You may have to explain what myrrh and frankincense are, and how they might be used.

Explain that the magi brought very special gifts for Jesus. They gave the best they could. We can also give special gifts to Jesus. Recall that when we show love to others, we are showing love to Jesus. What kinds of gifts might we bring to Jesus this year? Write the children's suggestions on sticky notes and place them on the worship table.

Pray with the children, giving thanks for the coming of Jesus and offering the children's special gifts.

The Sermon

Another Way

Hymns

Beginning of Worship: "Bring We the Frankincense of Our Love"
Sermon Hymn: "Rise up, Shepherd, and Follow"
Closing Hymn: "All Hail to God's Anointed" (based on Psalm 72)

Scripture

Matthew 2:1-12 (For additional sermon materials on this passage, see the October 2006 issue of *The Clergy Journal;* for sermon materials on Ephesians 3:1-12, see the 2006 May/June planning issue of *The Clergy Journal.*)

When I was in high school, most everyone knew I was a preacher's son. I remember times when guys (mostly bigger) would cunningly try to coerce money from me by forcefully asking me for, say, a quarter. Since I rarely had extra money, I would say, "I don't have an extra quarter." The request would then drop to a dime, still prompting a polite, "I don't have an extra dime" from me. At this point I would immediately hear a diatribe concerning my lack of unwillingness to give, and on top of that came a veiled threat of something terrible happening to me in the future because of it – "What? You're not going to give me even a dime? Okay, I'm gonna remember that!" This was, of course, done in the presence of that person's friends, and done in an intimidating manner, with the strategy being that next time they asked, I would be more likely to give than to receive another guilt-intended word lashing. Ultimately, it just made me avoid them and go another way.

These street-smart young men were attempting to use my kindness against me – their cunning versus my honest spirit. I have seen this contest played out many times with others; sadly, cunning wins most times. The Christian call and character trait of giving of ourselves is taken advantage of by those who know *how* we are suppose to respond. As an adult the same is true. There are people of great cunning who attempt to use our kindness and desire to do good against us for their own selfish profit and motives.

King Herod the Great tried to use the kindness of the wise men against them – to get to Jesus that he might kill him. He heard the news that magi had come from the east to see the One who had been born King of the Jews. This news was greatly disturbing to King Herod. He called all the chief priests and scribes of the people and asked where this child was to be born. When they said Bethlehem, he then met secretly with the wise men, who were Zoroastrian priests. Herod, inquiring of the exact time the star appeared, asked them to go to Bethlehem and make a careful search, and then to come back to tell him where the child could be found so that that he could go and pay homage to him.

Now, you might imagine the kindness and sweetness of voice with which Herod made this request. In his eyes may have been the affect of sincerity. Evil is a great actor and this Herod was cunning indeed, and cruel. He was ruthless in his need for power and control and destroyed any perceived threat to his rule. He murdered his wife, three of his six sons, mother-in-law, brother-in-law, uncle, and many others. He was set on protecting his throne for himself and his surviving sons (all three becoming rulers).

After the wise men visited Jesus, they were warned in a dream not to go back to Herod. And they went back to their country another way. It is interesting that the Bible says, "and having been warned in a dream." It seems these men were given a shared vision, which powerfully demonstrates God's ability to get through to us. There was agreement, and instead of going back to Herod, they went back to their country another way.

After Herod realized he had been outwitted, he became furious and had all the boys in Bethlehem and surrounding areas who were two-years-old or younger killed. But Jesus was unharmed because Joseph obeyed directions to escape to Egypt, given to him in a dream. So, because of two dreams – and obedience to the God who gave the dreams – we are here today. Because Joseph followed his dream, and because the wise men obeyed and followed the shared dream God had given them, Jesus survived. It must be remembered that Jesus was a human being and could have been killed along with the other children.

When we follow the leading of the Spirit, our dreams truly can come true. In addition, God's dreams for us benefit not only ourselves, but also others. We do not always get to know who or how, but we can have a feeling of peace trusting that God is in control.

Have you ever felt the leading of the Spirit and didn't follow it – only to find out later you had missed out on a blessing or could have prevented someone from doing harm to themselves or someone else? Has anyone ever told you, "Don't go down that road, go another way"?

Whatever brought you to Jesus probably sent you out in a different direction. You did not go back to your life the same way, but were sent on a different path. You didn't go back to the Herod that wanted to kill the Christ in you. When we come to Christ, God will direct our path. We are pointed in the direction of life and are steered away from that which seeks to destroy us along with the God in us.

There are Herods among us today – would-be tyrants that seek power and reign in our lives. These cruel and dangerous rulers range from life-draining addictions to joy-stealing-*isms* (workaholism, racism, consumer-ism, etc.). But when we make the long journey to Christ and worship him, as the wise men did – and when we open ourselves and give Jesus the treasures of our hearts, whether it be our most precious pains, heartaches worries, fears, or hopes and dreams – he will send us away in a new direction. Christ will impart a new dream for our life and give us wisdom for the road ahead, that we might safely travel in the direction of his leading. There is no better road.

– David P. Sharp

January 7, 2007

1st Sunday after Epiphany/
The Baptism of Our Lord

Lessons

RCL	Isa 43:1-7	Acts 8:14-17	Lk 3:15-17, 21-22
Roman Catholic	Isa 40:1-5, 9-11	Titus 2:11-14; 3:4-7	Lk 3:15-16, 21-22
Episcopal (BCP)	Isa 42:1-9	Acts 10:34-38	Lk 3:15-16, 21-22

Introduction to the Lessons
Lesson 1
(1) Isaiah 43:1-7 (RCL)
Isaiah, whose name means "The Lord saves," speaks vividly of God's ability to save and keep Israel. There is no mistaking Isaiah's message of God's power and authority to protect those who belong to the Lord.

(2) Isaiah 40:1-5, 9-11 (RC)
After prophesies of judgment in earlier chapters, Isaiah begins to speak here of Israel's coming deliverance and God's provision.

(3) Isaiah 42:1-9 (Epis)
Isaiah paints a clear picture of what Israel could be, even as he points to the messiah to come as an ideal embodiment. "He will" is the repeated refrain, punctuating a theme of expectation and the call to righteousness.

Lesson 2
(1) Acts 8:14-17 (RCL)
Stephen has been stoned to death, with Saul's approval. Those who believe in Jesus are beginning to be persecuted. They scatter to avoid death. However, the word of God continues to spread.

(2) Titus 2:11-14; 3:4-7 (RC)
Titus, an uncircumcised Gentile, was of great help to Paul in his work with other Gentiles. Paul instructs Titus here on the foundations of Christian living.

(3) Acts 10:34-38 (Epis)
This passage shows us the importance of "hearing" the word of God. Preached, taught, or simply expressed, Christ will always come to those with open hearts. This is the reason for the events unfolding here.

Gospel
Luke 3:15-17, 21-22 (RCL); Luke 3:15-16, 21-22 (RC/Epis)
John the Baptist is preaching in the 15th year of Tiberius Caesar's reign, and the people are wondering if he is the Messiah. He makes it unequivocally clear who the Messiah is and what he will do.

Theme
Power is even more powerful when it is seen in humility.

Thought for the Day
If you need to hear from God, pray. Pray until the Spirit rests lightly upon the mind. Then hear what God is saying.

Call to Worship
> **One:** The voice of the Lord is powerful;
> **All:** The voice of the Lord is full of majesty.
> **One:** The Lord is in this place.
> **All:** Praise be to God.
> **One:** May the Lord give strength to God's people!
> **All:** May the Lord bless God's people with peace!
>
> – based on Psalm 29

Pastoral Prayer
O Holy God, we thank you for the gift of life. We praise you for your mighty works, for the beauty of creation, for the vastness of space, and the mystery of spirit. You have fashioned a world so vast that it defies our logic, yet you know each of us by name.

We pray for peace in our lives and in the world around us. May we be the peace we are praying for; may our actions cause healing and wholeness, not division and tension. We pray for our church and for each member, that all needs will be met according to your grace. We pray for our community to be a safe place for our children to grow. We pray for our schools and for our teachers, that they may be inspired daily. We pray for the churches and pastors in our area, that we may be united in our mission to represent Jesus Christ. We pray for our brothers and sisters in Christ around the world, and rejoice in the knowledge that you love each one of us unconditionally. In the name of Jesus, we pray. Amen.

Prayer of Confession

Lord, we come to you humbly, knowing that we cannot hide our sins from you. We see people in pain and ignore the opportunity to help; we walk by the homeless on the street pretending we don't see them. We hear people speaking in ways that degrade other races and cultures; we laugh unashamed. We hear news reports of abuse and switch easily to the gossip and entertainment channels. We refuse to be immersed in the work of healing. We want easy lives. This we confess, Lord, and ask for your forgiveness. Help us to look longer at your people who are hurting and ask how we can help. Help us to listen, so that we might respond with compassion. Help us to live more for others than for ourselves, that the Christ in us will become visible to others. With thanks and praise to Christ Jesus, we pray. Amen.

Prayer of Dedication of Gifts and Self

We return to you, O God, a portion of what you have given us. We dedicate these offerings to the ongoing mission of the church in the cause of Jesus Christ. Keep us humble of spirit, so that we might remember those less fortunate. Help us to continually submit our ways to your ways, so that our ministry may truly be a blessing to those we serve. Amen.

Sermon Summary

The baptism of Jesus began his public ministry. In this act, he commits to us, bonds with our need to be cleansed from sin, and sides with those who are seeking to change their lives. The King of Kings begins his earthly work as humbly as he was born.

Hymn of the Day
"When Jesus Came to Jordan"

This hymn was written by British minister Fred Pratt Green in 1973
to meet the specific need for hymns celebrating the Baptism of Jesus.
Although not found in some hymnals, the hymn is worth locating and
singing. A variety of tunes have come to be associated with this text. The
tune COMPLAINER, unlike its name, provides a bright, major key setting.
In contrast, the tune DE EERSTEN SUN DE LAATSTEN gives a more somber,
minor key setting. Or, choose a 7.6.7.6.D. tune that's already known by
the congregation as the setting for this important text.

Children's Time

Jesus Is Baptized

Bring a jug of water and some cups, a sheet of drawing paper, and
powdered paint. Invite the children to join you for a drink of water. As
you pour and distribute the water have a brief conversation about the
wonder of water and all that it does.

Sprinkle a little paint powder on the paper. Lightly drizzle some
water from your cup on the powder. What happens when the water
touches the powder? Tip the paper up so that the paint runs down.
Observe that the water has made it possible for the paint to leave a mark
on the paper. Comment that in our Bible story today water is used to
help get Jesus ready to leave his mark on the world.

Tell the story of Jesus' baptism. Explain that Jesus' baptism marks
the time when Jesus started teaching about God's love.

Comment that people are still baptized today to show that they
are Jesus' followers. Encourage the children to share stories of their own
baptism or the baptism of other people, being sensitive to those who
have not been baptized.

Pray with the children, giving thanks for the story of Jesus' baptism.

The Sermon

The Greatest Little Beginning

Hymns
Beginning of Worship: "O, Christ, the Great Foundation"
Sermon Hymn: "Fill My Cup"
Closing Hymn: "Hail to the Lord's Anointed"

Scripture
Luke 3:15-17, 21-22 (For additional sermon materials on this passage, see the October 2006 issue of *The Clergy Journal* and the 2006 May/June planning issue of *The Clergy Journal*.)

This scripture passage captures the beginning of the public ministry of Jesus. We last saw him at the age of twelve, and now he is thirty. Eighteen years have passed. Emperor Tiberius has been in power for fifteen years. Pontius Pilate is governor of Judea, and Herod (son of Herod the Great, who tried to kill Jesus at birth) rules Galilee. For the Jews, Annas and Caiaphas are the high priests.

John the Baptist, the man who announced Jesus' coming, was a strange character who ate locusts and honey and preached vigorously about the coming Messiah. There had not been a prophet for 400 years in Israel, and though John the Baptist was recognized as a prophet, others wondered if he himself was the Messiah. He stirred the expectations of his listeners, from soldier to civilian, and raised the ire of politicians, most notably Herod, who had him jailed. John had paved the way for Jesus coming on the scene by raising awareness of the need to turn from sin and to turn to God. He preached this message in a manner that was immediate and urgent. One could evidently feel the pace of reality speeding up to a climactic moment, for people were coming to repent. And then it comes. History and prophecy meet as Jesus arrives.

Can you imagine being in the crowd when the revelation of Jesus' presence comes to pass? It must have been an amazing thing to behold. The Bible doesn't record the reactions of the people, but one can imagine the scene as the Spirit descended upon Jesus. "Here he is, the man who is God!" "The Messiah has come!" "He's actually here!"

Here is Jesus, a 30-year-old man, perhaps handsome and rugged from his work as a carpenter. No doubt beautiful of countenance because of the inner character he possessed. And now, he was about to create a beautiful moment – a powerful moment in history. Thirty was the accepted right age to begin one's important work. David was thirty when he became king. Joseph was thirty when he began serving the king of Egypt. Jesus, acting within the mores of the culture, would turn society upside down, from the inside out.

Jesus shows us many things in the way he begins his ministry. First, he chooses to begin his ministry in the company of those who have come to repent. This is auspicious, to say the least, for Jesus comes to all who repent even as he calls the world to repentance. He does not go to where he might have gained instant status in the eyes of the prominent religious leaders. He started out humbly – being born in a manger to humble parents – and he continues that pattern, beginning his ministry without fanfare among those who have come to humble themselves.

Second, Jesus chooses to begin his ministry at a site of water. He did not choose a site filled with the trappings of kings. No, this king begins at a humble place of cleansing, the Jordan River. Water is available to all, as is Jesus. It is a prime sustainer of life, even as the salvation he comes to bring is the prime ingredient for everlasting life with God.

Third, Jesus affirms baptism as a powerful symbol to express the human desire to be cleansed from sin. Jesus, in allowing John to baptize him, identifies with humanity, with our sin. He models submission. If Christ can, then so can we. That is the message. Jesus doesn't need baptism, but understands the powerful bonding it expresses to those watching; and to those who would hear about it.

So, it is telling that Jesus chooses to go into the water, to get wet. For it is a powerful testimony of Christ's willingness to go in with us – to join us and be right there with us in our need for spiritual renewal and transformation. He commits to us, choosing to be with us as opposed to being over us as other religious leaders of the day. Jesus is not watching from the sidelines or rooting us on from an elevated position that tempts condescension and arrogance. Jesus is proving his willingness to humble himself for our benefit, though he would know no sin. In his baptism, Jesus models what we all must do.

Jesus, in his baptism, sets up the coming baptism of the Holy Spirit and fire, as John the Baptist preached. In addition, Jesus' willingness to humble himself portends what he would do in the future. That is, he would go to the cross, taking on our sin when he didn't have to.

Finally, Jesus prays at the beginning of his ministry. As Jesus prays, the Holy Spirit descends on him. In this, the Bible records a connection between prayer and the Spirit. When we pray, we are opening the gates of heaven, as it were, and are able to receive its blessings. It is not that the Holy Spirit comes only when we pray – for God gives to us freely. However, we must pray to experience the guidance and power of the Holy Spirit in our lives.

After the baptism, four things took place: Jesus prayed, the heavens opened, the Holy Spirit descended upon Jesus in bodily form like a dove, and the voice of God came from heaven. In human terms: he was wet (drenched in the human condition); his heart was open (allowing him to commit to the task); he received power (to carry out his mission); and the voice of God came from heaven (to signal Jesus' readiness to speak to the world).

And Jesus did. And Jesus still does. Are you listening?

– David P. Sharp

January 14, 2007

2nd Sunday after Epiphany

RC/Pres: 2nd Sunday in Ordinary Time

Lessons

RCL	Isa 62:1-5	1 Cor 12:1-11	Jn 2:1-11
Roman Catholic	Isa 62:1-5	1 Cor 12:4-11	Jn 2:1-11
Episcopal (BCP)	Isa 62:1-5	1 Cor 12:1-11	Jn 2:1-11

Introduction to the Lessons

Lesson 1
Isaiah 62:1-5 (RCL/RC/Epis)

After twenty chapters of prophecies concerning Israel's deliverance and deliverer, Isaiah here speaks of the future of Jerusalem, using vivid imagery and powerful descriptions of its vindication and divine favor.

Lesson 2
1 Corinthians 12:1-11 (RCL/Epis); 1 Corinthians 12:4-11 (RC)

This letter to the church in Corinth, the most important Grecian city of Paul's day, is a collection of teachings on specific aspects of the Christian life. In this reading, Paul talks of the gifts of the Spirit.

Gospel
John 2:1-11 (RCL/RC/Epis)

Christ has chosen Andrew, Peter, Phillip, and Nathanael as disciples. At a wedding they attend with Jesus' mother, they witness a potentially embarrassing situation. Jesus meets this crisis with an astounding solution and a sign that he is the Christ.

Theme

When Jesus is present, miracles are possible.

Thought for the Day

If Jesus can turn water into wine, he can turn the water of your tears into tears of joy.

Call to Worship

One: O sing to the Lord a new song.
All: Sing to the Lord, all the earth.
One: Sing to the Lord, bless God's name.
All: Tell of God's salvation from day to day.
One: Declare the glory of the Lord among the nations,
All: God's marvelous works among all the peoples.
One: For great is the Lord,
All: And greatly to be praised.

— based on Psalm 96

Pastoral Prayer

We thank you, O God, for the blessing of life. We thank you for the celebration of worship and the hope for salvation that we have in you. We pray for those who do not know you, that they may receive the good news of Christ Jesus. We pray for those in leadership, that they may plan with insight and perspective that lead to wise decisions.

We pray for those who are making important commitments, that they will receive power to see them through. We pray for those who are in need, that they receive the blessing of fulfillment.

We pray for those who need renewal, that they may receive the newness of spirit available in Christ. We pray for those who face embarrassment or shame, that the power of God may change shame to praise and embarrassment to celebration. We pray for those who need faith, that they may ask and believe. Amen.

Prayer of Confession

God, we confess that we wrestle with our own image. We want to be humble, yet pride invades. We want to look good in the eyes of the world. We want what others have. And we want more when we have enough. We become envious when others acquire what we want. We admit frustration when we don't make as much money as our acquaintances. We question your love for us when we see those we consider equal in position or rank gaining material possessions as we struggle. We pray, O God, for a renewal of mind. Restore a right perspective, that we may be more like Christ. Help us to trust that you know what we need; and that you have the power to provide for us at all times. We ask these things in the name of Jesus Christ. Amen.

Prayer of Dedication of Gifts and Self

We present these tithes and offerings, generous God, thanking you for the blessings you have bestowed upon us. We ask your blessings on them, that they may truly serve the needs of the congregation and the community. As you have provided for us, may we provide for the hungry and minister to the poor in spirit. Increase our desire to be a blessing in the world, that we may ever seek to do all we can for the Kingdom of Heaven. Amen.

Sermon Summary

Jesus performs his first miracle at a wedding. There to celebrate, he obeys his mother by helping when a major problem develops. His own obedience sparks a miracle, and shows the power of God to renew, restore, and transform our circumstances.

Hymn of the Day
"Blessed Jesus, at Your Word"

We owe Catherine Winkworth our gratitude for this translation of the original German hymn, "Leibster Jesu, wir sind hier." The German hymn was written in 1663 by Tobias Clausnitzer and appeared in Winkworth's second series of *Lyra Germanica* in 1858. Clausnitzer, a pastor in Weiden, Saxony, intended the hymn to be sung just prior to the sermon. The text applies to the 21st-century church as well, as we acknowledge that "all our knowledge, sense, and sight lie in deepest darkness shrouded, till thy spirit breaks our night . . . " The German tune LEIBSTER JESU, written in 1664, has long been associated with this text.

Children's Time

Jesus Goes to a Wedding Party

Bring a party hat and a noisemaker. Get the children's attention by putting on the party hat and blowing the noisemaker. Ask the children about times they have gone to a party. What was being celebrated? Who was invited? Was there special food to eat? Observe that today's story is about a time when Jesus went to a wedding party.

Invite the children to help you retell the story. Ask for volunteers to play the different parts in the story – Mary, Jesus, the steward, the disciples, the servants. If you have a large group others can be guests. Explain that each time a new character is mentioned, the person playing that character can step forward and mime the actions. Retell the story of Jesus at the wedding in Cana. Tell the story slowly, pausing where necessary, to allow the children to play their parts.

Mention that the stories during Epiphany show us how the light of God's love shone out into the world through Jesus and Jesus' followers. Today we saw God's love in action at a wedding party.

Pray with the children, giving thanks for stories that show us God's love in action.

The Sermon

The Making of a Miracle

Hymns
Beginning of Worship: "Great Is Thy Faithfulness"
Sermon Hymn: "Trust and Obey"
Closing Hymn: "God of Our Life"

Scripture
John 2:1-11 (For sermon materials on 1 Corinthians 12:1-11, see the October 2006 issue of *The Clergy Journal;* for sermon materials on Isaiah 62:1-5, see the 2006 May/June planning issue of *The Clergy Journal.*)

The wedding at Cana was the occasion of Jesus' first miracle. It was an auspicious demonstration of God's ability to fill our needs and to transform the ordinary into the extraordinary.

Weddings are occasions when one hopes everything goes just right. The perfect day is planned long in advance, and the anticipation leads to a heightened sense of excitement. It is a special moment in the lives of the bride, the groom, and their families. Those in attendance share in the celebration as it reminds those who are married of their own wedding day and those who are single of the hope of marriage in the future.

Within the social norms of Jesus' day, it was considered an insult to run out of wine at an important celebration or event. Though the Bible does not record the emotion involved, one can imagine the panic the hosts must have felt in running out of wine at one of the most important events and social functions in life. It would have been seen as a bad omen.

Why they ran out of wine might be interesting to entertain. A wedding was usually a weeklong festival that included the whole town as invitees. Not to attend was considered an insult. So, perhaps just too many people showed up. Perhaps people drank more than was anticipated; perhaps this was the first big occasion the family had conducted and they simply underestimated the amount of supplies that would be needed. Perhaps they were on a budget and did what they could, hoping it would work out. When these kinds of things happen, whether then or now, there is little to mitigate the feelings of disappointment the hosts would likely feel. To the extent that provision was a sign of social position or financial well-being, running out of wine was certainly no small thing.

With this stage set, Jesus, along with his mother and the disciples, are present. Jesus, there to enjoy the festivities, was "a very present help in trouble" (Ps 46:1). Christ is with us in our times of joy just as much as in our times of struggle. Mary, no doubt feeling empathy, enlists Jesus' help. It is not so much that she was asking Jesus to perform a miracle as she was confident that whatever he did would be of great help in resolving the dilemma. It was Jesus' choice to act in a miraculous way, even as it is God's will that determines when to intercede and perform miracles in our own lives. And just as he responded to Mary, Jesus always responds to us. Later in John he says, "If in my name you ask me for anything, I will do it" (Jn 14:14).

When we invite Christ to be a part of our deepest commitments – marriage, career, or the work needed to fulfill a long-held dream – we can be sure he will be with us to guide us and make available the wisdom of God.

Christ will be there, if invited. And should our resources run low – patience, compassion, willpower, or even bodily strength – Christ has authority and power to supply our needs because of the abundance of God. Whatever problems confront us, whatever we lack in any situation, Christ can restore us. He can restore us to happiness, bring healing and restoration, and is able to renew our ability to enjoy life and celebrate fully, without worry or want. When we obey Christ, our faith is always rewarded with God's grace. Frustration turns to hope as faith is engaged. And faith is the assurance of the things we hope for and the evidence of the things we do not yet see.

Our best plans do not always succeed as planned. Life can throw us a curve. But as long as Jesus is present in the midst of what we are going through, there is hope. We cannot always see how God is going to provide for us. We do not know what the Lord is going to do to turn our circumstances around. And, we cannot predict what we might have to do to be a part of the solution. But we can remember that God works all things for good.

God honors our commitments, and when we act on them providence is employed. When we follow the leading of the Spirit, knowing it to be wise and for our greatest good, then we should not hesitate to follow the directions of God's guidance.

When the wine gave out, the water (set aside for ritual cleaning) became the new wine. In fact, it was the best wine. This is remarkable – Jesus turns social expectations completely around by saving the best for last. What Jesus has done at this wedding is a powerful analogy of his mission. He gave up his life on the cross – his blood poured out for our sins. But this was not the end of the story. It was the beginning of the greatest miracle in history. Jesus, the living water, was resurrected by the power of God. And now, because of his transformation from God incarnate to risen Savior, we who believe in Christ are cleansed of our sins.

Let the celebration begin! Become intoxicated with the Living Water who became the new wine, who saved the best for last by providing the way to salvation with the miracle of his life, death, and resurrection.

– David P. Sharp

January 21, 2007

3rd Sunday after Epiphany

RC/Pres: 3rd Sunday in Ordinary Time

Lessons

RCL	Neh 8:1-3, 5-6, 8-10	1 Cor 12:12-31a	Lk 4:14-21
Roman Catholic	Neh 8:2-4a, 5-6, 8-10	1 Cor 12:12-30 or 12:12-14, 27	Lk 1:1-4; 4:14-21
Episcopal (BCP)	Neh 8:2-10	1 Cor 12:12-27	Lk 4:14-21

Introduction to the Lessons

Lesson 1

Nehemiah 8:1-3, 5-6, 8-10 (RCL);

Nehemiah 8:2-4a, 5-6, 8-10 (RC);

Nehemiah 8:2-10 (Epis)

What a joy it must have been for the returning exiles to rediscover the Law and their special covenant with God. In this reading we hear about that rediscovery.

Lesson 2

1 Corinthians 12:12-31a (RCL);

1 Corinthians 12:12-30 or 12:12-14, 27 (RC);

1 Corinthians 12:12-27 (Epis)

This passage clearly points out that our personal relationship with God is incomplete. We need other members of the body of Christ if the work of God is to be accomplished.

Gospel

Luke 4:14-21 (RCL/Epis); Luke 1:1-4; 4:14-21 (RC)

Jesus spoke openly to the people of Nazareth about who he was. Here he clearly implies that he is the Messiah, the Christ.

Theme

Community is essential to bring to fruition our relationship with God.

Thought for the Day

Is community just a forum for expressing my personal faith, or a gift through which my faith can grow?

Call to Worship

Look around. We are surrounded by a great cloud of witnesses. Some we can see. Some are invisible to our earthly eyes. We recognize, too, the presence of Jesus Christ among us because we are gathered in his name. We recognize Christ in one another because we are members of his body. Let us come together and rejoice not just in the gift that God has given us in Christ, but in the gift God has given us in one another and in the entire church, that great mystery which is the body of Christ.

Pastoral Prayer

O God, let us recognize Christ present in this place. Let us recognize Christ in one another. Let us recognize Christ in those not present here. We are the members of your body and you have called us to do your work in the world, to show forth your love and your mercy until you come again. Let that work begin with those present here today. Enable us to carry your work into our community, and even throughout the world. Open our eyes of faith to see you, Lord, in all the peoples of the earth. In the power of the Spirit, enable us to be your instruments of peace, of grace, of redemption. Amen.

Prayer of Confession

All too often, merciful God, we have not recognized your presence among us. All too often, we have not seen you in one another, particularly in those we consider different from ourselves. All too often we have failed in proclaiming you to others through the way we live and act. Forgive us and open our eyes of faith that we may see you more clearly in the many ways you come to us. Help us ever to act toward our brothers and sisters as we would act toward you. Forgive us when we fail. May we, by your wisdom, recognize and learn from our failures that we may serve ever more faithfully day to day. Amen.

Prayer of Dedication of Gifts and Self

These gifts, Lord, represent our lives, our possessions, all that we are and have. We offer them now to you as symbols of ourselves, so that you may take us and bless us and, through the power of your Spirit, shape us into little Christs. Amen.

Sermon Summary

Christianity is not a do-it-yourself religion. Our faith may begin as a personal relationship with God, but it is supported, strengthened, and increased by our relationship with a Christian community. God gave us the church as a gift to enable us to grow spiritually.

Hymn of the Day
"God of Change and Glory"

For those looking for a fresh, contemporary hymn text and tune that celebrate the diversity of gifts as highlighted in 1 Corinthians 12, this is a match. The hymn was written in 1973 and is one of the earliest to acknowledge diversity as a gift from God. Its author, Al Carmines, in addition to serving as a United Church of Christ pastor in New York City, is a composer, playwright, performer, and teacher. He is a fellow of the Society for the Arts in Religion and Contemporary Culture. The hymn can be found in *The New Century Hymnal*, number 177.

Children's Time

Can You Spot Jesus?

Play a couple of rounds of "Can you spot?" Start the game by saying, "I'm thinking of a person in the church. She has blond hair and works in the church office. *(Adapt as needed.)*" The children work together to spot that person in the church. Comment that in order for the game to work you need a good description of the mystery person so others can recognize her or him.

Explain that many years before Jesus was born, the prophet Isaiah described a very special person called the "chosen one." Isaiah wanted the people to be able to recognize God's chosen one. This person would be filled with God's Spirit, bring good news to the poor, help the blind people see, and bring hope to those who had no hope. Ask the children if this description reminds them of anyone in particular.

Comment that in our Bible reading today, Jesus reads Isaiah's words in front of all the people. Then Jesus told the people that he was the one whom Isaiah had described. It was a very unexpected announcement.

Pray with the children, giving thanks for Jesus who came to bring good news, healing, and hope to the world.

The Sermon

Can We Be One with Christ?

Hymns
Beginning of Worship: "O God of Every Nation"
Sermon Hymn: "We Are One in the Spirit"
Closing Hymn: "Faith of Our Fathers"

Scripture
Luke 4:14-21 (For sermon materials on 1 Corinthians 12:12-31a, see the October 2006 issue of *The Clergy Journal;* for sermon materials on Nehemiah 8:1-3, 5-6, 8-10, see the 2006 May/June planning issue of *The Clergy Journal.*)

In case you had not noticed, there is an ambiguity in the title of today's sermon. Most of you will take the title to ask whether we can be united with Christ. Can we be so identified with our Savior that we might be said to be one with him?

But the way I want to read the question of the sermon title is this: Can we be alone with Christ? Can we be solitary Christians, having a personal relationship with Jesus, but disregarding the community of the local church and the community of the broader church – the entire body of Christ? In other words, can we, in the company of Christ, be "do-it-yourself" Christians?

To ask the question in this form is essentially to answer it. We are part of a larger company of members of Christ's body. Paul tells us that each of us has a role to play within that body, just as each of our organs has a role to play within our physical bodies. There are many more passages in scripture that underline our essential unity in Christ, a unity that is more than a number of humans who share the same beliefs or are members of the same organization. We are, as Christ taught, branches of the same vine. We are one as the Father and Christ are one. We are one in that we are all temples of the same Holy Spirit. We cannot ignore this unity and claim that our personal relationship with Christ is all that really matters. We need each other in a fundamental way to grow spiritually and to become all that Christ calls us to become.

Too many Christians, and one is too many, think they can grow spiritually by praying alone, studying the scripture in the privacy of their homes, and never attending church. And, no doubt, by the grace of God, some Christians have achieved significant spiritual growth in this way. But we can use all the help we can get in our spiritual journeys. Perhaps we think we come to church to worship God; thus, our attendance at services is our gift to God. But the reality is that the church is God's gift to us. We come to church not for God's sake, but for our sake. It is through our presence at worship that we can and should receive many spiritual benefits we would miss otherwise.

First, there is increased power in prayer when many Christians are gathered in prayer. Prayer generates spiritual power. If you have one lamp turned on in a room, the room is not as bright as if there are twenty lamps shining in that same room. When we pray together as the church, our prayer is more powerful than when we pray alone because we are praying as the church, not just as individuals.

Second, gathered as the people of God, we can learn from listening to the words we pray, listening to the sermon, listening to scripture read at the service. We can ask others to pray for us and we can exercise one of our great privileges as Christians to pray for the world and for the church. We can listen for the voice of God in others we meet. We do not know what words that others speak might touch our hearts, but we will not hear them if we are alone and not in church.

And, of course, it is at church and in community that we receive the sacraments. The sacraments are channels of grace given by God to help us. There is the Eucharist, for one, that is essential to a healthy spiritual life. The Eucharist is a reason to come to church if you can find no other reason convincing.

But I am sure at least a few of you are thinking that coming to church has disadvantages as well as advantages. We may have to put up with people we don't like. The sermon may be dull and uninspiring; it might even be a spiritual turnoff. We might be asked to become involved in activities that do not interest us and for which we do not have the time. We might indeed feel more comfortable curled up in our favorite easy chair at home reading the Bible than getting dressed up, driving to church, and sitting in a hard pew listening to babies squealing throughout the service.

All of these reasons given for not coming to church, however, can be turned around and made reasons why we ought to come to church. We need to recognize Christ in others, even those we do not like. We need to realize that Christ can talk to us even in the dullest of sermons if we are open to hear him. We should rejoice that there are infants in worship because if there were not, the future of the church would be dismal indeed. We should realize that the church is a gift. And I shall state frankly, if you do not find this particular church to be a place of comfort and healing, then find a church in which you will find what you think you need.

What we need most is God. And in church, God comes to us in a special way through the prayer of the body of Christ and the sacraments. Humans are weak and not always to our liking, but we are all in this together. We can separate ourselves from the church only by separating ourselves from Christ. We can ignore our membership in the body of Christ and the responsibilities that flow from that membership only at our spiritual peril.

Think carefully about the gift that Christ has given you through the church, the visible manifestation of his grace and his presence on earth. Take seriously your responsibilities as members of Christ's body and your essential bonds with all Christians everywhere. Come to church for your sake, not God's.

– Michael Gemignani

January 28, 2007

4th Sunday after Epiphany

RC/Pres: 4th Sunday in Ordinary Time

Lessons

RCL	Jer 1:4-10	1 Cor 13:1-13	Lk 4:21-30
Roman Catholic	Jer 1:4-5, 17-19	1 Cor 12:31—13:13 or 13:4-13	Lk 4:21-30
Episcopal (BCP)	Jer 1:4-10	1 Cor 14:12b-20	Lk 4:21-32

Introduction to the Lessons

Lesson 1

Jeremiah 1:4-10 (RCL/Epis); Jeremiah 1:4-5, 17-19 (RC)

Jeremiah recognizes his ignorance of the Lord's ways, so God gives him words and visions to teach him what he must say to the people of Israel who have forsaken the Law.

Lesson 2

(1) 1 Corinthians 13:1-13 (RCL);
1 Corinthians 12:31—13:13 or 13:4-13 (RC)

Paul's hymn describing Christian love and its preeminence over all other spiritual gifts is one of the finest passages found in all of his epistles.

(2) 1 Corinthians 14:12b-20 (Epis)

Paul admonishes the Corinthians to strive for excellence in their spiritual gifts in order to build up the church.

Gospel

Luke 4:21-30 (RCL/RC); Luke 4:21-32 (Epis)

How quickly public opinion can turn! One moment the people are praising Jesus and moments later they are ready to stone him. But they cannot kill Jesus because his time to die has not yet come.

Theme
Listen for God's voice in all voices.

Thought for the Day
God speaks to us in many ways: through coincidences, chance remarks of friends and strangers, successes, and even failures. We must listen for the voice of God at all times and in all places.

Call to Worship
We gather now to praise the Lord, but also to learn how we might better serve God. We are here not for God's sake, but for our own, for it is through the church that God showers many gifts on us – to strengthen us in our journey and to feed us that we might grow into spiritual maturity. We gather now to pray through word and song. We gather now to be taught through scripture and sermon. We gather now to be fed with the Lord's supper. Let us joyfully gather in the name of Christ.

Pastoral Prayer
We cannot thank you enough, dear God, that through Jesus you have made us your children and heirs of heaven. You have united us to your own life by bringing us into the body of Christ, your church, and making us temples of the Holy Spirit. Allow us to recognize the dignity you have freely poured out on us, not through pride and boasting, but through humility that recognizes our full dependence on you to be successful in your work. Give us discerning and faithful hearts that we may hear you when you speak and have the courage to follow wherever you might lead. Amen.

Prayer of Confession
How often, Lord, have we failed to listen for your voice, or, having heard it, have chosen to ignore it so that we might choose our wills over your own. We repent that we so often have failed to seek your holy will and have not come when you call us to follow. Strengthen us to prefer your will always to our own. Give us wise discernment that we might recognize your words when you speak to us. Keep us safe from deception and ever walking in your holy ways. Amen.

Prayer of Dedication of Gifts and Self

We dedicate these gifts and ourselves to you, generous God. They represent who we are, what we have, and what we do. As we offer them to you, we also thank you for the great gifts you have given us through Jesus Christ and the Holy Spirit. May our gifts be used in your service, and may the gifts you give to us inspire us to be ever faithful in your service. Make us aware of your sacred presence in our lives and give us the grace to hear your voice and answer its call. Amen.

Sermon Summary

The prophets and apostles were given revelations to teach God's people. God acts through the Spirit and the circumstances of our lives to teach us as individuals and to draw us more into the life of Christ. We must listen with the ears of the heart for what God wants us to hear.

Hymn of the Day
"My Faith Looks Up to Thee"

Ray Palmer wrote this hymn in 1830 after his graduation from Yale University as he was preparing for ordination in the Congregational Church. Directing the hymn's words to the "Lamb of Calvary," Palmer used them as a personal expression of what Christ meant to him. Shortly after writing the hymn, he gave it to composer Lowell Mason who wrote the tune OLIVET for it. The hymn helps us to acknowledge our divine Savior and to express the desire for our love of the Savior to be "pure, warm, and changeless . . . a living fire!"

Children's Time

Some Didn't Follow

Bring a box of toy figures of people. Place the toy figures on the floor and invite the children to pick one to represent Jesus. Explain that when Jesus was on earth he traveled around teaching about God's love and God's way for our lives. (Place Jesus in front of the toy figures.) Some of the people who heard Jesus' message followed Jesus. (Invite the children to place some of the toy figures in a group around Jesus.) And some of the people did not. (Have the children move the other figures away from Jesus.)

Mention that in the Bible story today we hear about a whole town of people who decided not to follow Jesus. (Move all the figures away from Jesus.) In fact some people got so angry at what Jesus had to say that they tried to hurt him. Jesus had to slip away quietly. Comment that Jesus must have been sad about this, but nothing would keep him from talking about God's love.

Comment that eventually some of the people from that town changed their minds and did follow Jesus. (Place some of the toy figures in a group around Jesus.)

Pray with the children, giving thanks for Jesus, who never stops telling people about God.

The Sermon

How God Speaks to Us

Hymns
Beginning of Worship: "God Has Spoken to His People"
Sermon Hymn: "The King of Love My Shepherd Is"
Closing Hymn: "Lead Us, Heavenly Father, Lead Us"

Scripture
Luke 4:21-30 (For sermon materials on 1 Corinthians 13:1-13, see the October 2006 issue of *The Clergy Journal*; for sermon materials on Jeremiah 1:4-10, see the 2006 May/June planning issue of *The Clergy Journal*.)

We have no trouble reading scripture and believing that we are hearing the word of God. But, though few will argue that scripture is not important as an aid to learning about how to live in relationship with God, there are other ways God communicates with us as well. It is important that we listen for God's still, small voice wherever it might be found – otherwise, we may miss lessons that God wishes to teach us.

One of the ways in which God speaks to us is in the ordinary circumstances of our lives. No, God does not micromanage our lives, nor does God generally intervene in our lives in a miraculous or extraordinary way. But faith tells us that God is with us in all times and places. God can instruct us and help us grow spiritually through successes, failures, joys, sorrows, sickness, or health. Paul tells us that God works to the good in all things for those who love the Lord. This does not mean that God invariably causes good things to happen to those who love God, but that the Lord can enable us to learn how to love God and our neighbor more whatever befalls us. Indeed, key questions we can ask ourselves at any time are: Where is God in what I am experiencing? What would God like me to learn? What would Jesus say to me at this time?

God does not cause every event in our lives. We have been left with free wills to make choices and God has set in motion natural laws that sometimes cause us grief. If God made all our choices for us, we would have no moral responsibility for our actions and there would be no such thing as sin. If God suspended the laws of nature to prevent harm, as in canceling the law of gravity so an airliner would not crash when a wing fell off, the world would become an unpredictable and chaotic place. But God can use the events of our lives to teach, no matter how tragic those events may seem at the time they happen. And God will teach us love and wisdom, and give us understanding of spiritual matters, if we allow God to do so.

Although God may have spoken directly to prophets like Isaiah, today God rarely speaks directly to individuals. If you think you hear the actual voice of God, you should test what you are being told against the scriptures and trusted advisors. We are easily deceived in such matters, particularly when God is supposedly telling us what we want to hear.

But this does not mean that God does not communicate with us. Here are some ways in which we can try to open our minds to God. First, as I mentioned earlier, we can look at the Bible to see if it provides guidance. We ought to read scripture as a prayer that God will give us light and wisdom. Our reading of God's word ought to be a prayer that God will guide us, even when we find scripture confusing and the words inapplicable to our needs. There are other fine spiritual books available, too, that might help us gain greater clarity about our relationship with God. Study groups, in which we exchange ideas with others about the Bible and other aspects of our faith, also can help us seek the mind of Christ in our regard.

Second, we should not hesitate to talk about our deepest concerns with trusted friends and advisors. Finding such spiritual companions may not be easy, but it is worth the effort to try. We all need someone with whom we can share our deepest thoughts and questions, someone who will listen sympathetically and pray with us, someone who can view us more objectively than we can view ourselves. This person does not have to be an ordained minister, but it probably should not be a spouse. We may ask God to help us identify such a person to walk with us in our pilgrimage.

Third, there is prayer. We must ask God to help us open our hearts and minds to what God wants of us. At times in prayer we will receive valuable insights that may not even be related to the subject matter of our prayer. We might even sit silently, reminding ourselves that God is present with us at all times, reminding ourselves that we are in the presence of our beloved Lord, and simply being available to God to do with us as God chooses. If we are ever afraid that we may be deceived if sit in silence and make ourselves available to God in quiet meditation, we can begin the session with a prayer that Jesus will protect us and keep us from all harm. Surrounding ourselves with God's protection is always a good way to begin meditation.

Fourth, God sometimes addresses us through the circumstances of our lives. Someone once said that coincidences are God's way of remaining anonymous. Two questions we should ask ourselves often are: Where is God in this? What does God want me to learn from this?

God rarely, if ever, speaks to us directly, but has given us many means to know of God's will and love for us, so that we might draw closer to the Lord. Never neglect these means. God is with us always and loves us more than we can possibly imagine. God wants to help us and will do just that. We only need to open ourselves to this help.

– Michael Gemignani

February 4, 2007

5th Sunday after Epiphany

RC/Pres: 5th Sunday in Ordinary Time

Lessons

RCL	Isa 6:1-8, (9-13)	1 Cor 15:1-11	Lk 5:1-11
Roman Catholic	Isa 6:1-2a, 3-8	1 Cor 15:1-11 or 15:3-8, 11	Lk 5:1-11
Episcopal (BCP)	Jud 6:11-24a	1 Cor 15:1-11	Lk 5:1-11

Introduction to the Lessons

Lesson 1
(1) Isaiah 6:1-8, (9-13) (RCL); Isaiah 6:1-2a, 3-8 (RC)

Each one of us is called by God for some holy work. Isaiah's call was more dramatic than most.

(2) Judges 6:11-24a (Epis)

Though Gideon objects that he is too weak to carry out a great mission, God chooses him anyway to drive out the oppressors of Israel.

Lesson 2
1 Corinthians 15:1-11 (RCL/RC/Epis)

Paul, though confessing his own weakness, exhorts Christians to hold fast to the gospel because of the saving power of Jesus Christ who proved he was the Son of God by rising from the dead.

Gospel
Luke 5:1-11 (RCL/RC/Epis)

Peter, suddenly recognizing the power of Jesus, can only fall to his knees and confess his sinfulness, yet Jesus chooses him to be an apostle.

Theme

God's power is present in the world.

Thought for the Day

Of ourselves we can do nothing, but the power of God can enable us to do more than we can ask for or imagine.

Call to Worship

We come together, Lord, knowing that you are present with your people in a special way when we gather in your name. The prayers of your children acting as your church have special power. Through our prayers, we gain strength to do your work. Through our prayers, we serve as channels for your grace to this troubled world. Through our prayers, we share in the restoration of all things in Christ, that your reign may come. Teach us, Lord, to pray and to do your work.

Pastoral Prayer

Dear God, give us the strength to do whatever you would have us do. We recognize that without the help of your Spirit we cannot even say, "Jesus is Lord," much less can we bring others into your kingdom. Let our common prayer bring us uncommon faith and willingness to do whatever you ask us to do in your name. May the power of your Spirit guide our every word and action. Fill us with your Spirit, that our prayers and works may proclaim your glory and work to the coming of your reign. Amen.

Prayer of Confession

All too often, O God, we have not recognized the mission you have committed to us – transforming the world, or at least our small portion of it, in the name of Christ. We have trusted in our ability to get things done rather than in your power. We have trusted in our wisdom instead of the wisdom of the Holy Spirit. May we always seek your will above our own wills. May we always pray for your strength and aid in all we do. Turn our hearts, minds, and wills completely to you, that we may serve you at all times and in all places. Amen.

Prayer of Dedication of Gifts and Self

Bountiful God, accept these gifts and bless those who have given them. Increase in us the gift of your Holy Spirit, that as our church takes these offerings and uses them for your work, we may be used for your work in whatever way you choose to use us. Amen.

Sermon Summary

God is active in the world in many ways. We must depend on God's power to carry out the work Christ has given us to do. Prayer is one of the most powerful tools God has given us.

Hymn of the Day
"Dear Lord, Lead Me Day by Day"

This hymn provides a bright expression of discipleship and praise. The text and tune were written by Francisca Asuncion in 1976, adapted from a popular Filipino folk song. It was first published in *Hymns from the Four Winds* in 1983. The tune lends itself to having a group of children introduce the hymn to the congregation. Perhaps guitar accompaniment could be used with the first two stanzas, followed with the entrance of the organ or piano on the final stanza. We express our desire for discipleship in "make me follow and obey" and our joyful praise in "praise to God…from morn till the set of sun."

Children's Time

Passing on the Good News

Bring two balls. Have the children stand in two lines facing you. Give a ball to the person at the head of each line. Invite them to say the name of someone who has told them about Jesus and pass the ball to the next person. When the balls get to the ends of the lines, pass them out to the congregation. Encourage the children to watch the balls travel from one person to the next. Let the excitement build! After a few moments, bring the balls back to the front.

Comment that sharing the good news of Jesus is a bit like passing the balls. The good news is passed from one person to the next. The Bible reading today was part of a letter written by the apostle Paul to the early church. Paraphrase verses 3-6. Comment that Paul was one person in a great chain of people who received the good news about Jesus and passed it on.

Observe that now it's our turn. Someone has told us about Jesus and now we can tell someone else. Pray, asking that God would help you share the good news of Jesus with others.

The Sermon

God, Help Us!

Hymns
Beginning of Worship: "O God, Our Help in Ages Past"
Sermon Hymn: "God of Grace and God of Glory"
Closing Hymn: "A Mighty Fortress Is Our God"

Scripture
1 Corinthians 15:1-11 (For sermon materials on Luke 5:1-11, see the October 2006 issue of *The Clergy Journal* and the 2006 May/June planning issue of *The Clergy Journal*.)

We are familiar with the concept of the body of Christ. We are members of that body and, therefore, as St. Paul tells us, we each have certain roles to play within that body to maintain its health, just as each organ of our physical bodies has a unique role in keeping us healthy. But as Jesus told us, "Apart from me you can do nothing" (Jn 15:5). And as Paul tells us, "No one can say 'Jesus is Lord' except by the Holy Spirit" (1 Cor 12:3). We, thus, are confronted with the fundamental truth that we are expected, indeed commanded, to carry out Christ's work in the world, but we are unable to carry out that work without the help of Christ and the Holy Spirit.

As always, our example must be Jesus. It is important to note that Jesus was always the Son of God, always the Messiah, always both human and divine. But even Jesus did not begin his public ministry until he had been anointed by the Holy Spirit at his baptism, when the Spirit descended on him in the form of a dove. He was then led by the Spirit into the wilderness for a 40-day retreat, and only then began his public ministry.

It has been said by some that spiritual growth involves turning more and more control of our lives over to God. But control is one of the hardest human possessions to give up. We want to do things our way. We want to choose the ministries we will participate in and then ask God to bless them. We depend on our own cleverness, our own abilities, our own strength to get things done; and, no doubt, we can accomplish a great deal on our own. But we can accomplish far more if we do what God wants to us to do – in the way that God wants us to do it – because then we are conforming our wills to God's will and depending on God rather than on ourselves.

There are objections that some raise against this line of reasoning. First, we object that we rarely know exactly what God wants us to do. If we are not sure what God's will might be, then we ought to do something rather than just wait around doing nothing at all in the hope that God will reveal what we should be doing. Surely God will bless our efforts if we are trying to work in the name of Christ and on behalf of Christ's mission, even if it might not be the work God intended us to do.

Second, we do have abilities and skills that have been given us by God to use in serving. What is wrong with depending on these skills and using them to work for God's glory? Are these not gifts from God, and, therefore, tools the Lord has given us? Though we depend on these gifts for success, we are still honoring God who gave us the tools in the first place.

In response to the objection that we ought to do something to serve the Lord even if we are not sure it is God's will, I offer the following. Certainly, I believe it is true, to paraphrase Thomas Merton, that it is pleasing to God that we want to please God, even if we are not sure that we are doing exactly what God wants us to do. But if we are constantly in motion, it may be harder for us to hear the still, small voice of God calling us to move in another direction.

Moreover, we may become so pleased with what we are doing, or the attention and praise that it attracts, that we are distracted from seeking God's glory. Though this temptation can occur even when we are carrying out God's will, it is easier to delude ourselves when we are doing what we ourselves have chosen. If we begin some work because we believe that God has called us to that work, we can remind ourselves why we are engaged in it and may be able to keep a better focus on God than on ourselves.

As to the objection that we ought to use the skills we are born with, I agree that these may indeed be valid indicators of the work God wants us to do. But, as Paul tells us, God is glorified most in weakness where the only credit for success belongs to God. If we shine brightly in some work, we must guard against putting ourselves first and God second. We may more easily attribute success to ourselves and congratulate God for having us on the team – forgetting that true holiness and success comes only from God.

Finally, God may not want us to do much at all except stand ready to serve and to listen carefully for God's call. We do not have to be busy all the time, since busyness itself can distract us from attention to God. As the great poet John Milton wrote, "They also serve who only stand and wait." Sometimes we grow more spiritually by waiting than by rushing headlong into activity.

We must try to please God in all we do, but we also must recognize our complete dependence on God to be truly holy and to be in control of bringing in the eternal reign of heaven. Pray to be faithful. That is what God asks for. Faithfulness is what matters, whether our human activity succeeds or fails.

– Michael Gemignani

February 11, 2007

6th Sunday after Epiphany

RC/Pres: 6th Sunday in Ordinary Time

Lessons

RCL	Jer 17:5-10	1 Cor 15:12-20	Lk 6:17-26
Roman Catholic	Jer 17:5-8	1 Cor 15:12, 16-20	Lk 6:17, 20-26
Episcopal (BCP)	Jer 17:5-10	1 Cor 15:12-20	Lk 6:17-26

Introduction to the Lessons
Lesson 1
Jeremiah 17:5-10 (RCL/Epis); Jeremiah 17:5-8 (RC)

We are called to keep our hearts and minds focused on the Lord and trust in God, rather than depending on our own strength.

Lesson 2
**1 Corinthians 15:12-20 (RCL/Epis);
1 Corinthians 15:12, 16-20 (RC)**

Without the Resurrection, Christianity makes no sense.

Gospel
Luke 6:17-26 (RCL/Epis); Luke 6:17, 20-26 (RC)

Many Christians feel that God's will is represented primarily by the Ten Commandments, but the beatitudes set an even higher standard.

Theme
Jesus calls us to a higher standard of living.

Thought for the Day
Many believe that if they obey the Ten Commandments, they are leading a godly life. But Jesus gives us an even higher way of life.

Call to Worship

We are the people of God gathered together, but why are we here? Lord, you know our hearts. We want to be here so that we might glorify you and receive your blessing. We want to be here so that we can support one another in our pilgrimage. We want to be here because the church is your gift to enable us to grow into your life. If we are here for a lesser reason, turn our hearts more fully to you.

Pastoral Prayer

Mighty God, you promised that where two or three are gathered in the name of Christ, you will be with them. We are gathered in the name of Jesus Christ. We pray that you will let us see you with eyes of faith. We pray that you will let us hear your voice with the ears of faith. We pray that you will let us sense your special presence here with us. And when we go forth from this place, be our unseen companion on our journey, guiding us to bring you to others and carry on your work of redemption. Amen.

Prayer of Confession

How often, merciful God, have we acted to please others rather than acting to please you! How often have we thought first of ourselves and only then, if at all, of you! We repent, for you alone must be the highest priority, the supreme goal of our lives. We must live for you alone; all we say and do must be out of love for you. Yet, Lord, you know how hard this ideal is for us to achieve. We need your help, your grace, your strength, and your wisdom to sustain and guide us, or we will fail. We turn to you to teach us to love you with all our hearts and minds and souls and strength. Be with us always. Amen.

Prayer of Dedication of Gifts and Self

These gifts we bring to you represent the fruit of our labors. They also represent our acknowledgment that we are dependent on your help if we are to bear true and enduring fruit in what we do. Accept these gifts, O God, as our prayer that we may receive your abundant strength and grace to enable us to carry out your work, that we may bear good fruit for the spread of your commonwealth. We come to you through your beloved Son, our Savior, Jesus Christ. Amen.

Sermon Summary

Jesus teaches that it is why we do what we do that matters more than the outward act. Christians must get away from legalism and think about their motives and priorities.

Hymn of the Day
"Rejoice, the Lord Is King"

Written by Charles Wesley, this hymn first appeared in *Hymns for Our Lord's Resurrection* in 1746. It begins with a reference to the first and last verses of Psalm 97 and then transitions to New Testament and creedal imagery of the exalted Christ. The tune DARWALL is most often associated with this powerful text. It first appeared in *The New Universal Psalmodist* compiled by Aaron Williams in 1770. The combination of text and tune provides a triumphant expression of the reigning lordship of Jesus Christ. Establish a lively tempo to give life to such phrases as, "give thanks and sing" and, "rejoice in glorious hope!"

Children's Time

Great News!

Talk about sharing good news: Has anyone had any good news this week? Invite the children to share stories of times when they were so excited about something that they thought they would burst if they didn't tell someone.

Explain that the first four books of the New Testament are called the "Gospels of Jesus." Explain that the word *gospel* means "good news." Why would that be a good name for a book about Jesus? What do you think is the best part about Jesus' story? Accept all the answers.

Comment that in the Bible reading today the apostle Paul shares what he thinks is the best part of the story. God raised Jesus to new life, and when we die God will raise us to new life, too. Express excitement about this marvelous news.

Comment that Paul was really excited about the new life God brings. Paul was so excited that that he couldn't stop talking about it. We can talk about it, too! How might we spread the good news of Jesus in the world? What could we say or do? Whom can we tell?

Pray, giving thanks for God's gift of new life in Jesus.

The Sermon

Paved with Good Intentions

Hymns
Beginning of Worship: "I Sought the Lord"
Sermon Hymn: "Come, Labor On"
Closing Hymn: "Onward, Christian Soldiers"

Scripture
Luke 6:17-26 (For additional sermon materials on this passage, see the October 2006 issue of *The Clergy Journal* and the 2006 May/June planning issue of *The Clergy Journal*.)

There is an old saying that the road to hell is paved with good intentions. I interpret this odd saying to mean that we can wind up hurting someone, even though we intended to help. Perhaps it is intended to mean what Paul meant when he lamented in Romans 7 that the good he wanted to do, he did not do; but the evil he did not want to do, that is what he did.

Many Christians place their religious emphasis on sin. They are certain they know what God requires of every human being who wants to avoid going to hell. Human beings, so they believe, are stained by original sin from birth due to the fall of Adam and Eve and deserve nothing more than condemnation. They believe that God has provided a means to rid humans of the punishment and guilt due them because of both original and actual sin, and bring them into a right relationship with God once again.

My point, though, is not that humans do not commit sins, but, rather, that the emphasis on sin often is an obstacle to spiritual growth and a loving relationship with both God and other human beings. For if we view God primarily as a stern judge, though with a certain measure of mercy – and we view the chief characteristic of human beings as sinfulness – we are not likely to come to the full love of God to which God calls us. Fear of sin and punishment is an obstacle to perfect love, because perfect love casts out fear.

We can look at the cross, the primary symbol of our faith, from the viewpoint of sinful humankind, or we can look at the cross as a symbol of the lengths to which God is willing to go to give us the means to grow into God's own life. We can look at Jesus primarily as a sacrifice, or we can look at Jesus as the Incarnate God through whom creation is joined to its Creator. We can view Jesus as a bridge over a chasm between creation and Creator – a chasm that we previously had no hope of crossing. Indeed, we can look at the cross as a symbol of tests we must pass in order to earn our way into heaven, or we can look at the cross as a symbol of the lessons we must learn in order to be joined more completely to God in love. If life is a school in which we are to learn how to love and be transformed into what God calls us to become, it calls for a different understanding of how we relate to God in our daily lives than if we place our stress on our sinfulness.

Thomas Merton was a Roman Catholic Trappist monk whose numerous writings are read and respected not only by Roman Catholics, but by many other Christians and even some adherents of other religions. I love reciting one of his most famous prayers, although I paraphrase it here because my memory is not exact. Merton prayed: "I do not know if what I do pleases you, Lord, but I know that my wanting to please you pleases you." Our desire to love God is a sign of our love for God. God honors our honest efforts, even if we make mistakes, which we are certain to do.

St. Augustine once said, "Love God and do as you please." Augustine was not urging us on to unbridled license to do whatever we want to do. The key is that we are to love God first and then do what we please. But if we love God, we will try to do what pleases God. If we deliberately set our wills against God's will, we cannot say that we truly love God.

Jesus chided the scribes and the Pharisees because, although their outward actions were entirely in keeping with the Law of Moses, their inward intentions too often were contrary to the spirit of the Law – unloving of both God and neighbor. Jesus taught that why we do something matters more than what we actually do. And he taught that when disciples act out of faith and love, the results may not be measured as successful by the world's standards.

We must, I suggest, still seek the loving and faithful thing to do and not merely assume we are doing the loving thing because what we are doing is what we want to do for our own selfish ends. It is better to make a mistake and act because we wish, first and foremost, to serve God and

237

neighbor, than to always do the safe thing because we want to be well thought of or to please others. It is better to be a fool for Christ than wise in the eyes of the worldly. The blessings of following God's wisdom are of more value than the woes of living for one's own self.

No, we do not have to go out of our way to make fools of ourselves, but we should be willing to go out of our way to do what we believe God wants us to do. We should pray that God will teach us how to love both God and our neighbor. We should search our hearts to see if we are acting out of love of God or for some lesser motive.

The road to hell is not paved with good intentions. When our intentions are truly good – when our intentions are to love and serve God above all else – our actions lead us to closer union with God. And we will be blessed. The road to heaven is paved with truly good intentions.

– Michael Gemignani

February 18, 2007

Transfiguration/Last Sunday after Epiphany

RC: 7th Sunday in Ordinary Time

Lessons

RCL	Ex 34:29-35	2 Cor 3:12—4:2	Lk 9:28-36, (37-43)
Roman Catholic	1 Sam 26:2, 7-9, 12-13, 22-23	1 Cor 15:45-49	Lk 6:27-38
Episcopal(BCP)	Ex 34:29-35	1 Cor 12:17—13:13	Lk 9:28-36

Introduction to the Lessons
Lesson 1
(1) Exodus 34:29-35 (RCL/Epis)
Moses' encounter with God on Mt. Sinai leaves his face radiant and signifies Moses special status as messenger of God's glory and a vision of the face of God for the community of faith.

(2) 1 Samuel 26:2, 7-9, 12-13, 22-23 (RC)
King Saul and David are involved in a struggle for the throne of Israel, which is full of conflict and tragedy. David will be victorious because of God's protection and plan.

Lesson 2
(1) 2 Corinthians 3:12—4:2 (RCL)
The apostle Paul is confident that God's promises will be made good in God's own time, and that in Christ we can know the freedom and glory of a new relationship with God.

(2) 1 Corinthians 15:45-49 (RC)
Our passage is part of the apostle Paul's teaching about the resurrection, in which he makes the point that just as we share in Adam's mortality, we also now share in Christ's immortality.

(3) 1 Corinthians 12:17—13:13 (Epis)
The apostle Paul emphasizes that there are a variety of gifts in the body of Christ and all are important. However, the greatest spiritual gift, which never ends, is love.

Gospel
(1) Luke 9:28-36, (37-43) (RCL); Luke 9:28-36 (Epis)
Jesus has been teaching about his coming death and resurrection, but the disciples do not understand. God transfigures Jesus on the mountaintop to confirm Jesus as the chosen one.

(2) Luke 6:27-38 (RC)
Love is an important part of a new life in Christ. The love that Jesus calls us to is gracious, determined, and actively interested in the welfare of the neighbor.

Theme
A vision of Christ's suffering and glory sustains us.

Thought for the Day
Our ministries today are held in the context of God's eternal saving plan.

Call to Worship
> **One:** The Lord our God is Holy and brings justice and salvation.
> **All:** Bless the Lord, O my soul.
> **One:** God is merciful and gracious, abounding in steadfast love.
> **All:** Bless the Lord, O my soul.
> **One:** Cry out and the Lord will answer.
> **All:** We give thanks and praise to the Lord our God.
>
> – based on Psalms 99 and 103

Pastoral Prayer
We give thanks to you, Holy God, for your saving purpose for the world, especially as it is revealed to us in the death and resurrection of Jesus Christ. Help us to keep our hearts and minds fixed on Christ as we follow him in our daily lives. Through him, strengthen us to do your loving will, and

give us the courage to follow even when our work is difficult and the way unclear. Bless the whole church with your Spirit of wisdom and strength, so that it may continue to be a faithful witness to the grace received through Jesus Christ and a beacon of hope in our troubled world. Amen.

Prayer of Confession

Gracious God, we confess to you that we grow weary in following Christ and doing your good will. We become lost in our own agendas and priorities; we often desire only glory and victory for ourselves and our families. We prefer to stay on the mountaintop, rather than serve in the valley. We can be discouraged easily by opposition and disappointments, fearing the criticism of others and, then, giving up quickly. Forgive our faint-hearted efforts and lukewarm devotion in our attempts to follow. Open our hearts and minds to the good news that Christ is with us in our suffering and struggle, and that he will never abandon us. Give us the faith to live for Christ and to trust in the gift of his presence with us and the promise of the kingdom for all eternity. In Jesus' name. Amen.

Prayer of Dedication of Gifts and Self

You have richly blessed us, O God, and we give you thanks with our offerings here today and with our lives of service each day. Reveal to us your loving will for our lives and give us the faith to go where you call us. Draw us together in your name that we may strengthen one another in all our ministries. Give us joy in the talents and abilities you have given to us, so that we may delight in doing your will. Amen.

Sermon Summary

In the transfiguration, God confirms Jesus' ministry of healing and his call to suffer and die. We can take heart from this as we face hardships and challenges in our own daily ministries.

Hymn of the Day
"O Wondrous Sight, O Vision Fair"

This hymn helps paint a picture of Christ's brilliant glory in his transfiguration. It also provides encouragement that those who "joy in God" will one day share in a similar glory. The text is an anonymous Latin hymn written for the Feast of the Transfiguration in the 15th century. It first appeared in *Sarum Breviary* of 1495. The English translation first appeared in the 1868 edition of the British *Hymns Ancient and Modern*. The tune WAREHAM, first published in 1738, provides a strong musical setting for a triumphant and somewhat mystical expression of the text. A broad and majestic tempo is suggested.

Children's Time

God's Glory

Bring a bright flashlight, something that sparkles in the light such as a cut crystal ornament, and some sparkling stickers. Shine the light on the glittering object, admire it together, and enjoy the sparkles. Explain that the object looks so pretty because it reflects the beauty of the light. Tell that the Bible story today is about a time when Peter, John, and James saw God's beauty reflected in the face of Jesus. Tell the story of the transfiguration. Discuss what it might have been like on the mountaintop with Jesus, Peter, James, and John. What words might the disciples have used to describe what happened to them?

Gather the children in a circle around you and one by one shine the flashlight on their faces. Comment on how beautiful they look as the light reflects off their faces. Explain that as God's children, they show the beauty of God's love in their faces, in their smiles, in their eyes, and in the way they care for others. Place a sparkling sticker on each child's hand as a reminder that they reflect the beauty of God's love.

Pray with the children, giving thanks for the exciting story of Jesus on the mountaintop.

The Sermon

On the Right Track

Hymns
Beginning of Worship: "Jesus on the Mountain Peak"
Sermon Hymn: "Arise, Your Light Has Come"
Closing Hymn: "Love Divine, All Loves Excelling"

Scripture

Luke 9:28-36, (37-43) (For additional sermon materials on this passage, see the November/December 2006 issue of *The Clergy Journal;* for sermon materials on Exodus 34:29-35, see the 2006 May/June planning issue of *The Clergy Journal.*)

Long ago my husband was working to persuade me to take my first backpacking trip in the mountains of the Pacific Northwest. I had hiked before, but not in a place that involved gaining and losing thousands of feet in altitude, and not with a 50-pound pack on my back. As you can imagine, it wasn't easy to convince me that this would be worth the effort.

It was the pictures that finally won me over. My husband brought out pictures of the trail he hoped we would hike, and dazzled me with views of cascading waterfalls; deep, green, lush forests; and breathtaking panoramic views of mountain valleys and distant peaks. These pictures inspired me to attempt that backpacking trip, and they helped to energize me when we were struggling up those steep trails and enduring the weight of our heavy packs.

Whether it is a backpacking trip or some other journey, it helps to be able to picture what the journey will entail and what the end will be like. In our journey of faith, the story of Jesus' transfiguration is something like the pictures I viewed before attempting my first mountain hike.

Jesus' transfiguration happens just after Peter has confessed that Jesus is the Messiah and Jesus announces that he must suffer, die, and on the third day rise. Jesus' coming death looms large on the landscape of his ministry. Peter and the disciples can hardly believe it, let alone begin to accept such a tragic fate for their beloved savior.

But then comes the transfiguration. Jesus glows with the light of God. Moses, the bearer of law, and Elijah, representing all the prophets, are right beside him there. It is as if God is saying through them, "Jesus, you are on the right track." Then the words from the cloud – "This is my Son, my Chosen, listen to him!" (9:35) – further confirm that Jesus' work, even if it means suffering and death, is exactly what God has in mind.

Not only is Jesus' ministry confirmed, but the disciples also are encouraged. They will need such a sign – a glimpse of glory – to steady them in the future. The transfiguration is glimpse of the resurrection, of the crown beyond the cross, and of the victory beyond the humiliation of crucifixion. These disciples have hard days and years ahead of them. They will need the memory of this day to strengthen them.

We know, in our own journeys of faith, that following Jesus is not one long march from victory to victory. When we are faithful to our Lord, we sometimes find ourselves in difficult situations: helping people who seem to be beyond help, struggling to forgive what seems unforgivable, giving one more ounce of care and concern when we think we're running on empty, and continuing to share our gifts and financial resources even when there is no immediate return.

Jesus' transfiguration is our signpost, telling us that this is the right way to go. Sacrifice, love, and generosity may not pay off immediately, but they are all a part of God's glorious plan. We are on the right track. One day, all that is good will be illuminated by the dazzling light of God. For now, the transfiguration is a signpost telling us that God is present in each and every day.

Consider the event that immediately follows the transfiguration on the mountain that day. A dad brings his son with seizures to Jesus and begs for Jesus to heal him. Down from the mountain, down from glorification, Jesus is called to get right to work again. The boy is healed, restored to his father, and all are astounded at the greatness of God. The cross awaits Jesus in Jerusalem, but God is determined to accomplish good things through him every day along the way. The entire ministry of Jesus makes this clear.

God's glory and God's good will are a part of each day in our lives, too. Even though the journey may be long and difficult, God is at work to accomplish good through our words and deeds. What good news for our daily walk of faith! This week none of us will probably have anything close to a transfiguration experience, but this doesn't mean that God isn't working through us and around us. God is at work every time you and I forgive a wrong and help restore a friendship; every time we are generous to someone in need, whether it be through a food pantry or a check to support cancer research; every time we stop to listen to someone's grief or teach a child about the faith; every time and any time we seek to bring hope and healing to a hurting world.

In our journeys of faith, remember the transfiguration. It is just one more sign that in Jesus Christ, crucified and raised, God is at work – bringing light and hope to the world God loves. Like the disciples, we also bear this light. It is a long journey, but with a promised and glorious ending.

– Jeanette B. Strandjord

February 21, 2007

Ash Wednesday

Lessons

RCL	Joel 2:1-2, 12-17 or Isa 58:1-12	2 Cor 5:20b—6:10	Mt 6:1-6, 16-21
Roman Catholic	Joel 2:12-18	2 Cor 5:20—6:2	Mt 6:1-6, 16-18
Episcopal (BCP)	Joel 2:1-2, 12-17 or Isa 58:1-12	2 Cor 5:20b—6:10	Mt 6:1-6, 16-21

Introduction to the Lessons

Lesson 1

Joel 2:1-2, 12-17 (RCL/Epis); Joel 2:12-18 (RC)

The prophet Joel, seeing the devastation of the land caused by a locust plague, calls God's people to repent and speaks God's gracious invitation for the people to return to God.

Lesson 2

2 Corinthians 5:20b—6:10 (RCL/Epis);
2 Corinthians 5:20—6:2 (RC)

The Lord has gone to extreme lengths to reconcile us to God. In sending Christ, God invites us not only to have our sins forgiven, but also to live in a new relationship with God.

Gospel

Matthew 6:1-6, 16-21 (RCL/Epis); Matthew 6:1-5, 16-18 (RC)

Jesus teaches about our sincere response to God in our almsgiving, prayer, and fasting. He counsels us to practice these privately and not as displays of our own righteousness.

Theme

Walk the walk of faith to the glory of God – not for personal recognition or public reward.

Thought for the Day

We repent because of the cross, which stands at the end of the Lenten pilgrimage.

— Herman G. Stuempfle, Jr.,
Proclamation: Aids for Interpreting the Lessons of the Church Year, Lent,
Fortress Press, 1973, p. 6

Call to Worship

One: Create in me a clean heart, O God.
All: Keep our eyes on Jesus, our crucified Lord.
One: Put a new and a right spirit within me, O God.
All: Keep our hearts in Jesus, our crucified Lord.
One: My footsteps falter and I lose my way.
All: Restore us to the joy of your salvation.
One: Turn me toward you, O God.
All: Open our lips, that we may declare your praise.

— based on Psalm 51

Pastoral Prayer

We give you thanks, O God, that in every age and time you call us to you. Open our hearts and minds to those who, like the prophet Joel, warn us of our sin and bid us to repent. In our repentance restore us in body and spirit, so that we may live with generous hearts toward all and seek your peace in our families and our world. During our Lenten journey keep our eyes on our crucified Lord Jesus, so that we may live faithfully, trusting only in Christ as Lord over life and death. May our prayers, offerings, and devotional life serve and glorify you. Let our mission together as God's people be centered on you and your saving purpose for our world, that we may walk this journey of faith with unity and clear purpose. Amen.

Prayer of Confession

Mighty Lord, we confess that we are lost without you. Gather us, so that we may join our hearts and voices together in seeking your forgiveness and direction. So often we would go our own way, desiring only our personal success and public glory. Forgive us. In our practice of the faith, may our right hand not be concerned with what the left is doing. So often we forget that without you we are but dust and ashes with no hope beyond this life. Forgive us. In our assembly and in our daily lives keep our hearts and minds fixed on the cross of Christ; remembering that our hope rests in his death and resurrection. May our journey be one of faith in you and generous service to your world. Amen.

Prayer of Dedication of Gifts and Self

Great God, who created us and continues to sustain us in this world, we give you thanks and praise for the blessings we have received through your bountiful grace. Use our lives and the resources you have given us, so that we may glorify you in all we say and do as we minister to all in need in this world. Unite us in our journey of faith, that we may strengthen and support one another in our walk of faith and our mutual ministry, all to your glory. Amen.

Sermon Summary

Jesus counsels us to practice our faith without calling attention to our own piety and good works. This is the way to journey faithfully in relationship to God. We keep our eyes on Jesus and his cross in our Lenten walk.

Hymn of the Day
"Jesus, Priceless Treasure"

This hymn is most often heard as a choral selection or organ composition and is not easily sung by a congregation. In the proper setting, however, this text and tune make a meaningful congregational statement. Perhaps a choir or soloist could sing the first stanza, setting the desired mood and providing a secure introduction to the hymn. The original German text was first published in 1653 and translated by Catherine Winkworth in 1864. The tune JESU, MEINE FREUDE appeared with the hymn in the 1653 publication *Praxis Pietatis Melica*, and is attributed to German composer Johann Crüger.

Children's Time

Ash Wednesday

Bring a container of ashes and a damp cloth. Ask the children to look around the church and notice the changes in the worship area. Explain that today is Ash Wednesday, the first day of Lent. Describe Lent as a special season of the church year when we think about being God's children and the things that Jesus did while he lived on the earth.

Tell how many people put ashes on their foreheads or hands this day. Invite the children to look at the ashes and touch them if they wish. (Have the cloth ready to wipe the children's hands afterwards.) Explain that ashes are used as a sign of sadness. Ash Wednesday is a time to think about how we could do a better job of being God's children. It is a day to say "sorry" to God. What kinds of things might we say sorry for? Wearing the ashes is also a sign that we want to change. What might we want to change? Conclude your time together with the simple reminder that God loves us very much and will forgive us when we say "sorry."

Pray with the children, giving thanks for the gift of God's forgiveness.

The Sermon

Journeying with Our Eyes on Jesus Christ

Hymns
Beginning of Worship: "O Lord, throughout These Forty Days"
Sermon Hymn: "In the Cross of Christ I Glory"
Closing Hymn: "I Want Jesus to Walk with Me"

Scripture
Matthew 6:1-6, 16-21 (For sermon materials on Joel 2:1-2, 12-17, see the November/December 2006 issue of *The Clergy Journal;* for sermon materials on 2 Corinthians 5:20b—6:10, see the 2006 May/June planning issue of *The Clergy Journal.*)

We could think of the season of Lent as a long road that stretches out before us. We walk along this road during the weeks of Lent, not concentrating on the tiny steps we take, but focusing on our destination: the cross of Jesus. The cross of Jesus Christ casts a long shadow over this Lenten road and this shadow reaches all the way back to the beginning, to Ash Wednesday. So tonight we lift our eyes to the cross as we begin our Lenten journey with confession, then ashes on our foreheads as a sign of repentance, and then, finally, the gift of Holy Communion.

The shadow of the cross is before us, not to make us feel bad and certainly not to make us feel so guilty that we will punish ourselves by giving up something for Lent. The cross, instead, comes to once again make real God's deep love and mercy for us and for our world. When we walk the road of Lent, we walk toward the love and mercy of God, given to us in Jesus Christ.

One simple meaning of the word *repentance* is "to turn around." Lent calls us to turn around toward God – toward our crucified Lord Jesus Christ. Once turned, we walk toward him. He is our focus this season. The focus of Lent is not ourselves and not the opinions of others.

Jesus talks about this in our gospel reading from Matthew chapter 6. Here Jesus warns you, me, and the whole Christian community not to lose our direction and our focus on God. As we walk our journey of faith, we are in danger of doing just this; it's too easy to start to concentrate on the little steps that we take – the good deeds that we do. When we do this, the opinions and approval of others begin to matter much more than they should. In Matthew's gospel, Jesus tells us that when we practice giving alms, when we pray, and when we fast, we must not do these things for public approval. This is like watching the little footsteps we take along our faith journey and waiting for the applause of others for our meager progress. When we live this way, it is all about the approval of others and not about our relationship with God.

This is how our society likes to work and we must be careful not to be entrapped by it in our walk of faith. Today we have society sections in our newspapers picturing who has attended the latest charity function and how much was raised. Very worthy charitable or non-profit groups are careful to publish donor lists on their programs or in their newsletters, bending over backwards to recognize all who contribute and to publicize how much was given. They've developed the "Gold Givers," the "Silver Givers," and the "Bronze Givers categories." This is not necessarily bad, until we transfer this approach to our practice of our life of faith. Jesus tells us that, for our own spiritual health, we need to practice our almsgiving, prayer, and fasting in private, and not seek any honor or earthly reward because of it. God does not have "Gold," "Silver," and "Bronze" categories for us.

On this Ash Wednesday, we lift our eyes and our hearts to the cross of Christ. Yes, we will pray; yes, we will give offerings; yes, some of us may even fast. But may all these things be because of Christ and not because of any hope for approval and recognition. Many of us will come forward to receive the sign of the cross in ashes on our foreheads as a sign of our true repentance. This can be very meaningful for us as individuals and as a worshiping community – we are all marked by sin and the power of death. Ashes, especially on the forehead of a baby, are a startling reminder of the harsh reality of sin and death, and our need for forgiveness and salvation.

This harsh reality comes home to us even more strongly when we stand at the open grave of a loved one. At the grave we have run out of things to do. Our hands are empty. Most likely everything has been tried: doctors, hospitals, prayers, positive thinking, good deeds, special diets, and whatever remedies are at hand. We are mortals, flesh and blood. We may be able to put death off sometimes, but we cannot stop it, and we certainly cannot raise ourselves from the grave.

Our hands are empty, but God's are not. Because God loves us and we are God's children through Jesus Christ, we have the gift – the absolute gift – of new life beyond the grave. This is the promise and the relationship that hold us in life and in death. This is a promise worthy of our attention, worthy of the commitment of our whole selves. This is why we walk the road of Lent with our eyes on our crucified Lord and Savior.

In this season of Lent, listen to Christ. Let's all stop looking at our own little footsteps and waiting for the approval of the crowd. As we live in relationship with Christ, our prayers don't have to be impressive and long; our giving should be generous, but done in secret; and our fasting or devotional reading or self-denial should never be flaunted for public consumption. God hears and sees us and, as Jesus promises in our gospel reading, we will be blessed by God.

You and I are on the road to the cross of Christ. Keep your eyes on Jesus and his saving death and resurrection for you. Do pray. Do help others. Do discipline yourselves with faithful practices. But do them all in thanksgiving and to the glory of the God who saves you.

– Jeanette B. Strandjord

February 25, 2007

1st Sunday in Lent

Lessons

RCL	Deut 26:1-11	Rom 10:8b-13	Lk 4:1-13
Roman Catholic	Deut 26:4-10	Rom 10:8-13	Lk 4:1-13
Episcopal (BCP)	Deut 26:(1-4), 5-11	Rom 10:(5-8a), 8b-13	Lk 4:1-13

Introduction to the Lessons

Lesson 1
> **Deuteronomy 26:1-11 (RCL);**
> **Deuteronomy 26:4-10 (RC);**
> **Deuteronomy 26:(1-4), 5-11 (Epis)**

The Israelites are settled in their new land, and God commands them to offer the first fruits of their harvest as a sign of their dependence on God and their gratitude for the land.

Lesson 2
> **Romans 10:8b-13 (RCL);**
> **Romans 10:8-13 (RC);**
> **Romans 10:(5-8a), 8b-13 (Epis)**

Paul writes that the goal of the law is Christ. Christ fulfills the law, bestowing righteousness on all who confess him as Lord, and giving them salvation.

Gospel
> **Luke 4:1-13 (RCL/RC/Epis)**

After Jesus is confirmed as God's beloved son in his baptism, God then sends Jesus into the wilderness to face temptation. Jesus refuses the devil's offers and remains faithful to his mission as God's Son.

Theme

Our identity is God-given.

Thought for the Day

It's a mind-blowing concept that the God who created the universe might be looking for company . . . Love interrupts, if you like, the consequences of your actions.

> — Bono, lead singer of the rock group U2,
> *The Christian Century,* September 6, 2005, p. 7

Call to Worship

One:	Come to the Lord, our strong fortress and deliverer.
All:	Let us find refuge in God's shadow.
One:	God will protect you; under the Lord's wings you will find refuge
All:	From snares, terror, and destruction.
One:	Seek the Lord and the Lord's dwelling place,
All:	That we may hear and follow.
One:	Call on the name of the Lord in trust and worship.
All:	All praise to our Refuge and Strength!

> — based on Psalm 91

Pastoral Prayer

We give thanks to you, O God, for the gift of your creation that continues to sustain us, and for all of your servants and witnesses in every generation. Help us to remember all that you have done for us since the beginning of time, that we may be inspired to serve you faithfully now. Give us thankful hearts, that we may share the gifts we have been given with those who are in need. Help us share our resources and talents in our congregations, to carry on ministry in your name and to your glory. Keep our eyes on our Lord Jesus Christ, in whom our lives – past, present, and future – are grounded. Amen.

Prayer of Confession

Almighty God, our refuge and strength, so often we forget that our lives are grounded in your grace. Protect us from the snare of pride and help us to remember that without you, we are imprisoned by our own sin and death. Guard us from the terror and despair within us, which separates us from you and our neighbor; help us, instead, to trust you to rescue and love us. Turn our hearts and minds to you, that we may live according to your purpose and saving will, and that our words and deeds may convey your love and grace to the whole world. When our courage and faith falter, give us the aid of your Holy Spirit, that we may look to our crucified Savior, Jesus Christ, for direction and strength. In Jesus' name we pray. Amen.

Prayer of Dedication of Gifts and Self

Most gracious God, we thank you for the gifts of all creation and especially for the gift of your own dear Son, Jesus Christ. We thank you for your saving faithfulness from generation to generation. Receive these gifts we offer in thanksgiving for all your mercies, and use them to your good purpose. Renew us by the power of your Holy Spirit, that we may live in faith in you and gladly share your gifts in service to your world. In Jesus' name we pray. Amen.

Sermon Summary

When we remember the history of God's gracious dealings with us and the world, we gain a faithful perspective on our lives. God's grace shapes us and shapes the world. In giving thanks for this great gift, we also rededicate our lives to God.

Hymn of the Day
"Lord, Who throughout These Forty Days"

This hymn focuses on the fullest meaning of the Lenten season. Antiphonal singing between a soloist or choir and the congregation can be a meaningful way of singing the hymn. In a four-stanza setting, the soloist or choir would sing the first and third stanzas and the congregation the second and fourth. The text was written in 1873 by British hymn writer, Claudia F. Hernaman. Although the tune ST. FLAVIAN is most generally associated with the hymn, the tune LAND OF REST gives a poignant interpretation of the text.

Children's Time

Giving Thanks

Bring some loose change, a bag of groceries, and a calendar. Comment that we enjoy many good things in our lives. Have the children list some of the things that fill their lives with happiness – things for which they are thankful. Comment that there are many ways to say thank you to God. The Bible tells us that one way is to give back some of what we have to God, and it should be the first thing we do.

Show the loose change. How might we give some back to God? Accept all ideas, and if no one else says it, suggest you might put some of the money in the offering plate where it will get used for God's work.

Show the groceries and ask how we might give some groceries back to God. Invite the children to help you choose a few items and put them in the collection box for the food bank.

Open the calendar and observe that every day is a gift from God. How might we give some of our day back to God? Perhaps we could spend some time each day helping others.

Pray with the children, giving thanks for all God's blessings.

The Sermon

Remember, Rejoice, Rededicate

Hymns
Beginning of Worship: "O God, Our Help in Ages Past"
Sermon Hymn: "Be Thou My Vision"
Closing Hymn: "The Church of Christ, in Every Age"

Scripture
Deuteronomy 26:1-11 (For additional sermon materials on this passage, see the November/December 2006 issue of *The Clergy Journal;* for sermon materials on Luke 4:1-13, see the 2006 May/June planning issue of *The Clergy Journal.*)

"Oh, no! Not more heritage!" my youngest daughter protested one Sunday afternoon as we planned to visit yet another historical site in my home state of Wisconsin. Why was it, she wondered, that we had to talk about all this old stuff, walk through old buildings, and listen to tour guides. "It's history, your history!" I tried to encourage her, but, with little success.

Those days were long ago, but the reason for "more heritage," as my young daughter put it, remains. It was so that she would better understand where she had come from and who she is meant to be. I think many parents share this goal for their children. Sometimes it is the parent, and if we're fortunate, the grandparent, who takes the child on his knee and tells her about the old days. Suddenly the child's life is held in a much larger frame than before. She is here because someone before her took an ocean voyage from Norway to New York or endured a difficult resettlement from Vietnam to the United States.

Our reading from Deuteronomy 26:1-11 puts everything into larger perspective, too. One important part of this passage is full of remembering. The response God calls for begins this way: "A wandering Aramean was my ancestor . . . " Before God brought the Israelites into the promised land, they were wandering in the desert with no home and no clear idea of where they were or who they were to be as a people. These newly freed slaves were totally dependent on God for their present and their future. This liturgy of the presentation of the first fruits of the harvest calls for God's people to remember this heritage. And even more important for them to remember was that it was God alone who freed them from slavery and brought them to this land "flowing with milk and honey."

If God's people did not remember this history, then they might begin to think that it was because of their own virtue or perhaps even blind luck that they were finally settled in their own land. They might begin to think that their harvest and whatever else they owned belonged solely to them and was for their use and pleasure. They might begin to think that they were the captains of their own future and not indebted to anyone else.

One of the reasons I took my children to see not only state historical sites, but also the homesteads of their grandparents, was because I wanted them to understand the larger picture of their personal history and the history of the state and country. Great sacrifices had been made and daring moves taken so that they could be where they were and have what they had. What they saw and learned gave them a greater appreciation for their current place in the world.

As Christians we have a long history. A "wandering Aramean" was our father, too. God has been at work in our world since the beginning of time to draw us close to God and save us from the sin and evil in ourselves and in our broken creation. God is at the center of our history, especially through Jesus Christ who lived and died for us. Every time we confess our creeds together, we are celebrating that history. Every time we remember our baptisms, we are reclaiming our identity as God's forgiven and beloved children. This is our central story.

In this season of Lent, we would do well to remember our identity and celebrate it. Lent helps us focus on what God has done for us, and on our absolute need for the grace of God. We need to do this so that some false story does not obscure who we really are and who we are meant to be. There are plenty of false stories around: rugged individualism (I don't need anybody), consumerism (I am what I own), nationalism (my country is everything), hedonism (whatever feels good is my soul purpose), and whatever else gives us the idea that we are the center of the universe.

The writer of Deuteronomy calls the people to celebrate the true story of who they are: God's chosen and redeemed people. This remembering and rejoicing leads to renewed dedication and the humble offering of the first fruits of the ground. In this season of Lent, it is good for us to focus on this call for renewed dedication and the offering of what we have been given. When God rescued the Hebrew people from Egypt, when God sent Jesus to the world, when God baptized you and claimed you in Christ, it was to bring you into close, saving relationship. God loves you. God loves the world in which you live. Let's take time to see this grand picture of salvation and grace. It frames us, our whole life, and all of creation. And then we can respond in thanks and praise.

My youngest daughter is now an adult. She even has thanked me for making her spend time on her heritage. She says that it put things in perspective for her, helped her make decisions about what to do and what not to do. It still gives her determination to use her life as she believes God intends and as God has made possible. It's good to know one's history.

Your history – our history – is in relationship with God; the One who sent God's own Son to die and rise for us. This is our story, a true story. In this season of Lent, may we be reenergized to give God thanks and to offer our whole selves to God's good purposes.

– Jeanette B. Strandjord

March 4, 2007

2nd Sunday in Lent

Lessons

RCL	Gen 15:1-12, 17-18	Phil 3:17—4:1	Lk 13:31-35 or Lk 9:28-36
Roman Catholic	Gen 15:5-12, 17-18	Phil 3:17—4:1 or 3:20—4:1	Lk 9:28b-36
Episcopal (BCP)	Gen 15:1-12, 17-18	Phil 3:17—4:1	Lk 13:(22-30), 31-35

Introduction to the Lessons
Lesson 1
Genesis 15:1-12, 17-18 (RCL/RC/Epis)
God had promised Abram land and descendants, but Abram remains childless. In our passage God comes with the covenant promise once more to steady Abram in his uncertainty.

Lesson 2
Philippians 3:17—4:1 (RCL/Epis);
Philippians 3:17—4:1 or 3:20—4:1 (RC)
Paul affectionately exhorts the Philippians to remember that their true home is in heaven and to resist hedonistic ways. Their conduct should be in keeping with their God-given, eternal identity.

Gospel
(1) Luke 13:31-35 (RCL); Luke 13:(22-30), 31-35 (Epis)
On the road to Jerusalem, Jesus warns of coming judgment and anticipates his rejection in that city. Still, not even warnings about Herod's plan to kill him deter Jesus from faithfully completing his God-given mission.

(2) Luke 9:28b-36 (RC)
Jesus' transfiguration is God's confirmation that this chosen one who will die in Jerusalem is indeed the Son of God. Suffering and defeat will not have the last word over Jesus or his church.

Theme

Do not fear, God has the last word.

Thought for the Day

Do not be afraid, little flock, for it is your Father's good pleasure to give you the kingdom (Lk 12:32).

Sermon Summary

Foxy Herod seeks the life of Jesus. But, Jesus is not deterred from his God-given mission to go to Jerusalem. Many things in life threaten us and make us afraid. Still, we can live confident of God's saving love and continue our mission in the name of Jesus Christ.

Call to Worship

One:	The Lord is my light and my salvation,
All:	We will not be afraid.
One:	The Lord is the stronghold of my life,
All:	We will not be afraid.
One:	Even when our adversaries and foes seek to destroy us,
All:	We will not be afraid.
One:	Come to the house of the Lord and behold God's beauty.
All:	We will sing to the Lord and trust in God!
One:	We will see the goodness of the Lord.
All:	We will be strong and place our trust in God!

– based on Psalm 27

Pastoral Prayer

Gracious God, our rock and defender, we give you thanks for your faithful lovingkindness to your people of every age and time. Especially we praise you for our Lord, Jesus Christ, and his death and resurrection for us and our world. His courage and faithfulness to your loving purpose is our salvation. May we follow him with such faith and courage so that, despite adversity, hardship, and danger, we will truly serve you in all that we say and do. Make us bold in facing the foxes of our day, that we may not be undone. Help us to remember your love for us and to entrust our present and our future to you, so we may live unafraid as we seek to do your work in our world. Unite us in our mission with your universal church, that we may serve together in gladness. Amen.

Prayer of Confession

We confess to you, O God, that we are often afraid. The criticism of others, the uncertainty of our own time, the hardships that veil our eyes from your loving purpose, our own sin and failure, and the evils of terror and war threaten to undo us. Too often we despair and act as if you have abandoned us. We give into fear and retreat into self-preservation at the expense of others. Forgive us, God. By the power of your Holy Spirit, renew our faith and courage so that we may find in our Lord Jesus Christ your sure promise of love and salvation. Lead us along your way and help us to face each challenge in our lives. Give us strong hearts and clear vision to resist evil and trust in you until we are finally at table with you in our eternal home in heaven. Amen.

Prayer of Dedication of Gifts and Self

For the blessings of this beautiful creation, of health, of work, of community, and of family, we give you thanks, O Lord. Receive these gifts we offer and use them and us to continue to bring your blessing to the whole world. Empower us to be peacemakers in your name and to work for your justice and the welfare of all. When our courage falters, lift us up in our God-given mission, that we might persevere in confidence and joy. Make your way our way, and strengthen us for the journey. Amen.

Hymn of the Day
"O Jesus Christ, May Grateful Hymns Be Rising"

Based on Matthew 23:37-39 and Luke 13:34-35, this hymn enables us to reflect through a poetic prayer on our desire to minister by Christ's example. It is especially suited to a focus upon urban ministry. It was written by American Methodist minister Bradford Gray Webster in 1954 and chosen the same year by The Hymn Society of the United States and Canada for inclusion in its publication, *Five New Hymns on the City.* Various tunes have been associated with the hymn, including CHARTER-HOUSE, WELWYN, and CITY OF GOD, each lending special meaning to the request for "new courage . . . to venture and to dare."

Children's Time

Mother Hen

Bring some pictures of mother animals with their young, some feathers, and a large blanket. Show the children the pictures. Talk about some of the ways in which mother animals clean, feed, and protect their babies. Comment that the Bible story today is about a mother hen and her baby chicks. Explain that mother birds often cover their young with their wings to protect and shelter them. Comment that the chicks must feel very safe and warm. One day Jesus was talking to some people and said that he wanted to gather the people of Jerusalem like a mother hen gathers her chicks under her wings.

Ask the children to imagine what it would be like to be enfolded in Jesus' arms.

Unfold the blanket and place it over your shoulders, hold the corners, and spread out your arms like wings. Invite the children to become chicks resting safely under the mother's wings. Encircle and cover the children as you remind them that Jesus' love will enfold them like the wings of a bird.

Finish your time together by giving each child a feather as a reminder of Jesus' love.

Pray with the children, giving thanks that we are enfolded in Jesus' love.

The Sermon

Take Heart – the Foxes Will Fail

Hymns
Beginning of Worship: "We Are Marching in the Light of God"
Sermon Hymn: "My Song Is Love Unknown"
Closing Hymn: "Thy Holy Wings"

Scripture

Luke 13:31-35 (For sermon materials on Genesis 15:1-12, 17-18, see the November/December 2006 issue of *The Clergy Journal;* for sermon materials on Philippians 3:17—4:1, see the 2006 May/June planning issue of *The Clergy Journal.*)

A fox is a wild animal. A chicken is a domestic animal. Foxes slink about under the cover of darkness ready to strike quickly and tear animal flesh apart with sharp teeth. A chicken roosts at night, doesn't even have teeth, and feeds on insects and grain. These are two very different animals and yet here they appear almost side-by-side in our reading from Luke.

I grew up on a farm with a henhouse and have seen how defenseless chickens are against a predatory fox. A single fox can wipe out a small flock of chickens in just one night of havoc in the chicken coop. Once the fox is inside the coop and attacks, there's really no hope for hens or baby chicks.

The fox in our gospel reading is King Herod. He is a ruthless man. It is thought that he even had two of his own sons murdered because he feared their growing political power. Now Herod is out to kill Jesus. The Pharisees, pretending concern, come to warn Jesus of this. Maybe they hope to intimidate and frighten Jesus, for they are certainly no allies of his. But Jesus is not intimidated by either the Pharisees' scare tactic or Herod's threats.

Jesus declares that he must be "on his way" and that he will reach Jerusalem. There is something much larger than Herod the fox working in this world and in this ministry of Jesus. Often we hear in Luke's gospel that Jesus is on his way. Especially memorable is the time when the crowd outside of Nazareth sought to throw Jesus over the brow of the hill, but Jesus "passed through the midst of them and went on his way" (Lk 4:30). Jesus has a mission, and God is with him to complete it. No one but God is truly in control of Jesus' life and mission – not the crowd in the temple that day in Nazareth and certainly not Herod.

In our own Lenten journey and walk of faith, there are plenty of foxes – foxes that seem out to get us. Sometimes the fox is our own illness or despair, sometimes our own weakness and sin. Or we might face the situation of someone in the work place, someone we know socially, or even someone in our family who deliberately hurts us. Such foxes can be untruthful, false friends, sneaky, and deceptive. Worse is when we fear for our lives in a situation of domestic violence. We've also seen foxes in the public arena. Smear campaigns still take place in public elections, using the power of innuendo and scare tactics to intimidate and defeat many a good person.

This last summer I visited the new Abraham Lincoln Presidential Library and Museum in Springfield, Illinois. One of the most memorable parts of that museum is the whispering gallery. Abraham Lincoln and his wife Mary endured a great deal of criticism, ridicule, and gossip when they lived in Washington, D.C. during Lincoln's presidency. In the museum, the whispering gallery contains all of the foul, unkind, and untrue words being whispered about them by others in their community. When you walk through this gallery it is as if the whispers are coming at you from all directions. They seem to inhabit your own head. It's very powerful; it's also frightening.

There are a lot of foxes in our world. Jesus shows us how to deal with them. Jesus is clear about who holds his life and his future. God does. Jesus does not let Herod's threats stop him from doing what he knows is God's will for him and the world. Jesus will go to Jerusalem; Herod can't stop him. Jesus will be killed, but it won't be Herod's doing. And, his death will not be God's final word either. The final victory belongs to God and the risen Christ.

The foxes of this world don't have the last word over us either. Lent is a journey. Life is a journey. As we seek to live faithfully, it is important for you and me to remember who holds us, and who has the final word over us. God does. So we face the foxes with courage and determination, refusing to be drawn into their hurtful and evil ways. Their way is finally doomed. Instead, the way of love – God's way – will triumph.

Jesus uses the illustration of a hen gathering her chicks to describe what God is about. God desires to gather us all into a place of protection and safety. Seems hopeless, though – after all, what chance does a hen and her chicks stand against the wily fox? But we who know the whole story know that it is not hopeless. God will have the victory. God raised Jesus Christ from the dead and God will save us, too. The journey ends with the powerful grace of God.

The whispering gallery in the Lincoln museum was oppressive and made me claustrophobic. My walking pace quickened almost unconsciously and my shoulders shivered at the sound of so much meanness.

How telling, though, that this little whispering gallery is held within a much larger building that honors the very man those "foxes" sought to bring down. The truth, honor, and good that Lincoln strove to do far outshine any foxiness aimed against him.

Jesus followed God with courage and determination, sacrificing even his own life for us and the whole world. As his disciples, we are called to follow with courage and determination. God is with us, full of love and grace, seeking always to gather us as a hen gathers her brood under her wings. We need not let the foxes of this world frighten us and derail our mission.

– Jeanette B. Strandjord

March 11, 2007

3rd Sunday in Lent

Lessons

RCL	Isa 55:1-9	1 Cor 10:1-13	Lk 13:1-9
Roman Catholic	Ex 3:1-8a, 13-15	1 Cor 10:1-6, 10-12	Lk 13:1-9
Episcopal (BCP)	Ex 3:1-15	1 Cor 10:1-13	Lk 13:1-9

Introduction to the Lessons
Lesson 1
(1) Isaiah 55:1-9 (RCL)

This chapter concludes a section of the book called "Second Isaiah" by many scholars. The meal symbolizes God's love and abundance for all peoples.

(2) Exodus 3:1-8a, 13-15 (RC); Exodus 3:1-15 (Epis)

"I am," or YHWH, is a tetragrammaton – a four-letter word – used most often for God in Hebrew Scriptures. In Judaism it is not read aloud but replaced with *Adonai* ("my Lord") and sometimes *Hashem* ("the Name").

Lesson 2
1 Corinthians 10:1-13 (RCL/Epis);
1 Corinthians 10:1-6, 10-12 (RC)

The population of Corinth, a center for industry and shipbuilding, as well as the arts, came from many places. Paul here responds to two letters concerning lack of harmony and internal strife in the Corinthian church.

Gospel
Luke 13:1-9 (RCL/RC/Epis)

While the slaughter of Galileans as they brought sacrifices to the Temple cannot be confirmed, it is plausible given Pilate's reputation. The idea that a person's sin causes such brutal treatment is a long-standing belief.

Theme
There's no chance like the second chance.

Thought for the Day
People changed other people's lives every day of the year. There was no call to make such a fuss about it.

— Anne Tyler (*Saint Maybe,*
Random House Publishing Group, 1991, p. 373)

Sermon Summary
God has given us second chances in Jesus Christ. Our choice is what to do with them.

Call to Worship
One: O God, you are my God, I seek you, my soul thirsts for you; my flesh faints for you, as in a dry and weary land where there is no water.

All: So I have looked upon you in the sanctuary, beholding your power and glory.

One: Your steadfast love is better than life, my lips will praise you.

All: I will bless you as long as I live; I will lift up my hands and call on your name.

— based on Psalm 63:1-4

Pastoral Prayer
We pause to think about the fig trees of the world, O God – people and places where lives and ways of living do not bear good fruit. We pray for our brothers and sisters in places where war is real, and waging war is a way of life. Turn our hearts, that we might use our money, creativity, and passion to wage justice, love, and peace. We remember those who suffer in body, mind, and spirit. We pray that, through our compassion and actions, loneliness, pain, and sorrow may be replaced by the comfort and healing of Christ's spirit. But miracle of miracles, in the dailyness of all that is broken, the light and power of your goodness, grace, and joy flow steady. For all the blessings of this day – the people, moments, activities, and things that make our hearts sing – we give you thanks. Amen.

Prayer of Confession

God, you call us to honesty about who we are and all that we do. In these moments, make us honest with ourselves. We remember now those things we have done or left undone that have hurt others, that have caused suffering and pain to our world, that have betrayed our love for ourselves. *(Pause for silent reflection.)* Give us now the courage and the wisdom to do things differently, to change our behavior so that in asking for forgiveness we might lead forgiven lives. In the spirit of Jesus Christ who befriended and loved all sinners, we now pray. Amen.

Prayer of Dedication of Gifts and Self

Bountiful God, bless now these gifts, our giving, and the fruits of our actions, that in all of it your glory and work might shine in and through the opportunities and second chances they enable and empower. In Jesus' name, make this so. Amen.

Hymn of the Day
"There's A Wideness in God's Mercy"

Frederick William Faber wrote this hymn in 1854, 19 years after leaving the Anglican priesthood for membership in the Roman Catholic priesthood. The hymn helps us focus on the reality of the true expanse of God's greatness. The hymn offers illustrative comparisons between God's mercy and the expanse of the sea, God's justice and liberty, and God's love and the limits of our mind. Two tunes are most generally associated with the hymn: WELLESLEY, with its four stanza text arrangement; and IN BABILONE, with a two stanza text arrangement. Or, you may wish to use another 8.7.8.7.D. tune.

Children's Time

Growing and Blooming

Bring some seeds. Show the seeds and invite the children to choose a seed to examine. What will happen if the seeds are planted? What kinds of plants might grow? What might they look like? Ask the children to share experiences of planting seeds and caring for the seedlings. What do plants need in order to grow well?

Comment that the Bible story today is about a fig tree that wasn't growing very well. Tell the parable of the fig tree (13:6-8). Comment that Jesus didn't say what happened to the fig tree, he just left it to our imaginations. Invite the children to help you finish the story.

Observe that seeds given proper care will grow well. In the same way, through gentle care we can encourage and help others to grow to be healthy and strong. What kinds of things can we do to help others grow?

Pray with the children, giving thanks for Jesus whose love and care helped many people to grow.

The Sermon

Church of the Second Chance

Hymns
Beginning of Worship: "Come, O Fount of Every Blessing"
Sermon Hymn: "Amazing Grace"
Closing Hymn: "Take My Life, God, Let It Be"

Scripture
Luke 13:1-9 (For additional materials on this passage, see the November/ December 2006 issue of *The Clergy Journal;* for sermon materials on 1 Corinthians 10:1-13, see the 2006 May/June planning issue of *The Clergy Journal.*)

Ian Bedloe walked past the Church of the Second Chance. It might have been the sign at the intersection that said "DON'T WALK" that made him give it a second thought. Inside, it was ordinary, an abandoned store with about twenty people, standing, singing, and turning to look at him and smile when the bell clanged on the door as he entered. It was a Wednesday evening prayer service and Ian found a seat. Each time a member brought a concern to the congregation, the preacher led them in silent prayer, ending with a resounding "Amen."

Ian found himself standing when the preacher asked for the third time, "Any other prayers?"

"I used to be good," he told them. "Or I used to be not bad, at least. I don't know what happened. Everything I touch goes wrong . . . Pray for me to be good

267

again . . . Pray for me to be forgiven" (Anne Tyler, *Saint Maybe,* Random House Publishing Group, 1991, p. 129). Ian felt washed in their silent prayers that were just for his forgiveness. "How could God not listen?" he wondered (p. 129).

After the service, Ian was shocked when Rev. Emmett asked him what he'd done that needed forgiveness. Resisting the urge to run, Ian said he'd caused his brother's suicide by telling him that his wife had been unfaithful. His brother's wife had, in turn, killed herself. It looked like Ian's parents would be raising three more children. Ian asked Rev. Emmett if he was forgiven.

"Goodness no," Rev. Emmett said. Unfair! Ian thought God forgave everything. Yes, Rev. Emmett told him, "But you can't just say, 'I'm sorry, God.' Why, anyone could do that much! You have to offer reparation – concrete, practical reparation, according to the rules of our church" (p. 133).

That's how Ian ended up dropping out of school and helping his parents raise his brother's children.

Second chance. The fig tree got one because of a caring gardener – one last, important second chance.

This story is a paradigm for Jesus, bringer of second chances. At least twice in the Hebrew Scriptures, other religious leaders negotiate with God for second chances. In Genesis 18, Abraham gets God to agree to spare Sodom and Gomorrah if there are ten righteous men in the towns. When Moses was delayed on Mt. Sinai, and the people made idols of gold and worshipped them, God's anger was so fierce that it threatened to "consume them" (Ex 32:10). But Moses begged God not to do it, reminding God of the covenant made with the Israelites. "And the Lord changed his mind about the disaster that he planned to bring on his people" (32:14).

Second changes. The fig tree got it, but it had to change. No fruit next season – no tree next season. In human terms it's called reparation.

Often, we in the liberal Protestant church settle for what Bonhoeffer called "cheap grace" – forgiveness not only without reparation, but also without repentance. As we sit in the security of our pews on Sunday mornings, confessing sins through a prayer that someone else wrote, there's no Rev. Emmett to remind us that, in the realm of God, saying, "I'm sorry" is only the first step. It's too easy, even for pastors, to practice "cheap grace."

I know firsthand. I've had too many women tell me about abusive fathers or husbands, only to stand around talking with these men after worship as if their horrific sins had not been committed. While nothing might be the right thing to say in those moments, it seems like, "Good to meet you," and, "How are you" are ingenuous.

Twice in today's gospel reading Jesus says, "unless you repent, you will all perish" (13:3, 5). We tend to think of this perishing as happening at the end of time. In part, that is what Jesus means. But Jesus was also talking about present time. What we do or don't do always matters. Consider how very hard it is for most of us to even tell someone we've offended that we're sorry. Every time we fail to make things right, we erect barriers in our relationships, and behind those barriers we perish a little in the here and now.

Second chances. Usually, when Jesus forgives sinners, he tells them to go and sin no more. In other words, *do something about your situation.* That's what reparation is about. It's doing something not only to acknowledge that what we did was wrong, but also that what we will now do is, if not right, then on the right track.

Ian's parents were shocked and resistant when he told them his plan. When they asked him who would help, he told them about the church "that believes you have to really do something practical to atone for your, shall we call them, sins. And if you agree to that, they'll pitch in" (p. 138). His parents were shocked, ". . . have you fallen into the hands of some *sect?*"

His mother reminds him that her church doesn't ask them to "abandon our entire way of life." "Well maybe it should have." Ian responds (p. 138). Then, following Rev. Emmett's instructions, he tells his parents what he had said to his brother before his car hit the wall. In their silence, he left to check on the children. That night, in a dream, his brother came to him, smiling (p. 140).

"People changed other people's lives every day of the year. There was no call to make such a fuss about it" (p. 373). That's how Anne Tyler ends *Saint Maybe*, her story of Ian Bedloe.

Second chances. If we think hard enough, we see she's right. Each moment and every day is a second chance. Every church on every street is the Church of the Second Chance. We are each other's Rev. Emmett. The challenge for each one of us is the same as for that fig tree in the garden and Ian Bedloe waiting at the stop light – what are we to do?

– Rosemary A. Rocha

March 18, 2007

4th Sunday in Lent

Lessons

RCL	Josh 5:9-12	2 Cor 5:16-21	Lk 15:1-3, 11b-32
Roman Catholic	Josh 5:9a, 10-12	2 Cor 5:17-21	Lk 15:1-3, 11-32
Episcopal (BCP)	Josh (4:19-24); 5:9-12	2 Cor 5:17-21	Lk 15:11-32

Introduction to the Lessons
Lesson 1
Joshua 5:9-12 (RCL); Joshua 5:9a, 10-12 (RC); Joshua (4:19-24); 5:9-12 (Epis)
Under God's directive, Joshua has circumcised all males in preparation for their second Passover on the eve of entering the promised land.

Lesson 2
2 Corinthians 5:16-21 (RCL); 2 Corinthians 5:17-21 (RC/Epis)
Writing from Macedonia, stung by criticism, Paul plays with the noun and verb for reconciliation. In Greek these words can signify a change in relationship with financial overtones. The cost of faithfulness? A life lived differently.

Gospel
Luke 15:1-3, 11b-32 (RCL); Luke 15:1-3, 11-32 (RC); Luke 15:11-32 (Epis)
Today's gospel is about lost and found – animals, money, people. All are so important in God's realm that losing even one among many is reason enough to go looking for the one that got away.

Theme
With Christ, what is separated, lost, or broken is reconnected.

270

Thought for the Day

I am part and parcel of the whole and cannot find God apart from the rest of humanity.

– Gandhi

Sermon Summary

Faith seems to be a dance of brokenness and reconciliation within ourselves, with one another, with our world, and – most importantly – to and with God. When it comes to God, the ledger sheet is never balanced, at least not in this life. Always, it is open to the possibility of reconciliation.

Call to Worship

One: Let us bless God at all times; may God's praise be on our lips.
All: We will magnify God, who is with us; and together we will exalt God's name.

– based on Psalm 34

Pastoral Prayer

In this moment of thoughtfulness, thank you, Mystery of Life. For bodies that run and walk, hearts that beat, and lungs that pump; for days that turn to nights and suns that follow moons; for mountains, valleys, rivers, oceans, and puddles; for glimpses of holy and breathtaking opportunities for loving; for all of this and so much more, thank you. In the stillness of this moment, we bring our concerns, anxieties, fears – for ourselves, for families and friends, and for our world. We give thanks for all the nameless ones who work faithfully and selflessly in big and little ways to turn us away from violence and estrangement toward your way of peace and unity. We pray that your reconciling love will infiltrate the places of resistance in our hearts and in the hearts of our world communities, so that soon we might live united, supportive and loving of one another. Amen.

Prayer of Confession

Gracious God, sometimes we ignore the one who is lost in favor of the many who are available. But then, in the midst of a hundred good thoughts and ideas, we focus on that one remark or look that leads us down the path of self-doubt and fear. Help us understand which to seek after and which to leave behind. In the spirit of Christ, who promises to walk beside us on the path. Amen.

Prayer of Dedication of Gifts and Self

Can what we bring to this time of offering really heal a broken world? Can our hour of prayer and song transform our hearts and minds to doing your work in the world? In faith, we trust that we can and we will. Bless now our intentions and our offerings, Holy God. Bless now our lives and our commitments. By your Spirit, reform our lives into ones worthy of the task you place before us. In the spirit of Jesus our Christ, we pray. Amen.

Hymn of the Day
"Beneath the Cross of Jesus"

This hymn enables us to consider the implications that the cross of Christ provides for Christian discipleship. Even with the challenges of 21st-century Christian life, here we have the assurance that the cross of Christ is indeed "the shadow of a mighty Rock," and that we can be "content to let the world go by." The text was written in 1872 by Elizabeth Cecilia Clephane, Scottish humanitarian, poet, and member of the Free Church of Scotland. The tune ST. CHRISTOPHER was written by Frederick C. Maker for this text, and was first printed in the 1881 *Bristol Tune Book*.

Children's Time

Lost and Found

Bring a simple puzzle with large pieces. Place one of the pieces on the floor somewhere in your worship space. Invite the children to put together the puzzle. When it is discovered that one piece is missing, ask everyone to search around for it. Express joy when the piece is found. Invite the children to share stories of a time when they were lost, or something important to them was lost. Comment that today we hear a story that Jesus told about being lost and found.

Relate the story of the prodigal son. Talk about the different people in the story. How do you think the son, the servants, the father, and the brother felt after the son came home? Explain that Jesus told this story to remind everyone that God loves us as much as the father loved his son in the story. Comment that this is something to celebrate.

Play some lively worship music, and invite the children to join you in a dance of celebration. God really loves us.

Pray with the children, giving thanks for God's amazing forgiveness and love.

The Sermon

Prodigal Reconciliation

Hymns

Beginning of Worship: "Called as Partners in Christ's Service"
Sermon Hymn: "If I Have Been the Source of Pain, O God"
Closing Hymn: "What a Covenant"

Scripture

Luke 15:1-3, 11b-32 (For additional materials on this passage, see the 2006 May/June planning issue of *The Clergy Journal;* for sermon materials on 2 Corinthians 5:16-21, see the November/December 2006 issue of *The Clergy Journal.*)

There would be no need for reconciliation if there were not the reality of brokenness. Whether it's the story of the prodigal son, our families, or the global political scene, we know that brokenness is real. God's call to us, then, is all the more clear. As a community of faith we are, in Paul's words, ambassadors of Christ – called to live out a ministry of reconciliation in whatever context we find ourselves.

Reconciliation is an interesting word. In high school I worked for a man who was the secretary-treasurer of a union. Among other things, it was my job to record dues and each month to reconcile the accounts.

There was one problem. I had never seen a checkbook, and hadn't a clue about what to do with a ledger sheet! That first month was not pretty. Again and again, and again, my boss sat down with me and made me reconcile the accounts. Years later his daughter told me that her dad thought I had been the best secretary he'd ever had. He could have fooled me in those first weeks!

In the realm of finances, reconciliation is making peace with the numbers. In the realm of human endeavors, reconciliation is making peace with or within people; bringing conflicting and divergent things together so that they balance. Sometimes reconciliation is internal. In my 30s I had to reconcile myself to the fact that I would never be a biological mother before I could be a mother of children I adopted. Reconciliation can be personal, as when we restore a friendship and bring harmony to a relationship – like what happened between father and son in our story. Reconciliation can be communal as when countries, congregations, or communities work out differences.

Luke's story of the prodigal son is an all-too-familiar story of family estrangement. The reconciliation that takes place as the story progresses moves through several characters and scenarios, attempting to balance values and life choices.

The youngest son, intent on getting on with living his life, takes what would be due him at his father's death and moves out into the world. In the midst of his enjoyment and extravagance, he soon must reconcile himself with the fact that he is unable to make it on his own. His moment of internal reconciliation becomes the catalyst of interpersonal reconciliation with his father.

Janice is a methamphetamine addict. She is also a single mother of two children, both under the age of six. Most of the time she is high, getting high, or trying to figure out how to get high. When she isn't, she is angry, impatient, and on the brink of violence. One day she found her children eating cookies on the kitchen floor, happily sitting amidst the wrinkled wrappings and crumbs. She hadn't yet figured out how to get her meth needs satisfied, and the sight of her children enraged her. Screaming at them, she picked them up, put them in her car, and drove into the desert. She opened the door and made them get out. As she drove away and watched her children standing there, growing smaller in her rear view mirror, a voice filtered through her muddled mind. "What kind of parent does this?" Horrified, she turned around, picked up her children, and drove home. Today, Janice is in a treatment center. She lost custody of her children when her parents reported her to authorities. She knows – at least in theory – that the path to reconciliation with her children and her parents comes only through reconciliation with herself.

We are never really sure about the internal workings of biblical characters, but the fact that the father excitedly and graciously welcomed his wayward son back makes me think that he'd never reconciled himself to the idea that his son was truly gone. In his mind, the balance sheet was open. When he sees his youngest coming up the road, he doesn't wonder if it's a trick or a manipulative act to get more money. No, he assumes that things are coming into balance and throws a celebration to that end.

I finished college at a time when most women got married right after graduation. Instead, I left home the next day. I lived with a cousin and worked temporary jobs until a teaching position opened up. Eventually I got my own apartment. It was not what my parents wanted for their only daughter. For months we hardly spoke to each other. One day, I went home for a visit and my mother handed me a bag – nothing fancy, no ribbons or cards – just a bag from a discount department store. In it was a set of bed sheets. Acts of reconciliation happen often in very simple ways, yet the effect of such connections can change lives.

The one character in our story that doesn't seem to be reconciled is the oldest son. Perhaps he had been reconciled to the foolishness of his brother and to his own importance as his father's only responsible child. But his brother's return changed any emotional balance he might have had. For him, everything was turned upside down – his relationship with his father, with his brother, with himself. For him, the work of reconciliation had just begun.

The life of faith seems to be a dance of brokenness and reconciliation within ourselves, with one another, with our world, and – most importantly – to and with our God. Our story today tells us that when it comes to God, the ledger sheet is never balanced – at least not in this life. Always, it is open to the possibility of reconciliation. It seems to be left in our court as to whether or not we have the courage or the humility to move into that realm of hospitality and grace that is God's gift of reconciliation.

– Rosemary A. Rocha

March 25, 2007

5th Sunday in Lent

Lessons

RCL	Isa 43:16-21	Phil 3:4b-14	Jn 12:1-8
Roman Catholic	Isa 43:16-21	Phil 3:8-14	Jn 8:1-11
Episcopal (BCP)	Isa 43:16-21	Phil 3:8-14	Lk 20:9-19

Introduction to the Lessons
Lesson 1
Isaiah 43:16-21(RCL/RC/Epis)
In Babylon, Isaiah speaks to exiles – descendants of those taken before Jerusalem's destruction in 587 BCE. Beloved images of God's power to liberate hold the promise of a new exodus.

Lesson 2
Philippians 3:4b-14 (RCL); Philippians 3:8-14 (RC/Epis)
Imprisoned in Ephesus or Rome, Paul wrote to Christians in northern Greece, arguing, once again, that salvation comes through grace by faith in Christ, not through the adherence to ritual practices such as circumcision.

Gospel
(1) John 12:1-8 (RCL)
The Greek word for "dinner," (*deipnon*) – used only in John here and during the account of the last supper – sets the scene for Mary's faithful discipleship and Judas's rehearsal of his final faithlessness.

(2) John 8:1-11 (RC)
Jesus challenges the legal interpretation of the scribes and Pharisees in this text that contains the only occurrence in John's Gospel of the word *teacher* used in reference to Jesus.

(3) Luke 20:9-19 (Epis)
The death of Jesus is foreshadowed in his parable's thinly veiled images of ancient prophets' deaths and of the rejected stone as the cornerstone of a new creation.

Theme
The betrayal and death of Jesus is prefigured, but this time, Mary gets to anoint him.

Thought for the Day
The difficulty, my friends, is not in avoiding death, but in avoiding unrighteousness; for that runs faster than death.

– Plato, *Apology of Socrates*

Sermon Summary
Not everyone has the courage to face death honestly. But those who are able to do so are able to minister to others in their final time of need.

Call to Worship
One: O God, we stand on the brink of today; our future is unknown.
All: Anoint our heads with your Spirit, that we might know the way.
One: O God, we stand in this moment of uncertain needs and concerns.
All: Anoint our hands with your Spirit, that what we touch, we touch with love.
One: O God, we stand at this place of comfort and stability.
All: Anoint our feet with your Spirit, that wherever we walk, we walk your walk.
One: O God, we stand in love and affirmation of you and your world.
All: Anoint our bodies, minds, and hearts with your Spirit, that our worship will be filled with signs of your presence.

Pastoral Prayer
We pray, O God of life and death, for people and places, nations and leaders facing death. Too many are willing to slaughter in the name of some honor or misdeed long forgotten. We pray for people of all nations

who give their lives to the work of peace, to the binding up of broken bodies and wounded spirits – for all the heroic acts that never get recorded in history books. We pray, O God of life and death, for people and places facing death. And we pray, O God of blessings, for people and places, nations and leaders surrounded by peace and prosperity, wealth and opportunity. Open their eyes to look into faces and places where death walks. Impassion their minds and hearts to burn with your righteous anger at what should not be. Give them freedom and courage to use their giftedness and their gifts to change your world. Amen.

Prayer of Confession

How is it that we walk through each day and so many times do not see you in the faces and lives of the world around us? Can it be that too often our heads are bent on winning, achieving, and having, so that we miss chances to look into the lives of our family, our friends, the stranger? Help us, God of life. Give us the courage of Mary to befriend one in need, to do the right thing even in the face of criticism, to spend everything on the priceless ointment of loving you and your world. In the face of death, and in promise of love beyond death, we pray in Christ's name. Amen.

Prayer of Dedication of Gifts and Self

What we offer, God of life and death, we give in love and faithfulness to your call to serve the world in the way of Christ, who in the end as in the beginning, gave everything. Bless these gifts to your service in his name. Amen.

Hymn of the Day
"Awake, My Soul, Stretch Every Nerve"

Written by British Congregationalist pastor Philip Doddridge, this hymn was included in his *Hymns Founded on Various Texts in the Holy Scripture* in 1755, published four years after his death. The hymn's title in the collection is "Pressing on in the Christian Race." The hymn is based on Philippians 3:12-14, and was written to cap a sermon based on this passage. The hymn makes use of the imagery of the Greek games, with which the apostle Paul was quite familiar. The text uses the "race" as a symbol of the strong Christian life in which heaven is the prize. Many authorities believe this is the best hymn written by Doddridge. Some even call it "immortal."

Children's Time

A Special Gift

Bring a bottle of lightly scented nonallergenic oil (baby oil). Open it and let the children smell the contents. Ask if anyone would like to have a drop of oil placed on her or his hands. Encourage the children to rub it into their skin. Mention that oil can be very soothing when rubbed into dry skin.

Explain that in Jesus' time, people walked a lot wearing sandals and that their feet often got tired and dry. Sometimes when they stopped to rest, they would wash their feet and rub them with perfumed oil to keep their skin soft. The perfumed oil was very expensive, so people would only use a few drops. Comment that in our Bible story today someone gave some perfumed oil to Jesus as a special gift.

Relate the gospel story, emphasizing the extravagance of Mary's loving gift. Comment that Mary gave Jesus a special gift of love. Ask: How do you think Mary's gift helped Jesus? Invite the children to name some ways that they might show their love to Jesus.

Pray with the children, giving thanks for the story of Mary and her special gift of caring for Jesus.

The Sermon

Preparing to Die

Hymns
> **Beginning of Worship:** "Jesu, Jesu, Fill Us with Your Love"
> **Sermon Hymn:** "Said Judas to Mary"
> **Closing Hymn:** "A Woman Came Who Did Not Count the Cost"

Scripture
John 12:1-8 (For additional materials on this passage, see the November/December 2006 issue of *The Clergy Journal;* for sermon materials on Philippians 3:4b-14, see the 2006 May/June planning issue of *The Clergy Journal.*)

Mary loved Jesus. But, she knew he was going to die. She also knew she couldn't take away that journey. So she did the only thing she could, blessed the feet that would take him through it. When Judas criticized her for anointing Jesus' feet with costly, fragrant ointment, Jesus silenced him: "Leave her alone. She is preparing me for burial."

John's story fascinates me, in part because of how it differs from similar stories in Mark (14:3-9) and Matthew (26:6-13). In those gospels, the woman anointing Jesus is nameless, and it is implied that she is a prostitute. In those gospels, the woman anoints the head of Jesus, as Old Testament prophets anointed the heads of kings. In those stories, anointing is a way of saying that Jesus is king or Messiah, a word meaning "the anointed one."

We know the woman in John. She is Mary – Mary who sat at Jesus' feet another time, and her sister Martha got mad at her for not helping in the kitchen. While anointing Jesus' head in the other gospels was a sign of his leadership, feet were anointed only when embalming the body for burial. Mary was able to see that Jesus was going to die. Anointing his feet was a way of preparing him for that journey. Not many of us have the courage to face death like this.

Jane was 90 years old when she died. She wasn't the oldest member of our congregation, but she had been a member the longest – a month shy of 79 years. Jane's friends encouraged her to hang on. Her doctor assured her that she could survive her medical situation. But Jane said, "I'm 90 years old. I've lived a good life. I have no regrets." She told her nieces that she was not afraid to die. She was ready.

It's not easy to accept that someone we love is about to die. I suspect that Mary was able to face Jesus' death because she had come to see death differently after Jesus had brought her brother Lazarus back from death. But the raising of Lazarus was – in fact – Jesus' undoing. After that event, religious leaders grew concerned about his powers. They began to plan his death.

Even Jesus became cautious. He no longer went about in public in Judea (Jn 11:54). The chief priests and Pharisees had given orders: Anyone who knew where Jesus was should tell them, so that he might be arrested. As the Passover drew near, people wondered, will Jesus come to Jerusalem for the festival or will he stay away? Tension was high. And, given human nature, people had begun to take sides.

It is into this social and political climate that John sets the story of Jesus and Mary. Jesus has once more come to the home of his friends Mary, Martha, and Lazarus. But this time, he is a hunted man. He knows he will go on to Jerusalem for the Passover. He also knows that he will never leave. Mary, with a pound of pure nard, prepares Jesus' feet for the journey only he can take.

We find ourselves in places like that. Maybe we're not facing our own death, but then again, we might be. Or, perhaps we're facing the death of a loved one, or a career, or a marriage, or a particular period in our lives like high school or college. We know what it's like to find ourselves facing a road only we can walk – a journey from which there is no turning back.

Giving birth is one of those journeys. The water breaks, contractions begin, and there is no way on earth that a mother can change her mind. But, just as a mother in the delivery room needs a coach – a spouse or a partner – Jesus needs a friend. So, he lets Mary soothe his tired feet and ease his weary soul.

When we are in pain, allowing someone to minister to us takes courage. We often think that we must bear our burdens alone – that it is somehow nobler or better to keep a "stiff upper lip." Many of us have learned that Christian faith calls us to be servants only. Jesus does call us to serve, but he also shows us how to be served. When we only allow ourselves to be servants, we miss part of the gospel. In fact, we can even abuse our role as servant, because serving others can often be a position of power.

So Jesus allows Mary to soothe his feet. A few days later, at the Passover meal with his disciples, Jesus washes their feet. When Peter protests, Jesus reminds him that in order to serve, one must learn how to be served. In our story today, Jesus shows us that to be God's servant means knowing when to do unto others, and when to let others do unto you.

Jesus said, "You always have the poor with you, but you do not always have me" (12:8).

If he was speaking about his physical presence, he was right. We do not have him here in the flesh. But we know that, in spirit, Jesus is with us always to strengthen and guide our lives. Jesus will not take our journey away from us, no matter how easy or hard it may be; but he does walk with us on the path. May we accept Jesus' presence and support, and may it be a balm to our souls from which we find the courage to face and walk the paths before us. Amen.

– Rosemary A. Rocha

April 1, 2007

Passion/Palm Sunday

Lessons

RCL	Isa 50:4-9a	Phil 2:5-11	Lk 22:14—23:56
			or Lk 23:1-49
Roman Catholic	Isa 50:4-7	Phil 2:6-11	Lk 22:14—23:56
			or Lk 23:1-49
Episcopal (BCP)	Isa 45:21-25	Phil 2:5-11	Lk (22:39-71),
	or Isa 52:13—53:12		23:1-49, (50-56)

Introduction to the Lessons

Lesson 1

(1) Isaiah 50:4-9a (RCL); Isaiah 50:4-7 (RC)

Part of a longer poem portraying the exile as the result of the nation's sin against God, this passage is seen by the early Christian church as a prophecy of Jesus' unjust trial and conviction.

(2) Isaiah 45:21-25 (Epis)

The fourth strophe of a longer poem addresses the victory of monotheism, God's invitation to the world, and the confession of the nations.

Lesson 2

Philippians 2:5-11 (RCL/Epis); Philippians 2:6-11 (RC)

Paul uses this early Christian hymn to make a point about choosing a lowly position in life in the service of others. Then, as now, the message was counter to the prevailing culture.

Gospel

(1) Luke 22:14—23:56 (RCL/RC)

Luke's passion story moves through Jesus' interactions with many people; yet, in the final scene, he is alone before the God he has lived and died to serve.

(2) Luke (22:39-71), 23:1-49, (50-56) (Epis)
Luke repeatedly portrays Pilate as believing Jesus to be innocent. Both Pilate and Jesus, however, remain powerless to change the unfolding future.

Theme
Imitation is a way to faithfulness.

Thought for the Day
The point here is that our way of being with and for one another flows from Christ's way of being with and for us. Our ethics are theological, not merely moral or moralistic.
– Tony Robinson (www.anthonybrobinson.com)

Call to Worship
One: Hosanna to the Son of David, the King of Israel. Blessed is he who comes in the name of the Lord.
All: Hosanna in the highest heaven!
– from Matthew 21:9

Pastoral Prayer
God, you move in the very fiber of our beings, pulsing through every cell, every heartbeat. So often we are unmindful of our intimate connection with you. In these moments help us to live in that connection, that we might courageously be your voice and hands and heart. We remember friends, family, and loved ones who live with terminal illness, who go about with chronic pain as their constant companion, who bear in their hearts and minds the reminders of past hurts, betrayals, and wrongs. In your love and grace heal them, comfort them, strengthen them. We remember people who live in war zones, who scavenge for food, shelter, and peace. Empower our commitments to them; show us in small and large ways how to work for their release from the results of human greed and vengeance, natural disaster, political negligence, and personal weakness. Amen.

Prayer of Confession

Gracious God, on this most holy day, when anticipation of what could be and foreboding of what will be meet, we pause to remember. We recall times of plenty, when we have been faithful to dreams and loyal to people and commitments, and times of difficulty when we have abandoned them. We remember fear that grows within our hearts and minds, and keeps us from standing by our ideals, our friends, our God. We remember despair that leads us to lose hope in ourselves, in you, in life itself. Gracious God, make us strong enough to walk the path as Jesus did. Give us courage and strength to face our trials, our abandonment, even our death. Renew in us hope that in suffering there is wholeness, in pain there is healing, and in death there is life. For it is the way of Jesus Christ, whom we seek to love and serve always. Amen.

Prayer of Dedication of Gifts and Self

We come before you, O God, asking for so much – time, possessions, our very lives. Forgive us for holding back when it is time to offer our gifts and ourselves to you. Shape our frame of mind and will so that giving to you becomes our privilege and our joy. Embolden us by your Spirit so that gladly we offer you everything. Amen.

Sermon Summary

Imitating Christ is the call of the gospel. It is a difficult and sometimes life-threatening challenge.

Hymn of the Day
"All Glory, Laud, and Honor"

The most well-known English translation of the ninth-century Latin hymn, "Gloria, laus et honor," was done by the Reverend John Mason Neale in 1854. Bishop Theodulph of Orleans wrote the original Latin hymn around 820 as a poetical rendering of the biblical story of the triumphal entry. Neale's translation offers us the opportunity to bring before Christ a triumphant song of praise, our modern day "hosanna." It can "set the stage" for Palm Sunday and its transition to a focus upon the passion of Christ. St. THEODULPH, written by Melchior Teschner in 1615 is the tune most often associated with the hymn text.

Children's Time

The Name of Jesus

Bring a book that lists names and their meanings. Invite the children to share something about their names, asking: Do you know why your name was chosen? Do you know what your name means? Comment that names are intriguing because most of them have a meaning. Use your book to look up your own name and some of the children's names.

Comment that in the Bible reading today we hear a very important name. That name is Jesus. Ask the children if they know what Jesus means. Jesus means "God saves." Explain that the name of Jesus is often joined with the word Christ, which means, "chosen one." If you put both names together, it means, "chosen by God to save." Jesus was chosen by God to show us God's love and forgiveness.

Explain that this Sunday begins Holy Week. This is the time when we remember the events of the last few days of Jesus' life on earth. One of the things that happened during that week was that Jesus chose to die on the cross rather than stop telling people about God's love. Jesus really did live up to his name didn't he?

Pray with the children, offering thanks for Jesus who was chosen to show us God's love.

The Sermon

The Sincerest Form of Flattery

Hymns
Beginning of Worship: "All Glory, Laud, and Honor"
Sermon Hymn: "Open Mine Eyes that I Might See"
Closing Hymn: "Ride on! Ride On in Majesty"

Scripture
Philippians 2:5-11 (For additional materials on this passage, see the January 2007 issue of *The Clergy Journal;* for sermon materials on Luke 22:14—23:56, see the 2006 May/June planning issue of *The Clergy Journal.*)

In his book, *A Pretty Good Person*, Lewis Smedes tells of spending a hot day at the Los Angeles County Jail, waiting for someone he was bailing out. Mid-afternoon, still waiting, he went out to get a cold drink and met a man in a black suit and clergy collar. Assuming he was a prison chaplain, Smedes asked the cleric to join him. The man was, Smede discovered, an insurance salesman. Once a week he visited prisoners and, he told Smede, the collar gave him entrance into the jail. (Lewis B. Smedes, *A Pretty Good Person: What It Takes to Live with Courage, Gratitude and Integrity*, Harper & Row, 1990, pp. 137-38)

"Let each of you look not to your own interests, but to the interests of others. Let the same mind be in you that was in Christ Jesus" (Phil 2:4-5).

What would it be like to walk around as someone else? Children do it, dressing up in mommy's shoes, daddy's shirt, or big brother's baggy jeans. Actors get paid for doing it. Watching the movie *Ray*, it's hard to remember that it's Jamie Foxx on screen and not Ray Charles. Identity fraud testifies to how lucrative it can be to walk around as someone else. The Federal Witness Protection Program offers government assistance to those who need to create new identities. If imitation is the sincerest form of flattery, then Paul's idea of letting "the same mind be in you that was in Christ Jesus" must be the ultimate act of honor.

In *The Imitation of Christ*, German mystic Thomas à Kempis (1379-1471) identifies ways in which a person can act more like Christ. The WWJD (What Would Jesus Do) movement underlines the idea that considering our behavior in light of Christ's is basic to our life together.

But United Church of Christ minister Tony Robinson, in his comments on this Philippians passage, asks an important question. "Is this way – Christ's way – practical? Can we live in this world and follow Christ in humility, in sacrifice, in placing the interests of others above our own?" (www.anthonybrobinson.com)

"Let the same mind be in you that was in Christ Jesus." This is, indeed, heavy stuff. We might have to get serious about life were we to take this passage to heart. Many do. A professor traveled with colleagues and students to help with recovery efforts after hurricane Katrina. While there, a student stole a large amount of money from an abandoned home. Returning to the dorm that night, the student bragged about "finding" the money. The professor was neither in charge of the group, nor directly responsible for the student's behavior. Yet the question of what to do plagued the professor, who confronted colleagues and the student both during and after the trip. In the end, the professor reported the situation to the school, the student was suspended, and the money returned.

The professor was living out the reality of having the mind of Christ. It's hard work. Too often we sanitize and "saccharin-ize" the Christian life. We make it about feeling good personally and being at peace within ourselves. But to have the same mind as Christ means that we are committed to living like the man who sacrificed and suffered in his faithfulness to God. Having the same mind of Christ means confronting the Pharisees of our world, challenging our version of Roman governors and political/religious dictators, and refusing to live by laws that are not of the Spirit.

The movie *Hotel Rwanda* tells the true story of how Paul Rusesabagina, a Hutu, saved the lives of more than 1000 Tutsi refugees by sheltering them in the hotel he managed. In that nightmare of human depravity, many clergy participated in the slaughter either by killing people or by helping trap them so that rebels could do their nasty work. Having the mind of Christ means, in many situations, a death or life calling, as people like Oscar Romero, Martin Luther King Jr. and many anonymous martyrs have testified to.

The Imitation of Christ, written by Kempis, is a dialog between Christ and "the disciple." In chapter three we read "The Voice of Christ" saying, "Do not think, therefore, that you have found true peace . . . or that all is well because you suffer no opposition . . . For the true lover of virtue is not known by these things, nor do the progress and perfection of a man consist in them.

"The Disciple: In what do they consist, Lord?

"The Voice of Christ: They consist in offering yourself with all your heart to the divine will, not seeking what is yours either in small matters or great ones . . . so that you will preserve equanimity and give thanks in both prosperity and adversity, seeing all things in their proper light."

In 2000, fashion designers Tara Subkoff and Matt Damhave, started a company called "Imitation of Christ." (newyorkmetro.com/fashion/fashionshows/05/spring/preview/brandhistory.htm) While they aim to "transform undesirables into desirables," a very Christly theme, I doubt that high-priced, hip clothing made from recycled designer cast-offs has much to do with imitating Christ. It just goes to show that there's a lot in life that is a bad imitation.

How do we know that we are imitating Christ, or that we have the same mind that was in Jesus? The answer, I believe, is biblical, simple, and the hardest thing we will ever do: love. Love God and love our neighbor just as if we were loving ourselves. To live every day in the excitement and challenge of this way of life is, I believe, to have the same mind that was in Jesus Christ. My friends, it is a challenge hard to live with, but one we cannot live without.

– Rosemary A. Rocha

April 5, 2007

Maundy Thursday

Lessons

RCL	Ex 12:1-4, (5-10), 11-14	1 Cor 11:23-26	Jn 13:1-17, 31b-35
Roman Catholic	Ex 12:1-8, 11-14	1 Cor 11:23-26	Jn 13:1-15
Episcopal (BCP)	Ex 12:1-14a	1 Cor 11:23-26, (27-32)	Jn 13:1-15 or Lk 22:14-30

Introduction to the Lessons

Lesson 1
> **Exodus 12:1-4, (5-10), 11-14 (RCL);**
> **Exodus 12:1-8, 11-14 (RC);**
> **Exodus 12:1-14a (Epis)**

This text follows the prediction of the final plague in Egypt, and comes right before the people leave Egypt. These words became important for the celebration of the Passover meal.

Lesson 2
> **1 Corinthians 11:23-26 (RCL/RC);**
> **1 Corinthians 11:23-26, (27-32) (Epis)**

Paul describes proper observance of the Lord's supper for the church at Corinth, in the face of some chaotic and exclusive practices. These words are key for the church in the practice of communion.

Gospel
> **John 13:1-17, 31b-35 (RCL); John 13:1-15 (RC/Epis)**

As Jesus moves closer to the cross in John's Gospel, this passage offers a key image of Jesus' example of serving others in love.

Theme

Let us remember God's power for possibility.

Thought for the day

When you feel fear or doubt about the future, remember all that God has done in the past.

Call to Worship

One: What shall I return to the Lord for all God's bounty to me?
All: I will lift up the cup of salvation and call on the name of the Lord.
One: I will offer to you a thanksgiving sacrifice and call on the name of the Lord.
All: I will pay my vows to God in the presence of all God's people,
One: In the courts of the house of the Lord, in your midst, O Jerusalem.
All: Praise the Lord!

– based on Psalm 116

Pastoral Prayer

Our God, we come before you tonight, remembering Jesus' last night with his disciples. We praise and thank you for his life, death, and resurrection, for the great and holy events we remember this week. We add our thanks for Jesus' ongoing presence with us and with the church around the world. We ask that you strengthen us through this service tonight and prepare us to be ever more faithful disciples. Renew our faith as we hear again the stories of your powerful work on behalf of your people. In the name of Jesus Christ we pray. Amen.

Prayer of Confession

Loving and gracious God, we need your grace. We ask your forgiveness for the times we have acted out of fear rather than faith. We are all too like Jesus' disciples, who also fled in fear. Forgive our forgetfulness, our difficulty in remembering your never-failing love and power. This night, tomorrow, and in the days ahead help us to leave our fears behind, and live out of your strength and hope, for Christ's sake. Amen.

Prayer of Dedication of Gifts and Self

Generous God, we offer these our gifts, together with ourselves, to support your work in our midst and in the world. May the result of our giving be that we come closer to your purpose. Amen.

Sermon Summary

The story of the exodus shapes us as we remember that God can do the impossible. God can deliver people from slavery. God can bring resurrection to Jesus. Our own stories remind us of the impossible things God has done. We can look ahead, expecting impossible things to be possible.

Hymn of the Day
"It Was a Sad and Solemn Night"

Also known as "It Happened on That Fateful Night," this is one of few hymns specifically based on the Maundy Thursday experience. This hymn provides opportunity for a poignant reflection upon what took place the night before Jesus' crucifixion. The hymn by Isaac Watts first appeared with the opening line, "'Twas on that dark and doleful night" and appeared in his 1709 publication, *Hymns and Spiritual Songs*. The pentatonic tune BOURBON first appeared with this text in 1825 in the American tune book, *Columbian Harmony*. The use of a soloist or choir may be most effective for this hymn.

Children's Time

A Meal to Remember

Talk about the kinds of things we do when we celebrate special events such as birthdays, Christmas, or Thanksgiving. Accept all suggestions; and, if no one else says it, mention that a good way to celebrate is to eat together. We might even have a feast. Encourage the children to name times when they have enjoyed a special meal with their families.

Comment that in the Bible reading today we read about a special meal that God told the Hebrew people to eat. Explain that this special meal is still eaten today and has become an important part of the celebration of Passover. This is the time when the Jewish people remember and celebrate their release from slavery into freedom.

Comment that in the church we also have a special meal that we share together. This meal helps us to remember and celebrate the life, death, and resurrection of Jesus. Talk with the children about communion and about how it is celebrated in your church.

Explain that when Jewish people share the Passover meal they are reminded of God's care for them. When we share communion, we also know that God cares for us.

Pray with the children, giving thanks for God's love and care.

The Sermon

Do This in Remembrance

Hymns

Beginning of Worship: "When I Survey the Wondrous Cross"
Sermon Hymn: "In the Cross of Christ I Glory"
Closing Hymn: "For the Bread Which You Have Broken"

Scripture

Exodus 12:1-4, (5-10), 11-14 (For sermon materials on John 13:1-17, 31b-35, see the January 2007 issue of *The Clergy Journal;* for sermon materials on 1 Corinthians 11:23-26, see the 2006 May/June planning issue of *The Clergy Journal.*)

What is your earliest memory? I remember sitting on the arm of a rocking armchair while my mother sat in the chair holding my baby brother, giving him a bottle and reading me a book at the same time. This is a memory that has shaped me over the years, and all my life I have been a reader, a book person.

Our text this evening is a story that has shaped the Jewish people from the first, right up to this day. Exodus 12 includes the instructions for the very first Passover. The people were to take a lamb and kill it and roast it. They were to eat a meal – this was not to be a relaxed family meal. They were to eat it with their shoes and their coats on, ready to go, because liberation from slavery was about to happen. In addition, the text says, "This day shall be a day of remembrance for you" (12:14). They

were to remember this story, to tell it again and again. This became a story
that shaped them. This was a night when the impossible happened, when
freedom came, and they were never to forget it.

This night, Maundy Thursday, we remember Jesus' last supper with
his disciples. Paul tells us in his description in 1 Corinthians that Jesus
said, "Do this in remembrance of me." Jesus' story also shapes us, and
we tell it again and again. His story tells us something important about
who we are.

We are a people who find the impossible possible. Who would have
thought that the people of Israel could have received freedom from slavery
in a night? This story tells us it is possible. Who would have thought that
Jesus could die and receive new life again? The stories of Holy Week tell
us it is possible.

Every church has stories of the impossible becoming possible, in big
and small ways. What's this church's story? A few people banding together
in hope and imagination, to begin a new community. An individual
coming to faith as an adult for the first time. A building being raised. A
conflict faced and overcome. A new spirit of vitality in the congregation.
Some of these stories are in the past, some are happening right now. When
we remember these stories and tell them again and again, we are reminding
ourselves of the God we have and serve.

Without these stories, big and small, it is easy for us to forget who
God is and what God can do. Our thinking remains too small. I recently
took a retreat at a Trappist monastery in Lafayette, Oregon. It was a mostly
silent retreat, which is something of an impossibility for a Baptist minister!
I did have one conversation with Brother Mark, who meets with guests in
the monastery. He quoted to me this phrase: "God does not believe in
our God." God does not believe in our God. Our God does not do
impossible things – but *God* does impossible things. The stories help us
believe in *God*, a God far bigger than "our God," that limited God we
imagine and create in our own minds. The disciples gathered with Jesus
on this night also had a hard time believing as the events of the next few
days unfolded.

In *Through the Looking Glass*, the Red Queen says, "Why, sometimes
I've believed as many as six impossible things before breakfast" (Lewis Car-
roll, *The Annotated Alice*, Clarkson N. Potter, 1960, p. 251). As Christians,
if we get up early to pray, we can believe even more than six. We could
go around the room tonight and tell six, eight, ten impossible stories of

how God has worked in our lives and in our midst. The fact that we are still remembering and telling these stories of the Passover and the last supper is impossible, but it is happening. God's story has been told, continues to be told, will continue to be told, and we are a part of that unfolding story.

So as we gather tonight around the table of the Lord, let us look not only to the past but also to the future. Let us put on our coats and our shoes, and be ready to go out the door in faith when God calls us. The events we remember tonight – the events of this week – are as much about what will happen as what has already happened. God wants us to be a presence in the world, on the journey as the people of Israel were, as the disciples came to be.

St. Francis put it this way: "Start by doing what is necessary, then do the possible, and suddenly you are doing the impossible." The necessary is the regular practice of communion, the yearly observance of Maundy Thursday and the other services of Holy Week. That practice prepares us to do the possible, to live as Christians as best we can each day and each week. Then suddenly we find ourselves doing the impossible things that God calls us to do, like working for peace in the world, sharing God's message of love with others, and being God's people.

– Margaret Marcuson

April 6, 2007

Good Friday

Lessons

RCL	Isa 52:13—53:12	Heb 10:16-25	Jn 18:1—19:42
		or Heb 4:14-16; 5:7-9	
Roman Catholic	Isa 52:13—53:12	Heb 4:14-16; 5:7-9	Jn 18:1—19:42
Episcopal (BCP)	Isa 52:13—53:12	Heb 10:1-25	Jn (18:1-40);
	or Gen 22:1-18		19:1-37
	or Wis 2:1, 12-24		

Introduction to the Lessons

Lesson 1
Isaiah 52:13—53:12 (RCL/RC/Epis)
This passage is one of the great songs in Isaiah that speak about the "servant of the Lord." Christians from the earliest days of the church have seen in these words a description of Jesus.

Lesson 2
(1) Hebrews 10:16-25 (RCL); Hebrews 10:1-25 (Epis)
The writer of Hebrews speaks about the new covenant under Christ. The author quotes the Old Testament liberally, including the words from Jeremiah that begin this passage, and also addresses the great theme of faith.

(2) Hebrews 4:14-16; 5:7-9 (RC)
The writer of Hebrews presents as a key theme Jesus as our high priest, who comes before God on our behalf. Jesus is the source of our salvation.

Gospel
John 18:1—19:42 (RCL/RC); John (18:1-40); 19:1-37 (Epis)
These chapters form the story of Jesus' passion according to John. It is important to remember that when John says "the Jews," the meaning is the religious leaders of the day.

Theme
Do we, like Jesus, thirst to do God's will?

Thought for the Day
Doing God's will can mean going through the darkness, yet God is with us.

Call to Worship
We gather in worship this Good Friday, a somber day, a day of darkness. We remember Jesus' suffering and death. We grieve over our own failure and sin. Yet we do not grieve as those who have no hope because we know that our loving God offers a powerful promise even in the darkness.

Pastoral Prayer
O God, we come before you today remembering this holy and terrible day, the day when Jesus died. We give you thanks for his faithfulness to the end, and praise you not only for this day, but also for the whole story of redemption, of which we are a part. We offer our prayers today for those around the world who suffer as Jesus did, and ask for your loving presence to be with them, in their hearts and in the hands of those who may touch them. We pray for those in this congregation who are suffering and wondering where you are. May we show your presence to them. May we all live through the Good Fridays of our lives to the new life that lies beyond. May we receive hope in the darkness, knowing that your love was and is shown to us in Jesus Christ, now and forever. Amen.

Prayer of Confession
Holy God, all we like sheep have gone astray; we have all turned to our own way. This Good Friday, we are mindful of this reality. But we know this does not have to be the end of our story. We ask that you would forgive us, and help us return to your loving care. May we walk more closely with you, as your servants and disciples of Jesus, for whose sake we pray. Amen.

Prayer of Dedication of Gifts and Self
We give thanks for your many gifts to us, O God. This day we give thanks most of all for the gift of your Son, our Savior Jesus Christ. His loving

sacrifice changed the world and changes us. In the same spirit of sacrifice, we offer our gifts to you – how can we do less? We owe our very lives to you, from birth to death and beyond. May our gifts be used to renew the lives of others, in the name of Christ. Amen.

Sermon Summary

Jesus thirsted to do God's will, even when it meant suffering. We, too, are called to follow in his footsteps in our longing to embrace God's will for us, looking beyond the immediate moment to God's ultimate hope.

Hymn of the Day
"Go to Dark Gethsemane"

This hymn gives us opportunity to reflect upon what happened in the final days before Christ's crucifixion, and how we may relate to Gethsemane, the judgment hall, the climb to Calvary's mountain, and the crucifixion. The words invite us to "early hasten to the tomb" of the risen Christ. The hymn concludes with our prayer, "Savior, teach us so to rise." Written by English poet James Montgomery, the text first appeared in print in 1820. The tune REDHEAD first appeared with this text in 1853. The hymn makes an excellent parting hymn at the close of the Good Friday service. It is also effective to sing only the first three stanzas and to leave the church building in silence.

Children's Time

Jesus Dies

Bring a newspaper or magazine photo that shows someone crying. Bring an ordinary candle and a trick candle that cannot be blown out. Show the picture and ask the children what the person in the picture is feeling. What kinds of things might cause someone to feel this way? Comment that sometimes when we feel very sad it seems as if the light of goodness has been blown out. Invite the children to tell of times they have felt sad. As the children share their stories, light and then blow out the ordinary candle several times.

Light the trick candle as you tell that in our Bible story today Jesus' disciples were very sad. When Jesus died on the cross, the disciples thought that the light of God's love had been blown out. They thought it was the end of everything. Invite the children to blow out the candle.

Comment that Jesus' death was not the end of the story. Nothing could destroy the light of God's love. Something amazing was about to happen. Explain that we will have to wait for a few days to hear the next part of the story, but it is wonderful.

Pray with the children, giving thanks for God's amazing love.

The Sermon

Thirsting for God's Will

Hymns
Beginning of Worship: "O Sacred Head"
Sermon Hymn: "Beneath the Cross of Jesus"
Closing Hymn: "Were You There?"

Scripture
John 18:1—19:42 (For additional sermon materials on this passage, see the January 2007 issue of *The Clergy Journal;* for sermon materials on Isaiah 52:13—53:12, see the 2006 May/June planning issue of *The Clergy Journal.*)

Every article on health suggests that we need water, eight glasses a day. I now notice more often when I am thirsty, and try to have water on hand to drink. It's quite a different thing to be thirsty with no water at hand. When Jesus is thirsty on the cross, what does he receive? A sponge of sour wine. Here is the one who produced gallons of wine for a wedding, the one who said he could provide living water, saying, "I am thirsty."

Here on the cross, Jesus thirsts to complete the work God has given him, as he approaches the end. Nothing could satisfy his thirst except that completion of his mission. (See Raymond E. Brown, *The Gospel According to John XIII-XXI*, Doubleday, 1970, p. 930.)

Are you thirsty? What do you thirst for? We all have longings and yearnings in our lives, and there are plenty of opportunities out there to try to satisfy those thirsts. Just look at the ads, whether for milk, vodka, or moisturizer, they all claim, "We will satisfy that part of you that thirsts."

Some people try to quench a thirst for meaning with alcohol and drugs, with sex, or with shopping. You can look for false satisfaction even in church, with lots of busy church activity, with good works. So we may seek to quench our thirst in all kinds of false ways. Yet we will find, sooner or later, that we have been drinking sour wine. We drink, and a moment later we are thirsty again. We go out searching for more ways to satisfy that thirst, which never goes away.

As followers of Jesus, we don't have to go looking for a way to satisfy our thirst for meaning. We don't have to accept the meager offerings of the world, which only serve to increase our thirst. The source of living water, Jesus, will satisfy all our thirst.

Now, it is a good thing we get thirsty. I'm often reminded to drink that next glass of water because I get thirsty. Thirst is our body telling us something – we are in need of water. And spiritual thirst is our spirit telling us something – we are in need of God.

The anonymous spiritual writer who wrote *The Cloud of Unknowing* put it this way: "One loving blind desire for God alone is more valuable in itself, more pleasing to God and to the saints, more beneficial to your own growth and more helpful to your friends, both living and dead, than anything else you could do" (Image Books, 1973, p. 60).

So if we understand that our thirst is for God and God alone, and direct our attention toward God, our lives can be changed. If we drink the living water that Jesus offers, our thirst will be satisfied not only now but forever. Jesus told the woman at the well, "Those who drink of the water that I will give them will never be thirsty" (Jn 4:14).

As we remember the cross this Good Friday, we are made vividly aware that the cup Jesus drank and offers to us includes suffering. Jesus did not thirst for suffering in some masochistic way, but he thirsted to do God's will, which included suffering.

To be Christians, to be followers of Jesus, to thirst not only for God but to do God's will, means we have to take some risks. It means we will not like everything that happens to us. If we thirst for God and for God's will as Jesus did, sometimes we will feel like we are in over our heads. We may say, "I just asked for a glass of water, and now these ocean waves are crashing over me!" At times like these, we can remember the cross and Jesus' own suffering. We are not alone in our struggles. The one who died for us lives with us.

And as we mature in our faith, we learn that God in Christ is not merely a cosmic soda machine to quench our thirst. We learn that true satisfaction comes not from getting what we want or even what we need, but from living out God's will. For each person, that may be something different. The Quaker Thomas Kelly puts it this way: "The loving Presence does not burden us equally with all things, but considerately puts upon each of us just a few central tasks as emphatic responsibilities. For each of us these special undertakings are our share in the joyous burdens of love . . . We cannot die on *every* cross, nor are we expected to" (*A Testament of Devotion,* Harper & Row, 1941, p. 109).

Jesus knew the cross was his responsibility. He took it on willingly, despite the suffering. As we drink his living water, we will learn where our responsibilities lie, and where the struggles may be. Jesus shows us the way. Yes, Jesus was as thirsty as any human would be thirsty in the agony of crucifixion. Yet beneath that surface thirst was a deeper thirst, a desire for God and for God's will to be carried out – a desire to do what God had called him to do, to complete the task.

At the deeper level is the thirst for what God wants for us, not merely what we want for ourselves. At that deeper level is the knowledge that what God wants for us is better for us and for the world. At that deeper level lies Easter knowledge – knowing that God can redeem suffering and bring new life even out of death. This Easter knowledge shows us that beyond the suffering is the promise of hope and joy and love. Or, as Carole King sings, "Way over yonder. That's where I'm bound."

Jesus, on the cross, looked beyond his physical thirst to the completion of his mission. Let us, too, look beyond and keep our eyes fixed "yonder," knowing that only God can and will satisfy our deepest thirst, now and forever. Amen.

– Margaret Marcuson

April 8, 2007

Easter

Lessons

RCL	Acts 10:34-43	1 Cor 15:19-26	Jn 20:1-18
	or Isa 65:17-25	or Acts 10:34-43	or Lk 24:1-12
Roman Catholic	Acts 10:34a, 37-43	Col 3:1-4	Jn 20:1-9
		or 1 Cor 5:6b-8	
Episcopal (BCP)	Acts 10:34-43	Col 3:1-4	Lk 24:1-10
	or Isa 51:9-11	or Acts 10:34-43	

Introduction to the Lessons
Lesson 1
Acts 10:34-43 (RCL/Epis); Acts 10:34a, 37-43 (RC)
Peter's words here in Acts follow the conversion of the first Gentile. Peter not only bears witness to the resurrection, but also proclaims the opening of the gospel message beyond the Jewish people.

Lesson 2
(1) 1 Corinthians 15:19-26 (RCL)
Paul devotes a whole chapter to a closely-reasoned discussion of the resurrection. These verses are part of his ringing affirmation of the reality of God's victory over death.

(2) Colossians 3:1-4 (RC/Epis)
The resurrection is not just about Jesus, but also about us and how we are to live in the world as his followers.

Gospel
(1) John 20:1-18 (RCL); John 20:1-9 (RC)
The climax of the gospel, and of our faith, is Easter, Jesus' followers discovering the empty tomb and meeting Jesus. Mary Magdalene plays a key role in John's version of the story that never grows old.

(2) Luke 24:1-10 (Epis)

This Easter story, of course, follows the sorrowful burial of Jesus, with the women preparing spices to anoint his body. The first day of the week changes things forever.

Theme

Christ is risen this day!

Thought for the Day

Because Christ is risen, we carry resurrection hope in our hearts.

Call to Worship

One: Christ is risen!
All: Alleluia!
One: Because Christ lives, we live now and forever.
All: Alleluia! Christ is risen indeed!

Pastoral Prayer

God of new life, we come before you with hearts filled with gratitude and praise. We praise you for your power even over death. We thank you for the newness of spring that surrounds us, lifting our spirits. And above all we thank you for the new life in Jesus Christ, which we can experience today and every day.

We pray for our world, and the places where death seems to reign supreme. We pray that your power for life might be seen in big and small ways, and that hope might shine through. May the same be true in the hopeless places of our own hearts. Give us hope for new life and new beginnings as, indeed, we begin again each day with you. Show us how to live as Easter people, as disciples of Jesus Christ, sharing this good news with others. Amen.

Prayer of Confession

We come before you to confess how slow of heart we are to believe your promise of new life. We expect the worst of the world and of those around us. We are equally hard on ourselves. Forgive us. Help us to receive the grace and hope you offer, and to give these same gifts to those around us. In the name of Jesus Christ, we pray. Amen.

Prayer of Dedication of Gifts and Self

We thank you not only for the special gift of Easter, Holy God, but for the daily gift of life – the sun that rises each day, the food on the table at breakfast, the smile across the room. We offer to you in return our gifts, both of money and of ourselves. Use us, we pray, to give gifts to others in your name. Amen.

Sermon Summary

Easter hope can permeate all of our lives, even in the middle of the sorrow and struggle, that is part of all our lives at times. Easter hope gives us a solid foundation for living.

Hymn of the Day
"Christ Is Risen! Shout Hosanna!"

This is a rather recent hymn for the celebration of the Resurrection. The hymn was written in 1984 by Brian Wren, British-born American minister, hymn writer, and educator. In 1989 Wren suggested the tune W ZLOBIE LEZY (best known as the Polish carol "Infant Holy, Infant Lowly") be used with his text. That request has been honored in most hymnbooks. The tune HYMN TO JOY is used in some collections. It's interesting to compare the settings. The hymn provides modern day encouragement to "see what love can do and dare" and to claim the reality that "God the First and Last is with us."

Children's Time

The Easter Story

Bring in an Easter basket containing a stone, an empty plastic egg, a small white cloth, a small container of water, an eyedropper, and a garden trowel. Bring some brightly colored streamers. Wish the children a happy Easter and invite them to sit in a circle. Explain that today is Easter Sunday, the day we celebrate how God raised Jesus to new life. Show the basket and comment that many people give and receive special baskets on Easter day. Explain that the things inside the basket will help you tell the Easter story.

Pass each object around the circle as you retell part of the story: stone – John 20:1; empty egg – John 20:2-3; white cloth – John 20:4-10; water and eyedropper – John 20:11-13 (Mary's tears: use the eye dropper to drip a "tear" onto the children's hands); garden trowel – John 20:14-18 (Mary thought she was talking to the gardener).

Distribute the streamers, play some joyful music, and invite the children to join you in a celebration dance; Jesus is risen!

Pray with the children, giving thanks for the new life of Easter.

The Sermon

Living Easter

Hymns

Beginning of Worship: "Christ the Lord Is Risen Today"
Sermon Hymn: "Alleluia, Alleluia! Give Thanks"
Closing Hymn: "Thine Is the Glory"

Scripture

John 20:1-18 (For additional sermon materials on this passage, see the 2006 May/June planning issue of *The Clergy Journal;* for sermon materials on Acts 10:34-43, see the January 2007 issue of *The Clergy Journal.*)

Early on the first day of the week, Mary Magdalene comes to the tomb. Then she goes to tell two other disciples – Simon Peter and the "one Jesus loved"– who themselves come to the tomb. Mary, Peter, and the unnamed disciple are the ones closest to Jesus, but none of them yet understands the significance of what they are witnessing.

After Mary sees the angels in the tomb, she sees Jesus himself. She doesn't recognize him at first. Not until Jesus calls her by name does she know who he is. She thinks at first he has returned as he promised, and now he will stay with her and the others, resuming their former relationships. But Jesus says, "Do not hold on to me" (Jn 20:17). Instead, he commands Mary to go and prepare Jesus' disciples for that coming of Jesus when the Spirit will be given.

As they approach the tomb, the disciples – first Mary and then the other two – are in the darkness of fear and pain. They are grieving their crucified Lord, and they are afraid. Mary says, "They have taken the Lord out of the tomb, and we do not know where they have laid him" (20:2).

We, too, experience pain, grief, and death in this world. There is plenty of suffering. We can turn on the television to see it up close. Some of you sitting here have lost loved ones this very year – you know suffering. We all know pain in our lives; it is part of the human experience.

Yet the disciples saw something surprising, which broke into their suffering and pain. Mary Magdalene saw Jesus himself, the first apostolic witness of the resurrected Lord. She saw that Jesus had passed into a different reality; something new was taking place.

Suffering is real, whether it is caused by overt decision, cowardice, disease, or the power of nature. And death comes to us all. But God's power triumphs over the realities of human life and death. We don't stop with Good Friday; we live on to Easter Sunday.

This good news affects far more than our individual lives. The hope brought into the world by the resurrection touches our whole world, and the cosmos itself. God's power is the real power – power over evil and power for good.

So we can look at our lives, even at the struggle and pain of life, through Easter eyes. It's as if we were color blind before and now can see the glorious colors brought into the world. The colors of Easter eggs and Easter baskets, Easter clothes and flowers remind us not only of spring, but of the new life Christ brings us.

We can live our lives with a new perspective. We can build on a new foundation, even when the buffeting in this life begins anew. We will be "rooted and grounded in love," as the apostle Paul says.

When we live our lives founded solidly on the hope provided by this Easter story, we will be prepared for even the hurricanes of life. And they will come, as assuredly as hurricanes will continue to come to the Atlantic coast. Yet the storms of life cannot destroy us because God's power is stronger than they are.

So what did the disciples do? First, we see Mary; she went and told the disciples, "I have seen the Lord." In the same way, we, too, can share the hope we receive in Jesus Christ. We can proclaim to other people that "I have seen the Lord" – no matter what we see in the newspaper or on television, no matter what our very real concerns are about our nation, our world, our community, our jobs, and our families.

Polly Berrien Berends wrote a little poem entitled "A Secret," which says, "God means good." (Polly Berrien Berends, *Gently Lead,* The Crossroad Publishing Company, 1998, p. 18) "God means good" says to us that God's power triumphs over evil and death. It means that none of the realities of this life, which weigh so heavily upon us, will ultimately prevail. It's "a secret" because we can't touch it or grasp it. "Do not hold on to me," Jesus said to Mary. Proclaiming the resurrection does not mean we marshal scientific data to "prove" anything. This is a secret of faith. We can't see or taste or touch Jesus. We see him with our Easter eyes, with the eyes of faith, and faith can be every bit as concrete in its impact on our lives as things that can be measured or weighed or put in the bank! This secret is one that must be told, proclaimed, shouted, and celebrated as we do today, this Easter Sunday.

As we receive this hope, we must share it with others in a world that increasingly needs hope. Let's tell the secret as we make it real in our own lives. The Easter story isn't one that we set away on a shelf after giving it a yearly reading. The Easter story becomes our story, as we affirm the great gift God has given us in the new life Jesus received and offers to us. Through this story in our lives, in the face of the worst that life can offer, we can affirm God's goodness and power.

Let me call each one of you, whether you're here every week or once a year, to commit yourself to the one whose good news we proclaim – to Jesus Christ our resurrected Lord. Make this story yours, let it renew your lives, share the story as did Mary and Peter. "I have seen the Lord," said Mary. Today, in this place, so have we. Jesus Christ transforms our lives and our world, despite the sin and suffering, despite our own failures. This new life offers us the power of hope, in Jesus Christ.

– Margaret Marcuson

April 15, 2007

2nd Sunday of Easter

Lessons

RCL	Acts 5:27-32	Rev 1:4-8	Jn 20:19-31
Roman Catholic	Acts 5:12-16	Rev 1:9-11, 12-13, 17-19	Jn 20:19-31
Episcopal (BCP)	Acts 5:12a, 17-22, 25-29 or Job 42:1-6	Rev 1:(1-8), 9-19 or Acts 5:12a, 17-22, 25-29	Jn 20:19-31

Introduction to the Lessons
Lesson 1
Acts 5:27-32 (RCL); Acts 5:12-16 (RC);
Acts 5:12a, 17-22, 25-29 (Epis)

As the popularity of the gospel message grew, so did opposition. The disciples were imprisoned, and then freed by an angel. Then they were brought again before the high priest to account for their actions.

Lesson 2
Revelation 1:4-8 (RCL);
Revelation 1:9-11, 12-13, 17-19 (RC);
Revelation 1:(1-8), 9-19 (Epis)

These verses are words of greeting to the churches in Asia, the area that is now Turkey. The salutation sounds much like other New Testament letters, although the content of Revelation is very different.

Gospel
John 20:19-31 (RCL/RC/Epis)

This text follows right after Jesus' appearance to Mary Magdalene. Jesus appears to nearly all the disciples. These stories continue to confirm Jesus' resurrection.

Theme
Live the Easter story daily.

Thought for the Day

Easter life is not just for Jesus, but for all of us in our daily lives.

Call to Worship

One: This is the day the Lord has made
All: Let us rejoice and be glad in it!
One: Christ is risen!
All: He is risen indeed!
One: Our celebration of Easter life continues,
All: Let us worship and give praise to God.

– based on Psalm 118

Pastoral Prayer

God of life, we offer to you the worship of our hearts and minds. You are worthy of all our praise, for you alone are God, with the power of life. Thank you for offering us the hope of Easter not just on one Sunday, but today and every day of the year. Help us to claim and live that hope in the everyday challenges of our lives and the big issues that face our world. We lift up to you today the needs of those in our midst who need that hope in a special way, who are struggling with the death of a loved one or the death of a cherished dream or with one of the other many losses life can bring to us. Send a beam of hope into their hearts, that they might be awakened anew to your presence. Amen.

Prayer of Confession

We come before you, O God, confessing the ways we have failed to live as Easter people this week. You know our hearts; you know our good intentions and our struggles to live as faithful people. We try; sometimes we succeed and sometimes we fail. Help us to be as gentle with ourselves as you are, and may we realize the true depth of your gracious love. Amen.

Prayer of Dedication of Gifts and Self

We thank you, O God, for your many gifts – for the fellowship among us, for food, for clothing, for water to drink. We offer our gifts today to support your work in this place and in the world. Receive these gifts together with our hearts and our thanksgiving. Amen.

Sermon Summary

Living out our faith may mean taking risks as we follow Jesus faithfully.
But the resurrection power shown forth by Jesus means we are more able
to see clearly what we are called to do, and to have the courage to do it.

Hymn of the Day
"New Songs of Celebration Render"

Is there a better way to celebrate the season of Easter than to sing
"new songs" of celebration? Erik Routley, British-born American hymnist,
church music apologist, author, and teacher wrote this hymn in 1972. It
is a paraphrase of Psalm 98, with grand, modern dimension. It encourages
us to offer to "God who has great wonders done" the most celebrative
praise possible. Here's an opportunity to use all the musical forces at your
disposal in grand celebration of God this Easter season. Yes, even on "low
Sunday." Routley set the text to the 16th-century tune RENDEZ A DIEU.

Children's Time

Good News!

Bring a newspaper, a large sheet of newsprint, and a marker. Briefly look
at some of the news items in the newspaper. Mention that a newspaper
is a really good way to pass on news. Observe that news spreads in many
different ways. Invite the children to think of other ways news might
spread in our world.

Comment that in the Bible reading today, Peter and the other disciples are starting to take the good news of Easter out into the world.
Paraphrase their message (Acts 5:30-31). Explain that this message has
been passed from one person to another down through the ages until it
reached us. Invite the children to name some of the people who have told
them about Jesus. Print the names on the newsprint.

Comment that now it is our turn. What might we tell others about
Jesus? Encourage the children to move among the congregation sharing the
good news, "Jesus is risen!" As they do this, add the children's names to
the list on the newsprint.

Gather together and pray with the children, giving thanks for the people
on the list and all those who have passed on the good news of Easter.

The Sermon

Free to Serve God

Hymns
Beginning of Worship: "Crown Him with Many Crowns"
Sermon Hymn: "My Faith Looks up to Thee"
Closing Hymn: "I Know That My Redeemer Lives"

Scripture
Acts 5:27-32 (For additional sermon materials on this passage, see the January 2007 issue of *The Clergy Journal;* for sermon materials on John 20:19-31, see the 2006 May/June planning issue of *The Clergy Journal.*)

Easter continues! Even if the Easter candy is gone, we are still celebrating. Easter life is a year-round reality for Christians.

Our text for today tells about the preaching of the apostles, and the challenges they faced as a result. According to Acts, they met with wild success, as more and more people listened, believed, and experienced healing. The religious leaders in Jerusalem were not happy, to say the least, and arrested them. An angel of the Lord came in the night, opened the door of the prison cell, and told them to go preach in the temple.

So at daybreak the apostles entered the temple and kept on preaching – just like they were doing when they had been arrested. The high priest sent police to the prison to find them, but the temple police came back and said, "We found the prison securely locked and the guards standing at the doors, but when we opened them, we found no one inside" (Acts 5:23). At that confusing moment, someone arrived and said, "The men whom you put in prison are standing in the temple and teaching the people!" (5:25).

Once again the apostles ended up in front of the council. We can imagine what the high priest said to them! "What are you doing? We ordered you not to do this, and here you are blasting that message all over the airwaves!"

Peter replied, "We must obey God rather than any human authority" (5:29). He summed up the message they had been preaching: God raised

April 15, 2007
2nd Sunday of Easter

Jesus and exalted him so he might give repentance to Israel and forgiveness of sins. And we are witnesses to it.

The leaders were furious and would have killed the apostles, except for the words of Gamaliel (Paul's teacher). "Keep away from these men and let them alone; because if this plan or this undertaking is of human origin, it will fail; but if it is of God, you will not be able to overthrow them – in that case you may even be found fighting against God!" (5:38-39)

This story in Acts is clear; the disciples, who were cowering before Easter, were different after. The Gospel of Luke vividly tells Peter's denial of Jesus. But once Peter and the others knew the reality of the resurrection and received the Holy Spirit, they were emboldened. Their experience of God's power gave them a new clarity and ability to take a stand for what they believed. The stand they took changed history.

Other Christians have found themselves able to take the same stand. German pastor Martin Niemoller preached in 1937, "We have no more thought of using our own powers to escape the arm of the authorities than had the apostles of old. No more are we ready to keep silent at man's behest when God commands us to speak. For it is, and must remain, the case that we must obey God rather than man." He preached this sermon on June 27, 1937, and was arrested on July 1 and imprisoned for eight years. (William L. Shirer, *The Rise and Fall of the Third Reich*, Simon & Schuster, p. 239.)

What about us? In what ways do we claim Easter power for ourselves? And when do we find it necessary to obey God rather than human authority? We cannot claim the power if we do not know the story – know it deeply, inside and out. We must know it not only in our heads, but also in our spirits. Peter says, "We are witnesses to these things, and so is the Holy Spirit whom God has given to those who obey him" (5:32). As we live faithfully, the Spirit is present with us.

Hearing the Easter story once a year is not enough (and let me commend you for showing up the Sunday *after* Easter)! Hearing it once a week is not enough. I find I need to listen for God's voice every day, even if I can only sit down for a few minutes. I need to read at least one verse of scripture (or more, I hope). I need to breathe deeply and be aware of the presence of God's Spirit for at least five minutes (or more, I hope). I find these moments allow me to be more aware of God through the day. I feel more grounded, more able to make choices that are courageous rather than fearful, not only on the big issues of the day but also on how I relate to my husband, my children, and the people whom I serve and encounter.

Sometimes people talk about "seeing red" in a moment of anger. Perhaps we are called to "see gold" – to have moments of blinding clarity of what God wants us to do. As the passage in Acts describes him, Peter didn't have to agonize over whether to preach the gospel even when it had been forbidden. Peter knew what his calling was, and he stepped forward to do it.

As a young woman, I had a secretarial job. One of our firm's clients was trying to infiltrate a consumer group that was critical of their policies. I felt very uncomfortable about this, both because I felt like the consumer group was doing the right thing and because of the deception involved. So I told my boss I didn't want to work on that account. It was frightening because I did not know whether I might lose my job. Of course the risk was minimal: I was never in any real danger; I could always have gotten another job. And fortunately, my boss excused me from the project. And I grew through facing the challenge of my conscience and making a choice that I believed was right.

We can find ourselves faced with such challenges in small and large ways. The better grounded we are in our faith and the scriptures, and the better connected we are to our church community, the more prepared we will be to "obey God rather than human authority." Easter power is for all Christians who want the courage to face both the worst and the best that life can offer. Easter power is for all Christians who want to make a difference, for the sake of our risen Lord.

– Margaret Marcuson

April 22, 2007

3rd Sunday of Easter

Lessons

RCL	Acts 9:1-6, (7-20)	Rev 5:11-14	Jn 21:1-19
Roman Catholic	Acts 5:27-32, 40b-41	Rev 5:11-14	Jn 21:1-19
			or Jn 21:1-14
Episcopal (BCP)	Acts 9:1-19a	Rev 5:6-14	Jn 21:1-14
	or Jer 32:36-41	or Acts 9:1-19a	

Introduction to the Lessons
Lesson 1
(1) Acts 9:1-6, (7-20) (RCL); Acts 9:1-19a (Epis)
Armed with letters from the high priest to allow him to arrest followers of the Way, Saul of Tarsus is stricken blind on the road to Damascus – an unexpected interruption to his otherwise promising career.

(2) Acts 5:27-32, 40b-41 (RC)
Peter and the apostles, enjoined from teaching in the name of Jesus by the high priest, continue to obey God in proclaiming Jesus as leader and savior.

Lesson 2
Revelation 5:11-14 (RCL/RC); Revelation 5:6-14 (Epis)
In his vision of heaven, John hears the angels, living creatures, and elders praising the Lamb as worthy of opening the scroll with seven seals, whose content is of supreme importance.

Gospel
John 21:1-19 (RCL/RC); John 21:1-14 (Epis)
Jesus appears to the disciples a third time after his resurrection, revealing his identity in the miraculous catch of fish and calling Peter to show his love by tending Jesus' sheep.

Theme
Transformed to Discipleship by Waiting

Thought for the Day

They also serve who only stand and wait.

— John Milton, "On His Blindness"

Call to Worship

One: To you, O Lord, we cry for help.
All: From you, O Lord, come health and healing.
One: To you, O Lord, our praise ascends.
All: From you, O Lord, comes joy in the morning.
One: To you, O Lord, our souls give thanks.
All: To you, O Lord, we dance in joy.

— based on Psalm 30

Pastoral Prayer

Exaltation and worship, honor and glory, majesty and power are yours, All-Sovereign God. We, whom you have created, find our hearts lifted in praise of your other-ness. To that heavenly glory, we praise you for your Son Jesus, whom you sent among us so that our sin and death might be vanquished, and the debt for our transgressions repaid. Such mysteries of love, beyond our comprehension, compel us to praise nonetheless. As you were present in the abundance of the disciples' catch of fish after the resurrection, so be present with us in bounteous ways. Teach us to perceive and receive your blessings with open, grateful hearts. All these prayers we offer, in and through and under your Mercy, who is our risen Lord Jesus Christ. Amen.

Prayer of Confession

How quickly we put aside the resurrection of your Son, O God, and return to the mundane pursuits that pass for the work of discipleship. How little difference his obliterating the power of death makes, as we return to pursuits of cultural death in gluttony, greed, anger, laziness, and pride. How much we need to return to you is evident in the myriad ways we run away from you, unable to bear the brightness of the light of your truth. Forgive us, we pray, for our deliberate blindness. Open our eyes to behold you in all your glory, and open our hearts to be ready to bring your love to all and among all in need. In Christ's name we pray. Amen.

Prayer of Dedication of Gifts and Self

God of generosity and blessing, sometimes your gifts come to us in comprehensible form, like the beauty of nature, the spectacle of the heavens, the depths of the seas. Sometimes your gifts come in packages that we wish contained instructions, so that we might know how to use them. For all your gifts, we offer you our thanks and praise. Guide us to use what you provide to transform ourselves and our brothers and sisters into your faithful disciples, under your Mercy. Amen.

Sermon Summary

A powerful insight gained by the poet John Milton – understood through the lens of Saul's encounter with the risen Christ on the Damascus road – is that faith, of necessity, is sometimes active, but also involves waiting for God's transforming power.

Hymn of the Day
"Ye Servants of God, Your Master Proclaim"

As we continue in the season of Easter, this hymn gives us further opportunity to celebrate and honor the Son. This is another of Charles Wesley's well-known hymns. It first appeared in his *Hymns for Times of Trouble and Persecution* in 1744. Although written as encouragement to those facing religious persecution in the 18th century, we can certainly use the hymn as a means of praising "God's triumphs." The principal biblical references for this hymn are Psalm 145 and Revelation 7:9-12.

Children's Time

Completely Changed

Bring some pictures of butterflies and caterpillars and butterfly stickers. Show the pictures and invite the children to tell you what they know about caterpillars and butterflies. Briefly list the differences between caterpillars and butterflies. Observe that when the caterpillar turns into a butterfly, its life is completely changed. Comment that our Bible story today is about someone whose life was completely changed by Jesus' love.

Retell the story of Saul's encounter with Jesus on the road to Damascus. Briefly talk about the story: How do you think Saul's life changed? Explain that Saul's life changed so much that he decided to change his name as well. Saul became known as Paul. Soon Paul began to tell others about Jesus. He went to many places and started many churches.

Observe that Jesus' love really makes a difference in the world. Place a butterfly sticker on each child's hand as a reminder of the new life that Jesus brings.

Pray, giving thanks for difference Jesus' love makes in the world.

The Sermon

They Also Serve Who Stand and Wait

Hymns

Beginning of Worship: "Christ Jesus Lay in Death's Strong Bands"
Sermon Hymn: "He Is the Way [New Dance]"
Closing Hymn: "I Want to Be Ready"

Scripture

Acts 9:1-6, (7-20) (For additional sermon materials on this passage, see the January 2007 issue of *The Clergy Journal;* for sermon materials on John 21:1-19, see the 2006 May/June planning issue of *The Clergy Journal.*)

The assignment seemed innocuous enough. Each of the students in my tenth-grade English class had to choose an author from a pre-selected list of names, then find a sonnet written by that person. We had to memorize the sonnet for recitation and learn something about the author's life. When the list came to me, I signed my name beside that of John Milton. Although I did not know it yet, I had embarked on an intense journey of learning and discovery that in time would prove very exciting.

When I started the project, I must admit, I had little use for poetry. The more I learned about him, the more unlikely John Milton seemed as a poet – a kindred spirit! Milton grew up in a home made comfortable by his father's success as a scrivener, or law writer. He studied Latin and Italian, as well as English, and later became a foreign language secretary to Oliver Cromwell. Born in 1608, Milton traveled to Italy and France as a young man and met Galileo Galilei in Florence. The vistas open to him through wealth and political connections must have seemed truly boundless.

Milton's life was forever altered when in 1651, at the age of forty-three, he became blind. He who had written biting political commentary and religious polemics turned inward to poetry. From this later period came Milton's epic work, *Paradise Lost* (1667), as well as the sonnet I chose to memorize, "On His Blindness."

The sonnet is Milton's measured reflection on the psychology of becoming blind. He struggles to find meaning by asking what God expects of him. He learns that God dos not need human works; God's works proceed because they are *God's works*. The closing line of the sonnet is Milton's hopeful apothegm: "They also serve who only stand and wait."

John Milton could simply have given up, finding in his blindness the final break between a life of public purpose and a life of crushing disability. Instead, he owned his blindness and used it as a new way of seeing. In so doing, he became one of the greatest poets of all time.

The unanticipated consequence of my study was that John Milton became a sort of role model for me, for I, too, had struggled with impaired sight. He helped me to envision myself as transcending and exceeding my congenital visual abnormalities and leading a creative, useful, imaginative life. For this, I am forever grateful.

"They also serve who only stand and wait."

Today's lesson from Acts concerns an adult who, like John Milton, is stricken blind at the height of his powers: Saul of Tarsus. We first meet Saul in Acts 8:1, where he is present at the execution of Stephen, deacon and martyr. Two verses later, Saul is functioning as an army of one – chief of the thought police – who is "ravaging the church by entering house after house; dragging off both men and women" and committing them to prison (8:3). Saul is on the fast track to becoming Persecutor of the Year. That is, until he carries his crusade to Damascus.

Saul is not invincible, whatever his intended victims might believe. He is armed with warrants, signed by the high priest, empowering him to round up followers of Jesus' Way and extradite them to Jerusalem for trial. Suddenly, Saul is stopped – *blind* – his tracks. A bright light from heaven flashes around him. Saul hears a voice, identified as that of Jesus, asking, "Saul, Saul, why do you persecute me?" (9:4). Then, the voice tells him,

"Get up and enter the city, and you will be told what you are to do" (9:6). Saul's companions lead him to Damascus, where he languishes for three days – blind, not eating or drinking.

Try to imagine Saul's frame of mind as he waits, helpless, in Damascus. There is no Braille for reading in Hebrew. No public works projects have made Damascus accessible for the visually impaired. There are no guide dogs, no laser surgeries. Blind is *blind*. How can he possibly salvage his independence? How can he persecute people he can't even see?

As promised, however, a disciple living in Damascus comes to Saul's aid. The man, Ananias, is no fool and tries to avoid the assignment; Saul's notoriety has preceded him. Ananias is told by the Lord to go to Saul anyway, because the Lord has plans for Saul. Ananias is the first to hear that Saul "is an instrument" chosen by the Lord to bring the Lord's name "before Gentiles and kings and before the people of Israel" (9:15). Ananias does his part, restoring Saul's sight. His priorities completely reversed, Saul is baptized, and the rest, as they say, is history.

For that three-day period, Saul must learn patience with his new disability. He must prepare for his blindness to be permanent. When his sight is restored, Saul completes the transformation from persecutor to proclaimer. Saul's encounter with Jesus on the Damascus road becomes a credential for his apostleship, as the only person outside the circle of the Twelve to witness a post-resurrection appearance of Jesus.

"They also serve who only stand and wait."

What of us, living so far removed from Jesus' risen form? What of us, who have such difficulty acknowledging the faith we profess? Do we even recognize our many forms of blindness? Perhaps, in our perceived ignorance and failure, we are actually performing some service for our Lord. Perhaps, in patient waiting, we render glory to God. Perhaps waiting is a form of discipleship, too.

"They also serve who only stand and wait."

Thank you, John Milton, for waiting through blinded eyes for your great vision of the cost and consequence of faith. Thank you, Saul of Tarsus, for doing as you were told, remaining and waiting to see what the Lord had in mind. Thank you both for the gift of transformation that catches us up short and helps each of us, in our own small way, to be Christ's witnesses.

This is our faith, under the Mercy.

– Nancy E. Topolewski

April 29, 2007

4th Sunday of Easter

Lessons

RCL	Acts 9:36-43	Rev 7:9-17	Jn 10:22-30
Roman Catholic	Acts 13:14, 43-52	Rev 7:9, 14b-17	Jn 10:27-30
Episcopal (BCP)	Acts 13:15-16, 26-33, (34-39) or Num 27:12-23	Rev 7:9-17 or Acts 13:15-16, 26-33, (34-39)	Jn 10:22-30

Introduction to the Lessons
Lesson 1
(1) Acts 9:36-43 (RCL)
Peter takes a mission to Joppa, where he heals Dorcas (also called Tabitha), a faithful disciple.

(2) Acts 13:14, 43-52 (RC); Acts 13:15-16, 26-33, (34-39) (Epis)
Paul and Barnabas travel to Antioch in Pisidia, where they convert many Gentiles by preaching faith in Jesus' life, death, and resurrection – the *kerygma* of the earliest Christians.

Lesson 2
Revelation 7:9-17 (RCL/Epis); Revelation 7:9, 14b-17 (RC)
John hears the praises offered to God by the multitude who have endured persecution, and have washed their robes in the blood of the Lamb.

Gospel
John 10:22-30 (RCL/Epis); John 10:27-30 (RC)
After refusing to answer directly the hostile questions of his adversaries about being the Messiah, Jesus testifies that he and the Father are one.

Theme
Transformed to Discipleship by Example

Thought for the Day

God does not lead all his servants by one road, nor in one way, nor at one time; for God is in all things..."

– Tauler, *Sermons*, quoted in Charles Williams (editor),
The New Christian Year, Oxford University Press, 1941, p. 52.

Call to Worship

One: Let all the earth praise God with joy.

All: We come to worship God in praise and thanksgiving.

One: Let all the earth praise God with joy.

All: We come as God's people, the sheep of God's pasture.

One: Let all the earth praise God with joy.

All: We come, blessing God's name, and celebrating God's goodness, love, and faithfulness.

– based on Psalm 100

Pastoral Prayer

God of Good Friday, God of Easter, God of all that was, and is, and will yet be: We know that you hold our lives in your hands – from conception to death and beyond. We yearn for the day when we will join the multitudes in heaven, giving honor and praise to you for your great, glorious love. Our grateful thanksgiving belongs with those who have gone before us, whose faithfulness was not easy, safe, or assured. Hold their fidelity before us as an example of the high calling to which we aspire as followers of your Son Jesus Christ. Help us to know that in life and in death, we are yours. We offer you these our prayers, in and through and under your Mercy, who is our risen Lord Jesus Christ. Amen.

Prayer of Confession

Your graciousness, your goodness, your loving care are around us and ever before us, O God. We know that your presence among human beings in the person of your Son is offered to heal the wounds of human sin and draw us closer to you. We speak as if we understand your nearness, but in reality, we would rather be alone with more attractive masters, who tell us it is all right to focus on personal advancement and acquisition. We shrink when you call us to account. Yet, speak those hard words that will renew our sense of purpose. Help us to return to you as those transformed, that we may once again do the work of disciples for which you have called us; through the merits and mediation of your Son, Jesus Christ our Lord. Amen.

Prayer of Dedication of Gifts and Self

We give thanks to you, God of all bounty, for the gifts with which you sustain and nourish us. In response to your extravagant generosity, we offer you our time, our abilities, our abundance, and our commitment, that what you have begun in us may be brought to fruition in your time. Help us to live as people transformed into your faithful disciples, under your Mercy. Amen.

Sermon Summary

Persons do not come to Christian discipleship fully formed, or by some instantaneous process, but rather are nurtured into the transformation of discipleship by others who offer their lives as examples.

Hymn of the Day
"Crown Him with Many Crowns"

English poet Matthew Bridges is remembered primarily through this hymn that he first published in 1851 in his *Hymns of the Heart*. The hymn is an imaginative search for what the "many crowns" of Revelation 19:12 may signify. The Rev. Godfrey Thring, Anglican priest, did some editing of the original text, resulting in the hymn that appears in most hymnbooks today. The buoyant tune DIADEMATA was written for Bridges' text in 1868 by British composer George J. Elvey. This hymn provides an opportunity for festive celebration of the resurrected "King of kings and Lord of lords!"

Children's Time

Acts of Kindness

Bring a piece of clothing that has been made by hand, a tray, some tea light candles, and matches or a lighter. Show the article of clothing and admire the workmanship. Comment that it takes a great deal of time to make something by hand. Invite the children to talk about clothes or special gifts that have been sewn or knitted for them. Comment that a lot of love is stitched into a handmade gift. Mention that the Bible story today is about a follower of Jesus who showed God's love by making clothes for others. Tell the story of Tabitha.

Observe that Tabitha showed God's love by showing kindness to others. As followers of Jesus we are called to do the same. How might we show kindness to others this week? Light a tea light candle for each idea mentioned and place it on the tray. Notice how brightly the candles are shining. Explain that when someone shows kindness, the light of God's love shines through them and lights up the world. Comment that the light of God's love will shine very brightly in *(name your community)* this week.

Pray, asking God to help you remember to show kindness this week.

The Sermon

Transformation: Discipleship by Example

Hymns

Beginning of Worship: "Come, Ye Faithful, Raise the Strain"
Sermon Hymn: "O For a Heart to Praise My God"
Closing Hymn: "Whom Shall I Send?"

Scripture

Acts 9:36-43 (For additional sermon materials on this passage, see the January 2007 issue of *The Clergy Journal;* for sermon materials on John 10:22-30, see the 2006 May/June planning issue of *The Clergy Journal.*)

During the winter of 1981, our family underwent one of the periodic reshapings that seem to be so much a part of our culture. Our oldest daughter, Cris, had given birth at the end of January to a little girl, named Erin – our first grandchild. Shortly thereafter, Erin's father, Ray, lost his job. So Cris, Ray, and baby Erin came to live with my husband Jack and me, in the parsonage provided by Jack's employing church. This arrangement continued until Erin was almost three years old. To all intents and purposes, Erin was as much our responsibility as she was her parents'.

Cris was just shy of twenty years old when Erin was born. I – her father's second wife – was twenty-seven. Neither Cris nor I had ever been parent to an infant. If the parental role had come to me fully formed when Jack and I married, the role of grandparent moved in with Erin. A whole new set of responsibilities and expectations had to be negotiated. Sometimes things went smoothly. Other times, tensions in the parsonage seemed ready to explode. All of us needed help – badly, immediately.

Into this void of inexperience came someone I am certain to this day was a gift of God, sent to us. Her name was Beatrice Hawk. As Erin learned to talk, Beatrice became "Mommy Hawk." All Erin had to do was lift her little arms over her head, and Mommy Hawk would pick her up and cuddle her. From the beginning, the bond between them was tight and close.

Mommy Hawk had been trained as a nurse. Her husband Kenneth – not surprisingly, called "Daddy Hawk" by Erin – had been supervising principal in the school district. The Hawks had one adult daughter, who was in Africa on a Fulbright Scholarship as she collected research data for her doctoral dissertation in anthropology. Their daughter's absence left Mommy Hawk (and, to some extent, Daddy Hawk) looking for ways to help other folks. Our needs intersected with theirs, and a deep friendship was formed.

We spent many a late night, playing board games at Hawks' dining room table, just being together. We spent hours and hours talking through issues related to three generations trying to live under one roof. Sometimes we just sat in the peace and quiet of Hawks' living room.

Erin never questioned why; she knew that Mommy Hawk was special, and was part of her network of protection and love. Mommy Hawk made banana bread to die for. I once overheard Erin describe the bread as a "warm hug from Mommy Hawk." To Erin in those early years, Mommy Hawk was one of the people she needed to remember with a "God bless" prayer each night at bedtime.

Time passed. Cris, Ray, and Erin moved into their own apartment. We moved to a new parish. As our paths took us gradually farther from one another, our connections remained nonetheless very strong. Then, in March of 1987, Mommy Hawk died very suddenly. The loss hurt us all.

All of us who had known and loved Beatrice Hawk gathered in the sanctuary of our former church to pay tribute to a most remarkable person. Her friends spoke of her gentle kindness, her generosity, her listening ear, her Christ-likeness. The church's pastor spoke of "Mother" Hawk, using an honorific for the remarkable women of early Methodism. To Erin, to this very day, Beatrice remains Mommy Hawk: a person fondly remembered for loving care, a surrogate grandmother, a gift of God.

Today's lesson from Acts tells the story of Tabitha, also called Dorcas, one of the most important disciples in the port city of Joppa. Her good works and acts of charity touched many lives, particularly among women. When Peter arrives in Joppa, he hears that this magnificent woman has died. Her friends, bereft, show Peter items of clothing Tabitha has made for them. Peter is moved by their devotion. He sends the mourners out of the room where Tabitha's body lies, ready for burial. Then he prays for her. "Tabitha, get up," he says. She awakens. Peter calls her friends to come and see her. The news of the healing spreads throughout Joppa, leading many to believe in the Lord Jesus.

The author of Acts is anxious for us to know that Tabitha's healing precedes a more significant event, the conversion of Cornelius in chapter 10. At the same time, however, the author notes Peter's compassion – a compassion that brings the healing power of Christ not only to Tabitha, but also to all those who know and love her.

The point of the story, beyond its message of Peter's healing Tabitha, seems to me to be that no matter who we are, we do not come to discipleship fully formed. We cannot take a pill and expect to wake up in the morning as mature followers of Jesus Christ. We cannot apply some potion to our bodies and anticipate that by repeating the application once or twice, we will be disciples. The transformation of discipleship is a gradual process of growth and change, whose gifts are taught by example. In a long line of relationships that extends from Jesus to those who became his followers during his lifetime to those they converted – on and on for generations – discipleship is a slow, painstaking, individual process.

The risen Lord continues to call to us in the voices of people who, like Tabitha and Mommy Hawk, have heard the risen Lord calling to them in someone else's voice. As we give thanks for these special people, we recognize that because of them, many have believed in the Lord. This blessing is limitless, magnificent to behold.

Are we ready to believe, and to join the hosts of those transformed, by example, into disciples? Are we? Are we?

This is our faith, under the Mercy.

– Nancy E. Topolewski

May 6, 2007

5th Sunday of Easter

Lessons

RCL	Acts 11:1-18	Rev 21:1-6	Jn 13:31-35
Roman Catholic	Acts 14:21-27	Rev 21:1-5a	Jn 13:31-33a, 34-35
Episcopal (BCP)	Acts 13:44-52 or Lev 19:1-2, 9-18	Rev 19:1, 4-9 or Acts 13:44-52	Jn 13:31-35

Introduction to the Lessons

Lesson 1

(1) Acts 11:1-18 (RCL)

When questioned about his consorting with Gentiles, Peter reports his vision of clean and unclean foods as a call to welcome Gentiles among the faithful.

(2) Acts 14:21-27 (RC)

Paul and Barnabas return to Antioch in Syria, meeting with many disciples along the way and praying for God to strengthen them in times of persecution.

(3) Acts 13:44-52 (Epis)

At Antioch in Pisidia, Paul and Barnabas testify publicly to the need for taking the salvation message to the Gentiles, and find themselves the objects of persecution by the Jews as a result.

Lesson 2

(1) Revelation 21:1-6 (RCL); Revelation 21:1-5a (RC)

John reports his vision of the new heaven and new earth, in which God dwells with mortals and makes all things new.

(2) Revelation 19:1, 4-9 (Epis)

John hears the praises of God sung by those who have come to celebrate the marriage supper of the Lamb, in one of the great paeans of the book of Revelation.

Gospel
John 13:31-35 (RCL/Epis); John 13:31-33a, 34-35 (RC)
After demonstrating how the disciples are to serve one another in washing each other's feet, Jesus calls them to love one another, thereby marking themselves as his followers.

Theme
Transformed to Discipleship by Love

Thought for the Day
Christian Love, either towards God or towards man [*sic*], is an affair of the will.

> – C. S. Lewis, *Mere Christianity,*
> The Macmillan Company,
> 1952, Book III, Chapter 9, p. 102.

Call to Worship
One:	Let us bless the Lord.
All:	Let us praise God's name forever and ever.
One:	The Lord does wondrous and awesome deeds.
All:	Let us praise God's name forever and ever.
One:	The Lord is faithful in words and gracious in deeds.
All:	Let us praise God's name forever and ever.
One:	The Lord is near to all who call upon God in truth.
All:	Let us praise God's name forever and ever.

> – based on Psalm 145

Pastoral Prayer
Surprising, resurrecting God, even now, we walk past your Son's burial place, hoping to peek inside, to reassure ourselves that he has, indeed, been raised from death. We have our moments of incredulous disbelief. But the proclamation of the church is ours as well – Christ is risen, indeed. That same risen Lord bids us who have witnessed his vindication to go into the world as his disciples, loving others as he loved us. For this inestimable blessing, we give you thanks and praise.

Because the tomb is vacant, we can yearn for your heavenly city, but we also long for an end to suffering here on earth, for needs spoken and silent. *(pause)* All these prayers we offer in, through, and under your Mercy, who is our risen Lord Jesus Christ. Amen.

Prayer of Confession

When your Son washed the feet of his disciples, O God, he set an example of love and service to others for us to follow. Peter and Paul and countless others have sought to be faithful to this high calling of love. It all looks so easy. Yet, when we are among those different from ourselves, and even among our own family and friends, we find ourselves holding back, as if loving others is someone else's job. Forgive our narrow and reluctant love, we pray. Open our hearts to one another, that we may become ever more faithful to your call to be loving disciples of Christ our Lord, in whose name we pray. Amen.

Prayer of Dedication of Gifts and Self

On the night before he suffered for us, O God, your Son offered his disciples the gift of love by washing their feet and instructing them to love one another. We who have received so bountifully of your gifts now offer them, and ourselves, back to you in love, that the work of faithful discipleship may continue in the world, under your Mercy. Amen.

Sermon Summary

One of Jesus' last instructions is that his disciples love one another – love shown in many human situations, love with the power to transform ordinariness to faithfulness.

Hymn of the Day
"The Gift of Love"

Appearing originally as a choral anthem, the text was written by American church musician and composer Hal Hopson in 1972. The hymn appears in some hymnal indices under its first line "Though I May Speak." The text, of course, is Hopson's paraphrase of 1 Corinthians 13:1-3. Hopson also made an adaptation of the traditional English melody O Waly Waly for the musical setting of the text. It was first set in its hymn form in 1984. At least one major hymnbook has chosen not to use Hopson's 2/2 meter in favor of the melody's original 3/4 meter, which allows the text to flow nicely in its hymn format.

Children's Time

Job Description

Bring an example of a job description, a sheet of newsprint, and a marker. Explain that most people who work have some kind of a job description. A job description lists all the things a person is expected to do at work. Read the example you have brought. Comment that a job description can be a very helpful thing to have. It helps a worker do her or his job well.

Comment that as followers of Jesus, we also have a job description. Ask the children if they can guess what might be on that description. What kinds of things do the followers of Jesus do? Explain that our job description was given to us by Jesus and can be found in the Bible. Paraphrase John 13:31-35.

Ask the children to list some of the ways they might show love to others. Print these on the newsprint in the form of a job description. When you have finished, read the list aloud and comment that it is easier to be a follower of Jesus when we know what our job is.

Pray with the children, asking that God would help you show love to others.

The Sermon

Transformation: Discipleship through Love

Hymns
Beginning of Worship: "Love Divine, All Loves Excelling"
Sermon Hymn: "Come Down, O Love Divine"
Closing Hymn: "Blest Be the Tie That Binds"

Scripture
John 13:31-35 (For additional sermon materials on this passage, see the 2006 May/June planning issue of *The Clergy Journal;* for sermon materials on Acts 11:1-18, see the February 2007 issue of *The Clergy Journal.*)

On a bitterly cold February morning, my husband and I were awakened just after dawn by a ringing telephone. Our friend and veterinarian, Dr. Jane, was on the line. The call was not unexpected, but it still came as a surprise, a shock. Dr. Jane told us that our ten-year-old miniature dachshund, Nadia Boulanger, had died during the night. Dr. Jane had performed surgery on Nadia three days earlier, in the hope that removing the stones that clogged her bladder would allow her a few more months with us. We went into the surgery with our eyes open. Dr. Jane thought it was worth a try. We trusted in both her judgment and her skill, for she had always dealt gently with us and with a succession of our dachshunds.

Dr. Jane was crying when she called us. "We did our best," she said, "but our best wasn't good enough this time."

If you have ever lost a beloved pet, you know the kind of anguished emptiness the end brings. We spent much of that bitterly cold February day looking for Nadia in the places she used to sleep, expecting to hear her throaty "woof" if a bird violated her air space, waiting for her to come to the kitchen table for a treat. But she wasn't there. Not in any of those places. Not any more.

That evening, we drove to Dr. Jane's office to bring Nadia home. The process of decay had already bloated her small frame. The Nadia we had known wasn't there any more. We touched her fur, stroking ever so gently. Jack took off her collar. We wrapped her for burial.

Dachshunds as a breed are scrappy little diggers, who worm and squirm and wriggle themselves into small spaces. They also like to nest, to root around in blankets and other soft things, and then snuggle down for a nap. True to her breed, Nadia had succeeded in worming and squirming and wriggling herself into empty places in our hearts, then nested there. With her death, those places were empty again.

Why do we love them so, these funny little creatures, when we know they're going to die? Why do we voluntarily subject ourselves to the anguish of losing them? After all, they're only animals – right?

Why do we love one another so, when we know we're going to die? More to the point, why does God love us so, when a consequence of the disobedience of our first ancestors is that every last one of us will die?

Part of the answer to these questions may be found in our gospel lesson for today: "I give you a new commandment, that you love one another. Just as I have loved you, you also should love one another. By this everyone will know that you are my disciples, if you have love for one another" (Jn 13:34-35).

Coming as they do in the midst of John's report of Jesus' last hours with his disciples, these instructions carry special weight for thoughtful readers. Not quite "deathbed instructions," they nonetheless are a marker, a signpost, pointing toward where Jesus wants his followers to go. He has shown them the transforming power of love by washing their feet. Now, Jesus' words spur them on: Go and do likewise. Love one another as I have loved you.

Part of the answer, too, lies beyond the text, in the nature of Love itself, as shown throughout the scriptural witness: Love that created us in God's image; Love that offered the first human being the chance to name the animals; Love that brought God's only Son to earth, to live and die as one of us; Love that raised God's Son from death and promises to raise us, as well.

Painful as love can be, especially when it ends in death, is not love a gift, wherever and whenever we find it?

The season of Easter shows us that Love's redeeming work is done – Love shown to us in Christ, Love that triumphs over death. This Love is not cheap, but comes at a cost: the cost of spending forty days in the wilderness, being tempted by Satan; the cost of setting his face to go to Jerusalem, waiting to be killed; the cost of losing this life, in order to find new life, resurrection life.

Sometimes the best love of all is given to us by small, insignificant, but treasured creatures, who reflect the love of God in our lives. Sometimes the best love of all is what we offer them in return.

Sometimes the best love of all is the love that connects us with one another – love that, whether given or received, transforms us, makes us into different people.

Sometimes the best Love of all must die, in order for us to live.

Two months after Nadia's death, we brought home an investment in love: a thirteen-ounce, squirming ball of downy-soft fur and needle-sharp teeth – an eight-week-old miniature dachshund, whom we named Dorothy L. Sayers. Yes, we know she is going to die someday. But in the meantime, she has joined our family, worming and squirming and wriggling herself into empty places in our hearts and nesting there. We love her with all our hearts.

This is our faith, under the Mercy.

– Nancy E. Topolewski

May 13, 2007

6th Sunday of Easter

Lessons

RCL	Acts 16:9-15	Rev 21:10, 22—22:5	Jn 14:23-29 or Jn 5:1-9
Roman Catholic	Acts 15:1-2, 22-29	Rev 21:10-14, 22-23	Jn 14:23-29
Episcopal (BCP)	Acts 14:8-18 or Joel 2:21-27	Rev 21:22—22:5 or Acts 14:8-18	Jn 14:23-29

Introduction to the Lessons

Lesson 1

(1) Acts 16:9-15 (RCL)
Called to Macedonia by a vision, Paul and Silas take their mission to the Gentiles of Philippi.

(2) Acts 15:1-2, 22-29 (RC)
In contrast to the insistence of some in the Jerusalem church on the necessity of converts becoming Jews before embracing Christ, Paul and Silas report the fruits of their mission to the Gentiles.

(3) Acts 14:8-18 (Epis)
A case of mistaken identity: after healing a crippled man, Paul and Barnabas are hailed as gods in Lystra.

Lesson 2

Revelation 21:10, 22—22:5 (RCL);
Revelation 21:10-14, 22-23 (RC);
Revelation 21:22—22:5 (Epis)
In a vision surely delectable to his exile on the water-poor island of Patmos, John sees the new Jerusalem basking in the glory of God and watered by the River of Life.

Gospel
John 14:23-29 (RCL/RC/Epis)
Jesus reminds his disciples one last time before he suffers: Live in love and draw strength and peace from his last gift to them, the Holy Spirit.

Theme
Transformed to Discipleship by the Spirit

Thought for the Day
"The whole offer which Christianity makes is . . . we can, if we let God have His Way, come to share in the life of Christ."

– C. S. Lewis, *Mere Christianity*,
The Macmillan Company,
1952, Book IV, Chapter 4, p. 137.

Call to Worship
One: Let us worship God, who is gracious and blesses us.
All: Let us worship God, who calls all nations to praise.
One: Let us worship God, who judges the peoples with equity.
All: Let us worship God, who guides all the nations of the earth.
One: Let the peoples praise you, O God.
All: Let all the peoples praise you.

– based on Psalm 67

Pastoral Prayer
How we long, O God, for the day when we will see your Son Jesus face to face, when we will hear his voice speaking our names. Until that day, you have sent the Holy Spirit to be your constant sustaining presence with us. For this inestimable gift, we lift our hearts in grateful thanksgiving.

How we long, O God, for the peace the world cannot give, for untroubled hearts, for calm that displaces fear. Through your Holy Spirit, be the One bearing peace to those in distress. Be the One bringing quiet to all who suffer. Be the One who enfolds us in your love and bids us not be afraid. Be the One who stands with your church in this suffering world. Be the One who hears our silent, needful petitions. *(pause)* All our prayers we offer in, through, and under your Mercy, who is our risen Lord Jesus Christ. Amen.

Prayer of Confession

Your Word comes clearly to us, O God, in words recorded in Holy Scripture. Through your Word-Made-Flesh, you bid us not to be anxious or afraid, to trust that Christ's comfort and peace will be his remaining, maintaining gifts to us. But in our ignorance and pride, we look to other sources of comfort and peace. So often we keep your saving words to ourselves, and hoard the overflowing bounty of your love as our exclusive property. We seek to control our own futures, when you call us instead to keep your words. Forgive us the arrogance of self-absorption. Free us to trust in your sustaining Spirit, even as you provide for all of your children, through all time. Restore us. Transform us to be faithful, loving disciples of the risen Christ; for it is in his name we pray. Amen.

Prayer of Dedication of Gifts and Self

Gracious and loving God, we rejoice in the promise of your Holy Spirit as both gift and blessing. In grateful response to all your gifts and blessings to us and to your church, we offer you our thanks and praise. Help us to use with joy and imagination your many mercies, that we may be constantly transforming into faithful disciples of our risen Lord Jesus Christ, in whose name we pray. Amen.

Sermon Summary

In the church, as well as in horticulture, if you're planting for yourself, plant plums; if you're planting for your children, plant pecans – that is, seek out the transforming power of the Spirit over the long term.

Hymn of the Day
"Guide Me, O Thou Great Jehovah"

The author of this hymn, William Williams, was never formally ordained. However, he reportedly traveled nearly 100,000 miles over the course of 43 years, preaching the gospel in his homeland of Wales. He wrote many hymns and used them as an educational and cultural force in his ministry. Few of his hymns have been translated into English. Originally written in Welsh by Williams in 1745, this hymn was translated into English during 1771 and 1772. Williams successfully transformed the biblical story of the Israelites' march into a hymn that can still sustain the modern Christian's spiritual march.

Children's Time

Peace Be With You

Bring a large paper heart for each child. Invite the children to share stories of times they were alone and afraid. Mention that in the Bible story today Jesus' followers were feeling alone and scared. They knew Jesus would not be with them for much longer. Jesus promises the disciples that they will be given a special kind of peace to help them through the difficult times. Paraphrase John 14:27.

Ask the children if they have heard the words, "Peace be with you." Mention that the early followers of Jesus used this greeting, and we still use it in our churches today. (If you have the tradition of "passing the peace" during worship, talk about it.)

Explain that greeting someone with the words "Peace be with you," is a way of passing along Jesus' love and peace. Distribute paper hearts and invite the children to pass a heart to someone in the congregation, saying, "Peace be with you." Encourage those who receive a heart to pass it on to the next person. Watch Jesus' love and peace travel around the church.

Pray, giving thanks for the gift of Jesus' peace.

The Sermon

Transformation: Discipleship by Plums or Pecans?

Hymns
Beginning of Worship: "Ask Ye What Great Thing I Know"
Sermon Hymn: "Christ Is the World's Light"
Closing Hymn: "Holy Spirit, Truth Divine"

Scripture
John 14:23-29 (For additional sermon materials on this passage, see the 2006 May/June planning issue of *The Clergy Journal;* for sermon materials on Acts 16:9-15, see the February 2007 issue of *The Clergy Journal.*)

Sometimes, to our immense surprise, actions taken by governments can offer entirely unintended interpretive possibilities. One such instance is the Homestead Act of 1862 and the lens it provides for viewing factors of growth and change within the church.

The Homestead Act was one of the most important pieces of legislation of the 19th century. It beckoned many hardy individuals to settle in the vast expanses of the great prairie of the American Midwest, promising the possibility of land ownership. If they could prove they were over 21 and were head of household, these pioneers could claim 160 acres from the United States government. Over a five-year period, the homesteaders were expected to build a house, make improvements, and farm the land of their tract. At the end of the five years, if they could prove they had met all the government criteria, the homesteaders paid a filing fee of $18 and were able to claim the land, free and clear. In this way, immigrants from overseas, former slaves, and many who otherwise would never have owned land, were able to establish homes and farms.

The psychology of homesteading is very interesting. For the first 20 years or so, homesteaders were focused on the need to make the land arable and wrest it from the seemingly endless stands of tall, waving prairie grass. Only when those essential tasks were completed did the settlers begin to think about how they might beautify and further domesticate the prairie by planting trees.

Native trees were few and far between on the prairie. Because of the expense involved, homesteaders had to choose their trees very carefully. For many, the choice came down to plums versus pecans.

Those who chose to plant plum trees achieved a relatively quick return on their investment. Because they grow fairly quickly, plum trees soon bring a shield against the weather. Homesteaders could expect to harvest plums after a few short years. The drawback is that plum trees run to brush and bramble as they get older and must eventually be cut down, burned, and replaced.

Those who chose to plant pecan trees did not receive immediate gratification. Because pecan trees grow and mature slowly, they could not be expected to provide either shelter or fruit until long after the plum trees did. The advantage of pecan trees is that they endure, providing benefits and beauty for many years to come.

When questioned about the choice between plums and pecans, one homesteader (whose response I remember reading in a United States history text in junior high) observed, "If you're planting for yourself, plant plums. If you're planting for your children, plant pecans."

One of the most difficult tasks we face, as thoughtful Christian disciples, is finding some balance between new insight and ancient truth – between what is relevant now and what was honored in the past. The choice is, in short, between plums and pecans.

When I was in seminary in the mid-1970s, theology's razor edge cut into what many would now describe as the "entitlements of dead white males." Liberation theologies – of the poor, of various racial groups, of one gender from another's political and economic domination – were the result. Such theological variants then superseded the doctrinal matters historically in the purview of Western theology, as political action replaced conciliar rumination. Now, 30 years later, it is fair to ask, What has happened to these new theologies and the individuals so passionately committed to them? What did the church catholic gain or lose, and how have the insights of liberation theologies changed the worldview of thoughtful Christians?

The 1970s also saw change in the role of language in the church. Gender-specific references to God, archaic pronouns, and grammatical constructions collided with a growing desire for inclusiveness, awakened by the liberation theologies. Language needed to reflect social change. Looking back now at all the fuss and fury, it is interesting to note that in many cases, the rich tapestry of church life has been further embroidered by new threads of language usage – a benefit that allows the church to move on in its constant self-reforming.

How do thoughtful Christians decide what is necessary for belief? Where, to cite just one example, do we place concerns about the use of electronic media in the contemporary church? How do we decide between plums and pecans?

"I have said these things to you while I am still with you. But the Advocate, the Holy Spirit, whom the Father will send in my name, will teach you everything, and remind you of all that I have said to you" (Jn 14:25-26).

As we seek some understanding of our present interpretive dilemma, the gospel lesson for today offers help: It is God's Holy Spirit, God's Advocate, who provides the bridge between what is taught in the present and remembered from the past. It is the work of God, in and through the Holy Spirit, which keeps us alive in and for the present, as well as sensitive to the past. It is the Spirit of God that brings us all to realize that when we set aside the encumbrances of culture, ideology, and class, we can begin to see the continuity and the connections over time – the linkages between

336

yesterday, today, and tomorrow. God's Holy Spirit enables us to hold it all together – with tension, certainly, but with *creative* tension.

I really like plum trees, and in terms of our life together in faith, I would not discourage planting a few. But for the sake of the church's mission and ministry, its ongoing programs, as well as our personal faith and its development and growth, I look back to the sage advice of the old homesteader:

"If you're planting for yourself, then plant plums. If you're planting for your children, plant pecans."

This is our faith, under the Mercy.

– Nancy E. Topolewski

May 17, 2007

Ascension Day

Lessons

RCL	Acts 1:1-11	Eph 1:15-23	Lk 24:44-53
Roman Catholic	Acts 1:1-11	Heb 9:24-28; 10:19-23	Lk 24:46-53
Episcopal (BCP)	Acts 1:1-11 or 2 Kings 2:1-15	Eph 1:15-23 or Acts 1:1-11	Lk 24:49-53 or Mk 16:9-15, 19-20

Introduction to the Lessons
Lesson 1
Acts 1:1-11 (RCL/RC/Epis)
The evangelist Luke transitions the story of faith from being Jesus-centered to one of the mission of the early church. At his ascension, Jesus gives a commission to his followers to spread the good news.

Lesson 2
(1) Ephesians 1:15-23 (RCL/Epis)
As Paul opens his letter to the Ephesians, he invokes the name of Jesus as the risen and ascended one, whose power rules above anything else.

(2) Hebrews 9:24-28; 10:19-23 (RC)
We are called to faith in Christ and his once-and-for-all sacrifice that bore our sins. With this, the writer calls us to persevere in hope.

Gospel
Luke 24:44-53 (RCL); Luke 24:46-53 (RC);
Luke 24:49-53 (Epis)
Jesus' ascension is not an end-all event; Christ promises to come even as his followers are reminded of all they have already witnessed.

Theme
We are empowered as witnesses to Christ's glory.

Thought for the Day

Physical absence does not mean the power, inspiration, and wisdom of a person is gone. With Christ, we have the promise of more.

Call to Worship

One:	Clap your hands, O people; shout to God with loud voices.
All:	Why should we cause such noise?
One:	Sing to God, Lord of the Most High, ruler of all.
All:	Why should we sing to the Lord?
One:	It is our God who chooses us, shielding us from everything.
All:	Ah, we can clap; we can shout; we can sing. For the Lord is good indeed!
One:	Give praise to our God, sing praises.
All:	We bring our hands together; we raise our voices; we sing, we sing, we sing.

– based on Psalm 47

Pastoral Prayer

We give thanks, God almighty, for the life, teachings, sacrifice, and resurrection of your Son. We continue to be guided by all that Christ stood for in his life and ours. It is through him that we can come before you as we continue to live the life he has given us.

We give thanks, God almighty, for your ascended Son. We continue to lift our eyes to the heavens while our hearts and minds remain focused on what lies below the mountain. It is through your Son that we can be strengthened to live lives of faith in this world.

We give thanks, God almighty, for the Spirit of your Son descended upon us. We continue to live, empowered by the Spirit sealed in us in our baptism and burning in our hearts. It is through the Spirit promised by Christ that we can be emboldened by your love. Amen.

Prayer of Confession

Lord Jesus Christ, we are not worthy to tie the thongs of your sandals; we are not worthy to even pick up the crumbs from your table. We fail to hear your voice; we fail to follow your call. We are easily distracted, and we do what is more convenient for us. And yet you call us to the mountaintop from where you point to both the heavens and the earth. As we walk our journeys, you embrace us, you guide us, you walk with us. Grant us the grace to hear you, and give us the confidence to proclaim your holy name wherever we go. Amen.

Prayer of Dedication of Gifts and Self

Grant, O God, the gift of your Son, risen and ascended not just to heaven, but also into our hearts. And through this gift of yours, empower us in our giving, that we may be a blessing unto others. Take our lives that we may be consecrated to you as we serve our neighbors. Take our hands and let them move at the guiding of your love. Take our mouths and let them be filled with the good news of Jesus. Amen.

Sermon Summary

Witnessing the truth of Christ, plus the power of God in our midst, makes for mission.

Hymn of the Day
"Hail the Day That Sees Him Rise"

This hymn by Charles Wesley first appeared in his *Hymns and Sacred Poems* in 1739. It provides a poetic commentary on Christ's ascension, as recorded in Luke 24. The "alleluias" were not part of Wesley's original text, but were later added by music editors. The tune LLANFAIR, by Welsh singer Robert Williams, became identified with the text around 1817. The modern church can celebrate the Ascension of Christ with this hymn. We find strong encouragement in the fourth stanza with its reminder that it is Christ who bestows "blessings on his church below."

Children's Time

Jesus Goes Home

Bring some helium-filled balloons with long strings. Have a brief conversation about things the children have seen that move up into the sky and may disappear (hot air balloons, kites, rockets, fireworks, smoke from a bonfire, an eagle soaring high). Note that some of these things go up with a bang – like rockets or fireworks – while other go up very gently.

Explain that today is Ascension Day, the day we remember when Jesus returned to heaven to live with God. Retell the story of Jesus' ascension as told in Luke 24. When you come to the part where Jesus is taken up into heaven, let go of the balloons and watch them float gently up to the ceiling.

Mention that the disciples weren't sad when Jesus left because they knew that he would send the Holy Spirit to help them. The Bible tells us they went back to Jerusalem filled with great joy.

Pray with the children, giving thanks for the joy that Jesus gives.

(At the end of the service, ask a few helpers to retrieve the balloons and give them to the children.)

The Sermon

I'm Expected to Do What?

Hymn
Beginning of Worship: "A Hymn of Glory Let Us Sing"
Sermon Hymn: "Alleluia! Sing to Jesus"
Closing Hymn: "A Hymn of Glory Let Us Sing"

Scripture
Luke 24:44-53 (For additional sermon materials on this passage, see the 2006 May/June planning issue of *The Clergy Journal;* for sermon materials on Acts 1:1-11, see the February 2007 issue of *The Clergy Journal.*)

Probably one of the worst things one can hear are the words: "I'm disappointed in you." Certainly these words can be harsh and demoralizing to anyone. We hear the words because expectations have not been met, conclusions not reached, ends not attained. Of course, some things we just can't do. We have our bad days, failed attempts because of external factors, things that just don't fit together.

Oh, we do have great expectations placed on us. Our parents teach us many things as we grow up, and we're expected to do them: eat properly at the table, tie your shoes, brush your teeth, say "thank you," clean up after yourself. We learn many things in school and we're expected to put it all together. All those math proofs add up to something useful. Science projects tell us something about life. Spelling is a way to put our thoughts into written words.

All the other training we receive helps hone our skills so we can function in particular spheres of life. We learn to work computers, strip wires, read blueprints, motivate people, take apart pistons, and recognize sounds. We learn, we observe, we question, we analyze, and we grow in understanding. And we're expected to function in this world. It should be easy enough if everything was learned well, information was absorbed, facts were set straight, practice was perfected.

One of the big concepts used these days is mentoring. Experts talk particularly about the value of mentoring youth and even young adults. Mentoring is different from teaching in that it acts more as a modeling and inspiration for life. Through mentoring one learns by experience, while being guided and encouraged, rather than as an intellectual exercise. It's a way to become all one can be for the sake of others, while seeing a wholeness of life.

That's where Jesus left his followers. Throughout his ministry, he made his disciples all they could be. And he now was sending them off for the sake of the world.

It was easy enough for the disciples to go off proclaiming Christ's good news. After all, Jesus himself was their teacher, their model, and their mentor. Of course, making Jesus into merely a mentor certainly downgrades all that he was. But there may be something to it as we look at what we see in Jesus and how we live our lives as his followers. And that was perhaps where his disciples were left. He opened their minds to understand the scriptures. He spoke about how their faith tradition was brought to fulfillment. He himself showed them what the Messiah was all about in his life, suffering, death, and resurrection. And Jesus tells them: "You've heard it; you've seen it; you understand it. Now go on and tell the rest of the world."

If only all these things actually were so easy. We know that, try as we may, things still go wrong. We may use the best of our abilities, recall the best of our experiences, find ourselves shaped by our mentors. And yet we are not always in control.

That may be the crux of things, and certainly that's the scary part: we are not in control – of things around us, sometimes even of things within us, and of things in this world. Regardless of the expectations placed on us – and no matter how much confidence we place in ourselves – ultimately we're just not in control.

Perhaps there's some wisdom in realizing and living with the fact that we're not in control. The wisdom is not in thus giving up, but in trusting something else. Here, Christ had some added things to tell his followers as he sent them off. "I am sending upon you what my Father promised." That's what Jesus' disciples could take with them. They knew what they had seen, what they had learned. They were mentored along the way – their questions addressed, their mistakes corrected. The disciples knew that their message came from God. They were not in control ultimately, for they were on a mission for God. Great expectations were placed on them, but they also had a promise from God to be with them.

We are expected to do the same. Our baptism sets us on a mission, too. The joy of receiving God's grace should compel us to share that good news. There's a slight problem here, though. Jesus reminded his disciples that they had witnessed so much. They had the tools with which to spread the news. Easy enough for them! They witnessed, they heard with their own ears, saw with their own eyes, touched with their own hands, walked with their own feet.

We don't have that benefit. We have not seen sight given to the blind. We have not taken bread and fish from some little boy's lunch and filled so many hungry stomachs. We have not seen the dead walk out of their graves. We have not heard words from Jesus' own mouth. We have not seen and touched the nail holes in Jesus' hands. We are not witnesses to these things.

But we are, my friends. We know of how the church has remained steadfast in its worship of God and love of neighbor for centuries. We have witnessed people turning to God, not for any self-serving reasons, but because they felt touched by God. We have seen our abundance turned into gifts overflowing for others. We have seen the power of words, even the simple utterance of "I forgive you" reshaping lives and bringing wholeness to our shared humanity. We have seen utter despair – as experienced by victims of disasters or those who have lost jobs – turned into hope because good people have dared to share something of themselves. And from all this, we have seen new life emerge, one in which the gift of faith showers new joys.

Oh, I'm not saying any of this is easy or comes easily. We have our doubts. We have our setbacks. Much is expected of us and we still stumble. But as we are sent down from the mountainside, we carry a promise. Christ promises to be with us, not just here in this holy place, but into all the world.

– Y. Franklin Ishida

May 20, 2007

7th Sunday of Easter

Lessons

RCL	Acts 16:16-34	Rev 22:12-14, 16-17, 20-21	Jn 17:20-26
Roman Catholic	Acts 7:55-60	Rev 22:12-14, 16-17, 20	Jn 17:20-26
Episcopal (BCP)	Acts 16:16-34 or 1 Sam 12:19-24	Rev 22:12-14, 16-17, 20 or Acts 16:16-34	Jn 17:20-26

Introduction to the Lessons
Lesson 1
(1) Acts 16:16-34 (RCL/Epis)
Everywhere it is preached, the gospel upsets the status quo. People complain, and Paul and Silas are imprisoned. But even in prison, the status quo is upset.

(2) Acts 7:55-60 (RC)
Despite conspiracies against him, Stephen proclaims the good news with increased fervor. He becomes the first martyr among the followers of Jesus Christ, with many more to come.

Lesson 2
Revelation 22:12-14, 16-17, 20-21 (RCL);
Revelation 22:12-14, 16-17, 20 (RC/Epis)
Even in times yet to come, Christ proclaims that he is both the beginning and the end. Therefore, Christ's promise to come again becomes a comfort because he was, he is, and he is to come.

Gospel
John 17:20-26 (RCL/RC/Epis)
Jesus' prayer for his disciples looks to the future, that unity in the one who sent Christ and love may prevail.

Theme
Rude awakenings can lead to renewal.

Thought for the Day
Repentance is more than turning around; it is the awakening to something totally new.

Call to Worship
One: Rejoice all the earth;
All: And the coastlands will be glad.
One: Rejoice all the heavens;
All: And all the peoples behold God's glory.
One: Rejoice in the Lord, all you people;
All: And give thanks to God's holy name.

– based on Psalm 97

Pastoral Prayer
We give you thanks, O God, for the gift of life – not just any life, but new life that comes through the redeeming death and resurrection of your Son, Jesus Christ. In him do we give you praise. In him do we live. In him do we set our eyes on the world. Grant us your Spirit to see you at work in us and in our world. And give us the strength to persevere in all that we do. Amen.

Prayer of Confession
Spirit of the living God, open our eyes even as we are blinded to you and all that you have placed around us. Spirit of the living God, open our minds even as we are weakened by the darkness that we create around us. Spirit of the living God, restore us, strengthen us, and lead us in service to all in need. Keep us in your truth and unite us in one hope. Amen.

Prayer of Dedication of Gifts and Self

God of all goodness, we give you thanks for all things in our lives. We are grateful for the gift of food, and the opportunity we have to feed others in your name; We are also grateful for the blessing of shelter, and the opportunity we have to care for the homeless. We give thanks for the love of friends and family, and your call to love even our enemies. You have given us much and you turn us to see more. Help us to receive your blessings and your challenges with gratitude. May we find that, through your grace, blessings become challenges and challenges become blessings. Amen.

Sermon Summary

God's many surprises include those moments when we are turned around by God. We are turned to something new and exciting, a life in Christ with all its promises.

Hymn of the Day
"Christ, Whose Glory Fills the Skies"

This poetic prayer was written by 18th-century English evangelist Charles Wesley. It originally appeared in Wesley's *Hymns and Sacred Poems* of 1740 with the title, "Morning Hymn." Various tunes have been associated with the hymn text, as reflected in current hymnbooks. A slightly different emphasis is enjoyed with the respective tunes, such as CHRIST WHOSE GLORY, DIX, and RATISBON. Although Wesley titled it "Morning Hymn," the sole emphasis of the hymn is upon Christ as the Light of the World, Sun of Righteousness, Dayspring, and Daystar. Biblical references are John 8:12; Malachi 4:2; Luke 1:78; and 2 Peter 1:19.

Children's Time

Risky Witness

Bring a length of chain and a padlock. Ahead of time recruit a volunteer to play the role of prisoner. Invite the children to build a jail by standing in a circle. Place your volunteer in the circle and padlock the chains around her or his feet. Invite the children to think about being in jail: What might it be like? (Be sensitive to those children who might know people who are or who have been in jail). Comment that today's story is about two followers of Jesus who were thrown into jail for helping someone.

Tell the story of Paul and Silas and their adventures in prison. Invite the children to mime the actions or stamp their feet to create an earthquake. Discuss what must it have been like for Paul and Silas to get into trouble for helping someone. Talk briefly about some of the unpopular and risky things other followers of Jesus have done to help others. If possible refer to things that have happened in your own area.

Pray with the children, asking God to help all those who take risks in order to help others.

The Sermon

Wake up!

Hymns
Beginning of Worship: "When in Our Music God Is Glorified"
Sermon Hymn: "All Are Welcome"
Closing Hymn: "Take the Name of Jesus with You"

Scripture
Acts 16:16-34 (For additional sermon materials on this passage, see the February 2007 issue of *The Clergy Journal*; for sermon materials on John 17:20-26, see the 2006 May/June planning issue of *The Clergy Journal*.)

Of all natural disasters, earthquakes are probably the most devastating. Certainly other disasters, such as tornadoes or hurricanes, wreak havoc. However, hurricanes can be tracked by satellite and even tornadoes have some forewarning based on weather patterns or sightings. There are other disasters, too, that can be predicted – volcanoes give off warning signs; tsunamis come in the aftermath of earthquakes; droughts come about slowly; floods follow great rains. Earthquakes, on the other hand, seem to just happen. At least, there is no certain predictability in earthquakes, making them silent and feared companions to all those who live within their grip.

In 1995, a devastating earthquake hit the Kobe area in west central Japan. One survivor, Kei *(pronounced Kay)*, recounts how she was rudely awakened in the dawning hours by the rumbling and rolling of this massive quake. Everything in her room was knocked over. But when she looked out her window after the quake subsided, her apartment building was one of few that was still standing. The devastation was overwhelming – miles upon miles of wasteland, thousands of deaths, tens of thousands of injured. Kei was fortunate to survive unscathed, but the rude awakening didn't end with the stop in tremors. She couldn't communicate with her parents who lived far away in Hiroshima. She couldn't get away easily. She walked miles to reach an operating train.

A rude awakening reverberated throughout Japan in different ways. Sure, the Japanese people know about earthquakes. They live in one of the most earthquake-prone areas of the world. And they know of devastation caused by earthquakes in the past. But it was a rude awakening when the newest of buildings collapsed, when railroad tracks twisted and were gnarled, and when everything came to a standstill.

What went wrong? Were not the best in earthquake-proof designs mandated by law? Were not people trained to react to earthquakes with swift attention? Where was all the preparedness?

The Japanese know that the "big one" has yet to hit key parts of Japan. Vigilance is still needed, and the lessons from the Kobe earthquake helped focus attention on new designs, new ways of thinking, new ways of managing crises. It was a rude awakening to all the dangers that exist in nature's power. But it was an awakening that hopefully will bring about change for the good.

The jailer guarding Paul and Silas was pretty certain he held them well. So he slept. That's why the earthquake was a rude awakening. Oh, it wasn't just an earthquake that rattled him awake. And it was more than being confronted with the prison doors wide open and the prisoners about to run for freedom. Ultimately, he was taken aback by those very prisoners not fleeing, but calling upon him. It was a rude awakening, and change for the good came out of it.

God is good at rude awakenings. The Bible tells of times when God used earthquakes, fire, floods, plagues, death, even the sudden appearances of angels. Scared to death may be an apt description of the fear people felt as they encountered the power of God.

The biblical witness includes some big events to demonstrate God's might. There are plenty of small nudges included, as well, and perhaps countless others not recorded. Of course, we need to remember that we ought not attribute to God just any devastating tragedy. But in all things, we can look at ways in which we are awakened anew to God at work in our lives.

We've had our share of rude awakenings these past several years. The Oklahoma City bombing woke the United States up to terrorism from within our midst. September 11, 2001 is engrained in our minds with the horrifying reality of terrorism going to the suicidal extreme. Both these incidents brought a new awareness of being caught in the middle of sheer hatred and have left us wondering how better to fight off terror.

The south Asia tsunami of December 2004 woke up the whole world not only to the devastation of that powerful wave, but also the realities of people living in great need in the first place. Hurricane Katrina and its aftermath in New Orleans and other parts of the Gulf coast made us realize not only the power of nature, but also how human lives entrenched in poverty are less able to escape the effects of such forces of nature.

Our human tendency is to point fingers in times of rude awakenings. We don't like them! So we blame others. Sometimes we even blame God, or at least we ask whether God is present in such challenging times.

As in all rude awakenings, regardless of the cause, God is about nudging people. Lest we get caught by complacency; lest we let sin put blinders on us and turn us in different directions, we have the opportunity to see God at work.

From the ruins of Kobe and the destroyed façade of the Oklahoma City federal courthouse, from the wreckage of the twin towers and from the flooded streets of New Orleans, comes God's call to something new. And also in the small things we find God nudging us – in the wrinkled faces of grandmothers, in the teeny hands of premature babies, in fields of crops, in inner cities whose vacant lots see renewed activity. In everything, God is there with something.

God has something in store for us. It's something newer, something better, something grander than anything we can imagine. In the rude awakenings that arrive at the most awkward moments, God has life in store for us. Yes, God gives us life that isn't bound up by the powers of this world, life that doesn't sway at whatever may come our way, life that isn't infused by promises that go unfulfilled.

God's promise of life is one that is filled with joy. No, this is not about happiness. Even Paul and Silas couldn't have been happy sitting there in prison. But they prayed and sang hymns to God. Theirs was a confidence in the presence of God. Theirs was a joy in the knowledge of God's presence with them.

That's why Paul and Silas didn't need to flee the moment the prison doors were open. Paul and Silas were compelled to put a stop to fear, to turn the fear that the prison guard was feeling into a joy of his own. And this joy is something that becomes our own. As we have put on Christ in our baptism, God works in us and the Holy Spirit flows through us. And this is good.

–Y. Franklin Ishida

May 27, 2007

Day of Pentecost

Lessons

RCL	Acts 2:1-21	Rom 8:14-17	Jn 14:8-17, (25-27)
	or Gen 11:1-9	or Acts 2:1-21	
Roman Catholic	Acts 2:1-11	Rom 8:8-17	Jn 14:14-16, 23b-26
Episcopal (BCP)	Acts 2:1-11	1 Cor 12:4-13	Jn 20:19-23
	or Joel 2:28-32	or Acts 2:1-11	or Jn 14:8-17

Introduction to the Lessons
Lesson 1
Acts 2:1-21 (RCL); Acts 2:1-11 (RC/Epis),
After his resurrection, Christ promised an advocate, the Spirit who would dwell within each of his followers. Now that day has come and great wonders are seen and heard, all witnessing to the power of God and the grace of God's Son.

Lesson 2
(1) Romans 8:14-17 (RCL); Romans 8:8-17 (RC)
We are made children of God, not just with a simple promise, but with a special gift that has been granted to us for the sake of life in Christ.

(2) 1 Corinthians 12:4-13 (Epis)
Spiritual gifts are more than simple abilities. They are gifts from God that raise us to life together in the full household of God in this world.

Gospel
(1) John 14: 8-17, (25-27) (RCL); John 14:14-16, 23b-26 (RC)
Jesus proclaims himself as the way to the Father. This happens as we come to a better understanding, through faith and by the indwelling of the Spirit, that the Son and the Father are in one another for our sake.

(2) John 20:19-23 (Epis)
Jesus comes to the disciples after the resurrection, bringing them peace and the Spirit.

Theme

God's Spirit comes to us just when we need it.

Thought for the Day

Receive the Spirit of truth.

Call to Worship

One: Come, O Holy Spirit, come.
All: Holy Spirit come.
One: Come, almighty Spirit come.
All: Almighty Spirit, come.
One: Come, come, come.
All: O Spirit, come.

Pastoral Prayer

Come to us, Holy Spirit, and be the source of life restored. Where lives are parched, send the waters of life. Where sins abound, wash these away. Where spirits are worn and wounded, be a healing presence. Where hopelessness abounds, ignite the fire of your love within our hearts. Where our ancient enemy binds us in apathy, loosen the reigns. Bring us to new life, we pray, O God, and may your Holy Spirit ever flow through us. Amen.

Prayer of Confession

Spirit of life, we confess that we fail to honor life. Blow your life-giving breath through us. Spirit of love, we confess that lovelessness prevails in our lives. Shower upon us the grace of your Son. Spirit of truth, we confess that our truths are put before your truth. Open our hearts to Jesus Christ, the Word and wisdom for this world. Spirit of gentleness, we confess the hardness of our hearts. Whisper new imaginations, new dreams into our minds. Spirit of unity, we confess our disunity in the church, community, and world. Bind us together and heal our divisions. O Holy Spirit, gather us in the power of your peace. Amen.

Prayer of Dedication of Gifts and Self

Gracious God, your Spirit has entered our lives that we may be blessed. We are indeed blessed with the many gifts of which we become aware through the power of your Spirit. We give you thanks for these and for the many other gifts yet unknown to us. As we dedicate ourselves to you with these gifts, continue to empower us to do your will in this world, for the sake of your Son, Jesus Christ. Amen.

Sermon Summary

Focusing on ourselves can result in an increased desire to make something of ourselves and also in the need for God. We celebrate the coming of the Spirit that blows new life into us, a life in God.

Hymn of the Day
"O Spirit of the Living God"

Can the postmodern church experience the power of Christ, and be filled with love, joy, and power? This hymn written by Yale Divinity School professor Henry Hallam Tweedy in 1935 assures us that it can. Although Tweedy was the winner of several Hymn Society contests, this hymn and his "Eternal God, Whose Power Upholds" are the only ones generally to be found in current hymnbooks. FOREST GREEN, ST. MATTHEW, and MELCOMBE are most often used with this text. A careful choosing of a hymn tune will greatly facilitate the use of the hymn as a prayerful celebration of the "light and fire divine."

Children's Time

The Spirit Brings Life

Bring some toys that need breath to make them work, such as pinwheels, whistles, or balloons. Bring bubble mixture and a bubble wand.

Invite the children to take a deep breath, hold it for a moment and then blow it out. Ask: Can we see your breath? How do we know it is there?

Show the toys and indicate that these toys do not work the way they are supposed to unless we breathe on them. Demonstrate, noting that even though we can't see it, our breath can have a powerful effect.

Explain that in the Bible the same word is used to describe both breath and God's Spirit. Even though we can't see it, God's breath fills us and helps us to live in God's way. God's breath, or Spirit, has a powerful effect.

Explain that today is the day of Pentecost, the day we celebrate the coming of the Holy Spirit on the church. Blow some bubbles over the children, praying with them to give thanks for the gift of new life that God's Spirit brings.

The Sermon

The Spirit's Way

Hymns

Beginning of Worship: "Gracious Spirit, Heed Our Pleading (Njoo kwetu, Roho mwema)"
Sermon Hymn: "Send Down the Fire"
Closing Hymn: "Spirit, Spirit of Gentleness"

Scripture

John 14:8-17, (25-27) (For sermon materials on Acts 2:1-21, see the February 2007 issue of *The Clergy Journal* and the 2006 May/June planning issue of *The Clergy Journal*.)

In the song, "My Way," Frank Sinatra sings a confession of sorts. He looks back at a life that had some regrets and sorrows, a life when at times he took on more than he could handle, a life that had its share of losses. But he claims he can stand tall in reflecting on this life because he did it "his way."

Confidence in oneself is important. Coupled with this is self-esteem. Most children are taught self-esteem by parents and teachers, which can help with self-confidence. The desire by all those who guide us in life is that we may have positive self-esteem. Many of those who are lacking in self-confidence spend years reading books or attending seminars that are intended toward motivating the self. "Eight Steps to Self-confidence" is just one of many titles in a self-help movement that is blossoming.

There is nothing new in this awareness of self. Sun Tzu, the Chinese scholar from 500 BCE, said, "You have to believe in yourself." This is not necessarily inward looking, for "Your chances of success in any undertaking can always be measured by your belief in yourself," says American motivational writer Robert Collier. And "Once we believe in ourselves, we can risk curiosity, wonder, spontaneous delight, or any experience that reveals the human spirit," as e. e. cummings put it. Of course, God is not left out when Benjamin Franklin said, "God helps those who help themselves."

There's something interesting, though, in all these approaches to "self." We know of the community style of life that predominated in the past. Interdependence was necessary for the sake of survival. One may have been strong, but one needed others to live. Community was important above anything else.

Today, we identify individualism as the norm. Note the shift in emphasis in magazine titles. There was *Life;* then came *People,* then *Self.* We now have *Me.* There is a trend here, from a broader look at life to a self-centered outlook on life. We've arrived at a strange oxymoron: to be self-centered and to have an outlook on life. One has to wonder about the difference between self-esteem and self-centeredness, between self-confidence and self-help. No wonder we have a confused society in which we need to "find ourselves" by helping ourselves.

We have a popular media that does so well in taking this "self" business as a self-help matter. It sells by convincing people that they can find their own way by doing it their own way. The message to each of us is strong: You don't have to learn things from teachers, mentors, or even parents; you can do it yourself. Watch an infomercial and buy equipment touted to build up your body. Get a few books to help yourself do everything from a home makeover to a self-makeover. And if things seem too complicated, there are plenty of "Dummy" guidebooks. I do wonder which came first, general observations toward this introspection to self or a media that encourages it. Maybe it's both.

The media of the Bible tells us an old story. Way before Easter and Pentecost are two events. The serpent in the garden placed in the minds of our first parents the idea of self-centeredness. "You will be like God, knowing good and evil," said the serpent as he tempted them with the fruit of the tree. "You can help yourself know good and evil, you can be free to make your own determination. God placed the tree at the center of the garden, and now you can place yourself at the center."

There was probably some hope for humankind as God, even through punishment, protected and blessed life. But humankind could not escape a sense of self-centeredness: "Let us make a name for ourselves," they declare

(Gen 11:4) as they proceed to build the tower of Babel.

There is a pattern here to what we know as sin – self-centeredness replacing God; self-help taking a front seat to trust in God; pride getting in the way of community. We don't want other powers in our lives; we'd rather do it our way. The consequences of this mindset can be devastating.

This side of Easter and Pentecost is a different story. God has already entered the picture, in person. From the quiet village of Bethlehem to the crowds on the hillsides of Galilee; from the individuals seeking healing to the masses seeking good words; the world has witnessed Immanuel, God with us.

On the cross, God suffered with us and died with us in our sins. Easter marks the ultimate breaking in of God into our lives, breaking in with the new life of the resurrection. And now, with that resurrected life, we have a further realization of Immanuel, God with us. God is now realized in the Spirit who remains with the disciples forever.

Self-centeredness is turned into life in Christ as we are sealed by that Spirit and marked with the cross of Christ forever. Self-help is turned into the interdependent spirit of the Christian community, a community that joins together in communion and service.

This comes with a promise. Jesus departed from his disciples with the promise to be with them through the Holy Spirit. And this was the power that would propel them as witnesses in "Jerusalem, in all Judea and Samaria, and to the ends of the earth" (Acts 1:8). As opposed to the self-centeredness and self-help that came in the garden of Eden and moved to the tower of Babel, the Spirit frees us to life and unity with God and one another. The Spirit is with us, in us, in this. By this we are made holy.

Certainly we can believe in ourselves. But believe in yourself as one marked with the cross. And not just any cross, but the empty cross that frees you to be the one God created you to be.

– Y. Franklin Ishida

June 3, 2007

Trinity Sunday

Lessons

RCL	Prov 8:1-4, 22-31	Rom 5:1-5	Jn 16:12-15
Roman Catholic	Prov 8:22-31	Rom 5:1-5	Jn 16:12-15
Episcopal (BCP)	Isa 6:1-8	Rev 4:1-11	Jn 16:(5-11), 12-15

Introduction to the Lessons

Lesson 1
(1) Proverbs 8:1-4, 22-31 (RCL); Proverbs 8:22-31 (RC)
While we can point to the power and life-giving Spirit of God at work in creation, it comes down to God's wisdom even "thinking" of creation, putting everything in its right place.

(2) Isaiah 6:1-8 (Epis)
The temple was understood to be the seat of God's power. Isaiah's vision is one of unworthiness to be in God's presence, and yet God chooses even the least to be a messenger of the Lord.

Lesson 2
(1) Romans 5:1-5 (RCL/RC)
Though always undeserving, we are made right again in God's sight by faith. The Holy Spirit gives us the wisdom to understand God's unconditional love for us.

(2) Revelation 4:1-11 (Epis)
A vision of heaven can be overwhelming. And yet, we are placed right before the one who brings us to that place, the Lord God Almighty.

Gospel
John 16:12-15 (RCL/RC); John 16:(5-11), 12-15 (Epis)
The complete truth comes not with Christ alone, but as the Spirit enters our lives as the promised advocate.

Theme

The gift of the Trinity is one that surpasses all wonders.

Thought for the Day

Three-ness, threefold-ness, three persons, three-in-one and one-in-three . . . no matter how we do it, the Trinity cannot be captured well. But then, can we ever capture God?

Call to Worship

One:	Come, O Holy Spirit, come.
All:	Spirit of wonder, come.
One:	Come, O Holy Spirit, come.
All:	Spirit of joy, come.
One:	Come, O Holy Spirit, come.
All:	Spirit of life, come.
One:	Come, O Holy Spirit, come.
All:	Spirit of truth, come. Come into our lives, O Holy Spirit, come.

Pastoral Prayer

Almighty and eternal God, you have revealed yourself as Father, Son, and Holy Spirit. You live and reign in the perfect unity of love, embracing us with your grace. Hold us firm in this faith, so we may know you in all your ways. Enlighten us to your truth, so we may witness to your eternal glory. Keep us in your holiness, so we may glow with your love. For all this, we give you thanks. Amen.

Prayer of Confession

Almighty God, who created the world and deemed it good: we confess our failure in being wise stewards. You have given us the bounty of the earth, and we have plundered it. You have gifted us with wholeness, and we have fragmented this gift.

Lord Jesus Christ, who showed the world mercy even unto death: we confess that we do not follow in your path of love and forgiveness. You have shown us compassion, but we have offered poor imitations in our daily living. You have given us yourself as a new covenant, but we have relied on our own gods.

O Holy Spirit, who continues to descend upon us: we confess that we are more often ablaze with other passions. You bring unity to your church, but we are confused over even small things. You have given us wisdom, but we have been content with convenience.

Grant us your forgiveness. Amen.

Prayer of Dedication of Gifts and Self

With these gifts we give of ourselves to the world you have created, to the love you have poured out, and to the work of your holy church. Grant us your mercy that we may be strengthened to walk in your ways, even as you walk with us. Amen.

Sermon Summary

While the Trinity is a doctrine, it is also a way of seeing God at work in and through us. This truth is given to us as a gift.

Hymn of the Day
"Maker, in Whom We Live"

This hymn first appeared with the title "To the Trinity" in Charles Wesley's 1747 publication, *Hymns for Those That Seek and Those That Have Redemption in the Blood of Jesus Christ.* Stanzas one, two, and three address the three persons of the Trinity. Stanza four emphasizes the undivided Trinity. The tune most generally used with this text is DIADEMATA, written by George J. Elvey in 1868. Since most congregations probably will know this tune, as used with the hymn "Crown Him with Many Crowns," it will be easier to introduce this valuable hymn of the Trinity, should it be new to the congregation.

Children's Time

Three and One

Bring three taper or birthday candles and some rubber bands. If possible the candles should be different colors, but the same length. Comment that today is Trinity Sunday, a day to celebrate the three ways we know God.

Explain that the word *Trinity* comes from two Latin words. *Tri* means "three" and *unity* means "one;" the word *Trinity* means "three and one."

Hold the candles up one at a time and count them. Then put the candles together in a bundle and secure with rubber bands, with all the wicks on one end. Light the candles and comment that you now have a kind of trinity – three separate candles and one flame.

Point to each candle in turn and explain how we know God as Father, a loving parent who made and loves us; as Jesus, God's Son who came to show us God's love and God's way; and the Holy Spirit, who helps us to learn about God. Comment that we have three ways of encountering God, (point to each candle) and one God (point to the flame).

Pray with the children, giving thanks for the mystery of the Trinity.

The Sermon

Bound to the Trinity

Hymn

Beginning of Worship: "All Creatures of our God and King"
Sermon Hymn: "All Glory Be to God on High"
Closing Hymn: "Blessed Be the Name"

Scripture

John 16:12-15 (For sermon materials on Romans 5:1-5, see the February 2007 issue of *The Clergy Journal;* for sermon materials on Proverbs 8:1-4, 22-31, see the 2006 May/June planning issue of *The Clergy Journal.*)

I once received an unsolicited email from someone in southeastern Asia. This person was struggling with faith, trying to comprehend the various religious teachings he was hearing. Specifically, he was torn between Islam and Christianity. To him, Islam made more sense; it seemed more straight-forward, simpler perhaps. But he admitted he was trying to comprehend the whole notion of the Trinity. It was something that attracted him, though he was not sure what to make of it. How do you explain the doctrine of the Holy Trinity in an email response?

We know that over the years, books, treatises, lectures – whole lives – have been devoted to contemplating the Trinity. St. Patrick, for example, expounded on the Trinity, in part to highlight the different kind of God we have as opposed to the varied beliefs he countered. Patrick considered the Trinity an evangelizing tool, something to which he felt "bound" and that he could proclaim. He saw God at work through the Trinity.

Likewise, we are bound even as we continue to proclaim the faith of the church, the faith into which we were baptized. We bind ourselves as we recall our baptism. We bind ourselves every time we repeat the historic words of the Apostles' Creed or Nicene Creed. We bind ourselves as we gather in unity around the Lord's table. Unfortunately, in our haste at times to "get through" the liturgy, proclaiming our faith too often becomes just words and repeated motions.

Live it, though. Feel the life that flows from the living God, a God that surrounds us with creative power and redeeming love as we are made God's holy people. God lives in us as we live in God.

It is my hope that we can see the Holy Trinity as something that is lived. The Trinity is God living in us, and our living in God. The creative power of God, the grace-filled redeeming work of God, and the life-giving Spirit flow around us. We, as created beings, live in this grace – God in us and we in God.

The truth can seem pretty simple, but is it? We live in a created world filled with ungodly things. Famine, disasters, wars, hatred – is this the kind of world God has created for us? And what have we done about this creation as we plunder the goodness that has been entrusted to us?

Then we have humankind, more often bent on retribution than justice, hatred than forgiveness, destruction than building up. Can we truthfully say that Christ lives in us? Despite the preciousness of life that we proclaim, we live in a world where despair and hopelessness prevail in the midst of both abundance and want. Where is the Spirit of life?

There is a *Peanuts* comic strip showing Lucy walking with a sign that reads, "Jesus is the answer." Along comes Snoopy with his own sign: "What's the question?" Indeed, what is the question? The question is whether we can see God in our world, whether we can see the Trinity at work in our world and in us. The question is how to struggle with the many questions we have before us about God, about human life, about reality, about truth.

As we live in this world, there are times when we wonder whether there is a God who is almighty, loving, forgiving. Where was God in the midst of the genocide in Rwanda? Where was God as Hurricane Katrina blasted its way through Louisiana and Mississippi? And where is God as we struggle with issues of sexuality? Where is God as we struggle with matters of racism, sexism, classism, and all the other "-isms"?

I know it often is overused and sometimes even misused, but you probably are familiar with the poem, "Footprints in the Sand" by Mary Stevenson. After walking in the sand with God, the words of the poem talk about seeing only one set of footprints in those moments of life that seem the lowest and saddest. God's response is that those are the times in which God carries us.

Yes, God does carry us and lives in us in so many ways. God does guide the thoughts in the compassionate words of caregivers. God does give strength to the hands of the emergency workers following disasters. God's hands are at work through the gifts of compassion shown to those who suffer. God's eyes do guide us to see the human face and soul in people around us.

When we were baptized, we put on Christ. Certainly Baptism is a washing of sins. Certainly Baptism regenerates us into new life. And certainly Baptism makes us members of the body of Christ. We have put on Christ and we become one with Christ. As we are baptized in the name of the Father, Son, and Holy Spirit, God lives in us; the Trinity lives in us.

Living in the Trinity, we are on a mission. We are baptized into a journey. God's mission for the sake of the world becomes our journey. God walks with us as we live this life. Yes, there will be times when we stumble. There will be times when we fall back. There will certainly be times when we doubt and stray from the path. But if we look where we're going, we'll know that it's not a solitary journey.

This is what I told my email inquirer: I can walk with trust in a God who comes to me and lives in me no matter what. God's life-giving power inspires me to new life. God's redeeming love frees me to live a life of wholeness. God's Spirit burns within me, giving me a passion for life. God the Father is the answer – only through the Father do we have life. God the Son, Jesus, is the answer – only through Christ can we live free from the bondage to sin. God the Spirit is the answer – only in the Spirit do we know the truth of the world around us.

May you remember that you are sealed with the Father, Son, and Holy Spirit. Amen.

– Y. Franklin Ishida

June 10, 2007

2nd Sunday after Pentecost (Proper 5)

Pres: 10th Sunday in Ordinary Time/
RC: Body & Blood of Christ (Not listed)

Lessons

RCL	1 Kings 17:8-16, (17-24)	Gal 1:11-24	Lk 7:11-17
Episcopal (BCP)	1 Kings 17:17-24	Gal 1:11-24	Lk 7:11-17
Lutheran	1 Kings 17:17-24	Gal 1:11-24	Lk 7:11-17

Introduction to the Lessons
Lesson 1
1 Kings 17:8-16, (17-24) (RCL); 1 Kings 17:17-24 (Epis/Luth)
God sends Elijah to Sidon, which is Gentile territory, and Elijah initiates a miracle. Later, Jesus uses this story to illustrate the faith of those that Israel views as pagans (Lk 4:25-26).

Lesson 2
Galatians 1:11-24 (RCL/Epis/Luth)
This passage contains part of Paul's defense of his apostolic calling. Paul emphasizes that his call is of divine, not human, origin.

Gospel
Luke 7:11-17 (RCL/Epis/Luth)
Luke's story of the raising of the widow's son at Nain has no counterpart in the other Synoptic Gospels. In some respects, however, it is an echo of the story of Elijah in Sidon (1 Kings 17).

Theme
Many hands lighten the load.

Thought for the Day
We as individuals cannot do everything, but each can do something.

Call to Worship

One: Praise the Lord, O my soul!

All: I will praise the Lord as long as I live; I will sing praises to my God all my life long.

One: Do not put your trust in princes, in mortals, in whom there is no help.

All: When their breath departs, they return to the earth;

One: Happy are those whose help is the God of Jacob, whose hope is in the Lord their God, who keeps faith forever; who executes justice for the oppressed; who gives food to the hungry.

All: The Lord will reign forever. Praise the Lord!

– based on Psalm 146

Pastoral Prayer

God of Grace and God of Glory, we thank you for calling us out as your people and naming us at our baptisms. We ask you to place in our hearts the desire to care for your world and keep your garden, which we call our home – Mother Earth. Help us be excellent stewards of that which allows us to live out our vocation as the church of Jesus Christ.

As we worship this day, send your Sprit to dwell in us as we pray, sing, and ponder the deeper things of scripture. Help us recognize that all we are, and all that we will be, is in your holy hands. Make us righteous, just as you have declared us justified in the life, death, and resurrection of Jesus Christ, our Lord and our Savior. Amen.

Prayer of Confession

God of all Creation, we confess this day that we have not been faithful in our thoughts, words, or deeds. You call us to show compassion to those who need our help, and we know that we can love because you first loved us. Yet, because of our fear or reluctance, we have failed to open our hands or our hearts to the poor. Inspire us with the example of Jesus and with the example of the saints who live in glory. By their sanctified lives, they show us the path that leads toward God's reign. Would we be those such as these?

We confess our sin to you, O God, because within your heart there is much forgiveness. Help us accept the forgiveness you offer us in Christ. Once again make us and claim us as your people. We pray this prayer of pardon in the powerful and holy name of Jesus Christ. Amen.

Prayer of Dedication of Gifts and Self

O God, you give and give and give to us each and every day. Help us, therefore, show gratitude to you not only in our worship of praise and thanksgiving, but also by the gifts we offer to you. Our offerings symbolize all that you have offered to us. Grant that our meager gifts may be joined with the gifts from others, that they may bring glory to your holy name. Amen.

Sermon Summary

Jesus raises a widow's son. Plainly, Jesus does not raise all the dead during his earthly ministry, but rather raises some. Our task as believers is not to resolve all the world's problems. Yet, God calls us to do what we can do. We trust God to care for the rest.

Hymn of the Day
"At the Name of Jesus"

Written by British poet Caroline Maria Noel in 1870, this hymn appeared in the enlarged edition of her book, *The Name of Jesus, and Other Verses for the Sick and Lonely*. Based on Philippians 2:5-11, the hymn is certainly not limited to being sung by "the sick and lonely." Used with the tune KING's WESTON by Ralph Vaughan Williams, this hymn provides quite a powerful and triumphant statement of Christian faith, exalting the majestic name of Jesus Christ. By contrast, the more modern tune CAMBERWELL, written in 1960 by Michael Brierley, provides a more upbeat setting.

Children's Time

When We Are Sad

Bring a bowl and some teardrops cut from paper. Show the teardrops and explain that they are tears. Scatter the tears on the floor and ask the children to name some of the things that make them sad. For each answer given, have a child pick up a tear shape and place it in the bowl. Express concern at the number of sad things the children have named. Observe that sometimes life can get very sad indeed. Comment that the Bible story today is about a time when Jesus met a woman who was very, very sad.

Tell the story about Jesus raising the woman's son. Emphasize the feelings of compassion Jesus had for the woman and her son. Comment that Jesus really cared about the sad widow and did something amazing to turn her sadness into joy. Observe that Jesus really cares about us, too. When life gets very sad for us we can know that Jesus is with us and that Jesus cares about our sad feelings. Comment that it really helps to have someone like Jesus around when we're sad.

Pray with the children, giving thanks for Jesus' loving presence with us.

The Sermon

Doing What We Can Do

Hymns
Beginning of Worship: "All Creatures of Our God and King"
Sermon Hymn: "Sois la Semilla" (You Are the Seed)
Closing Hymn: "Here I Am, Lord"

Scripture
Luke 7:11-17 (For additional sermon materials on this passage, see the February 2007 issue of *The Clergy Journal;* for sermon materials on 1 Kings 17:8-16, (17-24), see the 2006 May/June planning issue of *The Clergy Journal.*)

What could be a more appalling circumstance in life than to experience the grief related to the death of a child? Although our lesson today tells us that the widow's dead son was "a man," nonetheless, the age of a child rarely matters to the grief that a parent feels. Although the tragic death of an infant or a small child carries its own pathos, the grief that a parent feels for an adult child also devastates.

Sometimes I do not think that, as a preacher, I understand the depth of human love that people naturally have for their children. This is said despite celebrating dozens of children's funerals over the years for their parents who happened to be members of my church. I want to suggest that on a purely human level our gospel story today is something that we can never understand until we have given everything we have to give to God Almighty – and this includes giving God our children. Realistically, I'm certain I am not close to true understanding. I do, however, remember visiting one of my elderly church members who taught me a good deal about human loss.

I visited Mrs. Gregory when I was her pastor. She helped me learn something that I never want to experience. On my first visit, I discovered she was 91 years old. I entered her house and she sat me down in her front room. We chatted a few moments and then she fell silent. I chattered away – as I often do – but she made no attempt to speak.

After about 15 minutes, I stood up to leave. In an authoritative voice she commanded me to sit back down and so I did. She then said, "All three of my adult children have died before me, and although many of my friends say that long life is a blessing, I assure you preacher, in my case it has been a curse. I don't need to hear you jabber away. I need you to sit here with me while I argue and fuss with God in my mind."

I replied, "Yes, ma'am, I think I'll sit."

I sat silently. No noise passed through my ears except the dull street noise and that infernal clock. Finally, after another half an hour, she said, "It is all right now. You can say your little prayer and get along." She and I spent many long afternoons like that one, and after a while the visits seemed to help me understand her depth of faith and also her special burden.

Previous to today's gospel lesson, often called "the Raising of the Widow's Son at Nain," Jesus had been on his ministry tour. Jesus had been teaching and preaching throughout Galilee. The prior day Jesus had healed a centurion's ill slave who was at the point of death. Soon afterward, Jesus and his disciples came to a town called Nain, near the border of Samaria and Galilee.

What they saw was no doubt a common scene – a funeral procession leaving a house. Jesus and his disciples learned that the one who had died was the only son of a widowed woman. Undoubtedly, Jesus felt compassion for the poor woman. First, she had lost her husband to death. Now she had lost her only son. In the ancient world children were to families what "social security" is for us today – a safety net to provide food and shelter in one's later years. Clearly, this woman not only suffered from grief, but her visible means of support had essentially vanished.

You heard the story. You know that Jesus "touched the bier . . . [and] said, 'Young man, I say to you, rise!' The dead man sat up and began to speak, and Jesus gave him to his mother" (7:14-15). So, why did Jesus pick out this one mother, from all the grieving women, upon which to lavish this mercy?

Perhaps one answer is, as our young people might say, "Jesus raised the dead man because Jesus could." Nonetheless, I want to think Jesus raised the son because he saw a widow in need. Jesus made an appropriate response to the circumstance that presented itself. Clearly, Jesus did not heal every person he encountered, but he did what he could do when he could do it. The woman had a need and Jesus responded to it. Perhaps it is that simple!

For now, in our own time, we do not need everything set right in our world. Whether or not the church is full of problems and situations that need healing, ultimately, this is God's concern. However, we can ultimately do what we can do – for ourselves and for others.

I heard a speaker once relate a story about a large corporation in Chicago that addressed a concern of all its employees. The business had trouble with people who threw trash in their parking lots. This trash blew all over the business' beautiful grounds. The place was infested with beer cans, food wrappers, advertising circulars, coffee cups, and the like.

After a while the employees decided that rather than having the company hire expensive guards to protect their buildings and grounds from litterbugs, they would do something more proactive. They divided the whole business complex into sections and each person, both coming and going to work each day, would pick up the litter in her or his assigned area. Not one of them could have done it alone, but together they kept their buildings and grounds clear of trash. In this way, no one was responsible for everything, but each was responsible for something.

The church is like this, too. We can be responsible for our part. The rest we leave to God. Amen.

– David Neil Mosser

June 17, 2007

3rd Sunday after Pentecost (Proper 6)
RC/Pres: 11th Sunday in Ordinary Time

Lessons

RCL	1 Kings 21:1-10, (11-14), 15-21a	Gal 2:15-21	Lk 7:36—8:3
Roman Catholic	2 Sam 12:7-10, 13	Gal 2:16, 19-21	Lk 7:36—8:3 or Lk 7:36-50
Episcopal (BCP)	2 Sam 11:26—12:10, 13-15	Gal 2:11-21	Lk 7:36-50
Lutheran	2 Sam 11:26—12:10, 13-15	Gal 2:15-21	Lk 7:36—8:3

Introduction to the Lessons
Lesson 1
(1) 1 Kings 21:1-10, (11-14), 15-21a (RCL)
By remaining steadfast to his ancestral inheritance, Naboth unwittingly signs his death warrant. Jezebel plots a plan that thwarts the will of God for the faithful Naboth.

(2) 2 Samuel 12:7-10, 13 (RC)
The prophet Nathan speaks a strong word of judgment against the king. This prophetic judgment illustrates that no one, not even the king, is above the law of the Lord.

(3) 2 Samuel 11:26—12:10, 13-15 (Epis/Luth)
After his treachery against Uriah, David takes Bathsheba as his wife. Nathan's parable is a prelude to the harsh word the prophet delivers against King David.

Lesson 2
Galatians 2:15-21 (RCL/Luth); Galatians 2:16, 19-21 (RC); Galatians 2:11-21 (Epis)
Paul shares his deepest theological conviction that God saves human beings by grace. We receive the gift of God's grace through faith in Jesus Christ. Thus, the law no longer has a hold on humankind.

369

Gospel
Luke 7:36—8:3 (RCL/RC/Luth); Luke 7:36-50 (Epis)
Hospitality to Jesus, the Anointed One of God, appears to take precedence over a person's past sins as Jesus forgives "a sinful woman" at a Pharisee's house.

Theme
Authentic Christians understand that real freedom comes in service.

Thought for the Day
If "the Son of Man came not to be served but to serve," then what better example can we have as followers of God's Messiah?

Call to Worship
One: Happy are those whose transgression is forgiven, whose sin is covered.

All: Happy are those to whom the Lord imputes no iniquity, and in whose spirit there is no deceit.

One: I acknowledge my sin to you, and I do not hide my iniquity;

All: We will confess our transgressions to the Lord, rejoicing that God forgives the guilt of sin.

– based on Psalm 32:1-2, 5

Pastoral Prayer
God of everlasting peace, as we present ourselves in your holy presence this day, instill in each of us the deep desire for the grace you offer. As we gather to sing the established hymns of faith, help us recognize the sainted believers who have sung the same faith songs before us. Let us take their faithful example as a pattern by which we, too, might be faithful. As we worship today may we join the voices of those saints around the world and through the centuries as we exalt your holy name. Thank you, O God, for the bounty of the earth's blessing in which we stand and enjoy. We pray our prayer of thanksgiving in the powerful and holy name of the one who came to give us life and give it to us in abundance, Jesus Christ. Amen.

Prayer of Confession

O God, you have freed us to be your people and we pray today that we might catch a glimpse of your promise that would lead us toward your heavenly realms. Sometimes the Christian life is remarkably simple for us. We say our prayers, attend worship, study scripture, and tithe to the work you have given us to do. But too often life becomes difficult. We either have little inclination to follow the path you have given us; or worse, we see the path and in our dread we are reluctant to take it. We confess that we need more faith so that we can conjure. To this end we pray that you will send us the Holy Spirit to inspire in us the golden promises you offer. Let us soak in the scripture and its story of salvation, so that we might partake in its magnificent promise. Forgive us and set us aright on the path, which leads to you. Amen.

Prayer of Dedication of Gifts and Self

As a community of faithful people, you have bestowed on us unimaginable riches and made us stewards of it all. You have placed your trust in us, O Lord of heaven and earth, and for this we are grateful. Help us manage this sacred trust; remind us that all creation belongs to you, and that you have offered it to us to use for a while. As we return today a portion of what is yours, bless both those who give and those who receive in Jesus' name. Amen.

Sermon Summary

Paul writes to the Galatian churches about the matter of following Jewish ritual law. Paul urges these churches to remember that the only condition of their salvation is the fact that God has saved them by faith through grace. Faith in Christ is the solitary condition of salvation.

Hymn of the Day
"When Morning Gilds the Skies"

The anonymous German text for this hymn appeared in *Katholisches Gesangbuch* in 1828. It was translated into English by Edward Caswall in 1854. Of course this hymn of praise is not just a morning hymn. It is well suited for any time we wish say, "Jesus Christ be praised!" It is an eternal song, as stanza four suggests, appropriate for all eras of history and people of all ages. An additional element of praise can be experienced when the hymn is sung in an antiphonal manner with the tune LAUDES

371

DOMINI. A choir or soloist sings the first part of each line, and the congregation then responds, "may Jesus Christ be praised!"

Children's Time

Measuring God's love

Bring a measuring cup, a tape measure, some bathroom scales, and a watch. Ask the children to name each item. Explain that all these items are used to measure different things. If you want to measure time you use a watch. If you want to measure how long or wide something is, you use a tape measure (measure the length of a child's arm). If you need to measure how heavy someone is you stand on the bathroom scales (ask for volunteers to stand on the scales). If you need to measure the ingredients for a pie you use a measuring cup.

Ask the children if you could use any of these things to measure God's love. Say that you think God's love is so amazing, so big, and so huge that it cannot be measured.

Recall that Paul was a leader in the early church who taught and wrote about God's love. Explain that part of his letter to the church in Galatia was about God's love for us. We can't do anything to earn God's love. God just loves us. Comment that this kind of love is too big to be measured.

Pray with the children, giving thanks for God's amazing love.

The Sermon

Freed in Christ – for What?

Hymns
Beginning of Worship: "A Mighty Fortress Is Our God"
Sermon Hymn: "Thou Hidden Love of God"
Closing Hymn: "Take up Thy Cross"

Scripture
Galatians 2:15-21 (For sermon materials on Luke 7:36—8:3, see the March 2007 issue of *The Clergy Journal* and the 2006 May/June planning issue of *The Clergy Journal*.)

When my youngest son runs into a contentious person or hears an argument among adults, he sits back and with great solemnity announces, "These people have issues." What he is saying, of course, is that one or both of the parties in any argument have an agenda to push. Those who debate with passion are not disinterested persons in the discussion. To be more precise, verbal combatants advocate a strong point of view.

From our lesson today, it is clear that Paul has something that he wants to get off his chest. He writes to the Galatians. Those who know the Pauline letters understand that this audience is exceptional among all the recipients of Paul's letters. In every other case of an authentic Pauline epistle, Paul addresses his correspondence to a church, such as the church in Rome or Corinth. Where Paul does not write to an individual church, he writes to an individual person, such as the epistle to Philemon. So, who are "the Galatians" and why does Paul write to them in such strong language?

It would seem that the Galatians must be gentile Christians. They are apparently conversant with Jewish ritual practice and the Hebrew Scriptures, but it seems that the topic of circumcision is "up for discussion" in this church community. This theological business about circumcision was a major concern in the community (Gal 2:12; 5:6, 11; 6:15). The fact that these Gentiles understood Paul's nuanced argument about the circumcision rite suggests that they may have been gentile "God-fearers" on their way to becoming Christians, but also may have been contemplating participating in the Jewish faith and its rituals. In other words, "these people have issues."

Thus, the real issue in the Galatian churches is how Christians are to live within the faith. Are they to follow the Hebrew ritual law as Christians or are they freed from the strictures of the law? We might understand the issue of circumcision as a "code word" for what Paul understands as "a condition of salvation." Paul, of course, writes that "we have come to believe in Christ Jesus, so that we might be justified by faith in Christ, and not by doing the works of the law, because no one will be justified by the works of the law" (2:16).

This means that following certain Jewish rites – rites that Paul equates with "doing the works of the law" – does not bring salvation. However, Paul believes that God's grace through faith in Christ is what produces the change in a person's salvation status. Salvation comes, in other words, by faith apart from works of the law.

In every church that has ever existed, there are certain "obligations" for church membership. Some of these obligations are explicitly stated; other obligations are of a more implicit or assumed nature. For Paul, however, there is only one condition. This condition is that a person, or even a community of faith, receives the gift of salvation by faith in Christ.

One day a decade ago, I walked into a church to see the pastor. As I waited for him, I leafed through a brochure listing ten things a person must believe if he or she desires to be a member of this particular church. In a sense, this catalog was a laundry list of required beliefs for its members. This catalog of approved beliefs included the church's theological position on matters such as abortion, marriage, and the virgin birth. Although the educational intent of the catalog itself was worthy, it veered from Paul's mantra that "a person is justified by faith apart from works prescribed by the law" (Rom 3:28). No matter the intention we have for adding this or that obligation to the foundational requirements of what makes a Christian and what does not, for Paul, Christ's work on our behalf is the solitary condition of salvation.

Paul never tells his readers that the law is a "bad thing." Yet, Paul is always quick to point out that "if justification comes through the law, then Christ died for nothing" (Gal 2:21). Thus, Christ's death set us free to be what God created us to be – fully human people who can choose to be servants of one another and the risen Christ.

How does one become a servant of another? Perhaps this is a question that takes a lifetime to discover. I suggest that one way to appropriate salvation by faith is to imagine that we may be the only person that another individual will encounter who can offer the promise of salvation. We have the occasion to offer Christ by way of imitating Christ-like characteristics. For example, Paul wrote to the Philippian church about the "mind of Christ." Here some Christ-like traits surface. Paul wrote that the mind of Christ included "taking the form of a slave" and humbling himself (Phil 2:7-8).

Clearly, Christ did things that none of us could ever or would ever want to do. But each of us can stoop to serve other people. We are free to be servants of others because Jesus Christ first stooped to be a servant to us by being "obedient to the point of death – even death on a cross" (Phil 2:8).

By being Christ-like for others, we can offer the good news in non-threatening and non-menacing ways. Rather than hand a person a laundry list of appropriate things to believe, we can offer ourselves as living witnesses of what a person with Jesus in her or his heart looks like. For people in today's world, this witness is as effective as it is faithful. After all, the invitation to the reign of God is never coercive or bullying. It is always a gracious invitation given in love. Amen.

– David Neil Mosser

June 24, 2007

4th Sunday after Pentecost (Proper 7)
RC/Pres: 12th Sunday in Ordinary Time

Lessons

RCL	1 Kings 19:1-4, (5-7), 8-15a	Gal 3:23-29	Lk 8:26-39
Roman Catholic	Zech 12:10-11; 13:1	Gal 3:26-29	Lk 9:18-24
Episcopal (BCP)	Zech 12:8-10; 13:1	Gal 3:23-29	Lk 9:18-24
Lutheran	Isa 65:1-9	Gal 3:23-29	Lk 8:26-39

Introduction to the Lessons
Lesson 1
(1) 1 Kings 19:1-4, (5-7), 8-15a (RCL)
Poor Elijah; after his clash with Jezebel he heads for the hills. Yet, God will not allow him to hide, but rather calls him back into Yahweh's service through a theophany.

(2) Zechariah 12:10-11; 13:1 (RC);
Zechariah 12:8-10; 13:1 (Epis);
People in the most desperate circumstances cling to hope, and God, through the prophet, offers them this hope. Israel will be able to conquer because of God's power and not their own.

(3) Isaiah 65:1-9 (Luth)
Grace means nothing if God does not offer it as an alternative to judgment. Israel has been idolatrous, and the prophet gives ample warning about the penalty God will exact eventually from the rebellious people.

Lesson 2
Galatians 3:23-29 (RCL/Epis/Luth); Galatians 3:26-29 (RC)
In this part of his epistle, Paul explains the advantage of faith over the law. Also, because of faith in Jesus Christ, all human distinctions now fade away.

Gospel

(1) Luke 8:26-39 (RCL/Luth)

Although people today use the word *demon* largely in an allegorical way, for people in Jesus' time demons were real. The casting out of demons was a sign of Jesus' identity.

(2) Luke 9:18-24 (RC/Epis)

Jesus comes to give himself as a sacrifice and to call disciples to new life. The cost of discipleship will be great, but the realm of God is a place of salvation.

Theme

Faith in Christ has freed each of us to recognize other people's gifts and graces in Christ. We do not need to be alike.

Thought for the Day

"The letter kills, but the Spirit gives life" (2 Cor 3:6).

Call to Worship

One:	As a deer longs for flowing streams, so my soul longs for you, O God.
All:	My soul thirsts for God, for the living God.
One:	When shall I come and behold the face of God?
All:	My tears have been my food day and night, while people say to me continually, "Where is your God?"
One:	Why are you cast down, O my soul, and why are you disquieted within me?
All:	Hope in God; for I shall again praise you, my help and my God.

– based on Psalm 42:11

Pastoral Prayer

Almighty God, we gather as your people. We gather as those who live in hope. Our lives provide us many opportunities to speak words of peace and reconciliation, but often we have not the courage. Make us bold not only to speak your word, but also to live it. In order to live in the fullness of the gospel, remind us that it is by grace that we live and die. Keep the spirit of the gospel in front of us, so we are not tempted to fall back toward the law.

Help us remember those in our own community who suffer through no fault of their own. Make us members of a congregation who are willing to step out in faith and assist those who need our help. Make us ever mindful that we love because Christ first loved us. We pray in the name of Jesus. Amen.

Prayer of Confession

Most merciful God, we confess that we have sinned against you and our neighbor. We have taken incalculable benefits with little gratitude. Moreover, we have settled into complacency by claiming our own rights rather than seeking the welfare of all of your children. Help us see the needs of others and then respond to them as brothers and sisters in Christ. Have mercy and forgive us, for the sake of Jesus Christ our Lord. In this hour of worship, remind each of us of the wonderful life and ministry you have given us as a sacred trust. Make us believers who are worthy of sharing the mysteries of faith with our friends and neighbors. May we keep faith alive and vibrant in our community. All this we ask in Jesus Christ's sanctified name. Amen.

Prayer of Dedication of Gifts and Self

Blessed are those who can give without remembering and take without forgetting. As we offer ourselves and gifts, O God, bless these offerings and those who receive them. May these gifts be tangible signs of our relationship with you. Help us remember those who endure natural disasters, and make us mindful of their plight. We pray this in Christ's name. Amen.

Sermon Summary

The churches in the region of Galatia have dissenting opinions concerning obedience to the ritual Hebrew law, especially as it pertains to Christian believers. Yet, Paul tries to help these churches understand that depth of authentic life is not gained by fulfilling the letter of the law, but by living in the spirit of Christ.

Hymn of the Day
"O Worship the King"

Based on Psalm 104, this hymn was written in 1833 by the Governor of Bombay, Robert Grant. As the Governor of Bombay, Grant was a servant of the king of England and was quite accustomed to pomp and pageantry. He quite naturally adapts royal references in this hymn to honor his Divine King. The final stanza contrasts our human frailty with God's unfailing mercy. The hymn reminds us that we may also call God "Maker, Defender, Redeemer, and Friend." The tune LYONS is attributed to 18th-century Austrian composer Johann Michael Haydn.

Children's Time

God's Children

Bring a dark cloth, some cord, and a bowl containing a variety of large beads. Lay some of the beads on the cloth. Invite the children to look at them and notice the differences and similarities among the beads. Express appreciation for the different beads that are available. What would it be like if there were only one kind of bead?

Comment that even though the beads are different, they are all beads. They can all be strung on a cord to make a necklace. (Start stringing some beads onto the cord.)

Observe that people are a little bit like beads. At first we all look different. We are different sizes and shapes. We have different colors of eyes and hair. We like different things. However, even with all our differences, all of us are God's children.

Comment that in the Bible reading today, Paul says that when God looks at us, God doesn't see the differences. To God we are all wonderful, and together we make something special. (Hold up beads on the string and tie as a necklace.) Express excitement that we are members of God's family.

Pray, giving thanks that we are the children of God.

The Sermon

Coloring Outside the Lines

Hymns
Beginning of Worship: "To God Be the Glory"
Sermon Hymn: "Christ, from Whom All Blessing Flow"
Closing Hymn: "Blessed Be the Tie that Binds"

Scripture

Galatians 3:23-29 (For sermon materials on Luke 8:26-39, see the March 2007 issue of *The Clergy Journal;* for sermon materials on 1 Kings 19:1-4, (5-7), 8-15a, see the 2006 May/June planning issue of *The Clergy Journal.*)

The law in my state tells me that if I park in a parking space marked for "persons with handicapping conditions," then the law will prosecute me. Surely no death penalty is involved, but rather a ticket and the associated fine. The parking places I refer to are a great temptation to many able-bodied drivers – or parkers, that is. Handicapped parking spaces are usually in the prime spots near entrances to buildings. Perhaps, even to lawbreakers, it is obvious why the law situates the parking spots where they are. Yet the temptation still "is lurking at the door" (Gen 4:7), and I might add, in a most literal way. My church even has this problem on Sunday mornings, when some able-bodied persons park in the handicapped parking spaces as if no one will notice.

Similar to every breach of the law, we all offer our excuses. "Well, I'll only be a minute" or, "No one will park here for the next hour," and the like. The sad part is that able-bodied people who park in the handicapped parking spaces are not always held accountable. Some are caught, but many others violate the law with impunity!

The law is not a suggestion to us. The law is a rule or edict from an authorized group of people enabled to make regulations that bind a particular community of people. Sometimes the federal or state level government enacts the laws; but often laws are simply city ordinances. Sadly, unless enforced, laws are actually de facto suggestions.

We human beings have a funny sort of relationship with the law. On the one hand, we really don't like anyone telling us what to do. But, on the other hand, we also are rational enough to recognize that if we do not regulate our behavior in one way or another, then society will surely devolve into chaos. Therefore, we abide by the laws that none of us fancies as individuals. We comprehend them as a necessity for us to function as a community. Into this quandary of human consternation steps Paul.

First, Paul sets up his argument in today's lesson by writing that prior to faith, "we were imprisoned and guarded under the law until faith would be revealed" (Gal 3:23). Paul describes the law as our disciplinarian. One of my seminary professors said that the law was like a "nasty nanny" (he was British) or like a "bad babysitter." What this meant was that the law "watched over" people as if it had been hired by parents. Conversely, parents watch over children with the kind of loving care that can only be offered by people who are deeply involved in an intimate relationship. One who is hired does the baby watching as a hireling, while the parent who functions on the child's behalf behaves as only a mother or father can.

The book of Hebrews speaks of an analogous situation when it compares and contrasts Moses to Jesus. "Moses was faithful in all God's house as a servant . . . Christ, however, was faithful over God's house as a son" (Heb 3:5-6). Thus, the law may get the job done with respect to monitoring human conduct, but it cannot give depth of relationship. One either follows the law, or one does not. But the achievement of the law can never bring much joy to the practice.

For many people, "following the letter of the law" is a safe way to be obedient to God. The law may tell us exactly what we can and cannot do. Following the letter of the law is like a child who colors in a coloring book with lines that guide the art, rather than creatively fashioning something out of nothing that others might deem as art-worthy. Paul tries to help the Galatians see that now that Christ has come, a new and creative way to live is possible. We become children of faith because of Christ. And in Christ we are no longer bound, as Paul writes elsewhere, to the "letter [of the law] but of spirit; for the letter kills, but the Spirit gives life" (2 Cor 3:6). The spirit offers spontaneity for human benefit that adherence to the law can never give.

We, like Jewish people of the first century, reside in a world culture that divides people into legal categories. Today, people argue on legal grounds as to what constitutes legal marriage partners and when life legally begins. Perhaps this is well and good for us, so that we may abide in a society without tearing each other to pieces.

Yet, Paul believes that because of the spirit of Christ, the possibility exists that believers now can abstain from these legal categories. Paul tells us that, "There is no longer Jew or Greek, there is no longer slave or free, there is no longer male and female; for all of you are one in Christ Jesus" (Gal 3:28). When we live in faith, it seems that Paul thinks all human and legal distinctions between human beings dissolve into our belonging to Christ. In Baptism God has given us a tangible symbol of what our unity might look like. In Baptism God has clothed us with Christ.

Does this mean that differences between Christians disappear? No, we all retain our individual gifts and talents. Yet, we are not so prone to list them in some hierarchical order of excellence. Rather, we see them all for the unique gifts that God intended to bestow on us.

Paul writes as he does to the Galatians because evidently the differences among them had become points of contention. Some felt and acted superior to others based on these more-or-less legal qualifications. The people had returned to living by rules and distinctions and apart from a spirit that valued each and every person and the gifts that he or she offered to the community. Does this not describe some of us and our churches as well? Amen.

– David Neil Mosser

July 1, 2007

5th Sunday after Pentecost (Proper 8)

RC/Pres: 13th Sunday in Ordinary Time

Lessons

RCL	2 Kings 2:1-2, 6-14	Gal 5:1, 13-25	Lk 9:51-62
Roman Catholic	1 Kings 19:15-16, 19-21	Gal 5:1, 13-18	Lk 9:51-62
Episcopal (BCP)	1 Kings 19:15-16, 19-21	Gal 5:1, 13-25	Lk 9:51-62
Lutheran	1 Kings 19:15-16, 19-21	Gal 5:1, 13-25	Lk 9:51-62

Introduction to the Lessons

Lesson 1

(1) 2 Kings 2:1-2, 6-14 (RCL)

We obviously consider a double portion superior to a single portion, but how much more so with the spirit? Elisha requests a double portion of the prophet's spirit as God translates Elijah into heaven.

(2) 1 Kings 19:15-16, 19-21 (RC/Epis/Luth)

This is part of a continued story as God calls Elijah to anoint a new king over Syria and Israel. Elijah is also to anoint his successor, and finds him plowing.

Lesson 2

Galatians 5:1, 13-25 (RCL/Epis/Luth);
Galatians 5:1, 13-18 (RC)

The comfort of the previous ritual law seductively tempts those freed from the law by faith in Christ. Paul urges those who are justified in faith to produce "fruit of the Spirit."

Gospel

Luke 9:51-62 (RCL/RC/Epis/Luth)

Jesus begins his fateful journey to Jerusalem. We human beings have many excuses not to follow Jesus today, but Jesus puts into divine perspective all our feeble excuses.

Theme

Spiritual formation is seen by the fruit of the Spirit.

Thought for the Day

It is through discipline that God forms disciples for the realm of God.

Call to Worship

One: Let us rejoice in the day that God has given us!

All: Yes, may we once again worship the God who gives life!

One: May we all sing and pray with a singleness of heart and mind.

All: We pray that the Lord will bless us with truth and light and joy. Amen.

Pastoral Prayer

O God, in whom we live and move and have our being, bring us near to your throne of grace. Help us to leave our troubles and anxiety at the door of the church, so that we might better concentrate on the truth that you offer us today. As we read the Holy Scripture, may we be inspired with the same spirit that inspired those to whom you revealed your sacred message. As we sing the hymns of the faith, may these blessed tunes of heaven resound in our hearts, and may we hum these melodies as we work through our week. May our preacher be inspired with words from on high, so that we may discern and appropriate your ancient word for our day. We pray in the name of our great high priest, Jesus the Christ. Amen.

Prayer of Confession

When we measure our lives against the perfect standard of faithful living that we find in Jesus Christ, O God of forgiveness, we know that we "have been weighed on the scales and found wanting" (Dan 5:27). Yet, we also know the promise of scripture that calls us to turn to you in true repentance, O Merciful Parent, and be forgiven of our sins. Therefore we acknowledge and repent of our sin. We ask your divine pardon and ask that you offer us once again the opportunity to dwell in newness of life. Return us to lives that are full of meaning and value. In short, help us to return to the place where we first embraced your promise for abundant life. We pray this in the holy name of Jesus. Amen.

Prayer of Dedication of Gifts and Self

O God of unmatched splendor, give us a spirit of sincere gratitude for your mercy. Make us mindful of your manifold blessings. Give us compassion to pass along our material blessings to those who also stand in need of life's necessities. Make us a people known for benevolence and a spirit of loving charity. We pray this and everything in Jesus' name. Amen.

Sermon Summary

Christian life is more than a destination after death. God calls us to discipleship today. A way to grow as disciples is to observe spiritual disciplines, which help us endure tribulation and tribulation-producing circumstances. Moreover, spiritual disciplines allow us to cultivate the joy of God's "fruit of the Spirit."

Hymn of the Day
"Spirit of the Living God"

Presbyterian minister Daniel Iverson of Lumberton, North Carolina wrote this one-stanza hymn, perhaps better recognized as a "chorus," in 1926. He wrote the words and music the day he attended the George T. Stephans evangelistic crusade in Orlando, Florida, where he heard a message on the Holy Spirit. The song's popularity began that evening when it was sung at the crusade's meeting. This short hymn can be used as a call to prayer or a prayer response. Some hymnbooks include a second stanza, written by Michael Baughen in 1982. This addition gives the hymn more of a "corporate" expression.

Children's Time

Growing in God

Bring various items of clothing representing different ages from infant to adult. Invite the children to line up the clothes in order of size. Comment that people wear different sizes of clothing as they grow. Invite the children to name some of the clothes they can no longer wear. Talk about some of the other ways in which we grow physically. How do we know when we are growing?

Comment that we also are growing in ways that we can't see as easily. We are growing in knowledge and we are growing in our relationship with God. How can other people tell? Mention that in the Bible passage today Paul says that when we follow God's ways and love others, many good things will grow in our lives. List the fruit of the Spirit in verse 22.

Invite the children to name ways we can love and help others. Observe that there will be a lot of fruits of the Spirit growing in *(name your community)* this week.

Pray with the children, asking God to help you as you learn more about living in God's ways.

The Sermon

Spiritual Disciplines Form God's Disciples

Hymns
Beginning of Worship: "Guide Me, O Thou Great Jehovah"
Sermon Hymn: "Spirit of God, Descend Upon My Heart"
Closing Hymn: "How Firm a Foundation"

Scripture
Galatians 5:1, 13-25 (For sermon materials on Luke 9:51-62, see the March 2007 issue of *The Clergy Journal;* for sermon materials on 2 Kings 2:1-2, 6-14, see the 2006 May/June planning issue of *The Clergy Journal.*)

Our time together this morning will focus on the topic of spiritual formation. Honestly, like most of you, I'm not sure what this means. Being from a Wesleyan tradition, I suppose spiritual formation has something to do with the idea of practicing spiritual disciplines. These naturally include spiritual activities such as meditation, prayer, fasting, study, almsgiving, and worship. One thing I do know is that we all need time and a means to deepen our lives in God, so that we can deepen our relationships with other people and ourselves. "Our world is hungry for genuinely changed people," writes Richard Foster. Leo Tolstoy wrote, "Everybody thinks of changing humanity and nobody thinks of changing himself." Most of us know the absolute truth of Tolstoy's statement. We see it every day.

I have thought about spiritual formation quite a bit. If I had to name the goal or object of our congregation's journey of faith, then I would suggest hearing and revisiting something that the apostle Paul wrote. Clearly most Christians would confess that heaven or salvation is the aim of the Christian life, but I would like for us to stay on this side of the grave for a while. Paul got it right when he wrote, "The fruit of the Spirit is love, joy, peace, patience, kindness, generosity, faithfulness, gentleness, and self-control. There is no law against such things. And those who belong to Christ Jesus have crucified the flesh with its passions and desires" (Gal 5:22-24).

I think this is the worthy goal and object of the Christian life as we live it now.

If you are like me, your life does not always feel much like "love, joy, peace, patience, kindness, generosity, faithfulness, gentleness, and self-control." Rather, you have your problems and I have mine. Unfortunately, as members of the body of Christ, we sometimes must put on our game faces and go on. Deep in the dark night of the soul, however, we know that we need more of God than we ever manage to shoehorn into our lives. Thus we need the disciplines of the Spirit and the spiritual life just like we need the four major food groups to survive and to thrive. Spiritual formation is all about spiritual disciplines. Only by disciplining ourselves – after all, the word "disciple" does have its roots deep into discipline – can we assure ourselves of the double portion of God's grace so necessary to work with and among and for such a "stiff-necked people," as always seems our lot.

What kind of people do we do ministry with? Recently our young music director tried to teach our congregation a new and beautiful hymn. One older woman came out of church that morning and stomped her foot as she said to me, "I don't come to church to learn anything!" I had to hold my tongue, although I wanted to answer her and did so to myself, "Ma'am, you may count your objective for coming to church as a total success!"

Along the way there always seem to be moments of grace or chance or serendipity that help us move on toward God and the relationships that believers claim at their baptism as people of God's reign. Sometimes events occur that remind us of why we do what we do.

Through the years the Samaritans (a group of lay ministers in our church) made visits to James and Mary Youngblood in their home. After one of these weekly visits, a Samaritan came by the church office and asked if someone from the missions work group could repair the Youngbloods' front door knob – it wouldn't lock. This would be a simple repair, really, probably no more than a 30-minute job.

Upon inspecting the doorknob, it was recommended that the whole doorframe be replaced, and that perhaps a new front door would be nice. When this project was completed, the workers decided to continue inside and partition off a bedroom and then paint the walls. The carpet really needed to be replaced, and how about the kitchen and bathroom – these areas could use a little repair work, too.

As workers came by to complete one project, they were dreaming and planning the next project they wanted to do for James and Mary. The end result was a complete renovation of the inside of the little house on Plum Street. There were new chairs and a couch, a new kitchen stove, new mattresses, some new windows, and a handicapped bathroom. The kitchen floor was leveled so that they did not have to hold the refrigerator door shut with duck tape anymore.

Mary was so excited. "I never lived in a house as pretty as this. It's my dream house." James, who was recovering from a broken hip from a slip on the ice, returned to the house via a brand new "state of the art" wheel chair ramp. All in all, it was a project that started with a doorknob and ended up blessing the lives of all who had a part in it.

This experience with James and Mary makes me realize that even when life is hard and seems like divine testing, I am surrounded by a group of dedicated believers. Our church folk are people who want to live out the life of Christ in community. They give and live the faith. They take Paul's guidance to heart when they follow Paul's counsel to the church at Galatia: "Through love become slaves to one another" (Gal 5:13). Amen.

– David Neil Mosser

July 8, 2007

6th Sunday after Pentecost (Proper 9)
RC/Pres: 14th Sunday in Ordinary Time

Lessons

RCL	2 Kings 5:1-14	Gal 6:(1-6), 7-16	Lk 10:1-11, 16-20
Roman Catholic	Isa 66:10-14c	Gal 6:14-18	Lk 10:1-12, 17-20
			or Lk 10:1-9
Episcopal (BCP)	Isa 66:10-16	Gal 6:(1-10), 14-18	Lk 10:1-12, 16-20
Lutheran	Isa 66:10-14	Gal 6:(1-6), 7-16	Lk 10:1-11, 16-20

Introduction to the Lessons
Lesson 1
(1) 2 Kings 5:1-14 (RCL)
The Israelites were tempted, just as we are, to forget God's love and
concern for all nations. But now a foreign official comes to Elisha, a
prophet of Israel, seeking a cure for his leprosy.

(2) Isaiah 66:10-14c (RC); Isaiah 66:10-16 (Epis);
Isaiah 66:10-14 (Luth)
God is often compared to a loving Father. But here, in moving imagery,
God is likened to a young mother tenderly nursing her young.

Lesson 2
Galatians 6:(1-6), 7-16 (RCL/Luth); Galatians 6:14-18 (RC);
Galatians 6:(1-10), 14-18 (Epis)
Some in the church at Galatia think they are superior to other members
because they have undergone circumcision, a mark of Jewish identity. Paul
shines the light of the cross on such mistaken attitudes.

Gospel
Luke 10:1-11, 16-20 (RCL/Luth); Luke 10:1-12, 17-20 (RC);
Luke 10:1-12, 16-20 (Epis)
Jesus has just reminded his followers of the costliness and urgency of following
him. Now he sends 70 of them to proclaim the good news of God's reign.

Theme

By the life-changing power of Christ we can be and do all that God intends for us.

Thought for the Day

The way of Christ into our lives is such that grace always precedes law.

Call to Worship

One:	Make a joyful noise to God, all the earth.
All:	Sing the glory of God's name.
One:	Come and see what God has done,
All:	God's deeds are awesome!
One:	Bless our God, O peoples.
All:	Let the sound of praise to God be heard

– based on Psalm 66

Pastoral Prayer

Almighty God, you nourish and sustain the world from day to day, and you continue to bless and strengthen and guide us more than we could dare to think or ask. Thank you for your hidden and yet faithful presence. We pray for your church, established on earth as a loving witness to your nature and purposes for the world. May your people know in a fresh way the reconciling and restoring power of Christ, so that by their lives and witness, your realm may advance in this world. We pray for those who struggle to be and do all that you would have them be and do. We sense the painful gap between our present lives and your perfect will for us. Stir us afresh by your Holy Spirit. May the living Christ be seen in our lives as we point to him as the way, the truth, and the life. We pray these things through Christ our strong Savior. Amen.

Prayer of Confession

Merciful God, we confess that we often turn from you and hurt one another. We neglect the needs of those around us; we tune out the cry of the oppressed. Heal our divided hearts, deepen our love for you and for others, and strengthen our commitment to peace and justice in our world. We offer these prayers through Christ our Lord. Amen.

Prayer of Dedication of Gifts and Self

God, you have given us all things in Christ: life, love, forgiveness, purpose. You entrust us with so many blessings. Help us to be faithful stewards of your many gifts, and may these offerings further the work of your church here and around the world, through Jesus Christ our loving Savior. Amen.

Sermon Summary

Galatians 6 is filled with exhortations concerning sowing and reaping and well-doing, but we mistake their intent if we construe them as good advice, which well-intentioned people can fulfill apart from the gospel and apart from Christ. These words are addressed to those who are crucified with Christ, through whom we can make a difference that truly matters.

Hymn of the Day
"Ask Ye What Great Thing I Know

Based on 1 Corinthians 2:2 and Galatians 6:14, the original German hymn "Wollt ihr wissen, was mein Preis" was written by German pastor Johann Christoph Schwedler. It first appeared in *Hirschberger Gesangbuch* in 1741, seven years after Schwedler's death. The English translation used in most current hymnbooks is the 1863 translation by British pastor and writer Benjamin H. Kennedy. At least one hymnbook has altered the first line to read, "Ask me what great thing I know." A series of soul-searching questions are proposed in the hymn. The answer to each question is, "Jesus Christ, the crucified."

Children's Time

Bearing Burdens

Bring a sturdy plastic crate. Fill it with rocks or heavy books and place it in your worship area. The idea is to have a box that cannot be moved easily by one person. Gather around the crate and wonder what it is doing there. Comment that it is in the way and should be moved. Make a big show of trying to move the crate and exclaim that it is just too heavy for one person to lift safely.

Ask the children if they can think of a way to move the box. Accept all suggestions and if no one else says it, suggest that you might work together to move it. Divide the contents of the crate amongst the children and carry everything to another location. When you have finished, celebrate with a round of applause. Comment that it was much easier to carry the crate when the load was shared.

Comment that in the Bible passage today, Paul says followers of Jesus should stick together and help to carry one another's burdens – help one another when we need help. When we do this, the church will be strong. Pray with the children, asking God to help you as you help one another.

The Sermon

The Transforming Power of Christ

Hymns
Beginning of Worship: "Joyful, Joyful, We Adore Thee"
Sermon Hymn: "Love Divine, All Loves Excelling"
Closing Hymn: "Be Thou My Vision"

Scripture
Galatians 6:(1-6), 7-16 (For sermon materials on Luke 10:1-11, 16-20, see the March 2007 issue of *The Clergy Journal;* for sermon materials on 2 Kings 5:1-14, see the 2006 May/June planning issue of *The Clergy Journal.*)

I have a little confession to make. I have a tendency to latch onto verses that reinforce my philosophy of life and affirm my way of doing things. I like passages that give us warm, fuzzy feelings without challenging us. Simon and Garfunkel, popular folksingers of the 1970s, told the truth when they sang, "a man hears what he wants to hear and disregards the rest." I could latch onto the opening words of our passage from Galatians 6 about sowing and reaping, and make them fit popular notions about life being a do-it-yourself proposition. After all, doesn't the apostle Paul declare that "you reap whatever you sow" (6:7)?

Countless sermons are nothing more than pragmatic lessons on how to solve problems, create happiness, and get ahead. Of course, Christianity is practical, and the scriptures guide us in dealing with the challenges and possibilities of everyday life. But divorced from the gospel, preaching becomes nothing more than works religion. The bookshelves in our local Borders or Barnes & Noble are lined with self-help books. People desperately pour over these volumes, attend seminars, and watch Oprah and Dr. Phil, trying somehow to attain the good life.

To be honest, we ministers are aware of these trends, and, whether we like to admit it or not, are susceptible to worldly models of success. We sometimes think of ministry as a career rather than a calling; we measure success by things like building programs and attendance charts. We might cloak our thinking in benign phrases such as "being seeker sensitive," and think that our preaching must not be off-putting to visitors. After all, didn't Paul declare that he would be all things to all people in order to save some (1 Cor 9:22)? So marketing shapes homiletics, and we begin to hold forth about the importance of living a good life, so that we will receive wonderful rewards here and now. Preach like that and listeners might be inclined to nod their approval and feel reassured that they have the resources within themselves to earn the "good life." A popular prosperity gospel is making the circuit nowadays that asserts precisely this, and those who preach it are packing in the crowds.

But Paul aims broadside at that kind of bootstraps theology with his declaration, "May I never boast of anything except the cross of our Lord Jesus Christ, by which the world has been crucified to me, and I to the world" (Gal 6:14).

A man once announced to D. L. Moody, "Sir, I am a self-made man." To which the famous evangelist replied, "Congratulations. You have saved God a great responsibility."

There is brokenness in our world. The human race collectively and individually is at enmity with God. Look at the magazines that line our shelves at the check-out stands. They are not filled with stories about the despair and crying needs of our inner cities. Tabloids are not going to sell out by featuring articles about opportunities in the Peace Corps. They're crammed with leering accounts of the escapades of the rich and famous. Popular magazines tell us how to slim down, look younger, and get more pleasure. Evidence for the narcissistic obsessions of our society abounds. Luther was right when he said that, after the fall, the human race was "curved inward upon itself." The Beatles had a song that repeated endlessly the line, "I, me, me, mine."

A self-centered world like ours loves to hear sermons about self-improvement. But this is a world of urban blight, failed marriages, and empty lives. This world will never become the realm of God apart from the cross of Christ. Only through crucifixion can there be a resurrection. Only by dying to self can we begin to live for others. And this happens not by fresh resolution or greater effort. It comes through the cross of Christ.

The apostle Paul flatly asserts that something happened to him when Jesus Christ went to the cross. Paul, too, was an accomplice in the world's rebellion against God's way. There was a time when Paul lived for himself and his immediate desires. But the cross changed all that. Jesus was not just a solitary martyr going to his death. Jesus died as our representative, including us in his death. When he died, we died. And when he rose, we rose. Thus Paul could make the surprising assertion that, by the cross long ago, the world was crucified to him and he to the world. All humankind is bound up together in what Jesus did on Calvary.

Paul humbly confesses that the only thing he can boast about is that Christ died for him.

The great thing to which he wants to draw everyone's attention is that God incarnate, Jesus of Nazareth, donned flesh, took pain, ascended the hill, and in the mighty act of atonement, crucified the world and his former self. By faith, we can participate in what Christ did for us long ago.

If we extend our text to include the first six verses, we find three things about the Christian life. First, it is a caring life – lifting up the stumbling, hearing another's burdens, working for the good of all. It is not so much inward looking as outward looking. Second, the Christian life is a transformed life. We are no longer the same. Third, it is a Christ-centered life. The living reality of our lives is Christ. In Christ, we are new creations. It is striking that Paul declares the cross to have an *ongoing* impact. It is not, says Paul, merely the fact that I *was* crucified with Christ so that he took my place in the past. This is a fact with contemporary implications. I continue to be crucified with Christ; I continue to have victory over my selfish and sinful inclinations through the Crucified One.

Go forth, Christian friend, into your Monday morning and all the days beyond. Your life is a calling from God. Your relationships with your friends, your coworkers, and your neighbors all present opportunities to sow in fruitful ways, to make a loving difference. In due time you will reap. Lift up the stumbling one, encourage the fainthearted. Feed the hungry. In due time, you will reap a harvest through the Crucified One who died and now lives to walk every step with you.

– Daniel P. Thimell

July 15, 2007

7th Sunday after Pentecost (Proper 10)
RC/Pres: 15th Sunday in Ordinary Time

Lessons
RCL	Amos 7:7-17	Col 1:1-14	Lk 10:25-37
Roman Catholic	Deut 30:10-14	Col 1:15-20	Lk 10:25-37
Episcopal (BCP)	Deut 30:9-14	Col 1:1-14	Lk 10:25-37
Lutheran	Deut 30:9-14	Col 1:1-14	Lk 10:25-37

Introduction to the Lessons
Lesson 1
(1) Amos 7:7-17 (RCL)
The book of Amos was written during the eighth century BCE during a time of peace and prosperity for Israel and Judah. Amos warns the people of impending judgment.

(2) Deuteronomy 30:10-14 (RC);
Deuteronomy 30:9-14 (Epis/Luth)
Moses promises that obeying God's laws will be accompanied by blessing in everyday life.

Lesson 2
Colossians 1:1-14 (RCL/Epis/Luth); Colossians 1:15-20 (RC)
Colossians was written to respond to those who claim that the death and resurrection of Christ are not enough to make a person right with God.

Gospel
Luke 10:25-37 (RCL/RC/Epis/Luth)
A theological expert in the law of Moses – called here simply "a lawyer" – seeks to show up Jesus by asking him how one can earn eternal life.

Theme
Through Christ's love, we can love those rejected by society.

Thought for the Day
Christian discipleship is impossible apart from Christ.

Call to Worship
One: To you, O Lord, I lift up my soul.
All: O God, in you I trust.
One: Make me know your ways, O Lord,
All: And teach me your paths.
One: Lead me in your truth, and teach me,
All: For you are the God of my salvation.

— based on Psalm 25

Pastoral Prayer
Eternal God, we come to worship your greatness, to be lost once again in the wonder of who you are. We praise you for the splendor of the stars, the warmth of the sun, and for the rain you generously send on both the just and the unjust. We thank you for your providence in clothing the lilies of the field and your children as well. We are amazed that not a sparrow falls without your notice, and are moved to know that you care about the smallest details of our lives and the lives of our neighbors. We thank you that your love is not restricted to those we deem worthy, but is generous and unconditional. We ask that the love of your Son, our Savior Jesus, would overflow from our hearts and lives into the hearts and lives of those around us. Move us to weep with those who weep, and to ache with those who are unemployed, hungry, oppressed, powerless, or hopeless. Come alongside them through us, O Holy Spirit, so that all may know God's love. These things we are bold to pray, through Christ. Amen.

Prayer of Confession
Merciful God, you know every thought of our hearts, every word that we speak, and every temptation that attacks us. We have done that which we should not do, and have failed to love our neighbor for whom you died. Forgive us our sins and transform our hearts and minds, that we may walk in newness of life, through Christ our Savior. Amen.

Prayer of Dedication of Gifts and Self

Loving God, who in Christ has already come alongside our neighbors in this country and around the world, we bring these gifts and ourselves in fresh dedication to your service. May these offerings enable your church to render loving ministry to the those who need it most, through the same Christ our strong Savior. Amen.

Sermon Summary

Jesus, as Luther once said, is first gift and then example. Jesus' parable of the Good Samaritan is not intended to be a short course in self-improvement, but a description of the way Jesus ministers to those in need. In union with Christ, we are enabled to participate in his loving ministry.

Hymn of the Day
"Here I Am, Lord"

The words and music of the hymn were written by American Jesuit Daniel L. Schutte in 1981. In the hymn we have descriptions of God, of what God has done, and of what God continues to do in response to the cry of the people. The call to join in Christian mission is presented. As in Isaiah's time, we hear God asking: "Whom shall I send?" We may respond with our heartfelt "I will go, Lord, if you lead me." The hymn lends itself to creative singing options ranging from unison singing of the stanzas and part singing of the refrain to antiphonal singing between a choir and the congregation. Rhythm instrument accompaniment can be an effective addition.

Children's Time

The Good Samaritan

Bring a street map of your community. Show the map and identify some local landmarks. Explain that this is a map of your neighborhood. Talk about neighbors. Who are your neighbors? Do you ever do anything to help them, or do they do things to help you? Comment that in our Bible story today someone asks Jesus, "Who is my neighbor?"

Set the scene by explaining that Jesus often used stories to help people learn more about living in God's way. Tell the story of the good

Samaritan and ask the children to identify which person was the good neighbor in this story and why.

Encourage the children to recognize that our neighbors are not only the people who live near us, but anyone who needs our help. When we show care and love for others, we are being good neighbors. Have the children name some ways we might love and care for others. If you have time, talk about some of the ways your church acts as a good neighbor, both in your community and in the world.

Pray with the children, asking God to help you follow the example of the Good Samaritan.

The Sermon

God's Love and Ours

Hymns

Beginning of Worship: "Praise to the Lord, the Almighty"
Sermon Hymn: "Won't You Let Me Be Your Servant?"
Closing Hymn: "Guide Me, O Thou Great Jehovah"

Scripture

Luke 10:25-37 (For additional sermon materials on this passage, see the March 2007 issue of *The Clergy Journal* and the 2006 May/June planning issue of *The Clergy Journal.*)

Sometimes the familiar can become the unknown. Some well-worn stories in the Bible elude us because we've heard them so often. The good Samaritan is a case in point. Most of us could retell the story from memory, and all of us understand the image. The good Samaritan is somebody who goes out of the way to help the fallen one – the one in need – even at great inconvenience to self. We even have good Samaritan laws to protect one who stops to render aid from liability to prosecution should something go awry in her or his well-intentioned efforts.

But if this is just a morality tale about the importance of doing good deeds, then Jesus forgot his own message. You see, the lawyer whose question occasions this parable has a prior agenda. He's not interested in Jesus or the message about God's reign. He wants to put Jesus to the test so that he can show him up. The lawyer begins by asking what he can do to inherit eternal life.

In Scotland, home improvement stores are called "DIYs" – Do-It-Yourself shops. Many then and now have thought of religion in this way – as a Do-It-Yourself proposition. The lawyer bought into a DIY approach, which is really self-centered religion. He was preoccupied with his piety and his destiny. He wanted another good deed on his résumé to ensure approval at the heavenly gate. His love was a self-love.

Jesus takes him on his own terms. He could have flat-out scolded him for having such a bad theology. He might have declared, as he did to the Thomas in the upper room, "I am the way, and the truth, and the life" (Jn 14:6). The way to God is the way of grace. This way is constituted by Jesus, in his life, death, and resurrection for us. But Jesus always meets a person where he or she is. He begins by reviewing the law of God, encapsulated in the love of God and neighbor. Jesus even says, "Do this and you will live."

But *can* we, by our own strength, do these things? Can we love God with undivided hearts? Can we love others with total altruism, total unselfishness? If we could, then the cross was unnecessary. Jesus is gently showing this man that he, like the rest of the human race, is unable to be what he ought to be, to love as he ought to love, and to act as he ought to act.

At this point the lawyer starts to squirm. His selfishness and failure to love others has been exposed. If he cannot obey God's law, do God's will from his heart, then he has truly fallen short. And so Luke adds the telling observation: "But *wanting to justify himself,* he asked Jesus, 'And who is my neighbor?'" Most of us act with a certain measure of love and sacrifice toward those who are close to us, who love us back. We forego things and go out of our way to help our spouses, our children, and possibly our next-door neighbors.

But we find it far easier to help our daughter when her car breaks down than the anonymous stranger whose radiator is steaming on the shoulder of the interstate. In the story, the priest and the Levite have reasonable anxieties about helping this fallen man. Fred Craddock, who teaches at Candler School of Theology, notes that the body on the roadside may have been planted by thieves in order to trap somebody who stopped to help. A lot of us hesitate nowadays to render aid for fear of being carjacked or attacked. Touching a corpse would have made the priest and the Levite ritually unclean and disqualified them from ministering in the Temple.

The Samaritan goes far out of his way. Craddock says that he "delayed his own journey, expended great energy, risked danger to himself, spent two days' wages with the assurance of more, and promised to follow up on his activity" (*Luke: Interpretation,* John Knox Press, 1990, p. 151). Jesus is saying, if you want to save yourself, transcend yourself. Transform yourself from a taker to a giver. Come out of your selfishness and become sacrificially preoccupied with the needs of everyone you meet.

It calls to mind another self-made man who came up to Jesus and asked how to earn eternal life. Jesus took him through the commandments and then said, looking at his sharkskin suit, Rolex watch, and Mercedes, "Sell all that you own and distribute the money to the poor, and you will have treasure in heaven" (Lk 18:22). When Jesus explained this, he added a comment, which sheds brilliant light on that episode and the encounter with the lawyer: "What is impossible for mortals is possible for God" (18:27). With humans it is impossible. A leopard cannot change its spots; we cannot transform ourselves.

Karl Barth, the great Swiss theologian, declares that in the truest sense, Jesus is the Samaritan who shows mercy to the one left for dead on the roadside. In *Church Dogmatics* (Edinburgh, T & T Clark, 1958), Barth writes that Jesus alone could act as neighbor to the fallen ones, fulfilling to the ultimate the twin commands to love God and others. But he did all that for us. In and through Christ, we can act in deeds of love and kindness. That is why the gospel of Jesus is not "Good Advice," but "Good News."

There *is* a distinct ethical content to this story of the good Samaritan. The Christian life is a life of self-sacrifice and neighbor-love. But it is not undertaken autonomously. It begins at the foot of the cross and is carried out in the company of the Crucified One, by whom alone we can live such a life of love. The parable of the good Samaritan is not just a call to imitate Jesus. It's a call to participate in him.

– Daniel P. Thimell

July 22, 2007

8th Sunday after Pentecost (Proper 11)
RC/Pres: 16th Sunday in Ordinary Time

Lessons

RCL	Amos 8:1-12	Col 1:15-28	Lk 10:38-42
Roman Catholic	Gen 18:1-10	Col 1:24-28	Lk 10:38-42
Episcopal (BCP)	Gen 18:1-10a, (10b-14)	Col 1:21-29	Lk 10:38-42
Lutheran	Gen 18:1-10a	Col 1:15-28	Lk 10:38-42

Introduction to the Lessons
Lesson 1
(1) Amos 8:1-12 (RCL)

The prophet Amos speaks to people who scrupulously observe the Sabbath, but are guilty of blatant social injustice

(2) Genesis 18:1-10 (RC); Genesis 18:1-10a, (10b-14) (Epis); Genesis 18:1-10a (Luth)

God has promised Abraham the blessing of a multitude of descendants, but Abraham's wife Sarah has long since passed the age of childbearing.

Lesson 2
Colossians 1:15-28 (RCL/Luth); Colossians 1:24-28 (RC); Colossians 1:21-29 (Epis)

The author of Colossians quotes an ancient hymn to Christ to respond to those who think that what Christ has done is not enough for salvation.

Gospel
Luke 10:38-42 (RCL/RC/Epis/Luth)

Jesus is invited to Martha's home for dinner, and finds that Martha and her sister Mary have different priorities in their lives on that day.

Theme
Our life in Christ is the foundation for serving Christ.

Thought for the Day

Even in the midst of our busyness, we need to engage in what Brother Lawrence called "practicing the presence of Christ."

Call to Worship

One: O Lord, who may abide in your tent?
All: Who may dwell on your holy hill?
One: Those who walk blamelessly, and do what is right,
All: Who speak the truth from their hearts,
One: Who honor those who fear the Lord.
All: Those who do these things shall never be moved.

– based on Psalm 15

Pastoral Prayer

Eternal and ever-blessed God, we rejoice in the order and goodness of your creation. We praise you as our Creator and our Redeemer. We seek to worship you, and need your strength to do so. Transform our worship from its imperfection into an offering acceptable to you. O Christ, what a pure delight is a single hour spent in your presence. Cause us to see that we always live in your presence, and that by your companionship and constant help we can carry out the mission you give us in this world. O Holy Spirit, renewing all creation, transforming us from one degree of glory to another into the likeness of Christ, touch us and renew us in this hour. In Christ's name we pray. Amen.

Prayer of Confession

Forgive us, loving God, for hurrying past you in our daily lives. We crowd our lives with so many frenetic activities, many of them worthwhile, and yet we forget the one thing needful. We work hard to make ends meet, but forget the one thing needful. We spend time with our loved ones, but forget the one thing needful. We give to worthwhile causes, but forget the one thing needful. O Lord, may we never forget your presence again! Forgive us for self-preoccupation and neglecting our lives with you. Woo us to your heart all over again, and show us the joy, meaning, and purpose that come through living our lives in you. Through Christ our strong Savior we pray. Amen.

Prayer of Dedication of Gifts and Self
Gracious God, you have given us all things in Christ, and with thankful hearts we bring these gifts to further your church's ministry of worship, teaching, fellowship, and outreach, that you may be glorified. Through Christ our loving Savior, we are bold to pray. Amen.

Sermon Summary
Mary's life with Jesus was more important than her life of service. Does this minimize Christian action? Hardly. But it rivets our attention on the fact that the outward journey is rooted in and sustained by the inward journey. Life in Christ is a matter of moment-by-moment, living our lives out of who we are in Christ.

Hymn of the Day
"Be Thou My Vision"
The origin of this hymn is in eighth-century Ireland. Its original title is "Rob tu mo bhoile, a Comdi cride." It was translated into English prose by Mary E. Byrne in 1905 and put into current hymn form by Eleanor H. Hull in 1912. It can be sung by the church as an expression of its desire that God be its vision for all current and future ministries. Perhaps the personal pronouns could be replaced by the plural pronouns "our" and "we." Also, with a little creative rewriting, each Victorian "thou" could be dropped without destroying the intent of the text.

Children's Time

Mary and Martha

Bring a dusting cloth, broom, baking pan, and wooden spoon.

Invite the children to recall times when they have had visitors: What sorts of things did you do to get ready? How did you help you guests feel welcome? Together look at the cleaning and baking tools, and suggest ways they might be used to help get ready for guests. Comment that the Bible story today is about two sisters named Mary and Martha. They had a lot of preparations to make because Jesus was coming to their house. Tell the story of Jesus' visit with Mary and Martha.

Talk briefly about the story. Notice that each woman welcomed Jesus in her own way – Martha by working to make sure that everything was just right; Mary by sitting and listening to Jesus. Although Jesus appreciated Martha's hard work, he also wanted her to spend time listening and learning about God's love. There is a time to be busy, but it is important to take time to listen and learn about God. How might we do that?

Pray with the children, giving thanks for hands to work and ears to listen.

The Sermon

Your Life in Christ

Hymns
Beginning of Worship: "Morning Has Broken"
Sermon Hymn: "St. Patrick's Breastplate"
Closing Hymn: "O Master, Let Me Walk with Thee"

Scripture
Luke 10:38-42 (For additional sermon materials on this passage, see the March 2007 issue of *The Clergy Journal* and the 2006 May/June planning issue of *The Clergy Journal*.)

"I've been busy." That's one of our favorite self-descriptions. When asked how we've been or what we've been up to, we like to stress our high activity levels. It typifies our American culture, which has always emphasized initiative, hard work, and getting things done. We pastors are not exempt from this trend. Search committees are not terribly interested in our Christology or even our devotional lives. Committee members' attention is focused like a laser beam on church growth, community involvement, and our ability to connect with young people. Churches want their pastors to be busy.

Of course, that applies to church members, also. We applaud those who "wear several hats" – who serve on church council, teach Sunday school, cook for church dinners, and sing in the choir. At home, it's no different. How many parents set the alarm for 5:30, start breakfast, wake the kids up, get them dressed, send them off to the bus stop, dash to work, and after school, drive them to soccer practice, and then grab a few burger combo meals in the drive-through? Late at night, as we toss in our beds, we think about how we'd really like to write that letter or call our parents or even just sit close to our children and listen to them. Then we defend ourselves by saying, "I'm so busy."

Martha was busy, too – busy sweeping the floor, baking bread, and setting the table. When Jesus knocked at the door, she ushered him to a seat, gave him something to drink, and hurried out to check on the meal. Then she noticed that Mary was just sitting out there in the living room, listening to Jesus. How ridiculous! Here she was frantically managing a three-ring circus in the kitchen, while Mary just sat around.

She marched out to the living room and complained, "Lord, do you not care that my sister has left me all the work to do by myself? Tell her then to help me" (10:40).

But Jesus did not back her up. He surprised her by saying, "Martha, Martha, you are worried and distracted by many things . . . Mary has chosen the better part, which will not be taken away from her" (10:41-42).

It's a familiar story, but we can miss the point. Jesus is not simply telling Martha to take a break. Note that Mary was not stretched out on the sofa, taking a snooze. She was sitting at the feet of Jesus. I believe that Jesus is telling us that the core of our existence is our life with him. The Christian life *is* an active life, a life of worship and service, a life of telling the story of God's redeeming love. And its mainspring is Jesus.

At the center of our faith is the conviction that Jesus, who was crucified, is not a dead martyr but a living savior. Death could not hold him in its icy grip. Christ rose in triumph and reigns as the head over the church, the body of Christ. Jesus is present with us today at work, at play, at home, and at the mall. He is as close to us as the air we breathe.

The Christian life is life lived in the companionship of Christ. Henry Scougal was a devout young theologian who taught at the University of Aberdeen in Scotland. He died back in 1678 at the tender age of 28. He wrote an influential little book entitled, *The Life of God in the Soul of Man* (Inter-Varsity Fellowship, 1961). George Whitefield, one of the leading evangelists of the Great Awakening, passed on a copy to Charles Wesley in Oxford. It contributed to his conversion.

In his book, Henry Scougal laments that so few people seem to understand what true Christianity is. Some think, he writes, that Christianity is mainly orthodox notions. They imagine that all God wants is for us to have the correct mental understanding of Christianity. Others think it is a matter of external duties – obeying the laws of the Bible, keeping busy doing the right things. Still others believe that real Christianity is having the right affections and feelings toward God.

Each of these misses the point, according to Scougal. The essence of Christianity lies not in the realm of thought, performance, or feelings. Real Christianity is a union of the soul with God. The apostle Paul describes it as Christ "formed in" us (Gal 4:19).

Mary knew that. Her life with Jesus was more important than her life of service. Does this minimize Christian action? Hardly. But it rivets our attention on the fact that the outward journey is rooted in and sustained by the inward journey. Our life in Christ is the basis for our life in the world. The life of God in the human soul – that's the Christian life. Jesus makes this point when he tells the disciples that he is the vine, they are the branches, and that "apart from me you can do nothing" (Jn 15:5).

Your life in Christ is more than having devotions. It's not about "checking in" with God occasionally. It is a matter of, moment-by-moment, living our lives out of who we are in Christ. James Torrance, the beloved Scottish theologian and professor, emblazoned upon his students' hearts and minds this central New Testament insight. He was fond of quoting Galatians 2:19-20: "I have been crucified with Christ; and it is no longer I who live, but it is Christ who lives in me." That's the essence of the Christian life.

– Daniel P. Thimell

July 29, 2007

9th Sunday after Pentecost (Proper 12)
RC/Pres: 17th Sunday in Ordinary Time

Lessons

RCL	Hos 1:2-10	Col 2:6-15, (16-19)	Lk 11:1-13
Roman Catholic	Gen 18:20-32	Col 2:12-14	Lk 11:1-13
Episcopal (BCP)	Gen 18:20-33	Col 2:6-15	Lk 11:1-13
Lutheran	Gen 18:20-32	Col 2:6-15, (16-19)	Lk 11:1-13

Introduction to the Lessons
Lesson 1
(1) Hosea 1:2-10 (RCL)
The prophet Hosea speaks to a people who have been unfaithful to God.
They have been trying to cover their bets by worshiping both God and the
old Baals, the false gods of Canaan.

(2) Genesis 18:20-32 (RC/Luth); Genesis 18:20-33 (Epis)
God, the righteous judge of all the earth, is outraged by the sins of Sodom,
but Abraham represents God's own mercy and intervenes on behalf of sinners.

Lesson 2
Colossians 2:6-15, (16-19) (RCL/Luth);
Colossians 2:12-14 (RC); Colossians 2:6-15 (Epis)
Some in the Colossian church have a legalistic understanding of Christianity, and the author responds by pointing out that Christ has done
everything necessary to make us acceptable to God.

Gospel
Luke 11:1-13 (RCL/RC/Epis/Luth)
Impressed with the way Jesus prays, the disciples ask for guidance in how
to pray.

Theme

Jesus gives us the heart to pray, and then teaches us to pray.

Thought for the Day

Prayer is not our best efforts to reach heaven, it is God reaching down and lifting us up into God.

Call to Worship

One:	O Lord, where can I go from your spirit?
All:	Or where can I flee from your presence?
One:	If I take the wings of the morning,
All:	And settle in the distant reaches of the sea,
One:	Even there your hand shall lead me,
All:	And your right hand shall hold me fast.

– based on Psalm 138

Pastoral Prayer

Almighty God, we gather in praise and adoration to confess your greatness and goodness. Father, whose love is working in all creation, we praise you. Son of God, who left the safe immunity of heaven to bring us back, we adore you. Holy Spirit, empowering us to proclaim and manifest the good news, we glorify you. Receive our worship, O God, through the ongoing ministry of Christ.

We stand in awe before the life of Jesus – a life of humble service, of tender compassion, and of deep communion with you. Teach us to pray, O God! By your mighty Spirit lift us out of ourselves and our self-preoccupation to commune with you and to pour out our hearts in daily prayer. These things we would ask, through and with Jesus Christ. Amen.

Prayer of Confession

Gracious God, forgive us for prayerlessness. How seldom we seek your face! How infrequently we enter your presence! Our lives are consumed with our own wants and preoccupations. By the cross of Christ our Savior, deliver us from the dungeon of selfishness, and free us to love you and others with undivided hearts. In the name of Christ we pray. Amen.

Prayer of Dedication of Gifts and Self

Generous God, having given us all things, you give us your very self each time we commune with you. In gratitude we dedicate these offerings that the whole world might know the same joy. In Christ we pray. Amen.

Sermon Summary

When prayer is seen as an emergency measure or a natural inclination, it is not likely to be practiced in a meaningful way. But Jesus teaches us that prayer is communion with God, a communion that is actualized by his ongoing priesthood, as he takes our prayers into the presence of God.

Hymn of the Day
"What a Friend We Have in Jesus"

Although written as a personal message for his sorrowing mother, Joseph Scriven's hymn has become one of the most popular hymns around the world. Scriven was personally acquainted with great sorrow in his life. Twice he was engaged to be married and each time his fiancée died prior to the scheduled wedding. The hymn was written in 1855. The hymn provides encouragement to take our personal sorrows, hurts, and other needs "to the Lord in prayer." The tune CONVERSE was written by Charles C. Converse in 1868 specifically for this text.

Children's Time

Talking to God

Bring some newsprint and a marker. Talk with the children about prayer: When are some times that you pray? Do you have special prayers you use at home? Where do you pray?

Explain that we can talk to God anywhere, anytime. God is always ready to talk with us. Comment that in today's Bible story the disciples came to Jesus with a request. They had noticed that Jesus often prayed to God. They wanted to learn more about prayer, so they asked Jesus for help. Recite the prayer that Jesus taught, using the version that your congregation uses in worship.

Explain that ever since that day, the followers of Jesus have used Jesus' prayer. Comment that there are many ways to pray. We can use the prayer that Jesus taught, or we can make up our own prayers. God's not fussy! God just loves to hear from us.

Ask the children what they would like to talk to God about today. Do they want to say thank you for something? Do they want to pray for someone who is sick? Are they worried about something? List the children's suggestions on newsprint and offer them in prayer.

The Sermon

Teach Us to Pray

Hymns

Beginning of Worship: "I Sing the Mighty Power of God"
Sermon Hymn: "Lord, Take My Hand and Lead Me"
Closing Hymn: "Awake, My Soul, Stretch Every Nerve"

Scripture

Luke 11:1-13 (For additional sermon materials on this passage, see the March 2007 issue of *The Clergy Journal* and the 2006 May/June planning issue of *The Clergy Journal*.)

The story is told of a doctor who had some somber news for the family of a patient. "We have done everything that is possible medically. Now, all we can do is pray." The father, shocked, asked incredulously, "Doctor! Has it come to that?"

Our world is not naturally inclined to prayer. Prayer is not normally seen as ongoing communion with God. It's a practice left for emergencies, for desperation times. We keep tabs on the weather. If serious storms are forecast, we monitor the Weather Channel, and perhaps have the foresight to stock an emergency kit with a radio, flashlight, and bottled water. If the streets begin to flood, we contemplate evacuating. But we may not turn to prayer until the evacuation routes are impassable and all human means of escape are exhausted.

Jesus did not come to proclaim an absent God who could be reached long distance in an emergency. He lived his life in daily fellowship with God. He did pray on special occasions – in the Jordan River, when he was baptized, and in the garden of Gethsemane, when he struggled with his call to go to the cross. He spent all night in prayer prior to calling the twelve disciples. But Luke also informs us that prayer was Jesus' regular habit. In chapter 5 we learn that "he would withdraw to deserted places and pray" (5:16) And in our gospel reading today, Jesus has just finished praying when the disciples request, "Lord, teach us to pray."

Harry Emerson Fosdick, the famous pastor of Riverside Church in New York City asserted that prayer is a native tendency, a natural inclination for human beings (*The Meaning of Prayer*, Association Press, 1975, pp. 1-18). If that were true, we might have expected the disciples to be regular practitioners of prayer. Instead, we find no mention in the Gospels of their prayer habits at all. It is recorded that in Gethsemane, while Jesus wrestled with apprehension and fear as he prayed to God, the disciples promptly fell asleep. They were prayerless while Jesus was prayerful.

Could it be that this is one reason we do not pray more, because it is not an inborn drive, an automatic tendency? So many sermons and devotions seem to assume that prayer is natural and that all we need are a few pointers on how to engage in it effectively. People file out of the sanctuary uplifted by such a positive message and praise the preacher for her inspiring words. Then they go home and nothing happens. Prayer is one more "ought" that is not easily complied with, so they give up.

Prayer is not natural, because prayer is centered in God and not in ourselves. We're not naturally altruistic, looking out for the needs of others. We're not automatically desirous of worshiping God. The Westminster Shorter Catechism declares in the answer to the very first question that our "chief end" is to "glorify God" and "enjoy [God] forever." That's a wonderful sentiment and it certainly accords with Holy Scripture. But there is a wide difference between what our driving purpose in life ought to be and what it actually is.

Raymond Ortlund, when he was pastor of Lake Avenue Congregational Church in Pasadena, California, said that Jesus came to make worshipers out of rebels. He's right. That's why Jesus lived our life, died our death, and rose in triumph – to free us from ourselves so that we might love God and others.

The prayer that Jesus taught – the Lord's Prayer – is not a magic formula for getting what we want out of God. The disciples were taught this prayer in response to a request humbly addressed to Jesus as *Lord*. "Lord, teach us to pray." It can be prayed only by those who trust in Jesus as "Lord."

The only kind of prayer natural to fallen humans is the prayer of selfishness. One little boy was overheard giving God a long list of requests as he prayed. His mother wisely advised him, "Son, when you pray to God, don't give God instructions. Just report for duty."

I don't believe the mother meant to dissuade her son from bringing requests to God. God wants us to pour out our needs in prayer. After all, Jesus tells us to ask for forgiveness, our daily bread, and help in time of temptation. I think that the mother was concerned that the boy viewed God as some sort of cosmic bellhop, an errand runner whose role is to fulfill our wishes. When we pray the prayer Jesus taught, we pray, "Thy kingdom come, thy will be done." We blurt out our worries, anxieties, and perceived needs, but we humbly lay them before the throne of God and trust that God knows best.

If prayer is not a native tendency for us, if it is not natural for us to seek and practice communion with God, should we simply give up? Far from it. Helmut Thielicke, the German theologian and preacher of a generation ago, points out that Jesus Christ is the one who teaches us to pray the Lord's Prayer: "it is fatefully significant that *he* is the one from whom we have received this holy prayer of all Christendom" (*The Prayer that Spans the World*, James Clarke, 1965, p. 22).

Jesus is more than a teacher, more than an inspiring example. Jesus is the one who comes as our great high priest. He practiced prayer as communion with God, and comes to give us a share in his communion with God. Jesus not only offers himself as a sacrifice for us. He also inaugurates a holy priesthood and makes a realm of priests in him. As our great high priest, in the words of Hebrews 7:25, "he always lives to make intercession" for us. And Jesus gives us a share in his priesthood. When we pray as Christians, we enter into a prayer life that is always going on. We enter into the prayer life of Jesus, who always lives to pray for us. He strengthens our weak prayers. He converts our selfish prayers. He gives us the will to pray, "Thy will be done." He gives us the heart to pray and then teaches us to pray.

– Daniel P. Thimell

Appendices
Resources for Preparing to Preach
by David H. Schmidt

Of the writing of commentaries, there is no end. The following bibliography offers my review of commentaries and overviews that you might consult as you prepare the sermon. The first sections cover books and a few software resources that can be used all three years of the Revised Common Lectionary. These are followed by comments about books for the portions of the lectionary covered in this manual. They are presented in groups – gospels, then epistles, then Hebrew Scriptures. An effort is made to include some of the newer works coming on the market as well as some standard volumes that time has shown to be helpful to pastors. A variety of theological perspectives are included.

One-Volume Commentaries

One-volume commentaries that can be used throughout the three-year cycle include:

- *HarperCollins Bible Commentary,* Revised Edition, James L. Mays, general editor, Harper SanFrancisco, 2000. Published in cooperation with the Society of Biblical Literature, this one-volume commentary provides good, brief information that reflects the current state of scholarship. There are good overview articles as well as comments on each book, including the Deuterocanonical Books.
- *The New Jerome Biblical Commentary*, Revised Edition, Raymond E. Brown et. al., Paulist Press, 1989.
- Both of the above works are now available on a *Logos Bible Software* CD-ROM, which also includes *Matthew Henry's Commentary* and the *Bible Knowledge Commentary*. For information: www.logos.com.
- Logos Research Systems makes available electronically the *Harper's Bible Dictionary* and Doubleday's *Anchor Bible Dictionary*. They also have the *Interpretation Commentaries* series, *InterVarsity Press New Testament Commentary* series and others, and are working on the *International Critical Commentary* series. For information: www.logos.com.

- Abingdon Press has released the entire *New Interpreter's Bible* on CD-ROM. For information: www.abingdonpress.com
- *Word Biblical Commentary* is on a disc with Greek and Hebrew texts and numerous Bible translations. For information: www.logos.com.
- Biblesoft has packages that include such older series as *Matthew Henry's Commentaries, Wycliffe Commentaries, Keil & Delitzsch's OT Commentary, Adam Clarke's Commentaries,* and *Jamieson-Fausset-Brown* commentaries. For information: www.biblesoft.com.
- Several software companies provide the *Holman Bible Dictionary* and/or others with some of their packages.
- Zondervan has released *The Expositor's Bible Commentary*, edited by Frank Gaebelein on CD-ROM. For information: www.zondervan.com.

Books for Study of the Psalter for All Three Years

Overviews and Theology: H. J. Kraus's *Theology of the Psalms* (Fortress, 1992) is a good discussion by a scholar who has also published a major commentary (below). James L. Crenshaw's *The Psalms: An Introduction* (Eerdmans, 2001) offers a fairly thorough overview of recent discussion. For a work that invites looking at the Psalms in a new way, J. David Pleins's *The Psalms: Songs of Tragedy, Hope, and Justice,* The Bible & Liberation (Orbis, 1993). J. Clinton McCann and James C. Howell, *Preaching the Psalms* (Abingdon, 2001) challenges the preacher to recover the Psalms for sermon material.

Commentaries: H. J. Kraus's *Psalms 1-59* and *Psalms 60-150* (Fortress, 1990) are the standard works full of detail. J. Clinton McCann covers the Psalms in the *New Interpreter's Bible*, vol. 4 (Abingdon, 1996). Richard J. Clifford's *Psalms 1-72* and *Psalms 73-150*, Abingdon Old Testament Commentaries (Abingdon, 2002, 2004) provide an informed and relatively inexpensive set designed for the pastor. K. Schaefer's *Psalms*, Berit Olam: Studies in Hebrew Narrative and Poetry (The Liturgical Press, 2001) is a recent Roman Catholic study. James L. May's *Psalms,* Interpretation Commentaries (John Knox, 1994) is a fine expository work that can be used alongside any of the above commentaries.

Books for Study of Acts for All Three Years

Overviews: Mark Allen Powell's *What Are They Saying About Acts?* (Paulist Press, 1991) provides a good introduction to the state of research on Acts. Jacob Jervell's *The Theology of the Acts of the Apostles* (Cambridge University Press, 1996) offers a review of the some theological issues.

Commentaries: W. H. Willimon's *Acts,* Interpretation Commentaries (John Knox, 1988) gives a sound expository start for the pastor. Then use one or more of the following for exegetical support: E. Haenchen's *The Acts of the Apostles: A Commentary* (Westminster, 1971) is a significant reference. Robert W. Wall's "The Acts of the Apostles," *New Interpreters' Bible*, Vol. X (Abingdon, 2002) offers a Wesleyan exposition and exegesis. Beverly Roberts Gaventa's *Acts*, Abingdon New Testament Commentaries (Abingdon, 2003) adds an exciting study.

Luke Timothy Johnson's *The Acts of the Apostles*, Sacra Pagina 5 (The Liturgical Press, 1992) is a Roman Catholic study with a fresh translation, notes, and interpretation that provides another viewpoint. Joseph A. Fitzmyer's *The Acts of the Apostles*, Anchor Bible 31 (Doubleday, 1998) is a good replacement volume in that series. Howard Clark Kee, *To Every Nation Under Heaven: The Acts of the* Apostles (Trinty Press International, 1997) includes helpful notes from archaeology along with good commentary. C. K. Barrett's *Acts of the Apostles,* International Critical Commentary, 2 volumes (T & T Clark, 1993, 1998) is a significant study on the Greek text.

Books for Study of the Gospel Lessons
John (Years B, C)

Overviews: Gerard S. Sloyan's *What are They Saying about John?* (Paulist, 1991) provides a fine overview of scholarship. D. Moody Smith's *John*, Proclamation Commentary, 2nd ed. (Fortress, 1986) is an alternative. He also provides a theological overview in *The Theology of the Gospel of John* (Cambridge University Press, 1995). Wes Howard-Brook, *John's Gospel and the Renewal of the Church* (Orbis, 1997) can stimulate one's thinking. Robert Kysar's *Preaching John* (Fortress, 2002) also will prime many pumps.

Commentaries: Raymond E. Brown's *The Gospel According to John*, Anchor Bible 29, 29A (Doubleday, 1966, 1970) has become a standard two-volume work for exegetical study. Couple this with the expository effort of Gerald Sloyan's *John, Interpretation* (John Knox, 1988) for a solid set of resources. Gail R. O'Day's "The Gospel of John" in *The New Interpreter's Bible*, Vol. 9 (Abingdon, 1995) is an interesting study in a volume that also includes Luke.

Charles H. Talbert's *Reading John: A Literary and Theological Commentary on the Fourth Gospel and the Johannine Epistles* (Crossroad, 1994) is a fine study using the newer literary approach. Ben Witherington III, *John's Wisdom: A Commentary on the Fourth Gospel* (John Knox, 1995) offers another perspective. Bruce J. Malina, *Social Science Commentary on the Gospel of John* (Fortress, 1998) is study that can cause one to look at the text in a different way. Francis J. Moloney's *The Gospel of John*, Sacra Pagina (The Liturgical Press, 1998) is another recent study now in paperback. And Andrew T. Lincoln's *The Gospel According to Saint John*, Black's New Testament Commentary (Hendrickson, 2005) is a new update in that series.

Mark (Year B)

Overviews: Paul Achtemeier's *Mark*, Proclamation Commentaries, 2nd rev. ed. (Fortress, 1986) or Frank J. Matera's *What Are They Saying about Mark?* (Paulist Press, 1987) provide an opening overview. W. R. Telford's *The Theology of the Gospel of Mark* (Cambridge, 2000) will give a theological overview.

Commentaries: Expository studies include Lamar Williamson, Jr.'s *Mark*, Interpretation Commentaries (John Knox, 1983) or Bonnie Bowman Thurston's *Preaching Mark* (Fortress, 2002). Pheme Perkins's "The Gospel of Mark," *The New Interpreter's Bible*, vol. VIII (Abingdon, 1995) has both solid expository and exegetical material. Other options for exegetical study include John R. Donahue and Daniel J. Harrington's *The Gospel of Mark*, Sacra Pagina 2 (Liturgical Press, 2002), now in paperback; James R. Edwards's *The Gospel According to Mark*, Pillar New Testament Commentary (Eerdmans, 2002); or Morna D. Hooker's *The Gospel According to Saint Mark*, Black's New Testament Commentary (Hendrickson, 1992). Eduard Schweizer's *The Good News According to Mark* (John Knox, 1970) continues to provide solid help for preaching while Ched Myers's *Binding the Strong Man* and *Who Will Roll Away the Stone* (Orbis, 1988, 1994) challenge us to take a less familiar look at a familiar gospel.

Luke (Year C)

Overviews: Mark Allan Powell's *What Are They Saying About Luke?* (Paulist Press, 1989) provides the overview to what's happening in scholarship. F. W. Danker's *Luke*, Proclamation Commentary, 2nd rev. ed. (Fortress, 1989) might be an alternate. Jerome Neyrey, ed., *The Social World of Luke-Acts* (Henrickson, 1991) offers additional insight. Joel Green's *The Theology of the Gospel of Luke* (Cambridge, 1995) brings one up to date on some theological discussion.

Commentaries: Joseph Fitzmyer's *The Gospel According to Luke*, Anchor Bible 28, 28A (Doubleday, 1981, 1985) has been a standard set. Fred Craddock's *Luke*, Interpretation Commentaries (John Knox, 1990) has been the expository leader. R. Alan Culpepper offers both in his study in the *New Interpreter's Bible*, vol. 9 (Abingdon, 1995). Additional studies include: Luke Timothy Johnson's *The Gospel of Luke*, Sacra Pagina 3 (The Liturgical Press, 1991); Joel Green's *The Gospel of Luke,* New International Commentary on the New Testament (Eerdman's, 1997); Frederick Danker's *Jesus and the New Age*, rev & expanded (Fortress, 1988); and Francois Bovon's *Luke 1:1-9:50*, Hermeneia (Fortress Press, 2002).

Studies: Raymond E. Brown's *The Birth of the Messiah* (Doubleday, 1979) remains a classic detailed study of the infancy narratives. Loretta Dornisch's *A Woman Reads the Gospel of Luke* (The Liturgical Press, 1996) provides further insight into the gospel.

Books for the Study of the Epistle Lessons
1 Corinthians

William A. Beardslee's *First Corinthians: A Commentary for Today* (Chalice Press, 1994) is a good book aimed at the pastor and teacher. Richard B. Hays's *First Corinthians*, Interpretation Commentaries (John Knox, 1997) provides a good expository work. J. Paul Smalley offers exegetical and expository insight in "First Letter to the Corinthians," *New Interpreters' Bible*, Vol. X (Abingdon, 2002). Ben Witherington III, *Conflict and Community in Corinth: A Socio-Rhetorical Commentary on 1 and 2 Corinthians* (Eerdmans, 1995) offers a study by an evangelical. Gordon D. Fee's *The First Epistle to the Corinthians,* New International Commentary on the New Testament (Eerdmans, 1987) is a fine detailed evangelical study. Raymond F. Collins's *First Corinthians*, Sacra Pagina 7 (The Liturgical

Press, 1999) is a helpful addition in that series. Another helpful volume is Richard A. Horsley's *1 Corinthians*, Abingdon New Testament Commentaries (Abingdon, 1997).

Galatians

Richard B. Hays's "Letter to the Galatians," *New Interpreters' Bible*, vol. 11 (Abingdon, 2000) may be the place to start. Charles Cousar's *Galatians*, Interpretation Commentaries (John Knox, 1982) provides a fine expository reading. James D. G. Dunn's *The Epistle to the Galatians*, Black's New Testament Commentary (Hendrickson, 1993) offers his cutting edge interpretation. J. Louis Martyn's *Galatians*, Anchor Bible 33A (Doubleday, 1997) is a good theological study. Dieter Betz's *Galatians*, Hermeneia (Fortress, 1979) has become a standard on the Greek text. And Frank J. Matera's *Galatians*, Sacra Pagina 9 (The Liturgical Press, 1992) offers a clear Roman Catholic study.

Ephesians

Pheme Perkins's "Letter to the Ephesians," *The New Interpreter's Bible*, Vol. XI (Abingdon, 2000) is a good starting place. Markus Barth's *Ephesians*, Anchor Bible 34 and 34A (Doubleday, 1974) continues to provide a detailed study. Ralph P. Martin's *Ephesians, Colossians, and Philemon*, Interpretation Commentaries (John Knox, 1991) offers some additional expository material. Ernest Best's *Ephesians: A Critical and Exegetical Commentary*, International Critical Commentary (T & T Clark, 1998) provides a good study of the Greek text. Rudolf Schnackenburg's *The Epistle to the Ephesians: A Commentary* (T & T Clark, 1991) is a good Roman Catholic study. John Muddiman's *Letter to the Ephesians*, Black's New Testament Commentary, vol. 10 (Henrickson, 2004) is a recent addition in that series.

Colossians

Andrew T. Lincoln's "Letter to the Colossians," *New Interpreters' Bible*, vol. 11 (Abingdon, 2000) is a place to start. Ralph P. Martin (see "Ephesians") offers some additional exposition. James D. G. Dunn's *The Epistles to the Colossians and to Philemon*, New International Greek Testament Commentary (Eerdmans, 1996) or Robert Wilson's *Colossians and Philemon*, International Critical Commentary (T & T Clark, 2005) provide detailed study of the Greek text. Other exegetical support can be found in Petr Pokorny's *Colossians: A Commentary* (Hendrickson, 1991) or Markus Barth and Helmut Blanke's *Colossians*, Anchor Bible 34B (Doubleday, 1994).

James

Luke T. Johnson offers two recent studies, *Letter to James*, Anchor Bible 37A (Doubleday, 1995) or "James," *New Interpreters' Bible*, vol. 12 (Abingdon, 1998). Pheme Perkins's *First and Second Peter, James, and Jude*, Interpretation Commentaries (John Knox, 1995) provides an expository study. S. Law's *A Commentary on the Epistle of James*, Black's New Testament Commentaries (Hendrickson, 1980) remains helpful. Patrick J. Hartin's *James*, Sacra Pagina (The Liturgical Press, 2003) is a recent work, as is Christopher Church and Edgar V. McKnight's *Hebrews - James* (Smyth & Helwys, 2005) which includes a CD-ROM. Peter Davids's *Commentary on James*, New International Greek Testament Commentary (Eerdmans, 1982) provides a study of the Greek text.

Hebrews

Fred B. Craddock provides an exegetical and expository study in the *New Interpreters' Bible*, vol. 12 (Abingdon, 1998). Thomas G. Long's *Hebrews*, Interpretation Commentaries (John Knox, 1997) is a fresh exposition. David deSilva's *Perseverance in Gratitude: A Socio-Rhetorical Commentary on the Epistle to the Hebrews* (Eerdmans, 2000) applies new approaches to the text and may be used as a supplement. F. F. Bruce's *The Epistle to the Hebrews*, rev. ed., The New International Commentary on the New Testament (Eerdmans, 1990) continues to be a solid work as does Harold W. Attridge's *Hebrews*, Hermeneia (Fortress, 1989). See also Edgar McKnight under James.

Revelation

Christopher C. Rowland provides a study in the *New Interpreters' Bible*, vol. 12 (Abingdon, 1998). M. Eugene Boring's *Revelation*, Interpretation Commentaries (John Knox, 1989) has expository help. Other exegetical studies include Jürgen Roloff's *Revelation: A Continental Commentary* (Fortress, 1993); Mitchell B. Reddish's *Revelation* (Smyth & Helwys, 2001); or Wilfrid J. Harrington's *Revelation*, Sacra Pagina 16 (The Liturgical Press, 1993). David L. Barr's *Tales of the End: A Narrative Commentary on the Book of Revelation* (Polebridge, 1998) provides us with another current approach. Judith Kovacs and Christopher Rowland's *Revelation* (Blackwell, 2004) is a new study.

Books for the Study of Some of the Hebrew Scriptures Texts
1 and 2 Kings

Expository help is available in Richard D. Nelson's *First and Second Kings*, Interpretation Commentaries (John Knox, 1987) and Choon-Leong Seow in the *New Interpreters' Bible*, vol. 3 (Abingdon, 1999). A strong study in a work that includes a CD-ROM and contemporary applications is Walter Brueggeman's *1 & 2 Kings* (Smyth & Helwys, 2000). Volkmar Fritz's *1 & 2 Kings, A Continental Commentary* (Fortress, 2003) is a recent work. Less expensive helps include G. H. Jones's *1 and 2 Kings*, New Century Bible Commentary, 2 vols. (Eerdmans, 1984) or Donald J. Wiseman's *1 and 2 Kings*, Tyndale Old Testament Commentaries (InterVarsity Press, 1993).

Proverbs

Michael V. Fox's *Proverbs*, Anchor Bible 18A (Doubleday, 1997) or Raymond C. Van Leeuwen's "Proverbs," *New Interpreters' Bible*, vol. 5 (Abingdon, 1997) provide recent helpful studies for the pastor. Kathleen A. Farmer's *Proverbs & Ecclesiastes*, International Theological Commentary (Eerdmans, 1991) offers a fresh overview. Milton P. Horne's *Proverbs - Ecclesiastes* (Smyth & Helwys, 2005) is a creative new volume with CD-ROM.

Job

Expository insights abound in J. Gerald Janzen's *Job*, Interpretation Commentaries (John Knox, 1985). Supplement this with Carol A. Newsom's "Job," *New Interpreters' Bible*, Vol. 4 (Abingdon, 1996) or N. C. Habel's *The Book of Job: A Commentary*, Old Testament Library (Westminster, 1985). In addition one might look at Gustavo Gutierrez's *On Job: God-Talk and the Suffering of the Innocent* (Orbis, 1987) or John C. Holbert's *Preaching Job* (Chalice Press, 1999). David J. A. Clines's *Job 1-20* and *Job 21-42*, Word Biblical Commentaries 17 (Word, 1989, 2002) is a fine detailed study.

Isaiah

Joseph Blenkinsopp's *Isaiah*, Anchor Bible 19, 19B, 19C (Doubleday, 2000, 2002, 2003) is a replacement set in that series where one scholar studies the whole book. Brevard S. Child's *Isaiah*, Old Testament Library (Westminster, 2001) is another stimulating view of the whole book. Walter Brueggemann, *Isaiah 1-39, 40-66*, Westminster Bible Companion (John Knox, 1998) is a third such study.

Expository help for Isaiah of Jerusalem comes from Christopher R. Seitz's *Isaiah 1-39*, Interpretation Commentaries (John Knox, 1993). Seitz also edited *Reading and Preaching the Book of Isaiah* (Fortress, 1988), that can assist the pastor in thinking about the use of Isaiah during the year. He now is the author of "Isaiah 40-66" in *The New Interpreter's Bible*, Vol. 6 (Abingdon, 2001). Gene M. Tucker provides "Isaiah 1-39" in that same volume.

Paul D. Hanson's *Isaiah 40-66*, Interpretation Commentaries (John Knox, 1995) provides expository work on later Isaiah. R. Clements's *Isaiah 1-39*, New Century Bible Commentary (Eerdmans, 1980) and R. N. Whybray's *Isaiah 40-66*, New Century Bible Commentary (Eerdmans, 1975) provide good inexpensive commentaries. A more detailed set now in paperback would be O. Kaiser's *Isaiah 1-12*, Old Testament Library, 2nd Ed. (Westminster, 1983) and *Isaiah 13-39*, Old Testament Library (Westminster, 1974) plus Claus Westermann's *Isaiah 40-66*, Old Testament Library (Westminster, 1969).

2006–2007 Writers

Sermons and Prayers

Andrea La Sonde Anastos
(UCC) Littleton, CO
Oct. 31; Nov. 1, 5, 12

Rod Broding
(ELCA) Battle Lake, MN
Sept. 10, 17, 24; Oct. 1

C. Welton Gaddy
(Bapt) Monroe, LA
Nov. 19, 23, 26; Dec. 3

Michael Gemignani
(Epis) Freeport, TX
Jan. 21, 28; Feb. 4, 11

John Indermark
(UCC) Naselle, WA
Aug. 6, 13, 20, 27; Sept. 3

Y. Franklin Ishida
(ELCA) Chicago, IL
May 17, 20, 27; June 3

William L. Mangrum
(PCUSA) Princeton, NJ
Dec. 10, 17, 24, 25

Margaret Marcuson
(Bapt) Portland, OR
Apr. 5, 6, 8, 15

David Neil Mosser
(UMC) Arlington, TX
June 10, 17, 24; July 1

Rosemary A. Rocha
(UCC) Edina, MN
Mar. 11, 18, 25; Apr. 1

Melissa Bane Sevier
(PCUSA) Versailles, KY
Oct. 8, 15, 22, 29

David P. Sharp
(PCUSA) San Jose, CA
Dec. 31; Jan. 6, 7, 14

Jeanette B. Strandjord
(ELCA) Williams Bay, WI
Feb. 18, 21, 25; Mar. 4

Daniel P. Thimell
(UCC) Marshall, OK
July 8, 15, 22, 29

Nancy E. Topolewski
(UMC) Vestal, NY
Apr. 22, 29; May 6, 13

Children's Time

Sharon Harding
(Anglican) Athabasca, AB

Preaching Resources

David H. Schmidt
(UMC) Lafayette, IN

Hymn of the Day Selections

Roger Wayne Hicks
(UMC) Pinehurst, NC

Four-Year Church Year Calendar

	Year B 2005	Year C 2006	Year A 2007	Year B 2008
Advent begins	Nov. 27	Dec. 3	Dec. 2	Nov. 30
Christmas	Dec. 25	Dec. 25	Dec. 25	Dec. 25
	2006	**2007**	**2008**	**2009**
Epiphany	Jan. 6	Jan. 6	Jan. 6	Jan. 6
Ash Wednesday	Mar. 1	Feb. 21	Feb. 6	Feb. 25
Palm Sunday	Apr. 9	Apr. 1	Mar. 16	Apr. 5
Maundy Thursday	Apr. 13	Apr. 5	Mar. 20	Apr. 9
Good Friday	Apr. 14	Apr. 6	Mar. 21	Apr. 10
Easter Day	Apr. 16	Apr. 8	Mar. 23	Apr. 12
Ascension Day	May 25	May 17	May 1	May 21
Pentecost	June 4	May 27	May 11	May 31
Trinity Sunday	June 11	June 3	May 18	June 7
Reformation	Oct. 31	Oct. 31	Oct. 31	Oct. 31
All Saints' Day	Nov. 1	Nov. 1	Nov. 1	Nov. 1

Calendars for 2006 and 2007

2006

JANUARY 2006	FEBRUARY 2006	MARCH 2006	APRIL 2006
S M T W T F S	S M T W T F S	S M T W T F S	S M T W T F S
1 2 3 4 5 6 7	1 2 3 4	1 2 3 4	30 1
8 9 10 11 12 13 14	5 6 7 8 9 10 11	5 6 7 8 9 10 11	2 3 4 5 6 7 8
15 16 17 18 19 20 21	12 13 14 15 16 17 18	12 13 14 15 16 17 18	9 10 11 12 13 14 15
22 23 24 25 26 27 28	19 20 21 22 23 24 25	19 20 21 22 23 24 25	16 17 18 19 20 21 22
29 30 31	26 27 28	26 27 28 29 30 31	23 24 25 26 27 28 29

MAY 2006	JUNE 2006	JULY 2006	AUGUST 2006
S M T W T F S	S M T W T F S	S M T W T F S	S M T W T F S
1 2 3 4 5 6	1 2 3	30 31 1	1 2 3 4 5
7 8 9 10 11 12 13	4 5 6 7 8 9 10	2 3 4 5 6 7 8	6 7 8 9 10 11 12
14 15 16 17 18 19 20	11 12 13 14 15 16 17	9 10 11 12 13 14 15	13 14 15 16 17 18 19
21 22 23 24 25 26 27	18 19 20 21 22 23 24	16 17 18 19 20 21 22	20 21 22 23 24 25 26
28 29 30 31	25 26 27 28 29 30	23 24 25 26 27 28 29	27 28 29 30 31

SEPTEMBER 2006	OCTOBER 2006	NOVEMBER 2006	DECEMBER 2006
S M T W T F S	S M T W T F S	S M T W T F S	S M T W T F S
1 2	1 2 3 4 5 6 7	1 2 3 4	31 1 2
3 4 5 6 7 8 9	8 9 10 11 12 13 14	5 6 7 8 9 10 11	3 4 5 6 7 8 9
10 11 12 13 14 15 16	15 16 17 18 19 20 21	12 13 14 15 16 17 18	10 11 12 13 14 15 16
17 18 19 20 21 22 23	22 23 24 25 26 27 28	19 20 21 22 23 24 25	17 18 19 20 21 22 23
24 25 26 27 28 29 30	29 30 31	26 27 28 29 30	24 25 26 27 28 29 30

2007

JANUARY 2007	FEBRUARY 2007	MARCH 2007	APRIL 2007
S M T W T F S	S M T W T F S	S M T W T F S	S M T W T F S
1 2 3 4 5 6	1 2 3	1 2 3	1 2 3 4 5 6 7
7 8 9 10 11 12 13	4 5 6 7 8 9 10	4 5 6 7 8 9 10	8 9 10 11 12 13 14
14 15 16 17 18 19 20	11 12 13 14 15 16 17	11 12 13 14 15 16 17	15 16 17 18 19 20 21
21 22 23 24 25 26 27	18 19 20 21 22 23 24	18 19 20 21 22 23 24	22 23 24 25 26 27 28
28 29 30 31	25 26 27 28	25 26 27 28 29 30 31	29 30

MAY 2007	JUNE 2007	JULY 2007	AUGUST 2007
S M T W T F S	S M T W T F S	S M T W T F S	S M T W T F S
1 2 3 4 5	1 2	1 2 3 4 5 6 7	1 2 3 4
6 7 8 9 10 11 12	3 4 5 6 7 8 9	8 9 10 11 12 13 14	5 6 7 8 9 10 11
13 14 15 16 17 18 19	10 11 12 13 14 15 16	15 16 17 18 19 20 21	12 13 14 15 16 17 18
20 21 22 23 24 25 26	17 18 19 20 21 22 23	22 23 24 25 26 27 28	19 20 21 22 23 24 25
27 28 29 30 31	24 25 26 27 28 29 30	29 30 31	26 27 28 29 30 31

SEPTEMBER 2007	OCTOBER 2007	NOVEMBER 2007	DECEMBER 2007
S M T W T F S	S M T W T F S	S M T W T F S	S M T W T F S
30 1	1 2 3 4 5 6	1 2 3	30 31 1
2 3 4 5 6 7 8	7 8 9 10 11 12 13	4 5 6 7 8 9 10	2 3 4 5 6 7 8
9 10 11 12 13 14 15	14 15 16 17 18 19 20	11 12 13 14 15 16 17	9 10 11 12 13 14 15
16 17 18 19 20 21 22	21 22 23 24 25 26 27	18 19 20 21 22 23 24	16 17 18 19 20 21 22
23 24 25 26 27 28 29	28 29 30 31	25 26 27 28 29 30	23 24 25 26 27 28 29

Index of Sermon Texts